The Classical Theory of Economic Growth

Walter Eltis

St. Martin's Press　　New York

All rights reserved. For information, write:
St. Martin's Press, Inc., 175 Fifth Avenue, New York, NY 10010
Printed in Hong Kong
Published in the United Kingdom by The Macmillan Press Ltd
First published in the United States of America in 1984

ISBN 0–312–14264–1

Library of Congress Cataloguing in Publication Data

Main entry under title:

The Classical theory of economic growth.

   Bibliography: p.
   Includes index.
   1. Economic development—History.   I.Eltis, W. A.
(Water Alfred)
HD78.C57   1984   338.9′001   83–16154
ISBN 0–312–14264–1   66412

Contents

Preface   vii

Abbreviations for Much-cited Works and the Editions Used   xiv

1   FRANÇOIS QUESNAY'S *Tableau Economique*   1

2   QUESNAY'S THEORY OF ECONOMIC GROWTH   39

3   ADAM SMITH'S THEORY OF ECONOMIC GROWTH   68

4   MALTHUS'S THEORY OF POPULATION GROWTH   106

5   MALTHUS'S THEORY OF EFFECTIVE DEMAND AND GROWTH   140

6   RICARDO'S THEORY OF INCOME DISTRIBUTION AND
    GROWTH   182

7   MARX'S THEORY OF EXPLOITATION   233

8   MARX'S THEORY OF THE DECLINING RATE OF PROFIT AND
    THE COLLAPSE OF CAPITALISM   265

9   THE CLASSICAL THEORY OF ECONOMIC GROWTH   310

Notes   339

References   357

Index   366

Preface

This book seeks to provide an account of the theory of economic growth and income distribution as it was invented and developed successively by François Quesnay, Adam Smith, Thomas R. Malthus, David Ricardo and Karl Marx. These were five of the most original and distinguished thinkers to devote serious attention to economic problems, and they left important books which have enriched economics and exercised great political influence.

The classical theory of economic growth which they initiated, elaborated and corrected has two fundamental characteristics. Part and only part of the economy generates an investable surplus over costs; and growth depends on the reinvestment of a sufficient fraction of that surplus. In Quesnay's version of the theory, growth depends primarily on the reinvestment of the agricultural surplus, but it is also strongly influenced by the *demand* for agricultural produce which owes much to the extent to which rents are spent on food. The economy's full interrelationships are set out in the celebrated *Tableau Economique*, which Quesnay invented in 1758–9, and this is the subject of Chapter 1.

The theory of economic growth which follows from the conditions set out in the *Tableau* is the subject of Chapter 2. Economic advice streamed to Versailles, Baden Baden and even St Petersburg from Quesnay's Physiocratic school of *Economistes*, and many of his contemporaries were satisfied that profoundly important logical argument based on the *Tableau* underpinned the policy recommendations, but the *Tableau* itself, like much of the modern economics on which government decisions are based, was extremely obscure.

Smith visited Paris in 1765–6 while respect for Quesnay's economics was at its height, and it may be presumed that he achieved a complete grasp of Physiocratic economic theory. *The Nature and Causes of the Wealth of Nations* of 1776 which links the generation of an economic surplus to capital accumulation and economic growth contains the essence of Quesnay's argument, but Smith found a way of stating it which avoided the complexities of the *Tableau*. In Smith's version, moreover, industry and commerce contribute to the surpluses which influence the rate of growth, and this made more sense to his English and Scottish contemporaries than the Physiocratic propositions where only agriculture matters. Smith's explanation of the causes of economic growth, which is the subject of Chapter 3, was comprehensible to all who were literate and interested in economic questions, and these included Thomas R. Malthus, a Fellow of Jesus College, Cambridge, who sought to understand and account for the inevitability of population growth, and David Ricardo, a wealthy stockbroker who found a copy of Smith's great book in a circulating library in Bath in 1799, and like Malthus went on to correct and develop certain aspects of the argument.

Malthus's first important extension, his *Essay on the Principle of Population* of 1798, integrated into the argument the implications of scarce natural resources on the planet. Capital was the principal scarce factor of production so far as Smith and Quesnay were concerned, and they both took it for granted that if a country could expand its capital stock, then population and output would grow almost as rapidly. Malthus in contrast believed that the production of food could be expanded only slowly and with difficulty, and that it was this that fundamentally limited the scope for growth in population and hence in output. The economic and social conclusions which follow from his theory of population are the subject of Chapter 4.

Malthus also questioned Smith's belief in the overriding importance of capital accumulation as a determinant of growth. He believed that growth would cease if effective demand failed to expand. He considered that lack of effective demand provided an explanation of the underdevelopment of most of the world, which was no less important than a general inability to raise supply. Malthus's theory of effective demand which he set out in his *Principles of Political Economy Considered With a View to Their Practical Application* of 1820 is the subject of Chapter 5. It was remarkably prescient, and in several respects it anticipates the twentieth-century theories of Keynes and Kalecki.

Ricardo was entirely unconvinced that effective demand influences growth, and his great extension and correction of Smith was the powerful theory of income distribution which follows from a grafting of agricultural diminishing returns on to the argument of *The Wealth of Nations*. With this and other important new theoretical insights, he was able to evolve a precise and logically complete theory of the interactions of the economy which allowed him to offer a wide range of policy advice to the House of Commons, of which he was a member from 1819 until his death in 1823. His *Principles of Political Economy and Taxation* of 1817 had offered an analysis of the influence on income distribution of every kind of tax, and like Quesnay before him, he was able to offer his contemporaries a complete account of the underlying forces which produce economic growth or decline, and how these can be expected to influence wages, profits and rents. This is the subject of Chapter 6.

Marx absorbed *all* the economic writings of his great predecessors, and he wrote thousands of pages (which mostly remained unpublished until long after his death) to explain where they were correct and where they had been superficial. By 1867, when he published the first volume of *Capital*, Britain was far more industrialised than in the time of Malthus and Ricardo, and this had raised profits vastly more than wages. Marx believed that his predecessors had overlooked the fundamental explanation of this development. They had failed to appreciate that all surpluses over wage costs, on which profits and rents and a society's investment potential must ultimately depend, are due to the social, political and legal conditions which allow the capitalist class to squeeze more labour from the working class than the production of goods for workers' subsistence actually requires. To Marx, profits and rents were ultimately due to the power of capitalists to coerce workers to labour with unnecessary intensity and for excessive hours, and his theory of exploitation is the subject of Chapter 7.

Marx believed in addition that his predecessors had erred in taking it for granted that capital accumulation would raise the demand for labour. He believed instead that industrial and agricultural investment was beginning to displace labour, and that increases in the capital stock would in the end cease to create opportunities to raise employment. The fruits of technical advance would then go entirely to capitalists because competition for jobs from the growing reserve army of the unemployed could be guaranteed to hold wages down. Even capitalists would begin to suffer from a declining rate of profit as mechanisation continued to advance, though their aggregate profits would continue to grow for some time after the rate of profit began to fall. Moreover, capitalists could not be expected to spend all the gains which market forces together with these technical trends allocated to them. Hence capitalism would collapse because effective demand would cease to keep pace with the enormous growth in productive potential which increasing mechanisation was all the time creating. These technical trends and their implications are the subject of Chapter 8.

Finally, the way in which each of these theories of growth follows from its predecessors, which is merely touched on here, is the subject of Chapter 9, which sums up the classical theory of economic growth and explains why some aspects of these eighteenth- and nineteenth-century theories have become obsolete, while others are still vitally relevant to our world.

Restatements of the theories of the great eighteenth- and nineteenth-century economists present particular problems. What they had to say was of exceptional originality and interest, but they did not write with the clarity and rigour of modern economics, and the presentation of economic argument has advanced. Nowadays assumptions are stated clearly, and conclusions are derived from these and tested against the available data. Does logical theory of the modern kind underpin the far less clear writings of Quesnay, Smith, Malthus, Ricardo and Marx? It has been my assumption in writing this book that it does. The inferior economists of the eighteenth and nineteenth centuries are inconsistent and episodic in a way in which these great authors are not, and it has seemed overwhelmingly plausible that their argument rests on an underlying logical structure. The problem is to ascertain what that structure is.

Quesnay-like, Smith-like, Malthus-like, Ricardo-like and Marx-like theories can be constructed *ad infinitum*. How can there be any confidence that modern restatements amount to the theory which actually underlies the thought of the economists in question? For this two conditions must be met. The assumptions must be precisely those of these authors and the conclusions derived from the assumptions must be theirs. It is a relatively simple matter to set out a model which claims to be Smith's or Malthus's, to arrive at several of their results, and then to claim that those of their conclusions which differ from purported twentieth-century restatements do so because of eighteenth- and nineteenth-century logical error. Modern restatements are only likely to be the appropriate ones if the conclusions are overwhelmingly those arrived at by the original authors.

In the present book I have followed the procedure of stating the assumptions of these economists entirely through quotation from their own work. As well as ensuring that their own assumptions are indeed being followed, this should give readers some feel for the way in which they thought, which bald modern restatements of their assumptions can hardly provide. In the case of Malthus's theory of population, and Marx's theory of exploitation, with which Chapters 4 and 7 are concerned, a full statement of their assumptions in their own words was almost all that was needed. Their conclusions follow easily and naturally from these, and further problems of interpretation are only slightly controversial. For the explanation of Quesnay's *Tableau*, Smith's theory of growth, Malthus's theory of effective demand, Ricardo's theory of distribution, and Marx's theory of the tendency towards a declining rate of profit and a growing reserve army of labour, far more is involved. The conclusions do not follow at once from these authors' published premises, so it is necessary to find simple but convincing logical argument which leads from the assumptions to the conclusions.

The restatements which are offered here contain non-mathematical accounts of the argument, and in addition brief mathematical restatements. These are there to show how a mathematical argument would go, and to convince readers that the economists in question arrived at logically consistent conclusions which can be stated in the modern way. Such mathematics forms only a small fraction of the book, and readers will follow almost all of its argument if they are unable (or decline) to read the mathematical sections (which are preceded by an asterisk). I have however allowed a little mathematics to pervade the whole of the chapter on Ricardo. His work is so deep-rooted in abstract logic that a wholly non-algebraic statement confined to a single chapter could make known to readers only a travesty of his contribution. The present restatement which arrives at many of his principal results should be comprehensible to all who are not resistant to a little algebra of the most elemental kind.

My first effort to write about classical economics resulted from the invitation I received in 1972 to contribute an account of Adam Smith's theory of economic growth, set out in modern terms, to the *Essays on Adam Smith* which Tom Wilson and Andrew Skinner were editing for the Oxford University Press in connection with the bicentenary of *The Wealth of Nations*. Klaus Hennings gave me the admirable advice that when I was satisfied that I had found an appropriate modern representation of Smith's argument, I should re-read *The Wealth of Nations* and only be content if I found no passages in the book which were in conflict with my attempted restatement. I have followed this procedure with all the chapters, and I was fortunate enough to find a reformulation of Smith's argument which arrived at results which corresponded to all his statements about the growth process of which I was aware. This forms the basis of Chapter 3, but this has developed considerably from the version I published in *Essays on Adam Smith*. It has benefited especially from a reaction of Max Hartwell's. He believed that I had looked at Smith peculiarly as an economist, by focusing attention on technical connections such as those between investment, laws of returns and the rate of growth, and ignored Smith's deep concern with the nature of social institutions. Capital would inevitably accumulate in an environment in which individuals' natural motivations to increase their personal wealth could flourish, and the technicalities of the accumulation process were of secondary importance compared with this. That vital thread in Smith's argument, with its origins in *The Theory of Moral Sentiments*, and others which I neglected in my original version, are now very much a part of the argument.

I followed my essay on Smith's theory of growth with an attempt which began in 1973 to understand Quesnay's challenging *Tableau Economique* and its implications. In the next eighteen months I read everything I could find by Quesnay and about him, and I only fully grasped the richness and depth of his argument after the Library of the Taylor Institution in Oxford University had managed to obtain a copy of *L'Ami des Hommes*, which included the final volumes to which Quesnay contributed, through an intra-library loan from Berlin. Eighteenth-century Oxford had failed to appreciate that important economics was being published in France, and there were no copies of Quesnay's work in collaboration with Victor de Riqueti, Marquis de Mirabeau, in the Bodleian Library or in any of the twenty-eight College libraries. The explanation of the *Tableau* in disequilibrium in *L'Ami des Hommes* made it crystal clear to me for the first time that this eighteenth-century French doctor was actually making the Keynes-like assumption that the demand for food and manufactures depended upon the repeated expenditures of precise fractions of the coin originally received by landlords. Once I grasped this (and there had been several references to this multiplier process in other passages which I had not taken in because it had not occurred to me that Quesnay could have discovered anything so 'modern'), the rest fell into place quite naturally, and I was able to publish restatements of the *Tableau* and of Quesnay's theory of economic growth in *Oxford Economic Papers* in 1975. These two articles have been republished since in Italian and in Spanish, and they form the basis for Chapters 1 and 2. The versions here have benefited from literature which followed their publication including Guido

Candela's 'La Fisiocrazia Secondo Eltis' (1976), and from correspondence with the late Ronald Meek.

My subsequent work on Malthus and Ricardo which preoccupied me from 1976 to 1979 (although I had started to lecture on them in the early 1960s) has benefited immeasurably from the help and kindness of Samuel Hollander. He was instrumental in my receiving an invitation to spend a sabbatical year as a Visiting Professor in the University of Toronto in 1976–7, he read earlier versions of each chapter, and his comments and many insights into the work of Malthus and Ricardo have been of immense value to me. My restatement of Ricardo in Chapter 6 has more of the 'corn model' than his *The Economics of David Ricardo* (1979), though I have followed John Hicks (1972) in substituting 'necessities' – a workers' consumer basket which includes both food and manufactures – for the far more limited assumption which Ricardo rapidly discarded that workers consume only corn. My work on Ricardo has also benefited from comments and discussion with Carlo Casarosa, while my work on Malthus has been much assisted by the detailed and sharp criticisms of Robert Dixon when I spent a term in the University of Melbourne in 1979. The account of Malthus's theory of effective demand which appeared in *Oxford Economic Papers* in 1980 owes much to his advice. The version which appears here as Chapter 5 should be easier to follow than that 1980 version, as I believe I have been able to simplify the argument without losing anything essential.

My most recent work, which has been on Marx, has benefited greatly from comments by Wlodek Brus, Robert Dixon, Andrew Glyn, Geoffrey Harcourt and Michael Kaser, and above all, when I believed the work was done, from Alberto Chilosi. He uncovered a major weakness in Chapter 8 when I presented a seminar in Pisa in 1981 at the invitation of Carlo Casarosa, and the present form of Chapter 8 owes much to his criticisms, both personal and in subsequent correspondence.

Finally I am indebted to my colleague, Paul Slack, and to my pupils who have read most of these chapters in various versions in the past ten years. Their final form has been influenced by their often acute criticisms and comments.

WALTER ELTIS

Abbreviations for Much-cited Works and the Editions Used

FRANÇOIS QUESNAY

Q   *François Quesnay et la Physiocratie*, Institut National d'Etudes Démographiques, Paris, 2 vols, 1958, which contains the text of most of Quesnay's economic writings.

Tab   *Quesnay's Tableau Economique*, ed. Marguerite Kuczyinski and Ronald L. Meek, Macmillan, London, 1972.

AH   *L'Ami des Hommes*, Mirabeau (and Quesnay), a 1756–60 Avignon edition reprinted by Scientia Verlag Aalen, 1970.

PR   *Philosophie Rurale,* Mirabeau (and Quesnay), one of the 1764 Amsterdam editions (there is another with different pagination) reprinted by Scientia Verlag Aalen, 1972.

Where the letter [E] follows a page reference the responsibility for a translation is the present author's, while the letter [M] signifies that a translation is by Ronald Meek.

ADAM SMITH

TMS   *The Theory of Moral Sentiments*, ed. D. D. Raphael and A.L. Macfie.

WN   *An Inquiry into the Nature and Causes of the Wealth of Nations*, ed. R. H. Campbell and A. S. Skinner, 2 vols.

Jur   *Lectures on Jurisprudence*, ed. R. L. Meek and D. D. Raphael and P. G. Stein.

S.Corr *The Correspondence of Adam Smith*, ed. E. C. Mossener and
I. S. Ross.
These volumes are from *The Glasgow Edition of the Works
and Correspondence of Adam Smith*, Oxford University
Press, 1976 onwards.

THOMAS R. MALTHUS

Pop *Essay on Population*, 1st edn 1798, signified by edn 1; and
similarly for 2nd edn 1803; 3rd edn 1806; 4th edn 1807; 5th
edn 1817; and 6th edn 1826.

Pr *Principles of Political Economy*, 1st edn 1820; signified by
edn 1; and similarly for 2nd edn 1836.

Def *Definitions of Political Economy*, 1st edn 1827.

Ess *The Pamphlets of Thomas Robert Malthus*, Kelley, New
York, 1970, in which Malthus's shorter pamphlets are
reprinted.

Occ *Occasional Papers of T. R. Malthus*, ed. B. Semmel,
Franklin, New York, 1963, in which Malthus's articles in the
Edinburgh Review and the *Quarterly Review* are reprinted.

DAVID RICARDO

R *The Works and Correspondence of David Ricardo*, ed. Piero
Sraffa, Cambridge University Press, 11 vols, 1951–73.

KARL MARX

WPP *Wages, Price and Profit* (1865), reprinted in K. Marx and
F. Engels, *Selected Works*, 3 vols, Moscow, 1969.

Cap *Capital*, 1867–83, reprinted in Moscow for Lawrence &
Wishart, London, 3 vols, 1974. The pagination of the various
Moscow editions of *Capital* differs.

TSV *Theories of Surplus Value*, published in Moscow for
Lawrence & Wishart, London, 3 vols, 1969–71.

1 François Quesnay's *Tableau Economique*

François Quesnay's achievement is one of the most remarkable in the history of economics. He published his first article on an economic problem in 1756 when he was 62 years old, and in the following twelve years he produced a series of influential articles and successive versions of his famous *Tableau Economique*. He also became the centre of the first school of economists, the Physiocrats or *Economistes* of pre-revolutionary France. The *Tableau* has two multipliers, one of them almost Keynesian, and Leontief has said that he was following Quesnay when he constructed his input-output table of the United States economy in 1941.[1] Marx, who according to Schumpeter derived his fundamental conception of the economic process as a whole from Quesnay,[2] called it 'an extremely brilliant conception, incontestably the most brilliant for which political economy had up to then been responsible',[3] and in 1935 Schumpeter himself described Quesnay as one of the four greatest economists of all time.[4]

Born the son of a farmer, Quesnay first achieved distinction as a surgeon, becoming Secretary of the French Association of Surgeons, a member of the French Academy of Sciences, and a Fellow of the Royal Society of London. In addition he became one of four consultant doctors to King Louis XV, with an entresol at Versailles, where he was also Madame de Pompadour's private physician.[5] His first economic publications were two articles, '*Fermiers*' (1756) and '*Grains*' (1757), which Diderot and D'Alembert published in the *Encyclopedia*. These provide a more detailed account of the agriculture of the time than the work of any other great classical economist, and they set out the foundations of Quesnay's theory of the working of economies, and the policies needed to ensure France's recovery

1

from expensive wars and rural depopulation. The first edition of the *Tableau* followed a year later. This was gradually modified and refined until, in 1764, Quesnay's principal collaborator, Victor de Riqueti, Marquis de Mirabeau, was able to write in a Preface to *Philosophie Rurale*, the book (written with Quesnay) which 'provides the most complete and authentic account of the Physiocratic system considered as a whole',[6] that he was providing all the propositions needed to form an exact and complete theory of the working of economies, and:

> The *Tableau Economique* is the first rule of arithmetic which has been invented to reduce elementary economic science to precise and exact calculations ...
> Calculations are to economic science what bones are to the human body ... economic science is deepened and extended by examination and reasoning, but without calculations it will always be an inexact science, confused and everywhere open to error and prejudice. (PR XL–XLI [E])

By 1764 Quesnay had indeed evolved a complete model of the working of economies as Mirabeau claims, and this allowed the full dynamic effects of changes in, for instance, the productivity of the soil, taxation, and the propensities to consume food and manufactures to be estimated. However, subsequent writers who have attempted to reconstruct the model have faced considerable difficulties, for each version of the argument, read in isolation, contains assertions that have no clear logical basis and apparent gaps in the argument, inconsistencies, and puzzling calculations. Almost all the problems are solved, however, and the apparent inconsistencies removed when Quesnay's published works are read as a whole (most have still been published only in French), and in addition, the important books he wrote in collaboration with Mirabeau, in particular Part VI of *L'Ami des Hommes* entitled '*Tableau Economique avec ses Explications*', and *Philosophie Rurale*. Clearly only scholars with a particular interest in his work will go to this much trouble to understand him, but those like Schumpeter who persevered until they understood the model developed a great admiration for its originator.

In this chapter and the next on François Quesnay's theory of economic growth, an attempt will be made to present a modern reconstruction of Quesnay's account of the working of economies. In the present chapter an account will be given of the basic assumptions on which his analysis is based, and how these lead directly to the famous *Tableau Economique*. The successive versions of the *Tableau* will then be explained. In the chapter that follows on Quesnay's theory of economic growth, the effects of departures from the *Tableau's* equilibrium proportions will be shown. The scheme of simple reproduction depicted in the *Tableau* is merely the starting-point for the analysis of real problems, and any departure from the *Tableau's* exact equilibrium proportions must produce clearly analysable effects, including growth or decline in the economy's level of output and employment. The conditions which produce growth and decline will be systematically set out, and it will be shown that they are precisely those which Quesnay emphasised when he discussed real economies.

The exposition of his argument in this chapter and the next follows closely Mirabeau's plan for the teaching of economic science to French children in a school the Physiocrats set up in 1767:

> The class shall learn: 1° to know and understand the Tableau as it is ... 2° After this, the assumptions will be changed ... and they should be left to do the addition and work out the result themselves; this to be continued until they can work out each case easily, be it of growth or decline. 3° When they are at this stage, we should come to the problems, that is to say of arbitrary disturbances to distribution ...
>
> This completes that part of education of this type which is absolutely necessary and indispensable for all those who have received enough education to learn the four first rules of arithmetic.[7]

The Physiocrats were clearly convinced that they had discovered important truths about the working of economies.

QUESNAY'S ASSUMPTIONS

In this part of the chapter, Quesnay's basic assumptions about the factors which influence the development of economies will be outlined in turn. The first stage of the exposition is an account of his assumptions about techniques of production in agriculture and industry and their effectiveness, for this leads to the fundamental Physiocratic proposition that only agriculture produces a surplus or 'net product' over costs (where these arguably include a 'normal profit'), the size of the surplus depending on the capital intensity of agriculture. The second stage of the exposition, which follows directly from this, is an account of Quesnay's remarkable assumption that the economy's effective demand for marketable output depends on the expenditure of the agricultural surplus by landlords which has a multiplier effect on demand, and the further assumption that the relative size of the agricultural and industrial sectors of the economy depends upon how demand is distributed between them. The best known Physiocratic propositions all follow from these assumptions, that is, that agriculture which alone produces a 'net product' must be the ultimate source of all tax revenue; that the economy cannot grow without agricultural growth; and that the industrial sector is wholly dependent on the agricultural, since the demand for manufactures depends on the size of the 'net product' which is wholly derived from agriculture.

The foundation of the whole system of thought is Quesnay's analysis of agricultural techniques of production which he first outlined in his *Encyclopedia* articles of 1756 and 1757. There he distinguished three techniques of production: the cultivation of land with labour alone, cultivation with ox-drawn ploughs, and cultivation with horse-drawn ploughs.

Where labourers cannot find employment with a *métayer* using oxen or a farmer using horses:

> they leave the countryside, or else they are reduced to feeding themselves on oatmeal, barley, buckwheat, potatoes, and other cheap products which they grow themselves, and which they don't need to wait long to harvest. The cultivation of corn takes too much time and effort; they cannot wait two years for a crop.[8] Its cultivation is reserved for the farmer who can meet the expense, or the *métayer* who is helped by the landlord. (Q 446–7 [E])

and

> When the peasant works the soil himself, it is evidence of his wretchedness and uselessness. Four horses cultivate more than a hundred *arpents* [125 acres]; four men cultivate less than eight. (Q 453 [E])

and finally

A poor man who only draws from the land by his labour produce of little value such as potatoes, buckwheat, chestnuts, etc., who feeds himself on them, who buys nothing and sells nothing, works only for himself: he lives in wretchedness, and he and the land he tills bring nothing to the state. (Q 498 [E])

Thus, where farming must be undertaken without the capital of either a landlord or a rich farmer who employs others, there is no marketable agricultural surplus. The standard of living is so low that anything which reduces it further causes actual deaths through starvation (Q 553) and the peasant can pay no rent to the owner of the land. He thus makes no contribution to his landlord, the Church, or the State.

However, a surplus can be earned with two alternative techniques, the cultivation of the land with ploughs drawn by either oxen or horses, and Quesnay makes a series of detailed comparisons between these techniques.[9] Before the economic differences are examined, there is an important institutional difference:

It is only wealthy farmers who can use horses to work the soil. A farmer who sets himself up with a four-horse plough must incur considerable expenditure before he obtains his first crop: for a year he works the land which he must sow with corn, and after he has sown he only reaps in the August of the following year: thus he waits almost two years for the fruits of his work and his outlay. He has incurred the expense of the horses and the other animals that he needs; he provides the seed corn for the ground, he feeds the horses, he pays for the wages and the food of the servants; and all these expenses he is obliged to advance for the first two years' cultivation of a four-horse plough demesne are estimated to be 10 or 12 thousand livres: and 20 or 30 thousand livres in a farm large enough for two or three plough teams ...

In the provinces where there are no farmers able to obtain such establishments, the only way in which the landlords can get some produce from their land is to have it cultivated with oxen by peasants who give them half the crop. This type of cultivation calls for very little outlay on the part of the *métayer*: the landlord provides him with oxen and seed corn, and after their work the oxen feed on the pasture land; the total expenditure of the *métayer* comes down to the ploughing equipment and his outlay for food up to the first harvest, and the landlord is often obliged to advance even these expenses. (Q 428 [E])

Thus farming with horse-drawn ploughs which Quesnay calls '*la grande culture*' is undertaken by entrepreneurial *farmers*, while ox-drawn ploughs are used by *métayers* and Quesnay calls this kind of farming '*la petite culture*'. Where entrepreneur farmers are not available, landlords cannot have their land cultivated with horse-drawn ploughs, for:

> they would not find *métayers* or ploughmen [*charretiers*] able to handle and supervise horses in these provinces. They would have to arrange for them to come from far away, which could involve considerable inconvenience, for if a qualified ploughman falls ill or retires, work ceases. Such events are highly damaging, especially in busy seasons: and besides the master is too dependent on his servants, whom he cannot easily replace when they wish to leave, or when they work badly. (Q 429 [E])

This means that the availability of rich farmers is the crucial factor that determines which technique is used. As soon as *la grande culture* and *la petite culture* are compared in detail, it emerges that the use of ox-drawn ploughs has great disadvantages. First, many more oxen are needed:

> The work of oxen is much slower than that of horses: besides the oxen spend a lot of time grazing on the pastures for their own food; that is why normally twelve oxen, and sometimes as many as eighteen are needed in a farm which can be worked by four horses. (Q 429 [E])

These large numbers of oxen need to be fed:

> These oxen eat up the hay from his meadows, and a large part of the land of his demesnes remains fallow for their pasture; thus his property is badly cultivated and almost worthless. (Q 445 [E])

Moreover, the oxen will be used part of the time for the peasants' own profit:

> the *métayers* who share the crop with the owner keep the oxen

entrusted to them busy as often as they can by pulling carts for their own profit, which is more in their interests than ploughing the land; thus they so neglect its cultivation that most of the land stands fallow if the landlord fails to pay attention. (Q 431 [E])

The land which the oxen need for pasture, and the land that is otherwise uncultivated can be very profitably stocked with other animals. Quesnay specifies herds of sheep, beef cattle, calves, pigs, and poultry, but he points out that these cannot be entrusted to *métayers*. A particularly important point here is the manure that is obtained from the herds that can be stocked when the horse-drawn plough technique is used by rich farmers: Quesnay suggests that this may almost double grain yields (Q 430–1). Moreover, with the assumptions of *la grande culture* a wide variety of products can be grown by the rich farmers on land that is not quite good enough for wheat farming, and these are outlined in '*Grains*' (Q 477).

Quesnay makes detailed comparisons between the profitability of *la petite culture* and *la grand culture* in the context of the France of the 1750s, costing horses, oxen, animal feeding stuffs, farm workers, and so on, and making assumptions about soil yields with the various techniques, and the prices at which grains will be sold over an average of good and bad harvests. He summarises his results as follows:

It has been seen from the previous details that the cost of farming 30 million *arpents* of land with *la petite culture* is only 285 million [livres]; and that one would have to pay out 710 million to farm 30 million *arpents* with *la grande culture*; but in the first case the product is only 390 million [livres], and it would be 1,378 million in the second. Even greater outlays would produce still greater profits; the costs and men needed in addition with the best methods of cultivation for the purchase and management of farm animals bring in on their side a product which is scarcely less than that of the crops. (Q 504–5 [E])

With *la petite culture* the *net product* or the excess of output over the annual costs of agriculture is 390 *minus* 285 million livres, or 105 million livres, and the ratio of this to annual expenditure, one of the crucial ratios of the Physiocrats, is 105/285 or 36 per cent. With *la grande culture* the *net product is* 1378 *minus* 710 million livres, or 668 million livres, and 710 million livres of annual advances then yield a rate of return of 668/710 or 93 per cent, which Quesnay later rounds up to 100 per cent, legitimately in view of the fact that not all the products of agriculture have been included in the actual calculations.

These are rates of return on what Quesnay calls the 'annual advances' or circulating capital – the equivalence is nearly exact – of agriculture, that is, the investment in raw materials, wages and so on that must be made each year to produce a harvest. Farmers must also provide 'original advances' or fixed capital, that is, animals including horses in particular, ploughs, farm buildings and so on which do not need to be paid for each year, but these depreciate, or need regular replacement, and it is assumed that 'interest' at a rate of 10 per cent must be earned on the total capital of farmers to cover this.[10] In his later writings Quesnay assumes that the original advances of farmers are four or five times their annual advances with the methods of *la grande culture*[11] (no figure for *la petite culture* is given) and a rate of return on annual advances of 100 per cent will be 20 per cent on total farm capital if original advances or fixed capital are four times annual advances, so that total capital is five times annual advances. Similarly, the rate of return with *la petite culture* will be less than 36 per cent, and if original advances or fixed capital with this technique are twice annual advances, the rate of return on total capital will be about 12 per cent.

It will be evident that Quesnay attributes overwhelming importance to the agricultural technique of production. With no agricultural capital, grain farming is impossible, and the commercial yield of agriculture is zero, while the standard of living is barely sufficient to support life. With the low capital per acre ox-drawn plough technique, agriculture yields a return over annual advances of between 30 and 40 per cent and a return on total capital of perhaps 12 per cent, while with the capital intensive horse-drawn plough technique, agriculture can yield 100 per cent on annual advances and perhaps 20 per cent on total capital. With the assumptions of modern economics, the horse-drawn plough technique which is superior at virtually all factor prices would rapidly drive *la petite culture* out of existence, but it must be remembered that the institutional factors which Quesnay enumerated prevent this. Thus, only rich farmers can use the techniques of *la grande culture*, so landlords must have recourse to *métayers* who will farm with the techniques of *la petite culture* if there are too few rich farmers. Moreover, in the absence of banks able to lend at moderate rates of interest, farmers cannot add significantly to their own capital by borrowing, so the supply of capital of the rich farmers is inelastic.

It is interesting to contrast Quesnay's very detailed assumptions about agricultural techniques with the propositions of his great successors. Thus Ricardo, who believed that farm workers must generally produce high outputs on good land, apparently thought that 'the adoption of spade husbandry, and the dismissal of the horses and oxen from the work of the farm' might reduce agricultural output by about one-tenth.[12] According to Quesnay this would entirely destroy any agricultural surplus. In his account, it is capital and not labour or land that is of crucial importance:

> Inefficient cultivation however requires much work; but as the cultivator cannot meet the necessary expenses his work is unfruit-ful; he succumbs: and the stupid bourgeois attribute his bad results to idleness. They probably believe that all that is needed to make the land bear good crops is to work it and agitate it; there is general approval when a poor man who is unemployed is told 'go and work the land'. It is horses, oxen, and not men who should work the land. It is herds which should fertilize it; without these aids it scarcely repays the work of the cultivators. Don't people know besides that the land gives no payment in advance, that on the contrary it makes one wait a long time for the harvest? What then might be the fate of that poor man to whom they say 'go and work the land'? Can he till for his own account? Will he find work with the farmers if they are poor? The latter, powerless to meet the costs of good cultivation, in no state to pay the wages of servants and workers, cannot employ the peasants. The unfertil-ized and largely uncultivated land can only let them all languish in wretchedness. (Q 505 [E])

And finally, even the farmer must not be regarded as one who obtains his income from work. This is not what is needed:

> We do not see the rich farmer here as a worker who tills the soil himself; he is an entrepreneur who manages his undertaking and makes it prosper through his intelligence and his wealth. Agricul-ture carried on by rich cultivators is an honest and lucrative profession, reserved for free men who are in a position to advance the considerable sums the cultivation of the land requires, and it employs the peasants and gives them a suitable and assured return for their work. (Q 483 [E])

Thus capital in the hands of rich entrepreneurs who are willing to farm is the mainspring of an efficient agriculture, which will provide employment at good wages on the land. It is interesting in this context that Quesnay suggests that a rate of return of 100 per cent or more really is earned on annual agricultural advances in England where *la grande culture* predominates and there are sufficient rich entrepreneurs who are willing to farm. The contrast between England, which has an efficient agriculture, and France, which does not, is brought out several times.[13]

Quesnay assumes quite clearly that capital and entrepreneurs are the only factors of production which are needed to expand agricultural production, for he states quite specifically that the availability of land and labour is not a problem. So far as land is concerned, he writes:

The cultivation of corn is very expensive; we have far more land than we need for it ... (Q 473 [E])

In the Kingdom there are 30 million *arpents* of cultivable land which are fallow, and the rest is poorly cultivated; because the production of grains does not repay the outlay. (Q 549–50 [E])

and he quotes approvingly from Plumart de Danguel:

If one travels through some of the provinces of France, one finds that not only does much of the land that could produce corn or nourish animals lie fallow, but that the cultivated lands do not produce anything approaching what they could, given their fertility; because the farmer lacks the means to bring them to their true value. (Q 493 [E])

There are also numerous passages where Quesnay speaks of the rural devastation of whole provinces and the depopulation which followed taxes that were unfavourable to agriculture. Clearly scarcity of land will not act as an obstacle to development, nor will the availability of labour. Quesnay follows Cantillon who wrote 'Men multiply like mice in a barn if they have unlimited means of subsistence'[14] and it was very much his view that the growth of capital determines the growth of population. Thus:

It is however only with the help of wealth that an agricultural state can enrich itself more and more; *for an abundance of wealth contributes more than an abundance of men to the growth of wealth; but on the other hand the growth of wealth increases the number of men in all remunerative occupations.* (Q 570 [E]: the emphasis is Quesnay's)

It is therefore through the increase of wealth that a nation can achieve the greatest advances in wealth, population and power. It would then be in vain for it to try to increase the number of men without first setting out to increase wealth. (Q 571 [E])

Moreover:

If the government diverts wealth from the source which reproduces it perpetually, it destroys wealth and men. (Q 542 [E])

and more fully:

Men bereft of edible wealth could not live in a desert, they would perish there if they found no animals or other natural products to feed themselves on up to the time when by their labours they had forced the land to supply them with the products necessary to satisfy their needs continuously. Hence wealth is needed in advance to obtain in succession other wealth to live on, and to come to live in comfort which favours propagation. A Kingdom where revenues are growing attracts new inhabitants through the earnings it can procure for them; therefore the growth of wealth increases the population. (Q 537–8 [E])

Hence lack of population would not be an obstacle to growth. With land also available, it is abundantly clear that Quesnay believed that the accumulation of agricultural capital was what was primarily necessary to produce growth of output and population.

Quesnay gave a detailed account of his assumptions about how labour and capital had to be combined to produce food with the various techniques of production he described, but he was at no point so explicit about the sectors of the economy responsible for manufacturing, personal services, transport, commerce, and trade – which he called 'sterile'. The choice of the word 'sterile' to describe the sectors of the economy responsible for these activities proved unfortunate and many nineteenth- and twentieth-century economists concluded that Quesnay's and the Physiocrats' analyses of the working of economies need not be taken seriously because of the absurdity that they regarded manufacturing as sterile. However, if Quesnay's assumptions about manufacturing and commerce are followed carefully, and the world 'sterile' is put on one side until what he is saying becomes clear, it emerges that Quesnay's propositions are not very far from the analysis of the relationship between industrial costs and prices that subsequently became conventional. Thus in 1757 Quesnay gave the following account of the connection between industrial costs and prices:

> The works of manufacture demand from those who make them expenditures and costs which are equal to the value of the manufactured goods ... the workman who makes a cloth buys the raw material and lays out the expenditure for his own needs while he is making it; the payment he receives when he sells it reimburses him what he has bought and his expenses; what he receives from his work is only the restitution of the expenses he has incurred, and it is by this restitution that he is able to continue to live by his work. The competition of workers who seek a similar return to live on limits the price of the work of manufacturing to this same return. (Q 583 [E])

Thus competition ensures that the prices of manufactures are no more than the raw material and labour costs required to produce them. There is thus apparently no allowance for profits in the prices of manufactures. However, it is evident from Quesnay's work taken as a whole that the wages manufacturers receive include something that is very close to the modern concept of a 'normal profit'. In 1763 he set out the incomes of all the workers of the economy in very great detail in Chapter 7 of *Philosophie Rurale* which he contributed, and in manufacturing, commerce, etc., he assumed that there were 300 000 *Gagistes supérieurs* who earned an average of 2 000 livres each, and 1 800 000 *Gagistes inférieurs* or artisans who earned an average of 500 livres each (Q 712). The entrepreneurs in agriculture who farmed two four-horse plough demesnes had an average income of just 1 200 livres, while servants and agricultural workers had incomes ranging from 125 to 500 livres a year (Q 702–3). Of the 1 200 livres that the farmer or agricultural entrepreneur received, 600 livres were for 'their subsistence and that of their family', while the whole 1 200 livres were for 'the enterprise of working two demesnes', which include a return for 'the work and risks of his enterprise' (Q 702–3 [E]). Clearly the *Gagiste supérieur* in industry who received 2 000 livres also received a return for enterprise and risk, that is, a return which is not so far from the concept of a 'normal profit'.[15] There is no specific reference to a return to an entrepreneur's own capital, that is, to profits on capital, as part of this 'normal profit', but it is most reasonable to think of the excess of the entrepreneur's income over subsistence as a return to the entrepreneurial capital he has to supply, and a return to enterprise and risk taking, and several of the passages that have been quoted make it very clear that entrepreneurs had to provide a great deal of capital to earn the kind of incomes that have been set out. Unfortunately, the position is not quite as clear as this because agricultural entrepreneurs also receive 'interest' to provide for the depreciation and replacement of their capital, and to provide a margin against contingencies. There is no reference at any point to similar provisions in industry (although in the detailed account of the income and capital of the economy in the *'Explication du Tableau Economique'* of 1759, industry was assumed to require the same fixed and working capital in relation to output as agriculture).[16] Quesnay's failure to refer to 'interest' in industry is usually regarded as a simplifying assumption, and it is most natural to assume that the return to industrial entrepreneurs which is set so high in relation to subsistence includes a return to risk and enterprise, and sufficient income to make it worthwhile for industrial entrepreneurs to continue their activities, that is, it includes what is now regarded as a 'normal profit' – the return that must be earned if they are to maintain constant output.

A point that should be noted here is that industry resembles agriculture in that 'advances' are needed for production, and in the subsequent *Tableau Economique* these advances (principally raw materials which must be bought in advance) form half of industrial costs, so output is twice annual advances in both the 'productive' and the 'sterile' sectors. However, in agriculture this doubling of advances produces a surplus as substantial further costs are not incurred, while in industry further costs, mainly the wage costs of working up raw materials into manufactures, are incurred as production proceeds, so the fact that output is twice advances does not mean that a surplus is produced, and in formal terms, a rate of return of zero is earned on the advances of the 'sterile' sector. With the present interpretation of Quesnay's argument, the 'normal profits' on these are included in the exceptional income of the *Gagistes supérieurs*, which is part of total wage and salary costs.

The fundamental assumptions which underlie the basic Physiocratic propositions that industry produces no surplus over costs while agriculture can produce a surplus if it is sufficiently capital intensive have now been outlined. The argument is basically that agriculture can earn something over and above costs (where these include a 'normal profit') while industry and commerce cannot. The extra earning power of agriculture is called its 'net product', and this is paid as rent or 'revenue' to the landlords. It is, however, basically a return on capital and not land, and it varies with the capital intensity of agriculture.

The fundamental question arises of why 'labour and capital' can produce a surplus over wages and normal profits in agriculture and not in industry. Quesnay's argument is that competition between entrepreneurs prevents the emergence of a surplus over costs in industry and commerce, so an increase in industrial efficiency will eventually cheapen products and not produce a surplus for the producers. Quesnay was naturally asked to explain the existence of large commercial fortunes. For instance, in 1766 he discussed the problem of how ten manufacturers at Nîmes were able to make a profit of 150 per cent on costs by buying silk in Spain or Italy, and selling it as cloth in Germany. His explanation was that if there were perfect competition (*concurrence libre*) this could not occur, and that the abnormal profit that arose as a result of its absence was earned at someone else's expense (Q 759 and 771–80).

In contrast, an increase in agricultural efficiency supposedly increases the size of the agricultural net product or surplus. The fundamental assumption that allows Quesnay to arrive at this result, and it is also made by the great English classical economists, is that agricultural costs are largely fixed in terms of food. Thus the subsistence needs of farm labourers which determine what they are paid in the long run with an elastic supply of population are largely food[17] and the farmer-entrepreneur gets a multiple of what labourers get. As the product of a farm is also food, an increase in agricultural efficiency, that is, in food production per farm, must raise output relatively to agricultural costs (which can both be measured in food) and so increase profits which must go to someone. In stationary state conditions, Quesnay allows no more to the farmers than the multiple of the labourers' long-term subsistence needs that ensures constant output, and with growth farmers only receive more than this for a few years until leases come up for renewal, so what they receive is limited. There is no reference to the possibility that landlords might sometimes allow farmers to earn more, in order to attract tenants.

Hence the bulk of any agricultural surplus must go to the owners of the land in the form of rents or 'revenue' – or, indeed, to the Church or the King. At a more fundamental level, it is the institutions of society – limitation of land ownership to the nobility, and property rights, which give the surplus to the landlords, even though land is not scarce.[18] Voltaire's reaction to the role of the Sovereign in 1767 (and the hereditary landlords are similarly placed) goes to the root of the matter. 'It is quite certain that the land pays everything; what man is not convinced of this truth? But that one man should be the proprietor of all the land, that is a monstrous idea.'[19]

This account of how agriculture can produce a 'net product' which is paid to the landlords, the Church and the State, while industry cannot, concludes the present account of what would now be called Quesnay's microeconomic assumptions. His macroeconomic analysis of how effective demand for agricultural and industrial output is determined, and how this influences the growth of the two sectors of the economy, makes use of the propositions which have been arrived at.

The macroeconomic analysis of demand determination developed gradually. In his *Encyclopedia* articles of 1756–7 Quesnay makes it clear that the demand for manufactures and personal services, that is, the demand for the products of the 'sterile' sector, and therefore for labour in manufactures and services, depends on the expenditure of the revenue or surplus of agriculture by the landlords who receive it. Thus:

> Industry procures subsistence for a multitude of men by paying for their workmanship; but it produces no revenue whatsoever and it can only be sustained by the revenue of the citizens who buy the works of the artisans. (Q 480 [E])
>
> The works of agriculture make good their expenses, repay the costs of work, procure incomes for the workers; and in addition produce the revenues of the estates. Those who buy industrial goods pay for the costs, and the workmanship, and the merchant's return; but these goods produce no income beyond this.
>
> Thus all the expenditure on the works of industry only draws revenue from landed income; for works which do not generate revenue can only exist through the wealth of those who pay for them. (Q 496 [E])

And moreover:

The expenditure of these revenues constitutes the returns of the citizens who follow well paid professions. (Q 548 [E])

As well as emphasising the importance of the expenditure of the revenue, these passages make clear the full reasons for the total dependence of all other economic activities on agriculture, and therefore why Quesnay used the word 'sterile' to describe them. Not only does the production of industrial goods and services produce no surplus over 'normal profits', but in addition, because demand depends on the expenditure of the surplus, the markets for the output of the remainder of the economy depend on expenditure flows which originate in agriculture. Moreover, the 'sterile' sector is dependent on the 'productive' sector for its raw materials. Agriculture in contrast is in no way dependent on the other sector.[20]

Quesnay's *Encyclopedia* articles show that as well as creating demand for manufactures and labour, the revenue is spent several times. Thus:

> The wealthy must be left free to spend. If affluence brings them to feed and pay for useless people, one must not place these domestic servants, it is true, in the ranks of men who play a part in the production of wealth; but one must at least see them as consumers who ensure the distribution of the money of the rich to all the well-paid professions; for the servants do not pile up wealth taken away from the circulation of the money that is destined to return continually to the source of annual wealth... It is with these servants as it is with the workmen engaged in making luxury articles for the nation's use: as these workmen are useful only in so far as they cause the rich to spend and as they spend themselves what they draw from their work. (Q 568 [E])

The expenditure of rents or revenues is not merely necessary to produce demand for manufactures, services, and the lucrative professions, for it is clear from the above quotation that it is essential that there is sufficient expenditure that returns to 'the source of annual wealth', that is, to agriculture. Thus again:

> A farmer has sold 100 *setiers* of corn for 1,600 livres. The landowner has received 1,600 livres for the rent of the land; he uses this sum to build; the workers to whom he has distributed it spend it on corn to feed themselves; thus the 1,600 livres returns to

the farmer who sold them the corn. This farmer spends this sum on cultivation, to make more corn grow; thus the expenditure of the landlord becomes the returns of the workers, who restore to the farmer the sum that he has paid to the landlord. If this sum is taken away from the landlord, or from the workers, or from the farmer, its return in sequence is destroyed; the source will provide it no longer, neither to the landlord, nor to the workers, nor to the farmer. Its perpetual reproduction, the expenditure of the land-lord, of the workers, of the farmer, are all suppressed; the corn which was the real wealth, which came into being again, and which was consumed each year to feed the men is destroyed, and men must look elsewhere for their subsistence, and the State is impoverished and depopulated. (Q 541–2 [E])

The maintenance of a continuing expenditure flow is crucial:

It is necessary that the owners of landed property who receive these revenues spend them each year so that this kind of wealth is distributed to the whole nation. Without this distribution the State could not subsist; if the landlords held back the revenues, it would be essential to despoil them of these; thus this type of wealth belongs as much to the State as to the landowners themselves; the latter only have the enjoyment of it so that they can spend it. (Q 582 [E])

These passages outline the position Quesnay had reached in 1757, namely that the expenditure of rents or revenues has an important influence on demand for the products of both industry and agriculture, and he may have owed much to Cantillon's account of the role that rents play in the circulation of demand.[21] A year later Quesnay set out the effect of the expenditure of rents formally for the first time in his first draft of the *Tableau Economique*, and this is illustrated in Figure 1.1 which shows the circulation of the revenue as it is set out in the early editions of the *Tableau* of 1758–9, with the revenue changed to 1 000 livres. He assumed here that landlords, farmers, and artisans spend half the money they receive on the outputs of the 'productive' sector, that is, on the products provided by 'agriculture, grasslands, pastures, forests, mines, fishing, etc.', and the remaining half on the products of the 'sterile' sector, that is, on 'manufactured commodities, house-room, clothing, interest on money, servants, commercial costs, foreign produce, etc.' (Tab edn3 i [M]). It is also assumed that

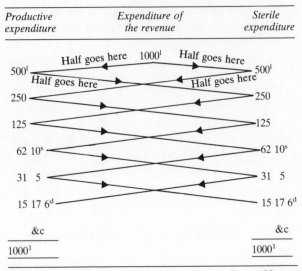

| Productive expenditure | Expenditure of the revenue | Sterile expenditure |

NOTE: l,s,d stand for livres, sous, and deniers; one livre = 20 sous, 1 sou = 12 deniers.

FIGURE 1.1

the expenditure flows between the classes, which are initiated by the expenditure of the 1 000 livres of revenue that the landlords receive, continue until the productive and sterile sectors have each received 1 000 livres, as in Figure 1.1. The expenditure of rents gives the productive and sterile sectors 500 livres each. Both sectors retain half of this until the end of the circulation process, supplying themselves with half their consumption needs from their own sector, and spend the remaining half of the 500 livres on the products of the other sector.[22] Both sectors therefore receive a further 250 livres from the other, and when this is spent, half on each side, they receive a further 125 livres each, and so on, as in the diagram, until total expenditure is twice the original expenditure of the landlords. Quesnay underlined precisely this aspect of the expenditure flows of the *Tableau* in 1763 in Chapter 7 of *Philosophie Rurale*:

With the assumptions of the present *Tableau* in which the advances of the productive class give rise to 100 per cent of revenue, this revenue which is spent in the year passes in its entirety to the productive class, and in entirety to the sterile class through the reciprocal transfers between one class and the other. (Q 699 [E])

Thus a multiplier of *two* can be applied to the expenditure of rents, and the aggregate domestic market demand for the products of the two sectors will be exactly twice the initial expenditure of rents – where the three classes (landlords, productive workers, sterile workers) always spend half the money they receive on the products of each sector. They may divide their expenditure differently, and a progression is illustrated in Part vi of *L'Ami des Hommes* which was published in 1760 where five-twelfths of all expenditures go to the productive and seven-twelfths to the sterile class. The revenue in the *Tableau* in question is 1 050 livres, and the zigzags then bring 915 livres in all to the productive and 1 146 livres to the sterile class, with the result that the expenditure multiplier is slightly less than two (AH vi. 192). The money receipts of the two sectors can always be inferred precisely from (i) total rents or revenues, and (ii) the proportion of money receipts that each class spends on the output of the productive sector of the economy. The precise formulae are set out in Figure 1.2, where total rents are R, and the proportion of all incomes that is spent on the productive side is q. The formulae set out in Figure 1.2

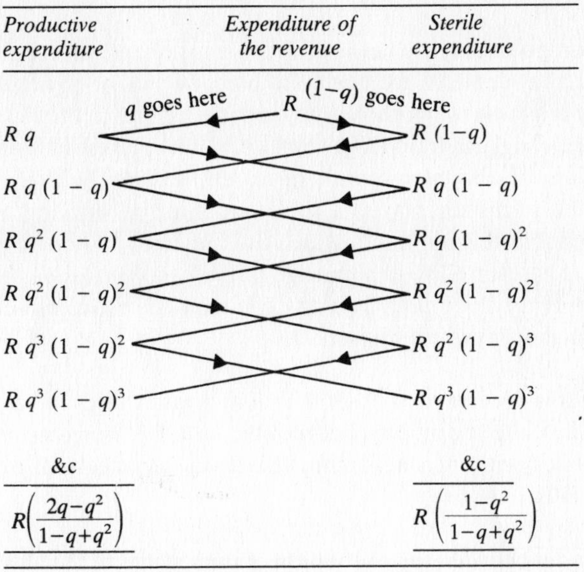

Productive expenditure	Expenditure of the revenue	Sterile expenditure
	q goes here ← R $(1-q)$ goes here	
$R\,q$		$R\,(1-q)$
$R\,q\,(1-q)$		$R\,q\,(1-q)$
$R\,q^2\,(1-q)$		$R\,q\,(1-q)^2$
$R\,q^2\,(1-q)^2$		$R\,q^2\,(1-q)^2$
$R\,q^3\,(1-q)^2$		$R\,q^2\,(1-q)^3$
$R\,q^3\,(1-q)^3$		$R\,q^3\,(1-q)^3$
&c		&c
$R\left(\dfrac{2q-q^2}{1-q+q^2}\right)$		$R\left(\dfrac{1-q^2}{1-q+q^2}\right)$

FIGURE 1.2

produce the exact totals outlined in the '*Tableau Economique avec ses Explications*' of 1760.[23]

The exact results arrived at by Quesnay and Mirabeau clearly depend on the assumptions that all receipts will be spent at every stage of the circulation process, and that none of the revenue is lost overseas, and these are Quesnay's first assumptions in each edition of the *Tableau* of 1758–9. Thus, from the first printed edition where the total revenue is 600 million livres:

> But in this distribution it is assumed:
> 1. That the whole of the 600 millions of revenue enters into the annual circulation, and runs through it to the full extent of its course; and that it is never formed into monetary fortunes, or at least that those which are formed are counterbalanced by those which come back into circulation; for otherwise these monetary fortunes would check the flow of a part of this annual revenue of the nation, and hold back the money stock or finance of the kingdom, to the detriment of the reproduction of the revenue and the well-being of the people.
> 2. That no part of the sum of revenue passes into the hands of foreign countries without return in money or commodities. (Tab edn2 3[M])

The assumption that the net product or rents of agriculture determine the effective demand for the marketed output of agriculture and industry is a most remarkable one, and it is unique to the Physiocrats. It has been suggested that Quesnay's previous published work on the circulation of the blood may have led him to believe that the circulation of money played a similar role in the working of economies, and that this led him towards the *Tableau*.[24] The circulation of the blood is referred to in a passage in *Philosophie Rurale*, but this is in a part of the book that Quesnay commented on extensively rather than one that he wrote himself:

> Here it is necessary to observe that it is with this circulation of the money of the revenue as it is with the blood. It is necessary that all circulates without slackening, the least stoppage will produce a clot. (PR i.66 [E])

The parallel between the circulation of money and of the blood is not, however, brought out in any passage clearly drafted by Quesnay himself.

The crucial assumptions on which Quesnay's analysis rests have now been outlined. It will be evident that his assumptions about the relationship between inputs and outputs in industry and agriculture, and about income distribution and the determination of effective demand for food and manufactures, produce an account of the working of economies that is far from simple. Quesnay could doubtless have set out his argument in algebra (for his last book was concerned with mathematical problems) but he chose instead to use diagrammatic methods of exposition based on the *Tableau Econo-mique* which he invented in 1758, and he later showed dynamic processes with a series of *Tableaux* which represented the economy in different years. Quesnay may well have believed that an argument based on the *Tableau* would be more widely accessible. The following passage from '*Tableau Economique avec ses Explications*' is interest-ing in this context: 'we have not claimed to make of it a work of Algebra, considered with all the relationships to which it is suscep-tible; that would be the amusement of a Geometer, useless to the aim of the Author, who has only presented in the *Tableau* the points of view that are indispensably necessary, and as it is, one will still find it only too complicated' (AH vi.129 [E]). Sadly, the failure to provide an algebraic account made it immensely difficult for later generations (and indeed for Quesnay's own contemporaries) to grasp the argu-ment fully, and this has actually added to the complications with which readers have to cope.

An attempt will now be made to supplement Quesnay's diagrammatic exposition with an account of the basic interrelation-ships that underlie the *Tableau Economique*.

QUESNAY'S *TABLEAU ECONOMIQUE*, AND ITS EXPLANATION

Quesnay's basic *Tableau* of the early editions of 1758–9 is set out in Figure 1.3, with Annual Agricultural Advances, the base of the *Tableau*, set at 1 000 livres. This *Tableau* incorporates the expendi-ture flows which were discussed in the earlier part of the chapter, and in addition some of Quesnay's other important propositions. Perhaps the most important of these is the principle that agriculture (or the productive sector) can produce a surplus or 'net product' of 100 per cent, while industry produces no surplus. This is firmly incorporated in the *Tableau*, for it will be noted that against each receipt of the productive sector in the left-hand column are the words 'reproduce net' followed by an identical sum of money printed in the column headed 'Annual revenue', so each 100 livres that the agriculturists receive from the year's expenditure flows reproduce and become 200 livres that can be disposed of in the following year. There is no extra column to the right of the 'Sterile expenditure' column, so 100 livres

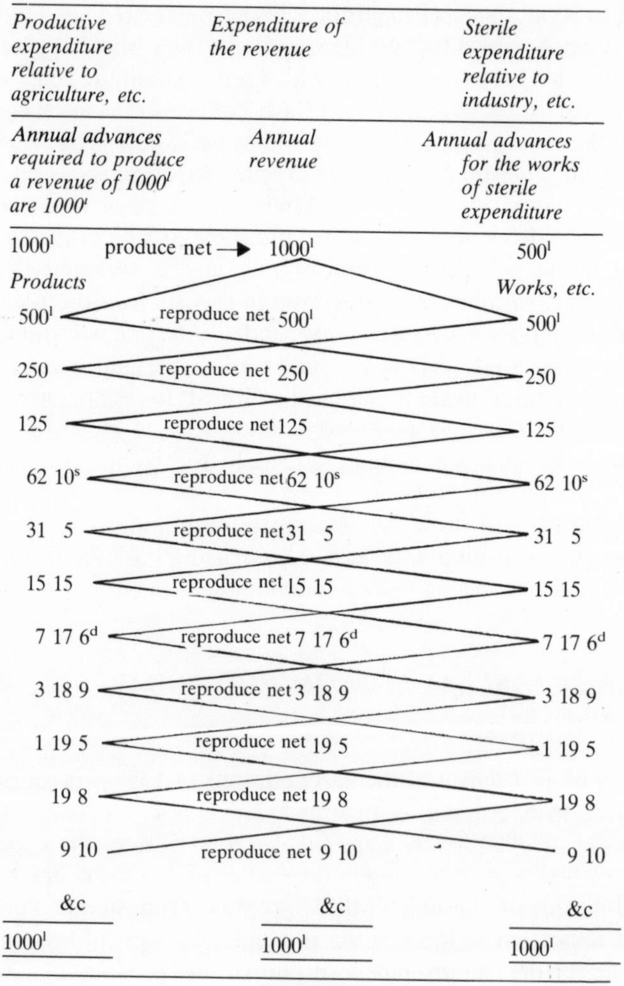

Productive expenditure relative to agriculture, etc.	Expenditure of the revenue	Sterile expenditure relative to industry, etc.
Annual advances required to produce a revenue of 1000^l are 1000^l	Annual revenue	Annual advances for the works of sterile expenditure

1000^l produce net ⟶	1000^l	500^l
Products		Works, etc.
500^l	reproduce net 500^l	500^l
250	reproduce net 250	250
125	reproduce net 125	125
62 10^s	reproduce net 62 10^s	62 10^s
31 5	reproduce net 31 5	31 5
15 15	reproduce net 15 15	15 15
7 17 6^d	reproduce net 7 17 6^d	7 17 6^d
3 18 9	reproduce net 3 18 9	3 18 9
1 19 5	reproduce net 19 5	1 19 5
19 8	reproduce net 19 8	19 8
9 10	reproduce net 9 10	9 10
&c	&c	&c
1000^l	1000^l	1000^l

Figure 1.3

spent on manufactures produce only 100 livres at the foot of the table. As a result of this asymmetry between the 'Productive' and 'Sterile' expenditure columns, the 1 000 livres of revenue that comes to the 'Productive' column generates a further 1 000 livres total in the central 'Revenue' column; while the 1 000 livres that goes to the right-hand 'Sterile expenditure' column produces a total of just 1 000 livres. The fact that the 1 000 livres that is spent on the products of agriculture becomes 2 000 livres shows that the land can produce enough to pay 1 000 livres to the landlords at the end of the year, and still retain 1 000 livres for the 'Annual advances' of the farmers, so that both the demand for food (which requires 1 000 livres of revenue) and its supply (which requires 1 000 livres of annual advances) can be maintained at the same level from year to year.

One point that is not clear from the *Tableau* alone is what happens to the economy's stock of money during the course of the year. This is 1 000 livres, and the landlords hold it at the beginning of the year.[25] They then distribute it equally to each class, and the *Tableau's* zigzags continue its distribution, but it would be wrong to think that the sterile class will be left with the stock of money at the end of the year. The sterile class consumes half of the 1 000 livres that it receives, and it uses the other 500 livres as advances for the following year (shown at the top of the 'Sterile expenditure' column), and these consist principally of raw materials which are bought from the agricultural sector for the next year's production.[26] The sterile sector will therefore exchange such money as reaches it in the course of the year for produce, with the result that the economy's whole stock of money will reach the productive sector by the end of the year. Thus, at the end of the year, the productive sector is left, not with 2 000 livres of 'food', but with 1 000 livres-worth of 'food' and 1 000 livres of money. The 1 000 livres of 'food' passes to the top of the 'Productive' column to become the productive sector's advances of the following year. The 1 000 livres of money passes to the top of the 'Revenue' column, that is, the money is paid as rent to the landlords, and this generates the following year's circulation or effective demand, while only 500 livres passes to the top of the 'Sterile expenditure' column to act as the advances of the sterile sector – for only the raw materials of the sterile sector actually remain in being from year to year.

The process can continue indefinitely if it is not disturbed. Each year 1 000 livres of annual advances in the productive sector in the form of food and raw materials, 1 000 livres of money in the hands of the landlords, and 500 livres of food and raw materials in the hands of artisans and merchants, become outputs of 2 000 livres of 'food' and 1 000 livres of manufactures. These are then marketed and leave precisely 1 000 livres of food and raw materials in the hands of the farmers, 1 000 livres of money in the hands of the landlords, and 500 livres of food and raw materials in the hands of the artisans and merchants at the end of the year. Quesnay's construction has been widely agreed to be a beautiful one, involving elegance, economy, and the several levels of meaning that characterise some of the eighteenth century's greatest works of art. The factors that may disturb the *Tableau's* equilibrium and so produce growth or decline will be discussed in the next chapter, but it may be noted here that both of Quesnay's multipliers have the same value. Thus the equilibrium of the *Tableau* depends partly on the fact that a multiplier of *two* can be applied to the Revenue to ascertain its effect on aggregate market demand, and the same multiplier of *two* is applied to what agriculture receives because of the proposition that agricultural outputs are twice agricultural inputs. Thus the multiplier involved in the expenditure of the revenue is the same as the multiplier of the soil, for it is only in these conditions that each class will get back at the end of a year what it had at the beginning.

Successive generations have found the *Tableau* exceedingly difficult to understand, and some of the reasons for this will already be evident. Quesnay's achievement in showing monetary flows with his zigzags, and the production of goods on a single diagram is a remarkable one, but the fact that these are both shown makes the *Tableau* that much more difficult to comprehend. A second difficulty is that the *Tableau* shows only part of Quesnay's model. Thus the 'interest' costs of farmers and the receipts they need to meet these are not shown, and international trade is also left out – which matters, for consistency between the demand and the supply of food and manufactures cannot be achieved in a closed economy. Only half the economy's consumer demand is for agricultural produce, but according to the *Tableau*, two-thirds of its output is agricultural. 'Food' must therefore be exported and manufactured goods imported, and Quesnay makes this clear in the '*Explication du Tableau Economique*' that he published with the *Tableau* in 1759 (Tab edn3 iii). Finally the *Tableau* leaves a number of questions unanswered. Thus, it is not clear from the *Tableau* alone just what goes where in the process of consumption, for exactly how the agricultural output of 2 000 livres and the industrial output of 1 000 livres is divided between the classes is not shown on the diagram. Quesnay had to supply his

'Explanation' to show that the food and manufactures produced were exactly what was needed by the various classes, and for international trade. Clearly the *Tableau* cannot give a full account of the economy's activities without some further information and interpretation.[27]

The complete interactions of the *Tableau* depend on a number of fundamental equations that must hold when it is in equilibrium. First, the productive class and the sterile class must each receive just enough money from the *Tableau's* zigzags, and so on, to meet their financial requirements. If they receive more money than they need, or less, their level of activity will rise or fall, so in the stationary state conditions that the *Tableau* describes, it is necessary that they receive exactly the right amount. In addition, there must be equality between the demand and supply of both agricultural and industrial production if the *Tableau* is to be in equilibrium. The fundamental interrelationships which determine the crucial values in the *Tableau* are completed with Quesnay's assumption that the costs of the industrial sector are half labour and half raw material costs,[28] and the further assumption that each class spends half its income on the agricultural and half on the industrial side of the *Tableau*. The equations that are produced by these conditions are outlined in the first section of the Appendix to this chapter, 'A Mathematical Explanation of Quesnay's *Tableau*'. The equations are in fact very simple and straightforward, and the solutions that result with Quesnay's specific assumptions about propensities to consume, and so on, are outlined in Table 1.1.

It will be seen that the solutions underline Quesnay's crucial argument that almost all the economy's quantities are multiples of

TABLE 1.1   The solutions to the original version of the *Tableau Economique*

	Solution
Annual agricultural advances	A
Rate of return on agricultural advances	100%
Total rents or revenues	A
Wages and entrepreneurial incomes in agriculture	A
Interest of agricultural entrepreneurs	any value
Raw materials used in agriculture	any value
Exports of agricultural produce	$\frac{1}{4}A$
Raw materials used by industry	$\frac{1}{2}A$
Wages and entrepreneurial incomes in industry	$\frac{1}{2}A$
Gross industrial output	A

annual agricultural advances, which are *A* in Table 1.1. Thus total rents or revenues equal annual agricultural advances, wages in agriculture equal agricultural advances, wages in industry are one-half agricultural advances, and therefore half wages in agriculture, total industrial production equals agricultural advances, exports are one-quarter agricultural advances, and so on. The capital of the entrepreneurial farmer therefore determines everything else, as Quesnay argued in everything he wrote from 1756 onwards, and if this can be doubled, then so can all the other quantities in the economy, once this reaches equilibrium. As for the details of the solution, the first crucial one is that the rate of return on annual agricultural advances is 100 per cent, and this is what he was at such pains to show to be practicable, both because it was achieved in part of the French economy, and more to the point, because it was achieved in the whole English economy. With a rate of return on annual agricultural advances of 100 per cent, total rents or the economy's aggregate revenues equal agricultural advances, and this is the case in every edition of the *Tableau*.

The result that the raw material and interest costs of the agricultural entrepreneurs can take any value without disturbing the equilibrium of the *Tableau* is an interesting one. It is arrived at because the raw materials that are used in agriculture, and the horses and so on that are bought to replace others with the 'interest' received are wholly supplied and used up within the same sector, so they must affect the costs and receipts of the agricultural class equally. This is not true of wages, rents, exports, and the agricultural raw materials which are used up in the industrial sector, and these must all be the precise proportions indicated in Table 1.1.

The result that industrial wages are half agricultural advances and half agricultural wages is exactly what Quesnay states, for with agricultural advances and therefore wages of 600 livres in the printed editions of both 1758 and 1759, the wages of the sterile expenditure class are said to be 300 livres (Tab edn3 iii), and in the economy as a whole it is said that there are 3 million workers' families (all quantities in the *Tableau* should be multiplied by a million to arrive at figures for the whole economy) which receive an average of 300 livres each, of whom 2 million are in the productive and one million in the sterile sector (Tab edn3 iv–v). Finally, it is specifically said that exports of agricultural products are 150 livres (where agricultural advances are 600 livres), so exports are one-quarter of agricultural advances as in Table 1.1 (Tab edn3 iii).

The fact that the results arrived at are precisely Quesnay's is a check that his fundamental argument has been followed. It also shows that it can be arrived at rigorously, and that his conclusions follow from his assumptions. He may either have followed the model through to the conclusions arrived at in Table 1.1 without publishing his actual reasoning, or he may have perceived intuitively that it all added up.

However he proceeded, he must also have appreciated that the *Tableau* as outlined in his diagram and in Table 1.1 can only take the argument so far. It presents a coherent account of an economy with one particular relationship between its various outputs and incomes: it is of course an economy in stationary state equilibrium, but the *Tableau* cannot be used to compare economies with different export ratios, or different rates of return on agricultural advances. This is because exports have to be one-quarter of annual agricultural advances and the rate of return 100 per cent in all economies that conform to the basic assumptions. Quesnay could not therefore use the *Tableau* to compare the French economy, where advances yielded much less than 100 per cent, with the English, so the *Tableau* was unsuitable for the kind of comparison that interested him most.

Quesnay and Mirabeau decided to deal with the problem by modifying some of the assumptions of the original *Tableau* so that an extra degree of freedom could be obtained. The crucial assumption they modified was the one that effective demand originates in the expenditure of the revenue, which is what limits the applicability of the *Tableau* because a very high revenue and therefore a very high rate of return on advances (that is, one of 100 per cent) is needed to produce sufficient effective demand. The opportunity which Quesnay and Mirabeau took to give the argument extra freedom was the publication in 1763 of *Philosophie Rurale* (its original title was to have been *Grand Tableau Economique*[29]), in which they planned to give a complete account of Quesnay's theory of the working of economies, and for this they needed a more flexible *Tableau*.[30]

They obtained this by inventing a *Tableau* which allowed the rate of return on annual agricultural advances to take any value whatsoever. The device they used to achieve this was the assumption that some agricultural incomes could be spent by rich farmers *as if they were rent*. Rich farmers could hold back some money after the harvest, and spend this for their consumption in the following year on the products of others, and this money would have the same effect on the circulation process as equivalent sums circulated by landlords. This is illustrated in Figure 1.4 which is based on a similar diagram in the section of Chapter 9 of *Philosophie Rurale* headed:

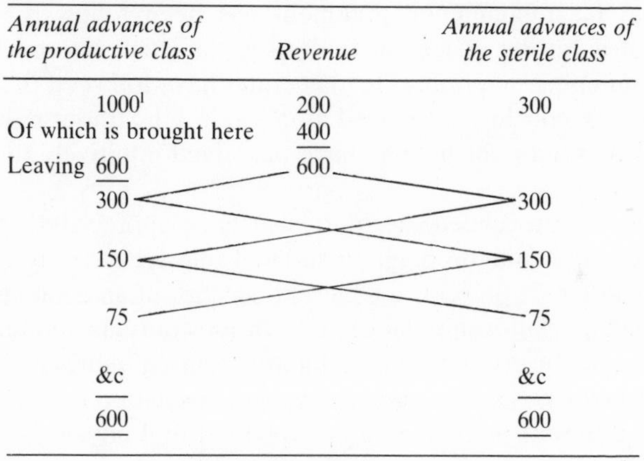

Annual advances of the productive class	Revenue	Annual advances of the sterile class
1000[1]	200	300
Of which is brought here	400	
Leaving 600	600	
300		300
150		150
75		75
&c		&c
600		600

FIGURE 1.4

RULES

To form an abridgement of the Tableau in all the different cases where the advances of the productive class yield more or less than 100 per cent of net product, and where it is supposed in addition that there are no causes of decline or growth in the annual reproduction.[31]

In Figure 1.4 the rate of return on the annual agricultural advances of 1000 livres is only 20 per cent, and a revenue of 200 livres will provide a total market demand of only 400 livres, which is much less than total production. However, if 400 of the agricultural advances of 1000 livres are spent as if they are revenue, leaving 600 livres to be spent as wages, the total expenditure of 'revenue' (including 400 livres of agricultural advances) is 600 livres, while the agricultural advances that are spent as 'wages' are also 600 livres and with industrial advances at 300 livres, the precise ratios of the original *Tableau* are obtained. This will be confirmed if Figure 1.4 is compared with Figure 1.3. The rule which must be followed to achieve this result is that equal total sums should be *spent* as agricultural advances and rent, and if poor landlords spend some of their income as if they are workers, and rich farmers some of theirs as if they are landlords, this can always be achieved. Quesnay and Mirabeau give several examples in the ninth chapter of *Philosophie Rurale*.[32]

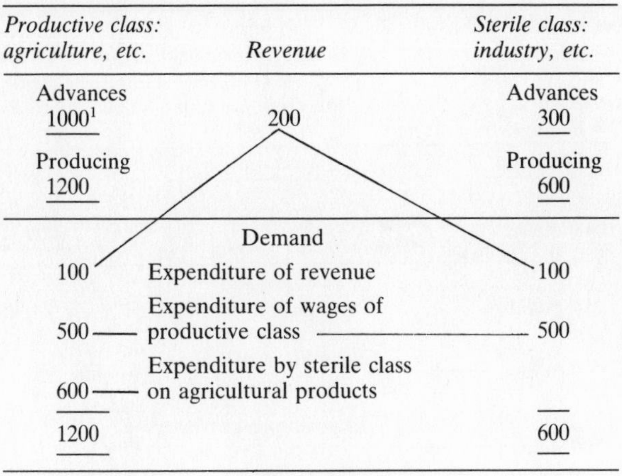

Productive class: agriculture, etc.	Revenue	Sterile class: industry, etc.
Advances 1000[1]	200	Advances 300
Producing 1200		Producing 600

Demand

100 — Expenditure of revenue — 100

500 — Expenditure of wages of productive class — 500

600 — Expenditure by sterile class on agricultural products

1200   600

FIGURE 1.5

With the assumption that the expenditure of some advances as revenue (and vice versa) always maintains the correct rate of effective demand, Quesnay and Mirabeau were able to drop the *Tableau's* zigzags and set out a much simpler diagram, while they explained that the economy's money stock was circulating as before, and producing precisely the same results. They called the result a précis of the original *Tableau*, and the one equivalent to the *Tableau* is shown in Figure 1.5.

All that needs to be said here is that half the revenue of 200 livres goes to each side: half the wages of the productive class go to each side: and the entire 600 livres the sterile class receives from the other two then comes back to agriculture, half being spent on agricultural products for consumption, and half on raw materials for the next year's advances. The assumption that the sterile class spends all it receives on the agricultural side of the *Tableau* is an apparent departure from the propositions of the original Tableau, of which more will be said below. A similar précis *Tableau* can be drawn at all rates of return on advances, and in each case demand from these sources will equal precisely what is produced on each side, as in Figure 1.5.[33]

The précis of the *Tableau* in *Philosophie Rurale* was modified further in Quesnay's final version of the *Tableau* which he published in 1766 as '*Analyse de la formule arithmétique du Tableau Economique*'.[34] This is the version of the *Tableau* that Marx admired

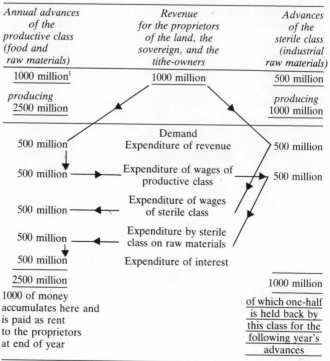

Annual advances of the productive class (food and raw materials)	Revenue for the proprietors of the land, the sovereign, and the tithe-owners	Advances of the sterile class (industrial raw materials)
1000 million[1]	1000 million	500 million
producing 2500 million		producing 1000 million
500 million	Demand Expenditure of revenue	500 million
500 million	Expenditure of wages of productive class	500 million
500 million	Expenditure of wages of sterile class	
500 million	Expenditure by sterile class on raw materials	
500 million	Expenditure of interest	
2500 million		1000 million
1000 of money accumulates here and is paid as rent to the proprietors at end of year		of which one-half is held back by this class for the following year's advances

NOTE: The arrows show monetary flows.

FIGURE 1.6

and discussed in 30 pages of his *Theories of Surplus Value*, and it has been turned into an input-output table.[35] The *Tableau* of 1766 is the précis *Tableau* of *Philosophie Rurale* with the single modification that the 'interest' costs of the agriculturalists (which are assumed to equal 50 per cent of annual agricultural advances)[36] are directly included in the *Tableau* for the first time. The final version of the *Tableau* is outlined in Figure 1.6, largely as Quesnay set it out, with a rate of return on agricultural advances of 100 per cent, but with some extra explanatory detail to help readers (and Quesnay's own text is printed underlined). Because of the inclusion of 'interest' at 50 per cent of advances, the annual agricultural advances of 1000 livres produce a total agricultural product of 2500 livres in place of the 2000 livres of the original *Tableau* of 1758–9, and the extra 500 livres is used up because farmers spend their 'interest' on the agricultural side to replace horses and so on. The final version of the *Tableau* is set out in

Figure 1.6 on the assumption of a rate of return on advances of 100 per cent, but it can be set out similarly with any rate of return, and there are examples of this version of the *Tableau* with rates of return of less than 50 and of 150 per cent in subsequent published articles of Quesnay's (Q 863 and 980). It is to be noted, however, that it is only where the rate of return is 100 per cent that there is the correct amount of revenue to carry through the financial transactions indicated by the lines of the diagram.[37] At all other rates of return, some farmers must spend like landlords, or vice versa as in *Philosophie Rurale*.

The final version of the *Tableau*, and the précis of the *Tableau* in *Philosophie Rurale*, both suffer from one serious weakness or omission: there is no reference in them to the consumption of industrial products by the sterile class, who are assumed to spend their wages exclusively on agricultural products. There is thus an apparent asymmetry of a highly implausible kind between the expenditure pattern of agricultural workers, who spend half their income on agricultural and half on industrial products, and industrial workers, who spend their whole income on food. Quesnay was far too subtle a thinker to have an asymmetry of this kind in his *real* or underlying model, and what he published always contained certain abstractions in the hope that this would make for easier comprehension.

One way of dealing with the difficulty is to examine the equations which lie behind the final version of the *Tableau*. These are outlined in the second section of the Appendix where the mathematical basis of the *Tableau* is discussed, and they produce the solutions that are presented in Table 1.2.

Table 1.2   The solutions to the final version of the *Tableau Economique*

	Solution
Annual agricultural advances	A
Rate of return on agricultural advances	r
Total rents or revenues	$A\,r$
Wages and entrepreneurial incomes in agriculture	A
Interest of agricultural entrepreneurs	$\frac{1}{2}\,A$
Raw materials used in agriculture	any value
Exports of agricultural produce	$\frac{1}{8}\,A\,(1 + r)$
Raw materials used by industry	$\frac{1}{4}\,A\,(1 + r)$
Wages and entrepreneurial incomes in industry	$\frac{1}{4}\,A\,(1 + r)$
Gross industrial output	$\frac{1}{2}\,A\,(1 + r)$

It will be evident that, as in the original *Tableau*, all quantities are multiples of annual agricultural advances, and moreover, here the rate of return on annual agricultural advances (r) can take the value that is appropriate to the economy in question. One of the most interesting conclusions that emerges from Table 1.2 is that Gross Industrial Output varies with both agricultural advances and the rate of return in agriculture – it is $\frac{1}{2} A(1 + r)$. An economy with a highly profitable agriculture will thus have a larger industrial sector than another with an equal agricultural wage bill but less efficiency on the land. These are among Quesnay's most basic propositions, and they are arrived at here as the result of a highly technical argument.[38]

Turning to the problem of the apparent asymmetry between the consumption patterns of agricultural and industrial workers which was remarked on above, Table 1.2 indicates that there is a solution to the problem. In this table, which is derived on the assumption that all classes have the same propensities to consume food and manufactures in Quesnay's underlying model, the discrepancy is removed because industrial workers export half the agricultural products they buy with their wages, and trade these for manufactures overseas. Their wages are $\frac{1}{4} A(1 + r)$, and if they export $\frac{1}{8} A(1 + r)$ of food and exchange this for manufactures, they will have the same proportion of food and manufactures in their own consumption as everyone else, and, as Meek who first discovered this solution points out, the precise manufactures they import could be consumed by anyone including the richest landlords. Exports of food equivalent to half of industrial wages and corresponding imports of manufactures will ensure that sufficient total manufactures will be available to allow each class to spend half of its income on food and half on industrial products.[39]

It can only be conjectured that this solution to the problem is part of Quesnay's underlying theory which he never published completely, but the ratio of trade to agricultural advances in Table 1.2 is the same as that in the original *Tableau* if $r = 100$ per cent, that is, one-quarter of agricultural advances, and there are two indications that Quesnay may have intended the precise solution of Tables 1.1 and 1.2 to apply to his final *Tableau*. In chapter 7 of *Philosophie Rurale* (which contributes so much to the interpretation of his thought) he set out a fully itemised *Tableau* showing each branch of agriculture and the sterile sector separately, itemising types of income in each branch, and arriving at equal totals for the output of agricultural products and purchases of these. In this *Tableau*, which

resembles modern national income accounts, he includes the following item among the purchases of agricultural products:

The Sterile Class buys of these	For the advances of its works and the business of exporting:
	1,437,066,667 (Q 712[E])

Now, if the formulae of Table 1.2 are applied to the itemised
Tableau, exports plus the advances of the sterile class come to
1 470 750 000 livres,[40] which is exceedingly close to the 1 437 066 667
livres that Quesnay allows for these items. There are a number of
small arithmetical errors in this detailed *Tableau*, and it contains
some more complex relationships than the simplified *Tableaux* that
have been outlined in this chapter, which must produce substantial
differences in some results. However, the fact that Quesnay's complete *Tableau* shows almost precisely the answer for exports plus
industrial raw materials that is arrived at in Table 1.2 indicates that
the solution suggested there may very well be the one he had in mind.
This is supported by the further evidence of a statement in the
'*(Premier) Problème Economique*' of 1766 (which is based on the
final version of the *Tableau*) where Quesnay says: 'Foreign trade can
be estimated at about one tenth of the total product [of agriculture]'
(Q 866 [M]) in a situation where the rate of return on annual
agricultural advances is 30 per cent. According to the solutions of
Table 1.2, the ratio of trade to agricultural output should be 9.03 per
cent in these conditions.[41]

This completes the present account of Quesnay's *Tableau Economique*. The importance of the *Tableau* is that it sets out with great
precision the conditions in which an economy will achieve continuous
reproduction with a constant level of output in each sector. The
conditions for stationary state equilibrium are, as Quesnay and later
Marx appreciated, the starting point for an analysis of the conditions
where growth will be achieved. Clearly there will be growth or
decline in aggregate output if the equilibrium of the *Tableau* is
disturbed. That is why the precise conditions in which the *Tableau* is
in equilibrium are of such importance, and why such care has been
taken to ascertain exactly what those conditions are. They form the
starting point of Quesnay's theory of economic growth, which is the
subject of the next chapter.

* APPENDIX: A MATHEMATICAL EXPLANATION OF QUESNAY'S *TABLEAU ECONOMIQUE*

1   *The original Tableau of 1758–9*

The best starting point for an understanding of the equations that underlie the original Tableau is to work out the implications of the condition that in equilibrium the total output or supply of the productive or agricultural sector, Y_a, must equal D_a, the demand for food and raw materials. Similarly, the total output of the sterile or industrial sector, Y_i must equal D_i, the demand for manufactures and services.

Y_a, the gross output of the agricultural sector, must be equivalent to the sum of the incomes earned in this sector plus raw materials used up in production. Thus if the raw materials and so on used up in agriculture are M_a, the 'interest' costs of the agricultural entrepreneurs I, the wages and entrepreneurial incomes earned in agriculture W_a, and R is written for the net product, that is, the total rents or revenues of the landlords:

$$Y_a \equiv M_a + I + W_a + R \qquad (1.1)$$

Similarly, Y_i, the gross output of the industrial sector, will be equivalent to the sum of wages and entrepreneurial incomes in that sector, W_i, and the raw materials used up, M_i, so that:

$$Y_i \equiv M_i + W_i \qquad (1.2)$$

D_a, the demand for agricultural output, is made up of the demand for the raw materials for both sectors, $M_a + M_i$, the expenditure of 'interest', I (for the replacement of farm animals that die, and so on, is always made good from the agricultural sector), that part of wages and rents that is spent on agricultural produce, $q\ (W_a + W_i + R)$ where q is the propensity to consume the products of agriculture of all classes,[42] and T_a, the net export demand for food and raw materials – and it is assumed by Quesnay that agriculture is always a net exporter. Then:

$$D_a = M_a + M_i + I + q\ (W_a + W_i + R) + T_a \qquad (1.3)$$

Similarly, D_i, the demand for manufactures and services, is made up of the demand of workers and landlords who all spend a proportion $(1 - q)$ of their incomes on the products of the 'sterile' sector, so they will spend $(1 - q)$ times $(W_a + W_i + R)$ on these. However, some manufactures come from abroad, and T_i, net imports of manufactures, must be subtracted from home demand to produce the demand for the output of the home country's industrial sector. Hence:

$$D_i = (1 - q) (W_a + W_i + R) - T_i \qquad (1.4)$$

In equilibrium, Y_a will equal D_a so that:

$$M_i + T_a + q W_i = (1 - q) (W_a + R)$$

and Y_i will equal D_i, so that:

$$M_i + T_i + q W_i = (1 - q) (W_a + R)$$

It will be seen that these equations are identical provided that T_a, net agricultural exports, equals T_i, net imports of manufactures. They are thus the same equation provided that trade is balanced as Quesnay always assumes. If T is written for both exports and imports, the equation becomes:

$$M_i + T + q W_i = (1 - q) (W_a + R) \qquad (1.5)$$

This is one of the fundamental equations on which the *Tableau Economique* is based. It will be noted that M_a and I, the raw material and 'interest' costs of the agricultural entrepreneurs, play no part in the equation, so any level of these is compatible with equality of supply and demand for food and manufactures.

The principal further condition which must be satisfied in the *Tableau* is that the money receipts of the farmers and artisans, which depend on the circulation of the revenue, must be just sufficient to meet their financial needs. This produces two further equations, one for each class.

The agricultural sector receives the expenditure flows that originate from the revenue, and the calculation in Figure 1.2 on page 19 shows that these amount to $R ((2q - q^2) / (1 - q + q^2))$. In addition, the agricultural sector receives M_i, from the sale of raw materials to the industrial sector for its advances.[43] It spends $(1 - q) W_a$ on wage goods from the industrial sector in the course of the year, and at the end of the year it pays rent of R to the landlords. In equilibrium, what it receives must equal what it spends, so that:

$$R\left(\frac{2q - q^2}{1 - q + q^2}\right) + M_i = (1 - q) W_a + R$$

that is:

$$R\left(\frac{3q - 2q^2 - 1}{1 - q + q^2}\right) = (1 - q) W_a - M_i \tag{1.6}$$

Turning to the industrial sector, this receives $R\left((1 - q^2)/(1 - q + q^2)\right)$ from the *Tableau's* zigzags in Figure 1.2, and it uses this to spend M_i on raw materials from the productive sector, T, on agricultural products for export,[44] and $q\,W_i$ on agricultural products for the consumption of its workers. Hence, in equilibrium:

$$R\left(\frac{1 - q^2}{1 - q + q^2}\right) = M_i + T + q\,W_i \tag{1.7}$$

(1.6) and (1.7) provide two equations that must be satisfied, given the circular flows of the original version of the *Tableau*, and (1.5) is an equation that a Physiocratic economy must always satisfy. These three equations can be supplemented by a fourth, because Quesnay states frequently through the various versions of the *Tableau* that the costs of the sterile sector are half wages and entrepreneurial incomes, and half raw materials, that is:

$$M_i = W_i \tag{1.8}$$

With this fourth equation, there are sufficient equations to express R, T, W_i and M_i in terms of W_a and q, that is:

$$R = W_a\left(\frac{1 - q + q^2}{2q - q^2}\right) \tag{1.9}$$

$$M_i = W_i = W_a\left(\frac{1 - q - q^2 + q^3}{2q - q^2}\right) \tag{1.10}$$

$$T = W_a\left(\frac{q - q^3}{2 - q}\right) \tag{1.11}$$

These are the general relationships which must hold in a *Tableau* of Quesnay's type. He at no point set them out in general terms, but he simply outlined the particular solutions arrived at where $q = \frac{1}{2}$, which he assumes wherever the *Tableau* is in equilibrium. Before the very simple results arrived at in the particular case where $q = \frac{1}{2}$ are presented, something must be said about a further assumption of Quesnay's which does not influence the results, but only the way in which these are presented.

In his various expositions of the *Tableau*, Quesnay assumes that annual agricultural advances, A, equal or nearly equal W_a, total wages and entrepreneurial incomes in the productive sector of the economy. Where the Tableau is set out in very great detail in Chapter 7 of *Philosophie Rurale*, annual agricultural advances at 1 921 million livres are close to the incomes of agricultural workers and entrepreneurs which total 2 180 million livres (Q 710–11), and everywhere else these totals are identical. Presumably the non-wage components of advances, and Quesnay mentions animal feeding stuffs in the '*Explication*' to the *Tableau* of 1759 (Tab edn3 iii), are just balanced by wages and entrepreneurial incomes which are not included in advances, and this allows Quesnay to assume that $W_a = A$.[45] With the simplifying assumption that annual agricultural advances equal labour costs, A can be substituted for W_a in (1.9), (1.10), and (1.11), and this allows the results to be presented as Quesnay actually presented them, so that where $q = \frac{1}{2}$, $R = A$, $M_i = W_i = \frac{1}{2} A$ and $T = \frac{1}{4} A$. The results are set out in this way in Table 1.1 on page 25. In addition, as rents are explained as a rate of return (of r) on annual agricultural advances in Quesnay's argument, $R = A r$, and r must then be 100 per cent where $R = A$.

2   *The final version of the Tableau of 1766*

There must be equality between the demand and supply of both food and manufactures when the final *Tableau* is in equilibrium, and if all classes have the same propensity to consume agricultural products (and it can be supposed that they do in Quesnay's underlying model), equation (1.5) must be satisfied as in the original *Tableau*. Moreover, equation (1.8) which states that the industrial wage bill equals the cost of industrial raw materials also definitely applies to the final *Tableau*.

However, because of the change in the circular flow assumption, the financial receipts of the two sectors are no longer derived directly from the zigzags originating from the revenue. This means that equations (1.6) and (1.7) do not apply to this version. There is, however, an equation peculiar to the final version that replaces them. This is the proposition that the advances of the sterile sector must be one-quarter of the sum of annual agricultural advances and rents; and it was seen on pages 28–9 (and note 33 on page 341) that this guarantees that the financial requirements of both sectors are always met. The equation that produces this result is written as:

$$M_i = \tfrac{1}{4} A + \tfrac{1}{4} R \tag{1.12}$$

and it replaces (1.6) and (1.7). Equations (1.5), (1.8) and (1.12) are sufficient to produce the results outlined in Table 1.2 on page 31 where $q = \tfrac{1}{2}$, and these are written down on the presumption that $W_a = A$ and $R = A\,r$.

2 Quesnay's Theory of Economic Growth

Quesnay believed that population and output had been falling in France for a century. He thought that the population was 16 million in 1758, and that it had been 24 million a hundred years earlier, and about 19.5 million in 1701 (Q 513–4). His detailed *Tableau* in chapter 7 of *Philosophie Rurale* was intended to show that France could support a population of 29.9 million, while the population in his final *Tableau* of 1766 was said to be 30 million (Q 712 and 795). These figures, and what growing and declining population and output meant in human and national terms, explain Quesnay's great concern with the causes of economic growth – and its opposite. He wished to explain the decline in France's output, population and wealth that he believed had occurred, and to discover how this trend could be reversed.

Modern research suggests that the population of France may have fallen from the latter part of the seventeenth century until 1720, but by much less than Quesnay believed. It is widely agreed that it increased slowly after this (with interruptions in years of famine) at an average rate of perhaps 0.2 or 0.3 per cent per annum, and reached 22 million by 1760 and 27 million by the end of the century: agricultural output increased at a similar rate.[1] Actual population and output trends were therefore far less desperate than Quesnay believed. Nevertheless, much of the population lived in conditions of such extreme poverty that death from starvation was the probable consequence of temporary economic misfortune.[2] At the same time, the royal finances were in perpetual crisis. Quesnay's belief that population, output and the tax base had been declining for a century was therefore understandable, as was his belief that there was great scope for expansion if only correct policies were pursued. The invention of the *Tableau Economique* provided the theoretical underpinning for the policies he believed that France should follow.

It will be evident that Quesnay had to use the *Tableau* to show two kinds of progression: to explain decline when the France of Louis XIV and Louis XV was under discussion, and to show growth when proposals to correct the weaknesses in the French economy were being put forward. The starting point for the sequences of *Tableaux* which showed decline was a *Tableau* in equilibrium with a rate of return on annual agricultural advances of 100 per cent, and in one case even of 150 per cent. The economy then fell from this state of 'bliss' for one of several reasons. Quesnay used so favourable a starting point because he believed that agricultural advances really had yielded rates like this in the past (Q 978) – when Sully had applied the correct policies to agriculture and the finances of France, which the Physiocrats were rediscovering. The downward progressions could then show realistically how Sully's successors had impoverished France, and Colbert was blamed in particular for the industrial and commercial bias of his policies. The upward progressions used the France of the 1750s and 1760s as their starting point, and these assumed an initial rate of return on annual agricultural advances of about 30 per cent, which was rapidly raised as 'correct' policies were applied to the economy.

The equilibrium of the *Tableau* can be disturbed in a number of ways to produce growth or decline, and it can be assumed that the sequences of *Tableaux* that Quesnay actually published were intended to demonstrate the causes of decline and the methods of achieving growth that he considered most important. He certainly believed that the *Tableau* was a powerful tool of analysis and exposition, and it is reasonable to suppose that he used it to explain what mattered most. He published two sequences of *Tableaux* in 1766 and 1767 to illustrate the applicability of the final version to practical problems,[3] and it was suggested in Chapter 1 that he was probably responsible for the many sequences of *Tableaux* that demonstate the causes of growth and decline in *Philosophie Rurale*, the book he wrote in collaboration with Victor de Riqueti, Marquis de Mirabeau, in 1763.[4] He was certainly at least part author of these. The accounts of the *Tableau* in disequilibrium in Part vi of *L'Ami des Hommes*, which Quesnay and Mirabeau published in 1760, add further information about Quesnay's theory of economic growth.[5]

An examination of this evidence suggests that there are three causes of disequilibrium which Quesnay and Mirabeau considered particularly important. First, the proportion of incomes that is spent on the products of agriculture may be less or more than the one-half that produces stationary state equilibrium. Second, a change in methods of taxation may affect the rate of return that farmers actually receive on their advances, with consequent decline or growth in these, and third, the rate of return may be raised in agriculture by increasing the price of food as a result of better marketing policies at home and overseas. Quesnay and Mirabeau used the *Tableau* to outline the dynamic effects of these three causes of disturbance, and they did this because they believed that the causes of French impoverishment were too much consumption of manufactures and services, and they attributed particular importance to excessive *luxe de décoration*, and methods of taxation which caused agricultural advances to diminish. In their opinion, the best way to restore the economy was to substitute taxes which did not fall on the capital of farmers for those which did, and to adopt commercial policies which restored the profitability of agriculture.

The effect of these on the growth of the economy can be shown quite straightforwardly with the assistance of the *Tableau*, and they will be outlined in turn below. Quesnay and Mirabeau usually gave an account of growth or decline by publishing two *Tableaux*, one for the beginning and one for the end of a period where the equilibrium of the economy was disturbed. Each *Tableau* described an economy in stationary state equilibrium, and their method of analysis was therefore generally that of comparative statics. The one exception to this is the analysis of the effects of a propensity to consume the products of agriculture which differs from one-half, and it will be shown below that this must continue to produce growth or decline for so long as the discrepancy persists. The other causes of growth and decline can all produce once-for-all effects which can be analysed with the methods of comparative statics, but they can also produce indefinite growth or decline. Both possibilities will be outlined in the present account of Quesnay's argument.

Quesnay and Mirabeau used the final version of the *Tableau*, or the précis of the final version in their accounts of growth and decline in *Philosophie Rurale* and the later articles. These versions are obviously superior to the original *Tableau* for the analysis of dynamic processes because they can show rates of return which differ from 100 per cent, and because they are more flexible and less cumbersome. The original version of the *Tableau* should, however, be used for the first of the problems which will be considered, the effect on the rate of growth of a propensity to consume the products of agriculture of more or less than one-half, for the final *Tableau* will only give an accurate account of the expenditure flows that go to each sector where the propensity to consume is exactly one-half.

THE EFFECT OF THE PROPENSITY TO CONSUME AGRICULTURAL PRODUCTS ON THE RATE OF GROWTH[6]

This is best analysed by focusing attention on the financial receipts of the agricultural producers. These receive money from the landlords and the artisans of the sterile class via the *Tableau's* zigzags, and in addition to this they receive money from the industrial sector for the sale of raw materials for its advances. The agriculturalists use the money they receive to buy manufactured goods for their own consumption, and to pay rent. This relationship is set out in detail in Table 2.1, where it is assumed that the rate of return on annual agricultural advances is 100 per cent, as in the original *Tableau*. In Table 2.1, it is assumed that the *Tableau* is in equilibrium initially with a propensity to consume the products of agriculture, q, of one-half. Annual agricultural advances are 1000 million livres in the initial year, and with a rate of return of 100 per cent, rents are also 1000 million livres. The agriculturalists then receive 1000 million livres in the course of the year from the circulation of the revenue, that is, from the *Tableau's* zigzags as in all of Quesnay's accounts of the original *Tableau*, and 500 million livres from the sale of raw materials to the industrial sector (that is, half of what this sector receives from the circulation of the revenue). The agriculturalists use this 1500 million livres for two purposes – to buy industrial products for their own consumption via the Tableau's zigzags which costs them 500 million livres, and to pay rent to the landlords which costs a further 1000 million livres. Then the 1500 million livres the agricultural class receives is just sufficient for its full financial needs when the *Tableau* is in equilibrium, as it is in the top line of Table 2.1 where the farmers have no financial surplus or deficit.[7]

Suppose now that q, the propensity to consume agricultural products, becomes 0.4 so that the propensity to consume manufactures is 0.6. The effects of this are outlined in the second line of Table 2.1. Here the *Tableau's* zigzags bring 842 million livres instead of 1000 million to the agricultural sector, and 1105 million instead of

TABLE 2.1 Declining production where the propensity to consume agricultural products (q) is less than 0.5

Annual agricultural advances A	Rents R = A	Farmers' receipts from circulation of revenue X_a	Industry's receipts from circulation of revenue X_i	Farmers' purchases from industry $(1 - q) X_a$	Industry's purchases for advances $\frac{1}{2} X_i$	Farmers' financial surplus (+) or deficit (−)
					millions of livres	
		initial equilibrium relationships where q = 0.5				
1000	1000	1000	1000	500	500	0
		q becomes 0.4: successive years				
1000	1000	842	1105	505	552.5	−110.5
945	945	796	1044.5	477.5	522	−104.5
893	893	752	987	451	493.5	− 98.5
844	844	711	933	426.5	466.5	− 93
797.5	797.5	671.5	881.5	403	441	− 88

$$X_a = R \left(\frac{2q - q^2}{1 - q + q^2} \right) \qquad X_i = R \left(\frac{1 - q^2}{1 - q + q^2} \right) \qquad \text{(See Figure 1.2, page 19.)}$$

1 000 million to the industrial – all sums of money being quoted to the nearest half million livres. The agricultural class receives a further 552.5 million livres from the industrialists for sales of raw materials, that is, half of the 1 105 million livres the industrial class receives, which is what Quesnay says this class puts aside for its advances. However, the agricultural class spends six-tenths of the 842 million livres it receives from the zigzags, or 505 million livres on manufactures for the consumption of its workers and entrepreneurs. When its full transactions are taken into account as in Table 2.1, it receives 842 + 552.5 = 1 394.5 million livres, and it spends 505 million livres on consumer goods and owes rents of 1 000 million livres so it requires 1 505 million livres. The agricultural class therefore has a financial deficit of 110.5 million livres which is shown in the final column of Table 2.1. If it pays the 1 000 million livres agreed to the landlords, the farmers must sell 110.5 million livres of their advances for the next year to get enough money to pay their rents. In the sequence of *Tableaux* that deals with this case in *Philosophie Rurale* Quesnay and Mirabeau actually assume that half the deficiency is met by the landlords who accept lower rents than those previously agreed (PR iii 33–53). Then half the farmers' deficit of 110.5 million livres is met by a fall in annual advances from 1 000 to 945 million livres, and half by a reduction in rents, so these will also become 945 instead of 1 000 million livres in the following year. It will be noted that the assumption that Quesnay and Mirabeau make in this case is the only one which keeps annual agricultural advances and rents in line with each other, which is necessary if the basic relationships of the *Tableau* are to hold from year to year.

While annual agricultural advances and rents both fall from 1 000 million livres in the first year of a lower propensity to consume food to 945 million livres in the second, Table 2.1 shows that the advances of the industrial sector increase from 500 million to 552.5 million livres. What has happened in general terms is that the circulation of demand has brought more money than before to the industrial sector and less to the agricultural, with the result that a higher proportion of the harvest has been allocated to the industrialists and a smaller proportion to the farmers themselves. This has produced the present situation where industrial advances are larger than usual, 552.5 instead of 500 million livres, and agricultural advances and rents are both 5.5 per cent lower. Looking further ahead, the 5.5 per cent fall in annual agricultural advances reduces agricultural output by 5.5 per cent in the following year, while the reduction in rents reduces demand for both food and manufactures by 5.5 per cent. The increase in the advances of the industrial sector will raise the following year's physical output of manufactures, but this has no effect on the *Tableau's* circular flows, and the amount of money the manufacturers receive for their increased production depends solely on the expenditure of rents and the subsequent zigzags, and these must bring 5.5 per cent less to the industrial class than in the previous year because rents are 5.5 per cent lower. In fact, an examination of Table 2.1 shows that each quantity is 5.5 per cent lower than in the previous year. Both sectors receive 5.5 per cent less from the circulation of the revenue, the industrial sector's purchases of raw materials (for advances) are reduced 5.5 per cent from 552.5 to 522 million livres, and the financial deficit of the farmers also falls 5.5 per cent from 110.5 to 104.5 million livres. However, the correction of this deficit requires a further 52 million livres reduction in both annual agricultural advances and rents in the third year, and this is again a fall of 5.5 per cent. Indeed it will be clear from Table 2.1 that with the present assumptions, all quantities in the *Tableau* must fall at an annual rate of 5.5 per cent after the first year, because annual agricultural advances fall at this rate. Because of this the advances of the sterile sector which rose from 500 to 552.5 million livres in the first year fall back below 500 million livres after only two further years. Hence an increased propensity to buy manufactures increases the wealth of the industrialists for only two years, and after this all classes become poorer at a rate of 5.5 per cent per annum because this is the rate at which annual agricultural advances are falling.[8]

The converse situation where the propensity to consume agricultural products rises from 0.5 to 0.6 is outlined in Table 2.2. Here, with the same assumptions as in the previous case, annual agricultural advances increase at a rate of 4.2 per cent per annum, and all other quantities grow with them. In the first year of the higher propensity to consume their products, farmers receive 1 105 instead of 1 000 million livres from the *Tableau's* zigzags, and when their other transactions are taken into account, they have a financial surplus of 84 million livres. If Quesnay's and Mirabeau's assumption that this is divided equally with the landlords is followed, their annual advances will then increase 4.2 per cent from 1 000 to 1 042 million livres in the second year, and this initiates growth at this rate which will continue for so long as the propensity to consume agricultural products remains 0.6. The advances of the sterile class are initially reduced from 500 to 421 million livres by the lower propensity to consume its products, but

TABLE 2.2 Growth where the propensity to consume agricultural products (q) exceeds 0.5

Annual agricultural advances	Rents	Farmers' receipts from circulation of revenue	Industry's receipts from circulation of revenue	Farmers' purchases from industry	Industry's purchases for advances	Farmers' financial surplus (+) or deficit (−)
					millions of livres	
		Initial equilibrium relationships where q = 0.5				
1 000	1 000	1 000	1 000	500	500	0
		q becomes 0.6: successive years				
1 000	1 000	1 105	842	442	421	+ 84
1 042	1 042	1 151.5	877.5	460.5	439	+ 88
1 086	1 086	1 200	914.5	480	457.5	+ 91.5
1 132	1 132	1 251	953	500.5	476.5	+ 95
1 179.5	1 179.5	1 303.5	993	521.5	496.5	+ 99
1 229	1 229	1 358.5	1 035	543.5	517.5	+103.5
1 281	1 281	1 416	1 078.5	566.5	539.5	+108

growth at 4.2 per cent will restore these to 500 million livres after five years, and raise them above this initial level from that point onwards. The industrialists will therefore become better off than they were originally, after the sixth year, as a result of a fall in the propensity to consume their products.

It will be evident that a propensity to consume agricultural products of more than 0.5 must produce growth, and that there must be declining output followed soon afterwards by declining population where this propensity is less than 0.5. There is naturally a formula which relates g_a, the rate of growth of annual agricultural advances, to q, the proportion of income spent on agricultural products, and if d is written for $(q - 0.5)$, that is, d is the excess of the propensity to consume agricultural products over one-half:[9]

$$g_a = \tfrac{1}{2}\,d\left(\frac{1 - 1\tfrac{1}{3}d - 1\tfrac{1}{3}d^2}{1 + 1\tfrac{1}{3}d^2}\right) \tag{2.1}$$

and where d is small so that terms in d^3, d^4, etc, can be disregarded:

$$g_a = \tfrac{1}{2}d - \tfrac{2}{3}\,d^2 \tag{2.2}$$

Thus the rate of growth varies with d, the excess of the propensity to consume agricultural products over one-half, provided that this excess is not very great, and quite small deviations from one-half produce very significant rates of growth or decline.[10] The maximum growth rate that the above formula (the completely accurate (2.1)) permits is 6.73 per cent per annum, which is reached where $d = 0.249$, that is, where the propensity to consume the products of the agricultural sector is approximately three-quarters. There is virtually no limit to the rate of decline of output that the formula can produce, and a propensity to consume agricultural products of only one-quarter (that is, a d of -0.25) will produce an annual reduction in agricultural advances and rents of 14.42 per cent if the landlords bear half the losses. Even a very modest departure of the propensity to consume agricultural products from one-half will suffice to produce massive growth or decline in output in eighteenth-century terms, in one or two generations.

Quesnay did not actually believe that the rates of growth or decline that can be inferred from his *Tableau* would be realised in the economies he wrote about, because of a number of further factors that the *Tableau* does not take fully into account, which will be discussed below. It is, however, best to start by confining the argument to the actual working of the *Tableau*, and this produces the formula for the rate of growth that is set out above.

There is no doubt that Quesnay fully recognised that the *Tableau* produced the result that there would be *continuing* decline in production where the propensity to consume the products of agriculture was less than one-half, and vice versa, and the following passage (among many) which is taken from the 'Maxims' that were published with the 1759 or 3rd edition of the *Tableau* brings this out very clearly:

> It can be seen from the distribution delineated in the *Tableau* that if the nation's expenditure went more to the sterile expenditure side than to the productive expenditure side, the revenue would fall proportionately, and that this fall would increase in the same progression from year to year successively. It follows that a high level of expenditure on luxury in the way of ornamentation and conspicuous consumption is ruinous. If on the other hand the nation's expenditure goes to the productive expenditure side the revenue will rise, and this rise will in the same way increase successively from year to year. Thus it is not true that the type of expenditure is a matter of indifference. (Tab edn3 12 [M])

Those who are only familiar with modern theories of growth will find it remarkable that the rate of growth can be a function of *what* is consumed rather than the ratio of investment to consumption. Just how different Quesnay's argument is can be seen from the following passage from one of the early *Encyclopedia* articles:

> [A nation which is reduced to subsisting on industrial activity] can only extend and sustain its trade, its industry and its shipping through saving; while those which have landed property increase their revenues through their consumption. (Q 499 [E])

This follows quite naturally if each livre spent on food produces an addition to rents, while no other form of expenditure has similar favourable 'external' effects. Quesnay was far from alone in believing that consumption of the 'correct' goods produced growth, for as will be shown in Chapter 3 it was a central argument in Adam Smith's *Wealth of Nations* that the rate of growth depends partly on the ratio of 'productive' to 'unproductive' consumption. Moreover, it will emerge that Ricardo and Marx followed Smith here, though each had borderlines between the 'productive' and 'unproductive' sectors of the economy which differed substantially from Quesnay's.

TAXATION AND THE RATE OF GROWTH

The propensity to consume the products of agriculture is not, of course, the sole factor that can produce growth or decline in Quesnay's argument, and according to the Physiocrats a major factor responsible for the supposed decline in France's population and wealth, in addition to excessive *luxe de décoration*, was the use of methods of taxation which fell on the capital of farmers, that is, on agricultural advances. One of the two articles which Quesnay published to illustrate the application of the final version of his *Tableau* to practical problems was concerned with the effects of indirect taxation, and there are two sequences of *Tableaux* in *Philosophie Rurale*, of which one is wholly Quesnay's, and two *Tableaux* in *L'Ami des Hommes* which demonstrate these.[11] There is no doubt that Quesnay thought that taxation which fell on agricultural advances was immensely harmful to production in the actual conditions of eighteenth-century France, and that the *Tableau* could be used to illustrate this.

With Quesnay's model the taxation of the revenue of the landlords has a wholly neutral effect on the economy, because it has no effect at all on the *Tableau*. It is clearly a matter of complete indifference to the workers and entrepreneurs of agriculture and industry whether the revenue is spent by the landlords themselves, or the Church, or the King and his Ministers. Their sole interest is that it be spent. If the King needs 30 per cent of the revenue for the government of the country and for military purposes (and Quesnay generally assumed that the government should have two-sevenths of the revenue, the Church one-seventh, and the landlords themselves four-sevenths), the arrangement that suits agriculture best is that illustrated in Table 2.3 where the landlords pay 30 per cent of their revenues directly to the government which can then spend this in place of the landlords. In Table 2.3 the *Tableau* in its final form is assumed with a rate of return on annual agricultural advances of 100 per cent. Then if annual agricultural advances are 1 000 million livres in the initial year, rents will also be 1 000 million livres, and agricultural output is worth 2 500 million livres, of which, in stationary state equilibrium, 1 000 million livres go to the farmers to allow them to maintain their advances, another 500 million livres go to them for their 'interest' costs, and the

TABLE 2.3   How taxation of rents at 30 per cent affects growth

Annual agricultural advances	Rents	Marketed farm output	Taxation of		Tax revenue	Farmers' financial surplus (+) or deficit (−)
			Farm output	Rents		
					millions of livres	
Initial year						
1 000	1 000	2 000	0	300	300	0
Second year						
1 000	1 000	2 000	0	300	300	0

remaining 1 000 million livres go to the landlords. However, of the 2 500 million livres that agriculture produces, half the agricultural wages or advances of 1 000 million livres are ,obtained by farmers from their own crops, so this 500 million livres of agricultural output does not need to be sold, leaving 2 000 million livres to be marketed.[12] It will be evident from Table 2.3 that if rents are taxed at 30 per cent while sales of farm produce are untaxed, farmers' incomes will be unaltered, for it is immaterial to them whether the revenue is spent by the landlords or the state. There is therefore no effect on the following year's annual agricultural advances (unless these are changing for some other reason) so the *Tableau* is in no way disturbed by the tax on rents, and constant output can be maintained from year to year as in Table 2.3. It is obviously assumed that the government spends the same proportion of its income on agricultural products as the landlords.

Suppose now that the landlords oppose a situation where they bear the entire costs of taxation, and that an alternative system is therefore adopted where an equal rate of tax is applied universally. The simplest case to take to obtain the essence of Quesnay's analysis is the one illustrated in Table 2.4 where the rate of return on advances and the other initial conditions are the same as in Table 2.3. The government seeks to obtain 300 million livres a year by taxing the landlords at 10 per cent, which is expected to raise 100 million livres, and in addition by taxing all marketed agricultural output at 10 per cent, which is expected to yield a further 200 million livres. The landlords apparently have their taxes reduced from 300 million to 100 million livres, but as Quesnay says of them in his similar but more complex example of 1767:

> Poor calculators that they are, they do not have an inkling that by entering into this plausible arrangement they are providing the spade which will be used to dig their own graves. (Q 987 [M])

The difficulty becomes rapidly apparent. When 2 000 million livres of agricultural products are marketed (and the cash flows of the *Tableau* will not allow the harvest to be sold for more than this – so the tax cannot be passed on), 200 million livres must be paid to the government, so the farmers will receive 200 million livres less than in the previous year when the *Tableau* was in equilibrium. They therefore have a financial deficit of 200 million livres in Table 2.4. If they split this loss equally with the landlords as is assumed in Table

TABLE 2.4 How the taxation of rents and marketed farm output at 10 per cent affects growth

Annual agricultural advances	Rents	Marketed farm output	Taxation of		Tax revenue	Farmers' financial surplus (+) or deficit (−)
			Farm output	Rents		
					millions of livres	
Initial year 1 000	1 000	2 000	200	100	300	−200
Second year 900	900	1 800	180	90	270	−180
Third year 810	810	1 620	162	81	243	−162

2.4, their advances for the next year will be reduced from 1 000 to 900 million livres, while rents will also be reduced from 1 000 to 900 million livres. With agricultural advances down 10 per cent to 900 million livres, the following year's taxable agricultural output will be 1 800 million instead of 2 000 million livres, and a 10 per cent tax on this will now yield only 180 million livres which, together with the 90 million livres the government now obtains from the landlords through the 10 per cent direct tax on rents, produces a total tax revenue of 270 million livres in place of the previous year's 300 million livres. Thus agricultural advances, rents and total tax revenues will all be 10 per cent lower than in the previous year. Moreover, Table 2.4 shows that annual agricultural advances will continue to fall at an annual rate of 10 per cent for so long as sales of agricultural produce are taxed at 10 per cent and landlords expect farmers to bear half the cost of this, and rents and total tax revenue will both fall with agricultural advances. There will thus be a continuing decline of all incomes at an annual rate of 10 per cent, and this is half the rate at which annual agricultural advances are taxed, for the 10 per cent tax on sales of food is, in effect, a 20 per cent tax on agricultural advances. The economy's annual rate of decline is thus half the rate at which agricultural advances are taxed, and it is half this rate because of the assumption that landlords accept a reduction in rents each year equal to half the farmers' financial deficit.

The argument can be put in the following way, which incidentally makes it quite clear why the farmers cannot pass a tax on sales of food on to another class. In the conditions assumed, the state uses its full powers to obtain 10 per cent of that part of each harvest which is marketed, and the landlords then take what is, in effect, one-half of the remainder, whatever this may be, or 45 per cent. This leaves the farmers just 45 per cent of each marketed harvest in place of the 50 per cent that they need in order to maintain constant output where annual agricultural advances yield 100 per cent. (They would need two-thirds of each harvest to maintain constant output if agricultural advances yielded 50 per cent.) With Quesnay's assumptions, if the farmers receive 45 per cent of the marketed harvest in place of the 50 per cent that they need in order to maintain constant output, production will fall in proportion, that is, at an annual rate of one-tenth. As agricultural output falls 10 per cent per annum, government revenue (which is one-tenth of output) and rents (which are half the remainder) will fall at the same rate.

The decline in the National Product will continue until the

landlords have sufficient appreciation of what is going on to accept a reduction in rents that corresponds to the full tax burden. When this happens, the landlords will agree to accept just 40 per cent of the harvest after the state has taken 10 per cent, and this will leave the farmers the 50 per cent of each marketed harvest that they need in order to maintain constant output. In Quesnay's view, the landlords are likely to appreciate this quite quickly, but the National Product, rents and government revenues will all fall during the year or years before they realise that taxation must not be allowed to fall on the farmers who work their land, and rents will decrease at a rate corresponding to half the effective rate of taxation that agricultural advances have to bear.

There are a number of points to note about this simplified account of Quesnay's argument. First there has been no reference to the industrial sector of the economy which is also taxed in Quesnay's examples. This can safely be omitted because the taxation of industrial output should have an approximately neutral effect on growth with Quesnay's assumptions. Industrial products are in no way *inputs* necessary for agriculture so their price has no effect on the proportion of agricultural output which can be reinvested by farmers, which is what determines the growth rate. Moreover, the government can be expected to spend any money it takes from industry so the aggregate demand for food will be unaffected. The essentials of Quesnay's argument can therefore be set out without reference to the 'sterile' sector of the economy, which obviously much simplifies the exposition.

A second point to note is that the above account greatly exaggerates the revenue the government will receive by assuming that it will actually obtain 10 per cent of the value of the food that is marketed. In his article of 1767 Quesnay estimated that the cost of collecting this kind of tax was generally about half the money paid to the tax collectors (Q 983), so the government might only receive about 100 million instead of 200 million livres in the first year from the tax on sales of food, the tax collectors, etc., receiving the other 100 million. This would not affect what is spent in the following year if the tax collectors spend what the government does not, but Quesnay in fact argues that they are likely to form monetary fortunes, and these are 'a clandestine form of wealth which knows neither king nor country' (Tab edn3 13 [M]) and their formation will certainly slow down the flows of the *Tableau*. The costs of collecting direct taxes on the rents of the landlords are always assumed to be very slight.

A third point to note is that the above account has understated the adverse effects of falling agricultural incomes on growth because it has been assumed throughout that annual agricultural advances yield 100 per cent. This is only possible with *la grande culture* which depends on the existence of rich farmers. As agricultural advances are taxed away, farms will increasingly revert to *la petite culture* which yields only about 30 per cent on annual advances, and this will accelerate the decline in production, rents, and tax returns.

Finally, as tax revenues fall as a result of the continuing decline in agricultural advances, the reversion to less capital intensive methods of farming, and the higher cost of collecting indirect taxation, the state will be under continuous pressure to raise rates of taxation, and this will especially be the case in time of war when revenue cannot easily be dispensed with. Clearly any increase in rates of taxation as government revenues fall will cause the fall in the National Product to accelerate.

It follows very strongly from the above argument that, given Quesnay's assumptions, there is an overwhelming case for taking tax revenue from the 'net product' of agriculture rather than from its whole produce, since this is where it must come from in any case in the end. Any departure from this rule will have highly adverse effects on growth. As Quesnay wrote in 1767:

The nobility and the clergy have demanded limitless exemptions and immunities, which they have claimed are bound up with their property and their estate. Sovereigns have also thought it appropriate to grant complete exemptions to their officers, and to all those who are invested with posts or employments in all the different branches of government administration. As a result of this state of affairs the revenue of the Exchequer has been reduced to such a low level, and the proprietors have put forward so much opposition to its direct increase, that sovereigns have had recourse to indirect taxes of various kinds, which have extended further and further in the proportion that the nation's revenue has diminished as a result of the deterioration which is the inevitable consequence of these taxes themselves. The landed proprietors, who did not foresee these consequences, and who during the time that they were destroying their revenue did not understand, did not even perceive the cause of the reduction in their wealth, gave their approval to these indirect taxes, by means of which they believed they could evade taxation, which ought to have been laid directly and immediately on the revenue of their property, where it would have caused no decline in the annual reproduction and would not have required to be successively increased; whereas in fact, as a result of the progressive increase and disastrous effects of the indirect taxes, successive increases in both indirect and direct taxes alike become necessary in order to meet the state's needs. In addition, the landed proprietors have not only got out of the payment of the *two-sevenths* of the revenue which belongs to the sovereign, but have also brought upon themselves indirect taxes, causing a progressive and inevitable deterioration which destroys their own revenue, that of the sovereign, and the wealth of the nation. (Q 982 [M])

Quesnay's final comment on what this meant in human terms looks forward to what was to happen twenty years later:

The increase of beggars, which is a consequence of the indirect taxes which destroy wages or subsistence by obliterating part of the reproduction of the nation's annual wealth. This increase of beggars is a large added burden on the cultivators, because they dare not refuse to give alms, being too exposed to the dangers which the discontent of vindictive beggars may draw down upon them. (Q 992 [M])

It is obviously an exaggeration to suppose that any taxation of sales of food must lead to the day of the vindictive beggar. The argument has superimposed taxation of the advances of farmers on a *Tableau* which is otherwise in equilibrium, that is, in a stationary state. Taxation of farm incomes need not produce actual falls in production if another factor, for instance a propensity to consume food which exceeds one-half, is simultaneously producing growth in farm incomes. Quesnay's analysis of the factors which produce growth and decline always takes a *Tableau* in equilibrium as the starting-point, and this is disturbed for one reason only, so he invariably shows the effect on a stationary state of one kind of departure from equilibrium proportions. The total effect on growth will be the sum of *all* departures from equilibrium proportions, so the taxation of farmers' receipts will be perfectly compatible with growth if its adverse effects, and these are undoubtedly very strong with his assumptions, can be outweighed by favourable effects from other directions. In Quesnay's view, there was a most important possible favourable effect (in addition to a high propensity to consume the products of agriculture) which could produce growth, namely an increase in the profitability of agriculture, and the effect of this on growth will now be outlined.

THE PROFITABILITY OF AGRICULTURE AND THE RATE OF GROWTH

The most obvious way to increase the profitability of agriculture is to increase its technical efficiency, and this requires either the application of new knowledge, which played no part in Quesnay's argument, or an increase in the capital of farmers, which he discussed at great length. However, with his analysis, farm capital can be increased only if growth is in any case occurring, and up to now this has been producible only by a propensity to consume the products of agriculture which exceeds one-half. If the technical efficiency of agriculture cannot readily be increased until growth is actually proceeding, then the profitability of agriculture must be increased in some other way, and Quesnay suggested that this could be achieved by improving the conditions in which its products were marketed, which was the only policy lever for raising farm incomes that made practical sense to him.

The first of Quesnay's two articles which illustrate the application of the final version of the *Tableau* to practical problems was concerned with the favourable effects that a higher price of food and better marketing policies should have on agricultural advances and rents; and there is a similar sequence of *Tableaux* in *Philosophie Rurale* which follows through, in a most detailed way, the effects over a nine-year period of the cumulative reinvestment of such extra advances as are obtained from an initial improvement in farmers' incomes.[13] In the mid-eighteenth century the free movement of food within France itself was only allowed intermittently, and sales abroad were generally only permitted in years of plenty. The object of these policies, for which Colbert was blamed, was to provide cheap food for the cities to help manufacturers. In his article of 1766 Quesnay argued that full internal and external free trade in the products of agriculture could be expected to increase the rate of return on annual agricultural advances from about 30 to about 50 per cent, for this should substantially *increase* the prices French farmers obtained for their products, turn the terms of trade in France's favour, and greatly reduce fluctuations in prices which affected farm incomes adversely.

This was the easy way, because it only required 'correct' decisions at Versailles, to set in motion a favourable sequence of *Tableaux*. Louis XV had in fact issued an edict permitting grain exports, subject to certain restrictions, in July 1764, largely as a result of the arguments and influence of the Physiocrats, and freer internal movements of food were also permitted for a time. Unfortunately, by 1767 the price of bread had risen 30 per cent and wages had not kept pace, whatever their long-run behaviour might have been, with the result that opposition to the edict became strong, especially in the cities, and it was suspended in 1770.[14] Turgot, however, managed to establish complete internal free movements of agricultural products in his brief tenure of the Finance Ministry from 1774 to 1776.

There is no need to go into the precise details of Quesnay's analysis of the effects of free trade in agricultural products because what is really important is the effect of an increase in farm incomes on growth. More favourable marketing conditions are just one way of bringing this about. Suppose that for some reason the rate of return on annual agricultural advances is raised from 30 to 50 per cent, and that, as has been assumed hitherto in this chapter, only half the increase in agricultural incomes goes to the landlords, while half is retained by the farmers. Then half of the 20 per cent increase in the rate of return will go to the farmers with the result that annual agricultural advances will increase 10 per cent, and this will raise agricultural output 10 per cent in the following year, and raise agricultural advances again if farmers are allowed to retain half the fruits of growth.

The argument corresponds to the one which showed that the taxation of agricultural receipts at a rate of 10 per cent should reduce output by 10 per cent per annum. In the present case advances yield 50 per cent, so farmers must reinvest 1 000 out of each 1 500 livres of agricultural sales to maintain constant output. However, the landlords were content to take 300 out of each 1 300 livres when agricultural advances yielded 30 per cent, and if they are content to take 400 out of 1 500 livres when the rate of return rises to 50 per cent, then the farmers will be left with 1 100 out of 1 500 livres which is 10 per cent more than the 1 000 out of 1 500 livres that they need in order to maintain constant output. With Quesnay's assumptions this will produce an initial 10 per cent rate of growth in agricultural advances and therefore in rents, government revenues, and industrial production also, and growth will continue for so long as landlords are content to leave farmers with half the increase in the returns to agriculture.

Where Quesnay discusses the effects on growth of an increase in farm incomes he does not actually make the mechanical assumption that half the benefits go to the farmers, but he assumes instead that farmers have fixed period leases, and obtain the whole benefit from an increase in the rate of return during the remainder of their leases, after which this goes in its entirety to the landlords (Q 870–1). In the passage cited from *Philosophie Rurale* of which Meek says 'All the evidence, stylistic and otherwise, points to Quesnay as its author',[15] the period of leases is assumed to be nine years, and farmers reinvest all the extra income they receive until their leases expire. The effect of an increase in the rate of return on annual agricultural advances from 30 to 50 per cent in these conditions is outlined in Table 2.5. This table is drawn up with the same assumptions as Tables 2.3 and 2.4. However, as the rate of return on advances is only 50 per cent instead of 100 per cent, marketed farm output is advances *plus* 50 per cent instead of advances *plus* 100 per cent. The farmers need to retain an amount equivalent to their advances to maintain constant output, and any excess they produce over this together with the previous level of rents is their potential surplus.[16] Thus in year 1, the first year in which a 50 per cent rate of return is earned, their output is 1 500 million livres, which exceeds advances of 1 000 million livres and rents of 300 million livres by 200 million livres, and this is the farmers' financial surplus. With the assumption of nine-year leases, one-ninth of the farms are in the final year of their leases, and in these cases the rent agreed for the next nine years will be based on the new 50 per cent rate of return, so one-ninth of the 200 million livre financial surplus will be absorbed in higher rents. The other eight-ninths, 178 million livres, will be reinvested as in Table 2.5, with the result that the second year's advances are raised by eight-ninths of the farmers' financial surplus of the first year. In the second year, a financial surplus will only be earned by the farmers whose leases have not yet come up for renewal, and one-eighth of these come up for renewal at the end of the year, so only seven-eighths of the surplus will be reinvested. Similarly, six-sevenths will be reinvested in the third year, five-sixths in the fourth year until finally, in the ninth year, the last leases expire, and the entire remaining farm surpluses are absorbed into rents. After this, in the tenth year of a 50 per cent rate of return in agriculture, rents will be 50 per cent of advances, so there will no longer be a financial surplus for farmers. There will therefore be no further growth in farm incomes and output, but Table 2.5 shows that

TABLE 2.5 Effect on growth of an increase in r, the rate of return on annual agricultural advances, from 30 per cent to 50 per cent in Year 1

Year	Advances	Rents	Marketed farm output	Farmers' financial surplus	Unexpired leases	Addition to	
	A	R	$A(1 + r)$	S	h	Advances hS	Rents $(1 - h) S$
						millions of livres	
0	1 000	300	1 300	0	—	—	—
1	1 000	300	1 500	200	8/9	178	22
2	1 178	322	1 767	267	7/8	234	33
3	1 412	355	2 118	351	6/7	301	50
4	1 713	405	2 569	451	5/6	376	75
5	2 089	480	3 133	564	4/5	451	113
6	2 540	593	3 810	677	3/4	508	169
7	3 048	762	4 572	762	2/3	508	254
8	3 556	1 016	5 334	762	1/2	381	381
9	3 937	1 397	5 905	571	0	0	571
10	3 937	1 968	5 905	0	—	—	—

in the nine years where there is growth, annual agricultural advances increase incredibly at an annual rate of 16.4 per cent from 1 000 million livres to 3 937 million livres, while rents increase at an annual rate of 23 per cent from 300 million to 1 968 million livres. The alternative assumption of an equal division of gains between rents and advances produced indefinite growth at an initial rate of 10 per cent per annum. Whichever assumption is used therefore produces growth that is quite capable of counteracting adverse effects from other causes, and thus achieving *la réparation de l'agriculture*. The actual growth rates produced by the argument are obviously implausibly high, as were the rates of decline that indirect taxation caused, but it is best to set out exactly what rates of growth and decline result from the direct application of the assumptions of the *Tableau* before the appropriate correction factors are applied.

A QUESNAY GROWTH FORMULA

Combining what has been said about growth so far, g_a, the rate of growth of annual agricultural advances, will depend on three sets of factors. First, if the propensity to consume the products of agriculture exceeds one-half by d, annual agricultural advances will grow at a rate of approximately, $\frac{1}{2}d - \frac{2}{3}d^2$ (from 2.2), if the dynamic assumption that all gains and losses in farm incomes are shared equally between farmers and landlords is made. Second, if annual agricultural advances are taxed at an effective rate of Γ_a, they will decline at a rate of $\frac{1}{2}\Gamma_a$ if gains and losses are shared equally by farmers and landlords; it was argued above that a 10 per cent tax on sales of food, which was in effect a 20 per cent tax on agricultural advances, would produce a 10 per cent rate of decline in incomes and advances in these conditions. Finally, if the actual rate of return on annual agricultural advances is r and rents are based on a rate of return of r^*, then agricultural advances should grow at an annual rate of $\frac{1}{2}(r - r^*)$ if farmers are allowed to reinvest half the excess, as in the example that has been outlined, and growth from this source will continue until r^* becomes as high as the new and higher r. Combining the three effects:

$$g_a = \frac{1}{2}d - \frac{2}{3}d^2 + \frac{1}{2}(r - r^* - \Gamma_a) \tag{2.3}$$

Quesnay believed that the French National Product had declined because d was negative, and because of Γ_a, while there was no compensation from an *r* in excess of *r**, that is, a more favourable rate of return in agriculture than the one on which rents were based. He believed, however, that the situation could be rapidly restored because it was open to the government to make Γ_a zero, and to make *r* exceed *r**, for nine years at any rate, which would produce considerable growth. It is now thought that there was, in fact, slow growth during much of his lifetime,[17] so there may have been favourable underlying factors that play no part in the formula, or *d* may have been positive and not negative. Growth was slow, however, there was great agricultural distress, and French governments went through a series of financial crises which contributed to the events of 1789, so Quesnay's proposals were very much to the point.

The formula can very easily produce extraordinarily rapid rates of growth or decline, and Quesnay was fully aware of this, and a number of correction factors are applied in *Philosophie Rurale* to produce more plausible rates of growth. These involve departures from the strict calculations of the *Tableau* in equilibrium, but this was not designed to deal with dynamic progressions in detail so some adjustment is appropriate. The principal adjustment, which is really all that is needed, is to bring the *original* advances of agriculture, that is, its fixed capital, fully into the argument. It has been assumed so far that agricultural output is proportional to *A*, the *annual* advances or circulating capital of farmers, and that in addition to this, farmers earn enough to cover 'interest' which can be regarded as the replacement of such fixed capital as wears out. It has therefore been assumed, in effect, that agricultural output can be doubled in the short period by doubling employment and seed corn without also doubling expenditure on horses, ploughs, and so on, which are part of the farmers' fixed capital. The assumption that more 'interest' is earned allows these to be replaced at a higher rate, but it does not allow for actual investment in more horses and ploughs as output expands. It is clear that more fixed capital is needed as output expands, as this is central to Quesnay's argument about the productivity of *la grande culture*, and the financing of any long-term growth process must require that fixed capital be increased at the same rate as circulating capital. Quesnay does not introduce this complication in the relatively small progressions and regressions that are shown in most of his published sequences of *Tableaux*, but the growth in farm incomes in the nine-year period where farmers continually reinvest what they gain until their leases expire is so great that the calculation in *Philosophie Rurale* concerned with this problem does allow for the need to expand fixed capital in line with circulating capital. It is assumed in this calculation that the fixed capital of farmers is four times their circulating capital, that is, four times annual advances, so total farm capital is five times *annual* advances.[18] Elsewhere in his writings, Quesnay sometimes assumes that fixed capital is five times annual advances so that total capital is six times annual advances.[19] With the assumption of *Philosophie Rurale* that total farm capital is five times annual agricultural advances, only one-fifth of any increase in the incomes that farmers receive can go to increase annual agricultural advances, and the remaining four-fifths has to be invested in new fixed capital which must grow at an equal rate in the long run. Applying the same principle, any shortfall in farm incomes can be partly made good at the expense of fixed capital in the long run, and this means that in periods of decline, annual agricultural advances need fall by only one-fifth of any fall in farm incomes, and Quesnay points out that fixed capital is run down where advances decline (Q 987). The long-term rise or fall of rents will depend on the rate at which circulating capital or annual agricultural advances rise or fall, and all the other important trends in the economy depend on this, and once the need for fixed capital is fully allowed for it becomes evident that annual agricultural advances will not grow or decline as rapidly as has so far been supposed.

The actual formula for the rate of growth of annual agricultural advances can be adjusted very simply to the need to expand the fixed capital of farmers in line with their circulating capital. If the ratio of total capital to circulating capital is F, and this is five or six in Quesnay's work, all growth rates will simply be reduced by a factor of F. Thus in the calculation in *Philosophie Rurale* where fixed capital is four times circulating capital, F is five, and the rate of growth of annual agricultural advances is one-fifth that so far supposed. More generally, with the need to invest in fixed capital allowed for, equation (2.3) will become:

$$g_a = \frac{1}{2F} (d - 1\tfrac{1}{3}\, d^2) + \frac{1}{2F} (r - r^* - \Gamma_a) \qquad (2.4)$$

In terms of modern growth theory, it would be said that (2.3), the earlier formula which neglected the need to expand fixed capital in line with annual advances, understated the capital–output ratio by a factor of F. Equation (2.4) recognises the existence of fixed capital, and that this raises the capital–output ratio F times, and an F-times increase in the capital–output ratio reduces the growth produced by given investments by a factor of F.

Equation (2.4) recognises the need to increase the fixed capital of farmers at the same rate as annual agricultural advances, but there has been no reference yet to the need to increase the money supply and landlords' own capital (*avances foncières*) at this rate. Quesnay assumes that countries will automatically obtain sufficient money for their needs through international trade (and that it will not be farmers who pay for it) and there is no reference to the possibility that insufficient *avances foncières* might restrict progress. The growth of farmers' advances will therefore be the growth rate that matters.

Much more plausible growth rates are obtained with (2.4) than with the earlier formula, which neglected the need to expand fixed capital. Thus if F is five, a propensity to consume the products of agriculture of 0.6 will produce a growth rate of about 0.8 per cent per annum instead of one of over 4 per cent, while a propensity to consume food of 0.4 will produce an annual rate of decline of only about 1.1 per cent. Similarly, the taxation of farm incomes at 20 per cent will produce an annual rate of decline of 2 per cent and not 10 per cent, while an increase in the rate of return on advances from 30 to 50 per cent will produce growth at just 2 per cent per annum. In the alternative calculation of the effect of the reinvestment of farm profits until all leases come up for renewal, the annual rate of growth in the nine-year period is 3.3 per cent, and not the incredible 16.4 per cent calculated previously. These slower and more plausible rates of growth and decline would be more than sufficient to account for any supposed decline or increase in population, incomes and wealth in France in the seventeenth and eighteenth centuries. They would moreover, as Quesnay says, allow a Kingdom to reach ' a high degree of strength and prosperity in a short period of time' (Q 504 [E]), where correct policies are pursued.

It is pointed out in *Philosophie Rurale* that an 'essential condition' that must be fulfilled if the calculated growth is to be achieved is that it must be possible to increase population and farm animals in line with production, which can expand only if this 'indispensable condition' can be fulfilled (PR ii.368). Hence it is recognised that the maximum achievable rate of population and animal growth sets an ultimate constraint to growth, and this could even affect the slower rates of growth produced by the modified formula. This could be particularly important in North America, for Quesnay's account of the effects of the reinvestment of the extra profits of agriculture over a nine-year period concludes with a few words about what could be achieved in a new colony:

> Nevertheless, if the rapid advance of the simple arithmetical progression shown above is applied to vigorous colonies with a large territory, which can be cultivated with the labour of animals, assisted by large advances supplied by a wealthy metropolis, it can be seen that such colonies may be able to make very great progress in a short time. 1. Because new land when it has been cleared yields a large product. 2. Because in such places little or no taxes are paid. 3. Because the cultivators are themselves proprietors, so that all the profits from cultivation are all the time continually used to increase the wealth employed in cultivation. (PR ii.369 [M])

With no taxation of the products of agriculture, and no diversion of growing farm incomes to landlords, r^* and Γ_a will be zero, and the basic growth formula will become:[20]

$$g_a = \frac{1}{F}\left(d - 1\tfrac{1}{3}d^2\right) + \frac{r}{F} \tag{2.5}$$

which will evidently produce more rapid growth than the earlier formula appropriate to the institutions of eighteenth-century France. Quesnay estimated that these, together with the other factors which held back the growth of French agriculture, reduced the growth which could follow from a given increase in the profitability of agriculture by nine-tenths (PR ii.370). Clearly, in North American conditions, the maximum rate at which population and farm animals can be expanded is likely to act as the effective constraint on growth, for the rate of capital accumulation produced by the above formula is likely to exceed any physically sustainable rate of growth.

This insight into what is achievable with the institutions of a new society concludes this account of Quesnay's theory of economic growth. It is an interesting, powerful and highly original theory, and it focuses attention on causes of growth and decline which are arguably of real importance. Moreover, no economist since has set out a growth model with plausible assumptions (once these are understood) where agriculture plays such a crucial role.

QUESNAY AND HIS SUCCESSORS

Quesnay's successors developed concepts which would have allowed him to express his argument more clearly. In particular, the adoption of Smith's division of the categories of income into wages the return to labour, profits the return to capital, and rent the return to land would have allowed Quesnay to say what he had to say much more comprehensibly. In his theory wages and the normal profits of both farmers and artisans are always expressed as a single total. They are already separated by Turgot in his *Réflexions sur la Formation et la Distribution des Richesses* of 1770, and Turgot even recognised that industrial as well as agricultural profits provide an investable surplus.[21] Quesnay may have believed that industry provided a negligible surplus in France at the time he wrote. His theories would have been taken more seriously if it had been appreciated that he was simply assuming that industry provided no taxable surplus, and not that it made no economic contribution to production, which is another interpretation of the word 'sterile'.

It would also have been helpful if Quesnay had been able to answer the criticisms of his theory which followed from the theory of rent which was developed by Ricardo, Malthus, and West forty years after his death, and which will be discussed in detail in Chapter 6. According to this, no rent accrues at the margin of cultivation, and given sufficient competition, an addition to agricultural and industrial investment must then produce the same total return, for agricultural capital will produce no return in addition to the normal profits that farmers receive (R I 67–84 and 327–37). Quesnay's response to this might well have been that agricultural output is principally a return to capital, and landlords must in all practical cases be able to obtain part of the return on this *once leases expire*. Then marginal industrial investments will yield wages and entrepreneurial returns, while marginal agricultural investments will yield wages and entrepreneurial returns, and an addition to rents on the expiry of leases, so agricultural investment must generally yield more. He would only have conceded the relevance of Ricardo's theory to a country where there was no need for farmers to invest at the margin of cultivation in any way that improved their farms in the course of their leases. These were not the conditions of eighteenth-century France where agricultural expansion meant taking the capital-intensive methods of *la grande culture* to land which was not being efficiently farmed. Thus

Ricardo's assumptions are appropriate to a country where all the land that can be farmed by efficient capital-intensive methods is already being so farmed, while Quesnay assumes a country where there is still some scope for the extension of these methods. This is often a more appropriate assumption than that of a fully stocked agriculture, and a particular case can be made for Quesnay's assumptions along these lines.

It is therefore arguable that Quesnay's theory of economic growth deserves serious attention. It is obviously of considerable historical interest for the light it throws on the underlying causes of the French Revolution, and for its undoubted influence on Smith, the subject of the next chapter. Smith met Quesnay in 1766, and would have 'inscribed' *The Wealth of Nations* to him if Quesnay had not died two years before its publication.[22] Through Smith, Quesnay went on to influence Malthus, Ricardo, and their successors including especially Marx: Quesnay was the only one of his predecessors who formulated a precise scheme of reproduction where attention was focused above all on the production of a surplus and its expenditure.

That is not, however, all that can be learned from Quesnay's theory of economic growth. His condemnation of Colbert's policies of taxing agriculture to subsidise industry has modern echoes, and Candela (1976) has shown that Mao Tse Tung criticised precisely this aspect of Soviet policies when he wrote: 'some socialist countries ... put too heavy a tax burden on the peasants, and they lowered agricultural prices in terms of industrial prices ... Any inadequacy, any neglect of the peasants' welfare, will result in a failure of the collective economy ... Unless under severe conditions of natural disaster, we must as far as agricultural production allows see to it that the peasant's income is higher than that of the previous year.'[23]

The relevance of Quesnay's critique of agricultural taxation to finance industrialisation is not confined to the centrally planned economies. He analysed the problems involved in achieving growth in an economy where land was not scarce in the sense that there was much land in use that was producing negligible rates of return because of the low capital intensity of the methods of production in use. These are precisely the conditions today in many developing countries, which have mostly adopted policies similar to Colbert's of favouring industries that can hardly produce a surplus at the expense of agriculture which can. The failures of these policies in the twentieth century would have surprised Quesnay no more than their failure in his own time.

3 Adam Smith's Theory of Economic Growth

Adam Smith's theory of economic growth is at first sight startlingly different from that of Quesnay and the Physiocrats. In their argument industry produces no investable surplus, and therefore makes no positive contribution to growth, which depends entirely on the reinvestment of the agricultural surplus. By 1776 when Smith published *The Wealth of Nations* the Industrial Revolution was transforming the North of England, and he perceived more of its implications for output and living standards than many of his successors. In the theory he developed both industry and agriculture play a vital role, but the agricultural surplus has a particularly important effect on growth and it will emerge that he took over crucial elements of Quesnay's argument which he greatly simplified. He also appreciated (from the 1750s onwards) the immense potential significance for growth of the division of labour in industry – the subject of the first three chapters of *The Wealth of Nations* – and this emerges as both a cause and a consequence of industrialisation. Moreover, he offers the prospect of rising living standards for the mass of the population – a possibility that Quesnay and indeed many of Smith's successors never perceived.

According to Smith, increasing returns in industry, and 'learning by doing' as growth theorists now call it can be expected to increase the *manufactured* goods that workers can afford to buy continuously in an economical and well-governed society. Right at the start of *The Wealth of Nations* Smith pointed out that as a result of the division of labour, an 'industrious and frugal peasant' enjoyed, as well as enough food for subsistence, a woollen coat, a coarse linen shirt, shoes, a kitchen grate, knives and forks and kitchen utensils, earthernware or pewter plates, and glass windows with the result that his 'accommodation' greatly exceeded that of an African King (WN 23–4). Workers, like peasants, gained from the division of labour which produced these benefits, and Smith certainly did not believe that the maximum possible advantages from this had been obtained by 1776.

Smith went on to develop a line of argument about the positive association between capital accumulation and productivity growth which modern theory has only recently begun to rediscover. Astonishingly, in much of twentieth-century growth theory, the rate of investment is predicted to have no effect at all on an economy's *long-term* rate of growth of output and living standards. This is true of all neoclassical growth theory and of a good deal of Keynesian growth theory in addition.[1] In Smith's theory, in contrast, capital accumulation leads to increased population and employment, and provided that the market for manufactured goods is widened by this, an increased division of labour will follow, which will have favourable effects on labour productivity. If competition is sufficient, and an increase in capital will generally increase competition, the prices of manufactured goods will then fall with unit labour costs, with the result that the quantity and range of manufactured goods which workers can afford to purchase will increase. It follows therefore that in Smith's account of growth, faster capital accumulation is associated with a faster rate of growth of employment and output, and faster growth in living standards. In modern growth theory, Arrow comes nearest to Smith's results with his 'learning by doing' model, where the rate of growth of labour productivity and wages per head depend on the rate of growth of employment opportunities provided by new machines.[2] Very few other modern theorists have arrived at Smith's results. Thus, if a strong interconnection between investment and growth is central to the development process, Smith's theory of growth must stand high, for it is one of the very few where investment has highly favourable long-term effects.

A number of problems are naturally involved in any attempt to present Smith's theory of growth in modern terms. *The Wealth of Nations* was not written with the rigour of modern growth theory. It is most unlikely that Smith's book would have had the vast influence it achieved if the argument had been presented in the form of a logical derivation of conclusions from carefully stated premises, with each term precisely defined. Because the book was written to persuade and to carry any literate reader along, definitions and assumptions often need to be inferred from the general argument, and as this deals with much more than growth and development, some of the propositions that relate to growth must be obtained from other parts of the argument.

In this chapter, an attempt will be made to present an account of Smith's theory of growth and development in modern terms, but before this is done, something must be said about Smith's basic assumptions, for these involve a number of problems of interpretation which must be resolved before a theory than can genuinely pretend to be his can be outlined. The first section of the chapter, 'Adam Smith's assumptions', will be concerned with these problems, and the various propositions that are to be found in *The Wealth of Nations* about returns to scale in industry and agriculture, the distinction between productive and unproductive employment and its relevance to the rate of capital accumulation, the effect of accumulation on wages, and so on. These are discussed with the object of arriving at the appropriate assumptions for a modern restatement of Smith's theory of growth. In the next section 'A *Wealth of Nations* growth model', the theory that follows from Smith's assumptions will be set out and discussed, and the results of the model will then be compared with various propositions and predictions about growth and development which are to be found in *The Wealth of Nations*. Smith does not merely predict continuing progress based on industry and agriculture, for he clearly believed that growth would eventually cease when a country's potential for development was fully realised, the development then achieved depending in part on a society's laws and institutions. He expected the rate of profit to fall as full development was approached, and this means that a model that predicted an indefinite continuation of growth would not be Smith's.[3] In addition, it is clear that Smith thought that agriculture provided a more useful foundation for growth than industry, even though industry offered greater potential benefits from the division of labour. This apparent paradox must be explained by any model that claims to be Smith's.

ADAM SMITH'S ASSUMPTIONS

In this part of the chapter, Smith's basic assumptions about four of the factors which influence the development of economies will be discussed, namely his assumptions about returns to scale in the different sectors of the economy; about the relationship between the ratio of productive to unproductive employment and the rate of capital accumulation and the principal considerations which motivate this; about how requirements for fixed and circulating capital vary with growth; and about how growth and income distribution interact. His assumptions about returns to scale in industry and agriculture will be considered first.

Chapter 1 of Book 1 of *The Wealth of Nations* opens with an account of the advantages to be derived from the division of labour, and after illustrations including the famous pin factory, Smith writes:

> This great increase of the quantity of work, which, in consequence of the division of labour, the same number of people are capable of performing, is owing to three different circumstances; first, to the increase of dexterity in every particular workman; secondly, to the saving of the time which is commonly lost in passing from one species of work to another; and lastly, to the invention of a great number of machines which facilitate and abridge labour, and enable one man to do the work of many. (WN 17)

The first two of these are now very familiar, but the third is less so, and it will be seen that it is important. It is obviously relevant to the correspondence between Smith's argument and Arrow's 'learning by doing' growth model that has been remarked upon.

The extent to which it is possible to take advantage of the division of labour depends on the number of workers who can be concentrated to manufacture a good at a single place, and this will depend on the market for the good. Smith points out that it takes 50–100 families to buy the product of a shoemaker working on his own, or an artisan in a single trade (WN 682), and many more where the division of labour is pushed far, so a workshop with 100 workers will produce for far more than 5000–10000 families. Such a workshop can only exist if transport facilities are available to distribute products widely, and as water transport was by far the cheapest form of transport until the nineteenth century, there is much in *The Wealth of Nations* about the influence of the Mediterranean and navigable rivers on the location of the areas of the world able to exploit the potential advantages inherent in the division of labour.[4] Provided that the extent of the market is sufficient (and that the division of labour depends on the extent of the market is one of the best-known propositions in *The Wealth of Nations*) industrial output can be expanded more than proportionately with the labour employed in industry. Each increase in employment will lead to a further subdivision of tasks, which will lead to higher labour productivity:

> What takes place among the labourers in a particular workhouse, takes place, for the same reason, among those of a great society. The greater their number, the more they naturally divide themselves into different classes and subdivisions of employment. More heads are occupied in inventing the most proper machinery for executing the work of each, and it is, therefore, more likely to be invented. (WN 104)

Thus with tasks further subdivided, new machines will be invented, and once they are, productivity will rise to the level appropriate to that degree of division of labour. A further increase in productivity will be achieved when tasks can be still more subdivided, and this will be possible when there is a further increase in employment.[5]

Thus, if employment per firm rises with total industrial employment, the economy will move up a line like *AB* in Figure 3.1, which shows the productivity level that is reached in the long run with each successively higher level of employment. The same diagram follows from Arrow's model, but there the horizontal axis would show

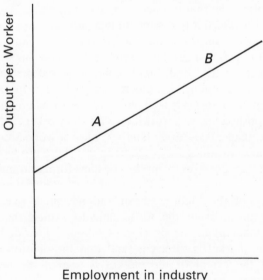

Employment in industry

FIGURE 3.1

successively produced machines, each worked by one worker, instead of aggregate industrial employment. However, the effect of these is the same, and in each case productivity advances at a rate depending on the rate at which the economy expands its industrial labour force and capital stock. An account of Smith's lectures delivered in the early 1760s in Glasgow suggests that he may have thought that AB rose very steeply, for the following statement has been attributed to him: 'For twenty millions in a society, in the same manner as a company of manufacturers, will produce 100 times more goods to be exchanged than a poorer and less numerous one of 2 mill' (Jur 392). A student who took lecture notes in a different year attributed a still more favourable statement to him: 'Twenty millions of people perhaps in a great society, working as it were to one anothers hands, from the nature of the division of labour before explained would produce a thousand times more goods than another society consisting only of two or three millions' (Jur 512). This student may well have added a nought to make a 'hundred' a 'thousand'. The first student implies that each 1 per cent rise in employment might be associated with an increase in labour productivity of 1 per cent,[6] which suggests exceedingly favourable production conditions wherever the division of labour can be usefully extended, and it was certainly Smith's view that it could be much further extended in industry.

Agriculture was, however, of considerably greater importance than industry in an eighteenth-century economy, and here two to four families can consume the output of a farm worker (WN 682), and:

> The nature of agriculture, indeed, does not admit of so many subdivisions of labour, nor of so complete a separation of one business from another, as manufactures. It is impossible to separate so entirely, the business of the grazier from that of the corn-farmer, as the trade of the carpenter is commonly separated from that of the smith. The spinner is almost always a distinct person from the weaver; but the ploughman, the harrower, the sower of the seed, and the reaper of the corn, are often the same. The occasions for those different sorts of labour returning with the different seasons of the year, it is impossible that one man should be constantly employed in any one of them. (WN 16)

The fact that a farm of maximum attainable efficiency requires few workers to work together, and few consumers to provide a market, means that the potential from the division of labour will be fully exploited in agriculture in most countries at most times. There will then be no reason to expect increasing returns in food production. Some foodstuffs will have the same real labour costs, however rapidly productivity advances elsewhere, for instance, corn:

> In every different stage of improvement, besides, the raising of equal quantities of corn in the same soil and climate, will, at an average, require nearly equal quantities of labour; or what comes to the same thing, the price of nearly equal quantities; the continual increase of the productive powers of labour in an improving state of cultivation, being more or less counter-balanced by the continually increasing price of cattle, the principal instruments of agriculture. Upon all these accounts, therefore, we may rest assured, that equal quantities of corn will, in every state of society, in every stage of improvement, more nearly represent, or be equivalent to, equal quantities of labour, than equal quantities of any other part of the rude produce of land. (WN 206)

Over much of the remainder of agriculture and mining, however, diminishing returns are to be expected: 'If you except corn and such other vegetables as are raised altogether by human industry, that all other sorts of rude produce, cattle, poultry, game of all kinds, the useful fossils and minerals of the earth, &c. naturally grow dearer as the society advances in wealth and improvement, I have endeavoured to show already' (WN 234). These all grow dearer in terms of both labour and corn. The exceptions in raw produce are vegetable foods, which fall in price relative to corn because they are a cheap by-product of improved methods of cultivation; and other by-products, for instance hides, which may fall in price because their supply is increased relative to demand because of a faster increase in the number of cattle than in the demand for leather.

It then turns out that Smith assumes increasing returns throughout industry, and with the exception of vegetable foods and hides, etc., that unit costs will be constant, or that they will rise as employment increases in agriculture and mining, where there is much less scope for the division of labour. It follows that whether the demand for manufactured goods grows as capital and employment rise will have a very great effect on the course that development follows. This is indeed the case, and it will emerge that the taste of the rich for manufactured goods, and potential export markets for these, have a very great effect on the growth of economies.

If there is increased employment, and increased demand for manufactured goods, productivity in industry will rise, and the next step in the argument is to discover what, according to Smith, determines the rate of growth of employment. This depends on the rate of growth of capital, for an increase in aggregate employment will only be possible if there is an increase in the capital stock, since more wage goods and raw materials will be needed in advance of production, if more workers are to be employed, and more fixed capital will be needed as well: 'As the accumulation of stock must, in the nature of things, be previous to the division of labour, so labour can be more and more subdivided in proportion only as stock is previously more and more accumulated' (WN 277). Clearly the rate of growth of capital is crucial, and here one comes to the line of argument in *The Wealth of Nations* which is furthest from modern economics. The best starting point for an understanding of Smith's approach to the determination of the rate of capital accumulation is perhaps the following passage:

> In all countries where there is tolerable security, every man of common understanding will endeavour to employ whatever stock he can command in procuring either present enjoyment or future profit. If it is employed in procuring present enjoyment, it is a stock reserved for immediate consumption. If it is employed in procuring future profit, it must procure this profit either by staying with him, or by going from him. In the one case it is a fixed, in the other it is a circulating capital. A man must be perfectly crazy who, where there is tolerable security, does not employ all the stock which he commands, whether it be his own or borrowed of other people, in some one or other of those three ways. (WN 284-5)

This immediately disposes of the possibility that part of a country's capital stock will not be fully utilised (provided that the institutions of a country maintain 'tolerable security' for creditors), and this proposition is a vital component of Say's law. Whatever goods are available that are not immediately consumed by their owners must either be used to make a profit or sold (or lent) to those who expect to be able to make a profit. No one (if the above proposition is accepted) will allow goods to stand idly in warehouses, for this would be 'crazy'.[7]

Now, so far as circulating capital is concerned, and attention will be focused on this for the moment, a profit is made by getting more goods back at the end of a period than went out at the beginning, for instance by feeding corn or its equivalent to farm workers who will then grow more corn than the cost of their wages and the necessary seed corn. Thus, that part of circulating capital that is not consumed by its owners must increase from period to period wherever profits are earned. However, circulating capital as a whole need not grow, because part of it is consumed (directly, or indirectly through the employment of unproductive workers, such as servants) by its owners each year. If the owners consume ¼ of circulating capital each year, and then receive back ⁴⁄₃ times the ¾ they employ productively, the capital stock will neither rise nor fall from period to period. If they consume ⅓, and receive back ⁴⁄₃ times the remaining ⅔, the capital stock will fall by ⅑ in each period; while it will grow by ⅑ if they consume only ⅙ and receive back ⁴⁄₃ times the remaining ⅚. Thus, whether the capital stock grows or declines depends on the proportion that is used productively, and on how productive this is:

> Both productive and unproductive labourers, and those who do not labour at all, are all equally maintained by the annual produce of the land and labour of the country. This produce, how great soever, can never be infinite, but must have certain limits. According, therefore, as a smaller or greater proportion of it is in any one year employed in maintaining unproductive hands, the more in the one case and the less in the other will remain for the productive, and the next year's produce will be greater or smaller accordingly; the whole annual produce, if we except the spontaneous productions of the earth, being the effect of productive labour. (WN 332)

Something must obviously be said about Smith's distinction between productive and unproductive labour, which has all but disappeared from modern economics. This distinction is clearly crucial to Smith's argument, and he says the following about it:

> There is one sort of labour which adds to the value of the subject upon which it is bestowed: There is another which has no such effect. The former, as it produces a value, may be called productive; the latter, unproductive labour. Thus the labour of a manufacturer adds, generally, to the value of the materials which he works upon, that of his own maintenance, and of his master's profit. The labour of a menial servant, on the contrary, adds to the

value of nothing...A man grows rich by employing a multitude of manufacturers: He grows poor, by maintaining a multitude of menial servants...the labour of the manufacturer fixes and realizes itself in some particular subject or vendible commodity, which lasts for some time at least after that labour is past...[the menial servant's] services generally perish in the very instant of their performance, and seldom leave any trace or value behind them, for which an equal quantity of service could afterwards be procured. (WN 330)

Here there are three criteria for the distinction between productive and unproductive labour: (i) whether employment produces a profit, (ii) whether employment produces something storable, and (iii) whether a particular kind of employment can be continued indefinitely without new infusions of capital. Some activities, for instance agriculture and manufacturing, are productive according to all three criteria, while others, for instance domestic services, are unproductive according to all three, while there are activities, for instance teaching or building an extension to a palace, which satisfy some and not others. There are obviously difficult borderline cases (as with the modern distinction between investment and consumption), but Smith's distinction may have force in separating activities which contribute directly to growth from those that do not. As he continues:

The labour of some of the most respectable orders in the society is, like that of menial servants, unproductive of any value, and does not fix or realize itself in any permanent subject, or vendible commodity, which endures after that labour is past, and for which an equal quantity of labour could afterwards be procured. The sovereign, for example, with all the officers both of justice and war who serve under him, the whole army and navy, are unproductive labourers. They are the servants of the publick, and are maintained by a part of the annual produce of the industry of other people. Their service, how honourable, how useful, or how necessary soever, produces nothing for which an equal quantity of service can afterwards be procured. The protection, security, and defence of the commonwealth, the effect of their labour this year, will not purchase its protection, security, and defence, for the year to come. In the same class must be ranked, some both of the gravest and most important, and some of the most frivolous professions: churchmen, lawyers, physicians, men of letters of all

kinds; players, buffoons, musicians, opera-singers, opera-dancers,
&c. (WN 330–1)

The labour of all these professions is included in modern national
income statistics, but if two countries had equal national incomes,
and one employed one-third of its labour in the above ways and the
other one-tenth, the latter would find growth easier to achieve.

In Smith's growth argument, the real distinction is between labour
that produces and makes available goods *that can be used as capital*
and labour that does not. Thus, as Smith points out, 'artificers,
manufacturers and merchants' (WN 674) and for the same reason
those concerned with transport, are productive. The above distinction will suffice for the argument that follows, so long as workers do
not consume services.[8]

The distinction between productive and unproductive labour is one
feature of Smith's account of growth that has become obsolete.
Another that is equally unfamiliar is the proposition that, so long as
investment in fixed capital (which was a small fraction of the national
product in 1776) is ignored, the entire national income is consumed in
each period:

> What is annually saved is as regularly consumed as what is
> annually spent, and nearly in the same time too; but it is consumed
> by a different set of people. That portion of his revenue which a
> rich man annually spends, is in most cases consumed by idle
> guests, and menial servants, who leave nothing behind them in
> return for their consumption. That portion which he annually
> saves, as for the sake of the profit it is immediately employed as a
> capital, is consumed in the same manner, and nearly in the same
> time too, but by a different set of people, by labourers, manufac-
> turers, and artificers, who re-produce with a profit the value of
> their annual consumption. (WN 337–8)

Thus, while part of the income of the rich is saved, the entire national
income is also consumed – saving by the rich amounting to the
employment of productive rather than unproductive workers.

The classical economists sometimes focused attention on an economy's total output, and at other times only on its net or disposable
revenue. The Physiocrats' '*produit net*' was rents alone, but for Smith
and his successors it also included profits. Because wages are wholly
consumed in all classical models, the '*produit net*' or rents plus profits

have to provide whatever a society can devote to net investment, luxury consumption and government consumption. Clearly extra capital investment from a given total of profits and rents will only be attainable if there is an equivalent reduction in consumption from these, so if attention is focused on profits and rents alone the modern result that an increase in investment is accompanied by an equal increase in saving always holds. Strangely, if attention is focused instead on the entire national income – the sum of wages, profits and rents – the modern proposition that an increase in investment entails an equivalent reduction in consumption (from an unchanged output) ceases to hold. The rate of growth of the capital stock of a classical *circulating capital* model will be raised if more of its output is consumed by the productive and less by the unproductive, but this will involve no reduction in aggregate consumption. Indeed, even when the rate of growth is being maximised, 100 per cent of output will still be being consumed each year – all by productive workers.[9] Investment, meaning increases in the real capital stock, will then much exceed that part of aggregate output which is not consumed. Where Smith makes a statement like the one just quoted that 'what is annually saved is as regularly consumed as what is annually spent', which appears to contradict modern accounting conventions, he is focusing attention on a nation's entire output including that part which is consumed by workers.

At the same time Smith considered frugality of vital importance:

By what a frugal man annually saves, he not only affords maintenance to an additional number of productive hands, for that or the ensuing year, but, like the founder of a publick workhouse, he establishes as it were a perpetual fund for the maintenance of an equal number in all times to come. (WN 338)

The prodigal...[b]y not confining his expence within his income ... encroaches upon his capital. Like him who perverts the revenues of some pious foundation to profane purposes, he pays the wages of idleness with those funds which the frugality of his forefathers had, as it were, consecrated to the maintenance of industry...If the prodigality of some was not compensated by the frugality of others, the conduct of every prodigal, by feeding the idle with the bread of the industrious, tends not only to beggar himself, but to impoverish his country. (WN 339)

Where Smith speaks of the overwhelming desirability of thrift in this way he is focusing attention on disposable income – the sum of profits and rents alone – where more consumption entails slower accumulation.

Smith believed that property-owning families would, on balance, wish to increase their fortunes for reasons which lay deep in human motivation, so private thrift would more than suffice to make good the depredations of families that were prodigal:

> It can seldom happen, indeed, that the circumstances of a great nation can be much affected either by the prodigality or misconduct of individuals; the profusion or imprudence of some being always more than compensated by the frugality and good conduct of others.
>
> With regard to profusion, the principle, which prompts to expence, is the passion for present enjoyment; which, though sometimes violent and very difficult to be restrained, is in general only momentary and occasional. But the principle which prompts to save, is a desire of bettering our condition, a desire which, though generally calm and dispassionate, comes with us from the womb, and never leaves us till we go into the grave. In the whole interval which separates those two moments, there is scarce perhaps a single instant in which any man is so perfectly and completely satisfied with his situation, as to be without any wish of alteration or improvement, of any kind. An augmentation of fortune is the means by which the greater part of men propose and wish to better their condition. It is the means the most vulgar and the most obvious; and the most likely way of augmenting their fortune, is to save and accumulate some part of what they acquire, either regularly and annually, or upon some extraordinary occasions. Though the principle of expence, therefore, prevails in almost all men upon some occasions, and in some men upon almost all occasions, yet in the greater part of men, taking the whole course of their life at an average, the principle of frugality seems not only to predominate, but to predominate very greatly. (WN 341–2)

The success of the principle of frugality depends, however, on the establishment and enforcement of property rights, and it will make little headway in their absence:

In the poor the hatred of labour and the love of present ease and enjoyment, are the passions which prompt to invade property ... Wherever there is great property, there is great inequality. For one very rich man, there must be at least five hundred poor, and the affluence of the few supposes the indigence of the many. The affluence of the rich excites the indignation of the poor, who are often both driven by want, and prompted by envy, to invade his possessions. It is only under the shelter of the civil magistrate that the owner of that valuable property, which is acquired by the labour of many years, or perhaps of many successive generations, can sleep a single night in security. He is at all times surrounded by unknown enemies, whom, though he never provoked, he can never appease, and from whose injustice he can be protected only by the powerful arm of the civil magistrate continually held up to chastise it. The acquisition of valuable and extensive property, therefore, necessarily requires the establishment of civil government. (WN 709–10)

The accumulation of capital can also be prevented by government extravagance, for the motives which promote frugality by individuals in no way apply to governments:

Great nations are never impoverished by private, though they sometimes are by publick prodigality and misconduct. The whole, or almost the whole publick revenue, is in most countries employed in maintaining unproductive hands...Such people, as they themselves produce nothing, are all maintained by the produce of other men's labour. When multiplied, therefore, to an unnecessary number, they may in a particular year consume so great a share of this produce, as not to leave a sufficiency for maintaining the productive labourers, who should reproduce it next year. The next year's produce, therefore, will be less than that of the foregoing, and if the same disorder should continue, that of the third year will be still less than that of the second...all the frugality and good conduct of individuals may not be able to compensate the waste and degradation of produce occasioned by this violent and forced encroachment. (WN 342)

Smith was, however, optimistic that private frugality would in general suffice to more than compensate for the extravagance of governments:

[F]rugality and good conduct, however, is upon most occasions, it appears from experience, sufficient to compensate, not only the private prodigality and misconduct of individuals, but the publick extravagance of government. The uniform, constant, and uninterrupted effort of every man to better his condition, the principle from which publick and national, as well as private opulence is originally derived, is frequently powerful enough to maintain the natural progress of things toward improvement, in spite both of the extravagance of government, and of the greatest errors of administration. Like the unknown principle of animal life, it frequently restores health and vigour to the constitution, in spite, not only of the disease, but of the absurd prescriptions of the doctor. (WN 342–3).

Smith did not believe that economy in government expenditure, leading to a high ratio of productive employment, was the sole factor behind rapid growth. It was equally important that the investment projects actually undertaken should create surpluses and not deficits:

The effects of misconduct are often the same as those of prodigality. Every injudicious and unsuccessful project in agriculture, mines, fisheries, trade, or manufactures, tends in the same manner to diminish the funds destined for the maintenance of productive labour. In every such project, though the capital is consumed by productive hands only, yet, as by the injudicious manner in which they are employed, they do not reproduce the full value of their consumption, there must always be some diminution in what would otherwise have been the productive funds of the society. (WN 340–1)

Smith was convinced that, so far as private decisions to invest were concerned:

the number of prudent and successful undertakings is every where much greater than that of injudicious and unsuccessful ones. (WN 342)

because

What is the species of domestick industry which his capital can employ, and of which the produce is likely to be of the greatest value, every individual, it is evident, can, in his local situation, judge much better than any statesman or lawgiver can do for him. (WN 456)

Governments are, in contrast, unqualified to assess the direction of investment:

The stateman, who should attempt to direct private people in what manner they ought to employ their capitals, would not only load himself with a most unnecessary attention, but assume an authority which could safely be trusted, not only to no single person, but to no council or senate whatever, and which would nowhere be so dangerous as in the hands of a man who had folly and presumption enough to fancy himself fit to exercise it. (WN 456)

Regulations to interfere with trade are liable to be equally damaging. Fundamentally, according to Smith:

The general industry of the society never can exceed what the capital of the society can employ. As the number of workmen that can be kept in employment by any particular person must bear a certain proportion to his capital, so the number of those that can be continually employed by all the members of a great society, must bear a certain proportion to the whole capital of that society, and never can exceed that proportion. No regulation of commerce can increase the quantity of industry in any society beyond what its capital can maintain. It can only divert a part of it into a direction into which it might not otherwise have gone; and it is by no means certain that this artificial direction is likely to be more advantageous to the society than that into which it would have gone of its own accord. (WN 453)

To give the monopoly of the home-market to the produce of domestick industry, in any particular art or manufacture, is in some measure to direct private people in what manner they ought to employ their capitals...

If a foreign country can supply us with a commodity cheaper than we ourselves can make it, better buy it of them with some part of the produce of our own industry, employed in a way in which we have some advantage. The general industry of the country, being always in proportion to the capital which employs it, will not thereby be diminished...but only left to find out the way in which it can be employed with the greatest advantage...According to the supposition, that commodity could be purchased from foreign countries cheaper than it can be made at home. It could, therefore, have been purchased with a part only of the commodities, or, what is the same thing, with a part only of the price of the commodities, which the industry employed by an equal capital, would have produced at home, had it been left to follow its natural course. The industry of the country, therefore, is thus turned away from a more, to a less advantageous employment, and the exchangeable value of its annual produce, instead of being increased, according to the intention of the lawgiver, must necessarily be diminished by every such regulation. (WN 456–7)

Indeed from Smith's assumption that a society's entire capital is always bound to find a use, 'In all countries where there is tolerable security', it naturally follows that the protection of relatively inefficient industries must reduce aggregate output. The capital employed in such industries would have found a use without protection, and it would have yielded more if its allocation had been left to market forces. More generally, Smith believed that:

every system which endeavours, either, by extraordinary encouragements, to draw towards a particular species of industry a greater share of the capital of the society than what would naturally go to it; or, by extraordinary restraints, to force from a particular species of industry some share of the capital which would otherwise be employed in it; is in reality subversive of the great purpose which it means to promote. It retards, instead of accelerating, the progress of the society towards real wealth and greatness; and diminishes, instead of increasing, the real value of the annual produce of its land and labour.

All systems either of preference or of restraint, therefore, being thus completely taken away, the obvious and simple system of natural liberty establishes itself of its own accord. Every man, as long as he does not violate the laws of justice, is left completely free to pursue his own interest his own way, and to bring both his industry and capital into competition with those of any other man, or order of men. (WN 687) by directing that industry in such a manner as its produce may be of the greatest value, he intends only his own gain, and he is in this, as in many other cases, led by an invisible hand to promote an end which was no part of his intention. Nor is it always the worse for the society that it was no part of it. By pursuing his own interest he frequently promotes that of the society more effectually than when he really intends to promote it. (WN 456)

It was thus Smith's belief that through the mechanism of the hidden hand, a system of natural liberty with entirely free trade would enable a society to make the best possible use of its capital, which would then create the ideal conditions for accumulation. The unproductive expenditures of government might of course be so high that they more than absorbed the surpluses that private thrift made available, but a system of natural liberty would readily provide surpluses more than adequate to cover the ordinary expenses of government.[10]

These are the principal elements of Smith's account of the considerations which influence the rate of capital accumulation. The proposition that a society will make the best possible use of its capital and so find it easiest to arrive at investable surpluses if it follows a system of natural liberty has had a long life and it is still believed by many. In contrast, the proposition that growth from this underlying basis of efficient resource allocation depends on the ratio of productive to unproductive employment has lapsed. In the nineteenth century there was growing recognition of the difficulties in drawing a sharp borderline between productive and unproductive employment.[11] In addition, as the world's economies expanded and the disposable incomes of societies rose, it began to appear less and less plausible that government extravagance was the principal obstacle to growth. However, the element in Smith's account of accumulation which seems most unusual in the twentieth century is the proposition that the entire output of a society is consumed each year, whether capital is expanding or declining.[12] This depends on the assumption that capital is predominantly circulating capital. Industrialisation gradually raised the ratio of fixed to circulating capital, and once fixed capital predominates, accumulation can only be increased if a smaller fraction of the *total* output of a society is consumed. That is the situation today, but with the circulating capital model Smith generally relied upon, it was only necessary to employ fewer servants to raise accumulation at once, and aggregate workers' consumption could be raised immediately after this, as output expanded, without any need for a transitional period when workers had to consume less.

There is of course fixed capital in *The Wealth of Nations*, and it will be seen that this plays an important role in the argument, but it plays no part in the passages that deal with consumption and thrift that have just been discussed.[13] Fixed capital is part of the gross product of productive labour, and once this is allowed for, the entire product of productive labour in one period is not used up in the next, and with growth, fixed capital per worker must evidently rise:

> The quantity of materials which the same number of people can work up, increases in a great proportion as labour comes to be more and more subdivided; and as the operations of each work-man are gradually reduced to a greater degree of simplicity, a variety of new machines come to be invented for facilitating and abridging those operations. As the division of labour advances, therefore, in order to give constant employment to an equal number of workmen, an equal stock of provisions, and a greater stock of materials and tools than what would have been necessary in a ruder state of things, must be accumulated beforehand. (WN 277)

Thus growth in industrial production will be accompanied by growth in both raw materials (in volume, and relative price also in the case of some minerals) and in fixed capital per worker.[14] The same is true in agriculture where there is an increase in cattle and sheep per worker as development continues, and in addition, as was noted earlier, the price of cattle will rise relative to the cost of labour.

Now because raw materials and fixed capital requirements per head grow as capital accumulates, employment will not increase as quickly as the capital stock. Smith has Malthus-type arguments, though it will turn out that there are important differences, to show that population will expand with the demand for labour: 'the demand for men, like that for any other commodity, necessarily regulates the production of men; quickens it when it goes on too slowly, and stops it when it advances too fast' (WN 98). However, increased raw material and fixed capital costs per worker will act as a leakage which prevents population and employment from growing *pari passu* with the capital stock. Moreover, if wages also rise as capital accumulates, there will be a further 'leakage' of circulating capital – to the payment of higher wages per worker – which would reduce the rate of growth of employment still further in relation to the rate of growth of capital.

Whether wages rise with the rate of growth of the capital stock is therefore a matter of some importance.

At first sight, it appears in contradiction to what was said at the start of the chapter that wages will not rise continuously as capital accumulates, for as Hollander points out, it is apparently the *level* and not the rate of growth of wages that depends on the rate of capital accumulation.[15] Thus:

> It is not the actual greatness of national wealth, but its continual increase, which occasions a rise in the wages of labour. It is not, accordingly, in the richest countries, but in the most thriving, or in those which are growing rich the fastest, that the wages of labour are highest. England is certainly, in the present times, a much richer country than any part of North America. The wages of labour, however, are much higher in North America than in any part of England. (WN 87)

> it is in the progressive state, while the society is advancing to the further acquisition, rather than when it has acquired its full complement of riches, that the condition of the labouring poor, of the great body of the people, seems to be the happiest and the most comfortable. It is hard in the stationary, and miserable in the declining state. (WN 99)

These passages, and others like them, suggest that Smith's theory of wages corresponds to that illustrated in Figure 3.2, where the wage at different rates of growth of circulating capital is shown by the schedule WW. Where there is no growth of capital, the wage is $0W_s$, Malthus's 'natural' or 'subsistence' wage, and it will exceed this if capital is growing as in England, or better still, North America, and fall short of it if capital is declining as in Bengal.

If this were Smith's theory, a country with a faster rate of accumulation than another would need to pay higher wages, but once the wage in each country reached that shown in Figure 3.2, no further increase in wages would be needed to produce the appropriate rate of population growth. Thus, if the rate of accumulation increased in any country, there would be a leakage into higher wages at first as part of the extra capital stock had to be diverted to the payment of higher wages per head, but this would cease once wages had risen sufficiently to produce the new rate of population growth. After this only extra fixed capital and raw materials per head would prevent employment from rising as fast as the capital stock.

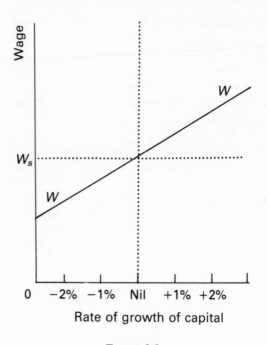

FIGURE 3.2

However, the view that wages will reach the *level* appropriate to the rate of accumulation and then rise no further is only correct if two important qualifications are made. First, it must be possible for employment and population to grow fast enough to prevent a continuous rise in wages. This, evidently, is not always possible: 'Notwithstanding the great increase [in population] occasioned by such early marriages, there is a continual complaint of the scarcity of hands in North America. The demand for labourers, the funds destined for maintaining them, increase, it seems, still faster than they can find labourers to employ' (WN 88). Wages must obviously go on rising so long as this situation persists – and similar conditions have applied to many countries since 1776.[16] The second qualification is that, as Smith points out, the argument represented in Figure 3.2 applies precisely to the wage measure in corn:

the money price of labour, which must always be such as to enable the labourer to purchase a quantity of corn sufficient to maintain him and his family either in the liberal, moderate, or scanty

manner in which the advancing, stationary or declining circumstances of the society oblige his employers to maintain him.
(WN 509)

Hence, Figure 3.2 corresponds to Smith's theory of wages if the
vertical axis shows wages measured in corn. Now, as capital accumulates and employment grows, the price of most manufactured goods
will fall continuously in relation to the price of corn as labour is more
and more subdivided in the manufacture of each good.[17] This means
that the wage will rise when it is measured in manufactured goods,
and this is precisely the line of argument that was presented at the
start of the chapter as the great feature that distinguishes *The Wealth
of Nations* from later classical writing.

To sum up Smith's theory of wages: measured in corn, only the
level of wages will vary with the rate of growth of capital, but
measured in manufactured goods, the rate of change of wages will
also vary with this, so the manufactured goods a worker can buy will
rise continuously with capital accumulation – as goods become
cheaper relative to corn and labour. Measured in cattle or poultry,
wages fall as capital accumulates because these become continuously
dearer in relation to corn, but measured in vegetables, wages rise,
and in Smith's opinion cheaper vegetables will matter more than
dearer meat to most poorer workers (WN 259). Thus as the wealth
and population of a country grow, workers may come to eat a little
better or worse (depending on the relative expenditure on vegetables
and meat), but they will enjoy a continuous growth in purchasing
power in terms of manufactured goods, and as only a small fraction of
the labour force is so poorly paid that most of its income must go on
food, the great majority of workers will gain substantially. Thus, as
capital accumulates, most workers will become better off, and they
will continue to become better off for so long as accumulation is able
to continue. This means that as a society advances, employment will
grow less quickly than the capital stock, both because of the need to
increase fixed capital and raw materials per worker, and because
wages per worker will rise – if these are thought of as a weighted
average of corn, meat and manufactures.

The above argument suggests that Smith's theory of wages differs
in several important respects from the 'iron law of wages' to which it
is often supposed that all the classical economists subscribed.

To turn now to profits, these are determined by two main
considerations in *The Wealth of Nations*. On the one hand, capital

accumulation reduces profits:

> The increase of stock, which raises wages, tends to lower profit. When the stocks of many rich merchants are turned into the same trade, their mutual competition naturally tends to lower its profit; and when there is a like increase of stock in all the different trades carried on in the same society, the same competition must produce the same effect in them all. (WN 105)

However, new investment opportunities raise the rate of return:

> The acquisition of new territory, or of new branches of trade, may sometimes raise the profits of stock, and with them the interest of money, even in a country which is fast advancing in the acquisition of riches...Part of what had before been employed in other trades, is necessarily withdrawn from them, and turned into some of the new and more profitable ones. In all those old trades, therefore, the competition comes to be less than before. (WN 110)

Perhaps the crucial factor is stock in relation to the business that is transacted, or in modern terms, the ratio of capital to output:

> In a country fully stocked in proportion to all the business it had to transact, as great a quantity of stock would be employed in every particular branch as the nature and extent of the trade would admit. The competition, therefore, would everywhere be as great, and consequently the ordinary profit as low as possible. (WN 111)

This suggests that the rate of profit may rise or fall in the course of development, and that it should certainly tend to fall where the rate of capital accumulation much exceeds the rate of growth of output.

This completes the consideration of *The Wealth of Nations* that enables us to state the assumptions about returns to scale, capital accumulation, fixed capital requirements, and wages that are appropriate to a modern restatement of Smith's theory of growth. The essential assumptions that must be carried forward to the next section are that there will be increasing returns to scale in industry until a country's full potential for development is realised, and constant or diminishing returns in agriculture and mining; that the ability to exploit the inherent potential for growth that follows from increasing returns depends on capital accumulation, which is a function of the ratio of productive to unproductive employment and the profitability of productive employment; and that fixed capital, raw materials, and wages per head (as a weighted average of manufactures and food) will all rise as the economy grows, while whether there is upward or downward pressure on profits should depend largely on the relative growth rates of capital and output. There is no production function where the substitution of capital for labour depends on relative factor prices in *The Wealth of Nations*.

A WEALTH OF NATIONS GROWTH MODEL

In this section of the chapter, the growth model that follows from the assumptions arrived at in the previous section will be presented in two stages. A very simple version of the model will be presented first, and in this the complicating effects of fixed capital will be ignored. It will emerge that it is possible to arrive at most of Smith's results with a very simple circulating capital model. However, fixed capital plays an important role in *The Wealth of Nations*, and it will be brought into the second stage of the argument to produce a richer and more general model, though one that is a little more complex than the circulating capital model which is presented first.

It has emerged that returns to scale play a crucial role in *The Wealth of Nations*, and that they depend on the extent to which the tasks performed by labour can be subdivided. A function which shows the effect of this is:

$$Y = J L_p^{Z} \tag{3.1}$$

where Y is the output achieved in the very long run at each level of productive employment, L_p, while J is a constant, and Z shows whether returns to scale are increasing, constant or diminishing. If there are constant returns, Z will equal 1 and doubling L_p will then double Y. If there are increasing returns, Z will exceed 1, causing Y to vary more than proportionately with L_p, while it will vary less than proportionately if Z is less than 1.[18] In the example from Smith's lectures that was quoted above, a ten-times increase in L_p raised Y a hundred times in industry, and this result would be produced by a Z of 2. It follows from (3.1) that:

$$g = Z n_p \tag{3.2}$$

where g is the long-term rate of growth of output $[(1/Y) \ (dY/dt)]$, while n_p is the rate of growth of productive employment $[(1/L_p) \ (dL_p/dt)]$, so the long-term rate of growth of output is Z times the rate of growth of productive employment.

Of course, employment cannot be increased without capital accumulation, and two equations are relevant to the relationship between the rate of growth of employment and the rate of capital accumulation. First, there is the population supply equation, where the rate of growth of population and the labour force (and these will be assumed to grow at the same rate) depend on the rate of capital accumulation. This equation can be written as:

$$n = E \, k_c \tag{3.3}$$

where n is the rate of growth of the total labour force $[(1/L) \ (dL/dt)]$, k_c is the rate of growth of circulating capital $[(1/K_c) \ (dK_c/dt)]$, and E is a constant. If the supply of labour available for employment was infinitely elastic with respect to the cost of employing labour, E would be 1, but it will be less than 1 in a *Wealth of Nations* growth model because raw material and possibly also wage costs per head rise with capital accumulation. It is to be noted that the proposition that E is less than 1 (which will prove to be of crucial importance) does not rest solely on the argument that wages rise with capital accumulation. An increase in raw material costs per worker as capital accumulates is quite sufficient to make E less than 1, even if wages are entirely unaffected by the rate of capital accumulation.

The second equation that relates the rate of growth of employment to the rate of capital accumulation is the 'wages fund' equation which follows from the proposition that circulating capital is used to provide wages and raw materials prior to production. If the proportion of the labour force that is employed unproductively is ψ so that the fraction which is employed productively is $(1 - \psi)$, it can be assumed, following Smith, that a fraction, $(1 - \psi)$ of circulating capital, that is, $(1 - \psi) \ K_c$, is used to provide wages and raw materials for L_p productive workers, and if the cost of providing wages and raw materials for each productive worker is W:

$$(1 - \psi) \ K_c = L_p \ W \tag{3.4}$$

Then, if $(1 - \psi)$, the proportion of the labour force that is employed productively, is constant, the rate of growth of circulating capital will equal the rate of growth of productive employment *plus* the rate of increase in the cost of employing a worker, that is,

$$k_c = n_p + w \tag{3.5}$$

where k_c and n_p are the rates of growth of circulating capital and productive employment as before, while w is the rate of increase in the wage and raw material costs of employing a worker $[(1/W)\,(dW/dt)]$.

If ψ is constant, $n_p = n$, and (3.2), (3.3) and (3.5) will then allow the long-term rates of growth of output, employment, and the wage and raw material costs of employing a worker to be expressed as multiples of the rate of growth of circulating capital. Thus:

$$g = E\,Z\,k_c \tag{3.6}$$
$$n = n_p = E\,k_c \tag{3.7}$$
$$w = (1 - E)\,k_c \tag{3.8}$$

Then the rate of growth of circulating capital determines the rates of growth of output, population, and wage and raw material costs per head, and a faster rate of capital accumulation will produce faster long-term rates of growth of each of these. Output may grow faster or more slowly than the capital stock, but population and wage and raw material costs per head must both grow more slowly than capital, since E must be less than 1.

To complete the model, what determines k_c, the rate of growth of circulating capital, must be set out. This has been worked out for a circulating capital model of the kind outlined here by John Hicks, and his equation can be arrived at as follows.[19] Y_t, the output of productive workers in period t, can be regarded as the economy's circulating capital in period $(t + 1)$, so $K_{c,t+1} = Y_t$. An expression for $K_{c,t}$ can be obtained from (3.4), that is:

$$K_{c,t} = \left(\frac{1}{1 - \psi}\right)(L_{p,t}\,W_t)$$

with the result that

$$\frac{K_{c,t+1}}{K_{c,t}} = (1 - \psi)\left(\frac{Y_t/L_{p,t}}{W_t}\right)$$

Then

$$\frac{K_{c,t+1} - K_{c,t}}{K_{c,t}} = (1 - \psi) \left(\frac{Y_t/L_{p,t}}{W_t} \right) - 1 \qquad (3.9)$$

Now $(K_{c,t+1} - K_{c,t})/K_{c,t}$ is the rate of growth of circulating capital per period. Up to now, k_c has been written for this, and these are equivalent, but the correct form of the accumulation equation is necessarily a period one since one year's output is the next year's capital. Equation (3.9) shows that the rate of growth of circulating capital depends on ψ, the proportion of the labour force which is employed unproductively, and on the ratio of output per productive worker, Y/L_p, to W, the cost of employing a worker, and this clearly corresponds to Smith's own argument. Thus, if two economies have equal technical opportunities for growth and one has more unproductive employment than the other, that economy will also have a slower rate of capital accumulation (from (3.9)), and therefore faster growth rates of output, population and wages per head (from (3.6), (3.7), and (3.8)).

The next step in the argument is to consider the question of whether the rate of capital accumulation will rise or fall through time. If ψ is given for various economies as is being assumed, the rate of capital accumulation will grow if $(Y/L_p)/W$ grows, that is, if Y grows at a faster rate than $L_p W$, and vice versa. The rate of growth of Y is g which equals $E Z k_c$ (from (3.6)), while the rate of growth of $L_p W$ is $(n_p + w)$ which equals k_c (from (3.5)), so the rate of capital accumulation will rise through time if $E Z k_c$ exceeds k_c, and fall if $E Z k_c$ is less than k_c. This leads to the very simple condition:

$$\text{Rate of change of } k_c \gtrless 0 \text{ where } Z \gtrless 1/E \qquad (3.10)$$

Then, whether an economy will enjoy a rising or a falling rate of capital accumulation will depend simply on whether Z, the returns-to-scale variable, is greater or less than $1/E$ and $1/E$ must exceed 1 since E must be less than 1. Then accumulation can only continue at an increasing or constant rate in conditions where increasing returns predominate, and these must be sufficient to hold Z at or above $1/E$. Thus, it is to be noted that the mere existence of increasing returns will not suffice to produce indefinite progress.

It therefore emerges that the relationship between Z and $1/E$ does not merely determine whether the rate of capital accumulation will rise or fall through time. It is evident from (3.6) that g will exceed k_c, that is, that an economy will enjoy a rising output-capital ratio, if Z exceeds $1/E$, and vice versa.[20] Moreover, as 'profits and rent' are the excess of output over wage and raw material costs, the share of 'profits and rent' in output will grow where $(Y/L_p)/W$ grows, and decline where this declines, so this too will depend on the relationship between Z and $1/E$. Where Z exceeds $1/E$, the share of 'profits and rent' in output will grow, and it will decline where Z is less than $1/E$. Furthermore, as 'output/capital' rises where Z exceeds $1/E$ and 'profits and rent/output' also rises:

$$\left(\frac{\text{output}}{\text{capital}} \right) \times \left(\frac{\text{profits and rent}}{\text{output}} \right)$$

which equals $\left(\dfrac{\text{profits and rent}}{\text{capital}} \right)$

must rise, and as profits are likely to gain in relation to rent where output grows faster than capital, it is particularly clear that 'profits/capital' or the rate of return on capital will rise through time where Z exceeds $1/E$.

Three possible development paths for growing economies can then be distinguished:

(1) Where Z exceeds $1/E$, the rate of capital accumulation will increase from period to period, while the capital-output ratio will fall and the rate of profit on capital and the share of 'profits and rent' in output will rise.

(2) Where Z equals $1/E$, the rate of capital accumulation, the capital-output ratio, the rate of profit, and the share of 'profits and rent' in output will be constant.

(3) Where Z is less than $1/E$, the rate of capital accumulation, the rate of profit, and the share of 'profits and rent' in output will fall continuously, while the capital-output ratio will rise continuously, until capital accumulation ceases, and once capital accumulation ceases, there will be no further change in the capital-output ratio, the rate of profit, and so on.

Thus, whether Z is greater or less than $1/E$ is a matter of the utmost importance. It is no wonder that there are numerous passages in *The Wealth of Nations* (which will be mentioned in the next section) where attention is drawn to the favourable effects on the long-term

growth opportunities of the economy of growing demand for industrial goods at home and abroad (as a result of the full exploitation of
trading opportunities), for these will increase the overall Z of the
economy since industry has a high Z.

The economy's Z will be high where the proportion of the labour
force employed in industry is high, and the opportunities to benefit
from a further subdivision of labour are still considerable. If a point is
reached where further subdivision produces diminishing benefits, Z
will fall from period to period, and it must then eventually become
less than $1/E$, however high its original starting point. The rate of
capital accumulation will slow down as soon as Z becomes less than
$1/E$, and the capital-output ratio will start to rise, while the rate of
profit on capital and the share of 'profits and rent' in output will both
start to fall – until a point is reached eventually where accumulation
ceases altogether, and a society will then have realised its full
potential for development, given its ratio of unproductive employment, and so on.

These are the principal results that follow from the circulating
capital model that has been considered so far. It is now time to
introduce fixed capital into the argument, and this can be done in the
following way. Up to now, it has been supposed that the employment
of L workers will merely require a circulating capital of $W\,L$, and it
can be assumed from this point onwards that a fixed capital of $G\,L^H$
will also be needed, where G is a constant, and H exceeds 1. With H
greater than 1, fixed capital requirements will grow more than
proportionately with population and employment as Smith assumed.
Writing K for total capital, K_c for circulating capital, and K_f for fixed
capital, it is being assumed that:

$$K = K_f + K_c = G\,L^H + W\,L \tag{3.11}$$

The introduction of fixed capital will not alter the basic returns-to-
scale equation which led to (3.2): more capital is now needed to
provide employment for a given labour force, but its output can still
be written as $J\,L^Z$.[21] Moreover, fixed capital will not affect the
population supply equation (3.3) or the wages fund equation (3.5), so
(3.6), (3.7) and (3.8) will be unaltered. It is only (3.9), the capital
accumulation equation, that will be altered, and this will be affected
in the following way. It was assumed earlier that the entire output of
period t became the circulating capital of period $(t + 1)$ so that $Y_t =
K_{c,t+1}$, but part of the output of period t will now need to consist of

additions to fixed capital. Provided that Y_t is the output of period t *net* of the depreciation of fixed capital, Y_t will become the circulating capital of period $(t + 1)$ *plus* the addition to fixed capital between periods t and $t + 1$. Thus:

$$Y_t = K_{c,t+1} + (K_{f,t+1} - K_{f,t})$$

Now $K_{c,t}$ will equal $\dfrac{1}{(1 - \psi)} L_{p,t} W_t$ as before, so that:

$$\frac{K_{c,t+1} - K_{c,t}}{K_{c,t}} = (1 - \psi) \left(\frac{Y_t/L_{p,t}}{W_t} \right) - 1 - \frac{K_{f,t+1} - K_{f,t}}{K_{c,t}}$$

As

$$E H K_{f,t} \left(\frac{K_{c,t+1} - K_{c,t}}{K_{c,t}} \right)$$

can be written for $(K_{f,t+1} - K_{f,t})$:[22]

$$\frac{K_{c,t+1} - K_{c,t}}{K_{c,t}} = \frac{(1 - \psi) \left(\dfrac{Y_t/L_{p,t}}{W_t} \right) - 1}{1 + E H(K_{f,t}/K_{c,t})} \tag{3.12}$$

Now a comparison between (3.9), the capital accumulation equation in the earlier circulating capital model, and the present capital accumulation equation shows that the rate of growth of capital in the earlier equation now has to be divided by $[1 + E H(K_f/K_c)]$. Thus the rate of growth of capital will always be lower, *ceteris paribus*, in the present fixed capital model. This is because the provision of fixed capital for extra workers is an additional factor in the capital cost of growth, so more resources will be needed, for instance a higher ratio of productive employment, to produce any given growth rate.

It was shown above that the critical condition for a constant rate of growth in the circulating capital model was that Z should equal $1/E$. Clearly, if Z equalled $1/E$ then in (3.12) as in (3.9), $(Y/L_p)/W$ would be constant, but the growth rate would still fall continuously if K_f/K_c was rising, and rise if this was falling. Thus, if the ratio of fixed to circulating capital rose through time, the need to invest in fixed capital as employment grew would act as an increasing brake on accumulation, while it would act as a brake of diminishing intensity if the ratio of fixed to circulating capital was falling. Whether this ratio rises or falls through time is therefore important.

The ratio of fixed to circulating capital will rise if k_f, the growth rate of fixed capital, exceeds k_c, the growth rate of circulating capital, and vice versa. k_f is the growth rate of K_f, that is, the rate of growth of $G L^H$, and this is $H n$, which equals $E H k_c$ (from 3.7) so that:

$$k_f/k_c = E H \tag{3.13}$$

Then the ratio of fixed to circulating capital will be constant if $E H = 1$, that is, if $H = 1/E$: and it will rise through time if H exceeds $1/E$, and fall if H is less than $1/E$. Hence, the need to provide fixed capital for a growing labour force will act as an increasing brake on growth if H exceeds $1/E$ and a diminishing brake if H is less than $1/E$.

In the earlier circulating capital model, the rate of capital accumulation and the economy's other major variables were constant through time when Z equalled $1/E$, and this proposition will not be disturbed if the ratio of fixed to circulating capital is also constant, that is, if H also equals $1/E$. Then the condition for a constant rate of growth, a constant rate of profit, a constant capital-output ratio, and constant income distribution is that $H = Z = 1/E$.

Clearly the development of the economy through time will depend on how high H and Z are in relation to $1/E$. The simplest way of analysing the effect of values of H or Z that are inappropriate for a constant rate of growth is to assume in each case that the value of the other is appropriate, that is, that $Z = 1/E$ where the value of H is inappropriate, and that $H = 1/E$ where Z is inappropriate. These possibilities will be considered in turn.

The effect of an inappropriate H

If H exceeds $1/E$ (and Z), the ratio of fixed to circulating capital will rise continuously, and this will reduce the rate of capital accumulation from period to period. Moreover, the capital-output ratio will rise continuously. Equality between Z and $1/E$ will ensure that the ratio of circulating capital to output is constant (from (3.6)), but as fixed capital rises continuously in relation to circulating capital, the overall capital-output ratio must rise from period to period. Equality between Z and $1/E$ keeps the share of 'profits and rent' in output constant, but if a rising capital-output ratio acts against profits relative to rent, then the share of profits will fall and the share of rents rise. A rising capital-output ratio will reduce the rate of profit on capital, even if the share of profits is constant, and if this falls, the rate of profit will be doubly reduced. Hence a higher H than Z and $1/E$ will produce a declining rate of growth, a declining rate of profit, a rising capital-output ratio, and possibly a declining share of profits also. A lower H will produce the opposite effects.

The effect of an inappropriate Z

If Z exceeds H and $1/E$ where these are equal, the ratio of fixed to circulating capital will be constant, so the model will behave exactly as the circulating capital model which was analysed earlier, that is, a higher Z will produce accelerating growth, a rising rate of profit, a rising share of profits, a falling capital-output ratio, and so on. A lower Z will produce the opposite effects.

It appears then that the effects on the economy of a high H and a low Z are rather similar. The analysis has, of course, been simplified by focusing attention on one variable at a time. Smith may well have envisaged a growing ratio of fixed to circulating capital, especially in view of what he said about cattle, that is, an H that exceeded $1/E$; and strong increasing returns for a time if a country could so arrange its affairs (through trading opportunities and so on) that it could take advantage of the potential gains from increasing returns in industry over a considerable range of its output; this being followed by a period where increasing returns became less important as the advantages from further subdivisions of labour diminished. Here Z would start high and then fall. If this was his view, then the present model would produce the result of either accelerating or declining growth while H and Z both exceeded $1/E$: the high Z would act as a stimulus and the high H as a brake, and either could exercise the dominant influence, though obviously a high enough Z would be bound to do so. Once Z fell, however, the high H and low Z (in relation to $1/E$ which must always exceed 1) would reduce the rate of profit from period to period, and the share of profits in output. More will be said about the relationship between Smith's predictions in *The Wealth of Nations* and the predictions of the model in the concluding section of this chapter.

However, before the present account of the model is completed, it may be worthwhile to relax one further assumption. Up to now, in the account that has been given, the various sectors of the economy have been considered together, so that Z has been a kind of weighted average of returns to scale in industry and agriculture, etc. Suppose instead that the various sectors are considered separately, starting with corn where it is clear that Smith thought that Z was 1 (since he assumed constant costs), and that $1/E$ and H exceeded 1 because of the need to increase fixed capital (that is, cattle) and raw materials per worker. With these assumptions, the rate of growth, the rate of profit, and the share of 'profits and rent' would all decline (at a rate depending on the extent to which H and $1/E$ exceeded Z), and the capital-output ratio would rise continuously when these were all measured in corn. Then a declining rate of profit in agriculture would be the only possible result of the model, and assuming that profit rates are equalised between sectors, manufactured goods would have to be so priced that a declining rate of profit was also earned on the manufacture of these, with the result that the entire benefits from increasing returns would be more than reflected in lower prices. Real wages (measured in manufactured goods) would then benefit sub-stantially. The agricultural part of this argument looks forward, perhaps too much so, to the 'corn model' version of Ricardo's theory of income distribution which will be discussed in Chapter 6. It may well be more sensible to think of Smith's as a 'weighted average' model with each sector playing a part, rather than one where production conditions in the corn sector determine the rate of profit in the other sectors of the economy. However, Smith's chapter on corn bounties has a lot of Ricardo in it (though there may be some special pleading in this chapter), and the possibility that he had an underlying corn model of the kind considered in this paragraph in mind cannot be excluded. Both this model and the 'weighted average of sectors' model can be set out with the help of the basic rela-tionships that have been outlined.

THE RESULTS OF THE MODEL AND SOME OF ADAM SMITH'S CONCLUSIONS

The model, like *The Wealth of Nations*, attributes overwhelming importance to the rate of capital accumulation. Without this, popula-tion and the labour force would not grow and industry would not expand, so the potential gains in productivity that could follow from increased subdivisions of labour could not be exploited, and the manufactured goods that workers could buy would not increase. The rate of capital accumulation itself depends on the proportion of the labour force that is employed productively, and on the efficiency of productive workers. The first three paragraphs of *The Wealth of Nations* bring out that these are, in Smith's view, the key factors, so the central features of the model certainly correspond to Smith's own view of what is crucial.

This preliminary correspondence is not surprising, because an account of *The Wealth of Nations* could hardly be produced which failed to attribute overwhelming importance to accumulation and what causes it, and the virtues of thrift: 'every prodigal appears to be a publick enemy, and every frugal man a publick benefactor' (WN 340), and of economies in public expenditure. These were among Smith's main legacies to the nineteenth century.

A second central feature of the argument of the model is the role of increasing returns, and Smith devoted the first three chapters of *The Wealth of Nations* to the division of labour, so a modern account of his argument must allow these to play an equally crucial role. In the model that has just been outlined, the relationships between Z, the returns-to-scale variable, and E and H are crucial, and Z is perhaps best thought of as a weighted average of returns to scale in industry and agriculture. Hence, if Smith's view was similar, there should be a number of passages in *The Wealth of Nations* which speak of the crucial effect on the rate of development of an economy of the size of the industrial sector of the economy in relation to the agricultural. Perhaps two quotations will suffice to demonstrate the importance of building up a manufacturing sector:

A small quantity of manufactured produce purchases a great quantity of rude produce. A trading and manufacturing country, therefore, naturally purchases with a small part of its manufactured produce a great part of the rude produce of other countries; while, on the contrary, a country without trade and manufactures is generally obliged to purchase, at the expence of a great part of its rude produce, a very small part of the manufactured produce of other countries. The one exports what can subsist and accommodate but a very few, and imports the subsistence and accommodation of a great number. The other exports the accommodation and subsistence of a great number, and imports that of a very few only. The inhabitants of the one must always enjoy a much greater

quantity of subsistence than what their own lands, in the actual
state of their cultivation, could afford. (WN 677–8)

And, two pages later:

Without an extensive foreign market, [manufactures] could not
well flourish, either in countries so moderately extensive as to
afford but a narrow home market; or in countries where the
communication between one province and another was so difficult,
as to render it impossible for the goods of any particular place to
enjoy the whole of that home market which the country could
afford. The perfection of manufacturing industry, it must be
remembered, depends altogether upon the division of labour; and
the degree to which the division of labour can be introduced into
any manufacture, is necessarily regulated, it has already been
shown, by the extent of the market. (WN 680)

There are also passages which speak of the benefits derived by
European industry from the colonisation of America (WN 592), and
of the advantages that are derived where the rich buy manufactures
instead of employing servants, and these refer to other advantages of
a demand for manufactures (WN 346–9).

Clearly capital accumulation and increasing returns play a central
role in *The Wealth of Nations*, but there are other propositions in the
book which do not at first sight fit the view that a thrifty society will
enjoy indefinite progress as a result of increasing returns, provided
that the market for manufactures grows. There are two types of
proposition in *The Wealth of Nations* that do not correspond with this
first approximation to Smith's argument, and these must be explained
in any attempt to provide a modern reconstruction.

First, Smith argued that a given employment of capital in agriculture would provide a larger surplus for reinvestment (and therefore
more growth of employment) than an equivalent investment of
capital in industry – which apparently contradicts the view that
growth is a function of the ratio of industrial to agricultural output.
Thus:

When the capital of any country is not sufficient for all...purposes,
in proportion as a greater share of it is employed in agriculture, the
greater will be the quantity of productive labour which it puts into
motion within the country; as will likewise be the value which its

employment adds to the annual produce of the land and labour of the society. After agriculture, the capital employed in manufactures puts into motion the greatest quantity of productive labour, and adds the greatest value to the annual produce. (WN 366)

For

The labourers and labouring cattle, therefore, employed in agriculture, not only occasion, like the workmen in manufactures, the reproduction of a value equal to their own consumption, or to the capital which employs them, together with its owners profits; but of a much greater value. Over and above the capital of the farmer and all its profits, they regularly occasion the reproduction of the rent of the landlord. (WN 363-4)

And, Smith adds:

It has been the principal cause of the rapid progress of our American colonies towards wealth and greatness, that almost their whole capitals have hitherto been employed in agriculture...Were the Americans, either by combination or by any other sort of violence, to stop the importation of European manufactures, and, by thus giving a monopoly to such of their own countrymen as could manufacture the like goods, divert any considerable part of their capital into this employment, they would retard instead of accelerating the further increase in the value of their annual produce, and would obstruct instead of promoting the progress of their country towards real wealth and greatness. (WN 366–7)

Now these statements, which superficially contradict what has been said so far, follow directly from the model that was outlined above. There, the rate of capital accumulation which determines the growth of employment depends very substantially on ψ, the ratio of unproductive employment, and on $(Y/L_p)/W$, the ratio of output per worker to the cost of employing a worker, and any increase in $(Y/L_p)/W$ will more than proportionately raise the rate of capital accumulation. Now, $(Y/L_p)/W$ is clearly highest in agriculture for the reasons that Smith gives, and it is even proper to include rent in Y/L_p for the purposes of this accumulation equation if there are constant costs in agriculture. However, the argument appeared incorrect to Smith's successors, in particular, Ricardo,[23] but it follows directly from the restatement of Smith's theory in this chapter. The unimpeded use of resources in agriculture is central to the achievement of an adequate rate of capital accumulation, because the ratio of output per worker to the cost of employing a worker is highest in agriculture. However, the *effects* of accumulation as distinct from what causes this depend upon Z, and the effect of a Z greater than 1 will be more favourable, the higher the ratio of industrial output in total output. There is thus a trade-off between agriculture which favours the *rate* of accumulation, and industry which favours the *effects* of accumulation. Smith was fully aware of both propositions, but in the context of a world where some countries achieved no accumulation at all, and Great Britain and most other European countries had taken five hundred years to double the population they could support (WN 88), the first priority could reasonably be the achievement of accumulation: and to obstruct this through *artificial* policies to raise Z by helping industry *at the expense* of agriculture was misguided, and these policies are criticised throughout Book III of *The Wealth of Nations*. In the case of North America, accumulation was so rapid that it was continuously raising wages even in terms of corn, and there was nothing to be gained by slowing down the rate of accumulation.

A second set of passages in *The Wealth of Nations* which stand in the way of the simple interpretation that accumulation and increasing returns will lead to unlimited progress are the passages which speak of the eventual completion of the accumulation process, after which wages and profits would both become low, for instance:

> In a country which had acquired that full complement of riches which the nature of its soil and climate, and its situation with respect to other countries allowed it to acquire; which could, therefore, advance no further, and which was not going backwards, both the wages of labour and the profits of stock would probably be very low. (WN 111)

Here, there are low wages, low profits and zero growth, even though thriftiness conditions may be very favourable. The implication of 'full complement of riches' is, however, that gains from the division of labour are no longer possible. Once increasing returns cease in the model outlined in this chapter, Z falls to 1 or below, and this leads to a declining rate of growth, a declining rate and share of profits, and a rising capital-output ratio, and so on. Now, as the rate of capital accumulation falls, the wage (measured in corn) will fall, which will restore profitability for a time, but the low Z will always set profits on a downward path again until, as Smith says, the wage (in corn) has become appropriate to a stationary state, and profits will also have fallen very low when this is reached. Thus, passages of the kind just quoted are fully in line with the predictions of the model if it is assumed that the benefits from the division of labour have upper limits.[24]

In the stationary state that has just been described, the wage is, of course, high in terms of manufactured goods, since the division of labour has reached an upper limit, and Smith did not mention this, though it follows from his argument, where there are many passages which explain that the relative prices of most manufactured goods must fall as a society progresses, and there is no suggestion that this trend is ever reversed. He spelt out the details of this eventual stationary state no more than Keynes bothered to provide a detailed description of the ultimate destination of a Keynesian economy with the *rentier* 'euthanised', and the rate of profit reduced to negligible proportions. Such propositions were not relevant to the main work of Smith and Keynes, which was to provide an account of the working of the economies in which they lived.

Smith was arguably as successful as Keynes in this great task. His was recognised by most of his contemporaries as an accurate and plausible account of the way in which eighteenth-century economies worked, and his influence on public policy was as great as that of Keynes, and far longer lasting, for the central policy propositions of *The Wealth of Nations* dominated British economic policy and legislation from the late eighteenth century until the 1930s.

Smith did not, however, write out an account of his theory of growth and development which had the impact that it should have had on the thought of professional economists. Something like the model in this chapter is needed to integrate increasing returns and the accumulation equation with his propositions about increasing raw material costs, etc., and while Smith may well have understood the full complexities of his argument – a great thinker will hardly arrive at consistent results by chance – he only published (and he may only have put on paper) what could be understood by all. Because of this, with the notable exception of Marx, increasing returns in industry played virtually no part in the thought of those who wrote about economics after Smith. Their books disregarded or discounted the significance of Smith's first three chapters with the result that a vital element in classical economics was lost.[25]

4 Malthus's Theory of Population Growth

There are striking statements about the explosive nature of potential population growth from Malthus's predecessors – such as those by Cantillon and Smith which were quoted in previous chapters.[1] It was Malthus, however, who fully and systematically set out the complete classical theory of population growth together with its powerful social implications. He was much impressed by the evidence of extremely rapid population growth in the North American colonies, and in 1798 when he published his first *Essay on Population* he quoted examples of population in the various colonies doubling or more than doubling in twenty-five years. The evidence he relied on was first published in Boston in 1761 by Dr Edward Styles, President of Yale College, and it was republished in London by Richard Price in numerous publications from 1769 onwards, and Malthus saw it in one of these.[2] He appreciated its full implications and the first of his famous propositions was based on this evidence:

> In the United States of America, where the means of subsistence have been more ample, the manners of the people more pure, and consequently the checks to early marriages fewer, than in any of the modern states of Europe, the population has been found to double itself in twenty-five years.
>
> This ratio of increase, though short of the utmost power of population, yet as the result of actual experience, we will take as our rule; and say, that population, when unchecked, goes on doubling itself every twenty–five years, or increases in a geometrical ratio. (Pop edn1 20–1)

That assumes, of course, that the American expansion was all natural increase when some must have been due to immigration.

Malthus's second celebrated proposition, that the supply of food would grow at most in an arithmetic ratio *was* a departure from the work of his predecessors. There is no reference to rising costs and diminishing returns in agriculture in the work of Smith and Quesnay. Both described economies where much land was very lightly farmed, and they both saw capital as the principal constraint that limited agricultural output. Both assumed that extra agricultural output was producible at constant costs. By the time Malthus wrote, the supply of good land to efficient farmers may have become inelastic. Perhaps the war with France had led to great extensions of ploughing. Malthus wrote significantly:

> In a country where all the fertile spots have been seized, high offers are necessary to encourage the farmer to lay his dressing on land, from which he cannot expect a profitable return for some years. (Pop edn1 90)

And:

> When acre has been added to acre, till all the fertile land is occupied, the yearly increase of food will depend upon the amelioration of the land already in possession; and even this moderate stream will be gradually diminishing. (Pop edn1 107)

There is nothing like this in the writings of his great predecessors. His main proposition of an arithmetic rate of increase in food production (and therefore a diminishing proportional rate of increase) is derived from his awareness that the land was fully occupied, and that there were diminishing returns from expenditures designed to improve its yield (which the above quotations indicate). He arrived at his precise proposition about the maximum possible growth of food production as follows:

> Let us now take any spot of earth, this Island for instance, and see in what ratio the subsistence it affords can be supposed to increase. We will begin with it under its present state of cultivation.
>
> If I allow that by the best possible policy, by breaking up more land, and by great encouragements to agriculture, the produce of this Island may be doubled in the first twenty-five years, I think it will be allowing as much as any person can well demand.

In the next twenty-five years, it is impossible to suppose that the produce could be quadrupled. It would be contrary to all our knowledge of the qualities of land. The very utmost that we can conceive, is, that the increase in the second twenty-five years might equal the present produce. Let us then take this for our rule, though certainly far beyond the truth; and allow that by great exertion, the whole produce of the Island might be increased every twenty-five years, by a quantity of subsistence equal to what it at present produces. The most enthusiastic speculator cannot suppose a greater increase than this. In a few centuries it would make every acre of land in the Island like a garden.

Yet this ratio of increase is evidently arithmetical.

It may be fairly said, therefore, that the means of subsistence increase in an arithmetical ratio. (Pop edn1 21–3)

There is, in fact, no simple diminishing returns production function which readily predicts an arithmetic growth of food production, but the underlying basis of Malthus's argument is clear enough. With his assumptions, if food supply is Y_a in 1798, it will *never exceed* the totals set out below:

Maximum food production

1798	1823	1848	1873	1898	1923	1948
Y_a	$2Y_a$	$3Y_a$	$4Y_a$	$5Y_a$	$6Y_a$	$7Y_a$

Population size, N in 1798, will on the other hand, if allowed to grow unchecked become *at least*:

Minimum population

1798	1823	1848	1873	1898	1923	1948
N	$2N$	$4N$	$8N$	$16N$	$32N$	$64N$

with the result that the supply of food per head *could not exceed*:

Maximum food production per head

1798	1823	1848	1873	1898	1923	1948
Y_a/N	Y_a/N	$0.75Y_a/N$	$0.50Y_a/N$	$0.31Y_a/N$	$0.19Y_a/N$	$0.11Y_a/N$

Malthus never considered it necessary to set out the underlying basis for these series. As he said in 1806 in the third edition of the *Essay on Population*:

> It has been said that I have written a quarto volume to prove that population increases in a geometrical, and food in an arithmetical ratio; but this is not quite true. The first of these propositions I considered as proved the moment that the American increase was related, and the second proposition as soon as it was enunciated. The chief object of my work was to inquire what effects these laws, which I considered as established in the first six pages had produced, and were likely to produce on society; a subject not very readily exhausted. (Pop edn3 ii.520)

It is of course the case that it is the implications of these series that are vital, and Malthus's contribution was that he introduced the concept of diminishing returns in agriculture, which was new, and set out the overwhelmingly important implications that this could have. The first implication is of course that no society can actually experience the great fall in food production per head that the third series shows. As Malthus puts it, a five-times increase in food production in a century and a sixteen-times increase in population would leave over two-thirds of the population 'unprovided for'. Hence population cannot in practice increase at the geometric rate set out in the second series. There must be checks to population growth which prevent the United States rate of increase from occurring in most countries and at most times. Malthus divides these into *preventive* and *positive* checks:

> a foresight of the difficulties attending the rearing of a family, acts as a preventive check...
>
> The preventive check appears to operate in some degree through all the ranks of society in England. There are some men, even in the highest rank, who are prevented from marrying by the idea of the expences that they must retrench, and the fancied pleasures that they must deprive themselves of, on the supposition of having a family...
>
> A man of liberal education, but with an income only just sufficient to enable him to associate in the rank of gentlemen, must feel absolutely certain, that if he marries and has a family, he shall

be obliged, if he mixes at all in society, to rank himself with moderate farmers, and the lower class of tradesmen...Two or three steps of descent in society, particularly at this round of the ladder, where education ends, and ignorance begins, will not be considered by the generality of people, as a fancied and chimerical, but a real and essential evil...

The labourer who earns eighteen pence a day, and lives with some degree of comfort as a single man, will hesitate a little before he divides that pittance among four or five, which seems to be but just sufficient for one. Harder fare and harder labour he would submit to, for the sake of living with the woman that he loves; but he must feel conscious, if he thinks at all, that, should he have a large family, and any ill luck whatever, no degree of frugality, no possible exertion of his manual strength, could preserve him from the heart rending sensation of seeing his children starve, or of forfeiting his independence, and being obliged to the parish for their support...

If this sketch of the state of society in England be near the truth, and I do not conceive that it is exaggerated, it will be allowed, that the preventive check to population in this country operates, though with varied force, through all the classes of the community. The same observations will hold true with regard to all old states. (Pop edn1 62–9)

Where the preventive check is weak, *positive* checks take over:

The positive check to population, by which I mean, the check that represses an increase which is already begun, is confined chiefly, though not perhaps solely, to the lowest orders of society. (Pop edn1 71)

In every state in Europe, since we have first had accounts of it, millions and millions of human existences have been repressed [directly or indirectly, for want of food]; though perhaps in some of these States, an absolute famine has never been known.

Famine seems to be the last, the most dreadful resource of nature. The power of population is so superior to the power in the earth to produce subsistence for man, that premature death must in some shape or other visit the human race. The vices of mankind are active and able ministers of depopulation. They are the precursors in the great army of destruction; and often finish the dreadful work themselves. But should they fail in this war of extermination, sickly seasons, epidemics, pestilence, and plague, advance in terrific array, and sweep off their thousands and ten thousands. Should success be still incomplete; gigantic inevitable famine stalks in the rear, and with one mighty blow, levels the population with the food of the world. (Pop edn1 139–40)

In the third edition of 1806 Malthus went on to argue strikingly that the mortality from particular diseases depends strongly on the relationship between population and the availability of subsistence. Disease is not the cause of depopulation – it is the positive check at work correcting for overpopulation:

In a country which keeps its population at a certain standard, if the average number of marriages and births be given, it is evident that the average number of deaths will also be given...the channels through which the great stream of mortality is constantly flowing, will always convey off a given quantity. Now if we stop up any of these channels, it is most perfectly clear that the stream of mortality must run with greater force through some of the other channels; that is, if we eradicate some diseases, others will become proportionally more fatal. (Pop edn3 ii.362–3)

... the extinction of the plague, and the striking reduction of the deaths in the dysentry. While these, and some other disorders became almost evanescent, consumption, palsy, apoplexy, gout, lunacy and the small-pox, became more mortal. The widening of these drains was necessary to carry off the population which still remained redundant...
I am far from doubting that millions and millions of human beings have been destroyed by the small-pox. But were its devastations, as Dr. Haygarth supposes, many thousand degrees greater than the plague, I should still doubt whether the average population of the earth had been diminished by them. The small-pox is certainly one of the channels, and a very broad one, which nature has opened for the last thousand years, to keep down the population to the level of the means of subsistence; but had this been closed, others would have become wider, or new ones would have been formed. (Pop edn3 ii.365–7)

Population indeed is determined by the supply of food, whatever the actual diseases which prevail. This is even true in the face of forced migrations of population which is a further positive check, alternative to famine and disease:

> Africa has been at all times the principal mart of slaves. The drains of its population in this way have been great and constant, particularly since their introduction into the European colonies; but perhaps, as Dr. Franklin observes, it would be difficult to find the gap that has been made by a hundred years exportation of negroes which has blackened half America. (Pop edn3 i.174)

Population is kept in line with the supply of food in these various ways and each involves either positive or preventive checks. The positive checks must be weak where the preventive checks are strong, and vice versa, and Malthus points out precisely this in his third edition:

> The sum of all these preventive and positive checks taken together forms the immediate check to population, and it is evident that in every country where the whole of the procreative power cannot be called into action, the preventive and the positive checks must vary inversely as each other, that is, in countries either naturally unhealthy, or subject to a great mortality from whatever cause it may arise, the preventive check will prevail very little. In those countries on the contrary which are naturally healthy, and where the preventive check is found to prevail with considerable force, the positive check will prevail very little, or the mortality be very small. (Pop edn3 i.21–2)

Since the control of the population through the positive checks involves either near-institutionalised warfare (to which Malthus attributes the stability of population in some of the most primitive societies he describes) or a standard of living where deaths through starvation are frequent, living conditions of the working class are most favourable in societies where the growth of population is limited through the preventive check:

> It is not in the nature of things that any permanent and general improvement in the condition of the poor can be effected, without an increase in the preventive check; and unless this take place, either with or without our efforts, every thing that is done for the

poor must be temporary and partial: a diminution in mortality at present, will be balanced by an increased mortality in future; and the improvement of their condition in one place, will proportionally depress it in another. This is a truth so important and so little understood, that it can scarcely be too often insisted on. (Pop edn3 ii.481)

Despotism weakens the preventive check, while liberal institutions and property rights strengthen it, and therefore have favourable effects on the standard of living of the poor:

Ignorance and despotism seem to have no tendency to destroy the passion which prompts to increase; but they effectually destroy the checks to it from reason and foresight. The improvident barbarian who thinks only of his present wants, or the miserable peasant, who, from his political situation, feels little security of reaping what he has sown, will seldom be deterred from gratifying his passions by the prospect of inconveniences which cannot be expected to press on him under three or four years. But though this want of foresight which is fostered by ignorance and despotism tend thus rather to encourage the procreation of children, it is absolutely fatal to the industry which is to support them. Industry cannot exist without foresight and security. The indolence of the savage is well known; and the poor Egyptian or Abyssinian farmer without capital, who rents land which is let out yearly to the highest bidder, and who is constantly subject to the demands of his tyrannical masters, to the casual plunder of an enemy, and, not unfrequently, to the violation of his miserable contract, can have no heart to be industrious, and if he had, could not exercise that industry with success. (Pop edn3 ii.286–7)

In such societies, the positive checks of war, famine and disease must be the means through which the growth of the population is kept in line with subsistence. The situation of England, where the preventive check was strong, was clearly far more favourable, and in his later editions Malthus became aware that the spread of manufactures to the working class would strengthen it further:

The condition of the labouring poor, supposing their habits to remain the same, cannot be very essentially improved but by giving them a greater command over the means of subsistence. But any advantage of this kind must from its nature be temporary, and is therefore really of less value to them than any permanent change in their habits. But manufactures by inspiring a taste for comforts, tend to promote a favourable change in these habits, and in this way perhaps counterbalance all their disadvantages. The labouring classes of society in nations merely agricultural are generally on the whole poorer than in manufacturing nations, though less subject to those occasional variations which among manufacturers often produce the most severe distress. (Pop edn3 ii.206)

The best and in every point of view the most advantageous manufactures in this country, are those which are consumed by the great body of the people. The manufactures which are confined exclusively to the rich, are not only trivial on account of the comparative smallness of their quantity; but are further liable to the great disadvantage of producing much occasional misery among those employed in them, from changes of fashion. It is the spread of luxury therefore among the mass of the people, and not an excess of it in a few, that seems to be most advantageous, both with regard to national wealth and national happiness...If indeed, it be allowed that in every society, not in the state of a new colony, some powerful check to population must prevail; and if it be observed that a taste for the comforts and conveniencies of life will prevent people from marrying under the certainty of being deprived of these advantages; it must be allowed that we can hardly expect to find any check to marriage so little prejudicial to the happiness and virtue of society as the general prevalance of such a taste (Pop edn3 ii.482–3)

The standard of living of a family and the wages of labour will not depend simply on the strength of the preventive check to population growth. It will also depend on the rate of growth of the 'funds for the maintenance of labour'. If the funds available for the maintenance of labour are growing, population will be able to grow, and therefore there will be less need for deaths as a result of positive checks to population amongst the poorest in the community.

Malthus states very clearly that the wage will tend to a level where it will induce a rate of growth of population which is in line with the rate of growth of the 'real funds for the maintenance of labour':

The price of labour, when left to find its natural level, is a most important political barometer, expressing the relation between the supply of provisions, and the demand for them; between the quantity to be consumed and the number of consumers; and taken on the average, independently of accidental circumstances, it further expresses clearly the wants of the society respecting population; that is, whatever may be the number of children to a marriage necessary to maintain exactly the present population, the price of labour will be just sufficient to support this number, or be above it, or below it, according to the state of the real funds for the maintenance of labour, whether stationary, progressive, or retrograde. (Pop edn3 ii.165–6)

There are in fact two general propositions about the real wage. First from the above passage, the faster the rate of growth of 'the real funds for the maintenance of labour', the higher the wage will be because there will be less need for the positive checks of starvation and disease to limit the rate of population growth. Second, as earlier passages demonstrate, stronger preventive checks will also be associated with a higher real wage because there will again be less need for the positive checks of starvation and disease.

The effect of these two propositions is illustrated in Figure 4.1. The schedule $L'L'$ shows the relationship between the rate of growth of the real funds for the maintenance of labour and the wage where the preventive check is strong, while the lower schedule $L''L''$ shows this relationship where the preventive check is weaker. The wage is higher at each rate of growth on $L'L'$ where the preventive check is strong, because less positive checks are needed than on $L''L''$ to keep population growth in line with the rate of growth of subsistence funds. Second, both schedules are drawn upward-sloping to show that with given preventive checks, the wage will be higher where subsistence funds grow faster, because fewer positive checks will be needed to keep population growth in line with a faster rate of growth of subsistence.

In Figure 4.2, a further schedule, $D_L D_L$, is drawn. This shows that the funds for the maintenance of labour which act as a demand curve for population will grow more rapidly where wages are low than where they are high. Where wages are low, profits will be high, and this will lead to faster capital accumulation. In addition, Malthus points out that where labour is cheap, cultivators will 'employ more labour upon their land; to turn up fresh soil, and to manure and

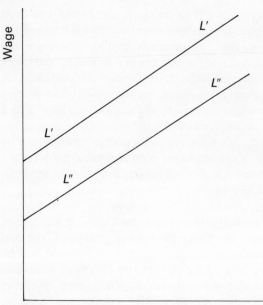

Rate of growth of real funds for the maintenance of labour

FIGURE 4.1

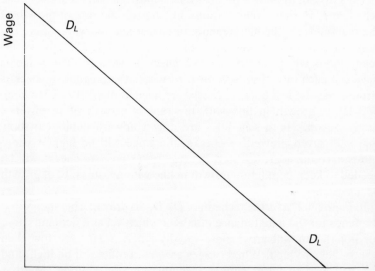

Rate of growth of real funds for the maintenance of labour

FIGURE 4.2

improve more completely what is already in tillage' (Pop edn1 30–1), which will raise the supply of food.

Figure 4.3 shows how the equilibrium wage and the equilibrium rate of growth of the subsistence funds for the maintenance of labour are simultaneously determined by the two schedules, LL and $D_L D_L$. The wage will clearly fluctuate about the equilibrium wage, $0W$, and the rate of growth will also fluctuate around $0g$, the equilibrium rate of growth. This is because many years will elapse before the extra population which will result from a wage of $0W+$ will join the labour force. When it does, the wage will fall below $0W$ to $0W-$, as in Figure 4.3, and many years will again elapse before this below-equilibrium wage produces the necessary contraction of the labour force. There will therefore be a series of 'cobweb' fluctuations like those indicated on the diagram.[3] That there will be such fluctuations was made very clear by Malthus himself in several passages including a very full one in the first edition of the *Essay on Population*:

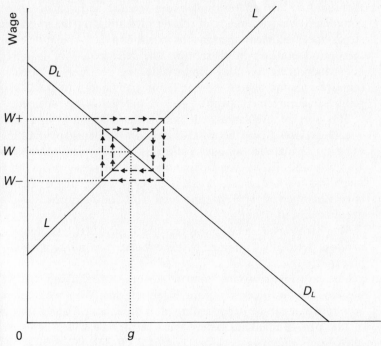

FIGURE 4.3

We will suppose the means of subsistence in any country just equal to the easy support of its inhabitants. The constant effort towards population, which is found to act even in the most vicious societies, increases the number of people before the means of subsistence are increased. The food therefore which before supported seven millions, must now be divided among seven millions and a half or eight millions. The poor consequently must live much worse, and many of them be reduced to severe distress. The number of labourers also being above the proportion of the work in the market, the price of labour must tend toward a decrease; while the price of provisions would at the same time tend to rise. The labourer therefore must work harder to earn the same as he did before. During this season of distress, the discouragements to marriage, and the difficulty of rearing a family are so great, that population is at a stand. In the meantime the cheapness of labour, the plenty of labourers, and the necessity of an increased industry amongst them, encourage cultivators to employ more labour upon their land; to turn up fresh soil, and to manure and improve more completely what is already in tillage; till ultimately the means of subsistence become in the same proportion to the population as at the period from which we set out. The situation of the labourer being then again tolerably comfortable, the restraints to population are in some degree loosened; and the same retrograde and progressive movements with respect to happiness are repeated.

This sort of oscillation will not be remarked by superficial observers; and it may be difficult even for the most penetrating mind to calculate its periods. Yet that in all old states some such vibration does exist; though from various transverse causes, in a much less marked, and in a much more irregular manner than I have described it, no reflecting man who considers the subject deeply can well doubt.

Many reasons occur why this oscillation has been less obvious, and less decidedly confirmed by experience, than might naturally be expected.

One principal reason is, that the histories of mankind that we possess, are histories only of the higher classes. We have but few accounts that can be depended upon of the manners and customs of that part of mankind, where these retrograde and progressive movements chiefly take place. (Pop edn1 29–32)

The diagram and the reasoning which lies behind it summarises

Malthus's theory of the interconnection between the wage, the rate of growth of subsistence and the rate of population growth. It shows also how it is fluctuations in the standard of living of the poorest groups in the community that are at the centre of his theory and how these keep the rate of growth of population in line with the rate of growth of subsistence.

THE SOCIAL IMPLICATIONS OF MALTHUS'S THEORY OF POPULATION

Malthus found the conclusion that population keeps in line with subsistence, as a result of deaths through malnutrition and hunger-induced disease among the poorest in the community, inescapable, and much of his essay is concerned with the social implications of this proposition which none before him had fully perceived. The essay grew out of discussions with his father about the feasibility of utopian schemes for the improvement of society, and the first edition of the essay is directed especially at Godwin's *An Enquiry Concerning Political Justice* which was published in 1793.[4] Malthus opens disarmingly, 'The system of equality which Mr. Godwin proposes, is, without doubt, by far the most beautiful and engaging of any that has yet appeared' (Pop edn1 174). Godwin proposed a society where there were no institutions to protect private property, where all worked only for the common good, and where there was no institution of marriage (which Godwin deplored since it involved the monopolisation of women by their husbands), while the population lived in plenty on land which was fairly shared out among the population. As Malthus writes, one consequence of this would be that:

> It would be of little consequence, according to Mr. Godwin, how many children a woman had, or to whom they belonged. Provisions and assistance would spontaneously flow from the quarter in which they abounded, to the quarter that was deficient. And every man would be ready to furnish instruction to the rising generation according to his capacity.
>
> I cannot conceive a form of society so favourable upon the whole to population. The irremediableness of marriage, as it is at present constituted, undoubtedly deters many from entering into that state. An unshackled intercourse on the contrary, would be a

most powerful incitement to early attachments: and as we are supposing no anxiety about the future support of children to exist, I do not conceive that there would be one woman in a hundred, of twenty three, without a family. (Pop edn1 183–4)

Malthus assumes that in these circumstances population would double each twenty-five years, from 7 millions when the scheme is first introduced to 28 millions after fifty years, when food supply, increasing only arithmetically, would suffice for only 21 millions, leaving seven millions 'unprovided for'. In consequence:

the corn is plucked before it is ripe, or secreted in unfair proportions…Provisions no longer flow in for the support of the mother with a large family. The children are sickly from insufficient food…Benevolence yet lingering in a few bosoms, makes some faint expiring struggles, till at length self-love resumes his wonted empire and lords it triumphant over the world. (Pop edn1 190)

No man had been goaded to the breach of order by unjust laws. Benevolence had established her reign in all hearts: and yet in so short a period as within fifty years, violence, oppression, falsehood, misery, every hateful vice, and every form of distress, which degrade and sadden the present state of society, seem to have been generated by the most imperious circumstances, by laws inherent in the nature of man, and absolutely independent of all human regulations. (Pop edn1 191)

Malthus goes on to point out that if the same trends continued for another twenty-five years, population would become 56 millions while food would suffice for only 28 millions, leaving 'twenty-eight millions of human beings without the means of support.' In another twenty-five years, 'the population would be one hundred and twelve millions, and the food only sufficient for thirty-five millions, leaving seventy-seven millions unprovided for. In these ages want would be indeed triumphant, and rapine and murder must reign at large: and yet all this time we are supposing the produce of the earth absolutely unlimited, and the yearly increase greater than the boldest speculator can imagine' (Pop edn1 192). At that point, 'some of the laws which at present govern civilized society, would be successively dictated by the most imperious necessity' (Pop edn1 194):

the goadings of want could not continue long, before some violations of public or private stock would necessarily take place...The urgency of the case would suggest the necessity of some immediate measures to be taken for the general safety. Some kind of convention would then be called, and the dangerous situation of the country stated in the strongest terms. It would be observed...that these violations had already checked the increase of food, and would, if they were not by some means or other prevented, throw the whole community in confusion: that imperious necessity seemed to dictate that a yearly increase of produce should, if possible, be obtained at all events: that in order to effect this first, great, and indispensible purpose, it would be adviseable to make a more complete division of land, and to secure every man's stock against violation by the most powerful sanctions, even by death itself...that the quantity of food which one man could consume, was necessarily limited by the narrow capacity of the human stomach: that it was not certainly probable that he should throw away the rest; but that even if he exchanged his surplus food for the labour of others, and made them in some degree dependent on him, this would still be better than that these others should absolutely starve.

It seems highly probable, therefore, that an administration of property, not very different from that which prevails in civilized States at present, would be established, as the best, though inadequate, remedy, for the evils which were pressing on the society. (Pop edn1 194–8)

It is not merely individual property rights over capital and land, and the death penalty to maintain them which would be restored, together with a return to a situation where those with only labour to sell were employed by those who owned part of the capital stock (that is, superfluous corn). Marriage too would need to be restored, and the obligations that accompany it:

It would be urged by those who had turned their attention to the true cause of the difficulties under which the community laboured that...yet still... the increase of food would by no means keep pace with the much more rapid increase of population: that some check to population therefore was imperiously called for: that the most natural and obvious check seemed to be, to make every man provide for his own children: that this would operate in some respect, as a measure and guide, in the increase of population; as it might be expected that no man would bring beings into the world, for whom he could not find the means of support: that where this notwithstanding was the case, it seemed necessary, for the example of others, that the disgrace and inconvenience attending such a conduct, should fall upon that individual, who had thus inconsiderately plunged himself and innocent children in misery and want.

The institution of marriage, or at least, of some express or implied obligation on every man to support his own children, seems to be the natural result of these reasonings in a community under the difficulties that we have supposed. (Pop edn1 198–200)

The restoration of marriage and of property rights would inevitably lead to inequalities of inheritance:

It has appeared, that from the inevitable laws of our nature, some human beings must suffer from want. These are the unhappy persons who, in the great lottery of life, have drawn a blank. The number of these claimants would soon exceed the ability of the surplus produce to supply...And it seems both natural and just, that [the choice of the owners of surplus produce] should fall upon those, who were able, and professed themselves willing, to exert their strength in procuring a further surplus produce; and thus at once benefiting the community, and enabling these proprietors to afford assistance to greater numbers. All who were in want of food would be urged by imperious necessity to offer their labour in exchange for this article so absolutely essential to existence. The fund appropriated to the maintenance of labour, would be, the aggregate quantity of food possessed by the owners of land beyond their own consumption. When the demands upon this fund were great and numerous, it would naturally be divided in very small shares. Labour would be ill paid. Men would offer to work for a bare subsistence, and the rearing of families would be checked by sickness and misery. On the contrary, when this fund was increasing fast; when it was great in proportion to the number of claimants; it would be divided in much larger shares. No man would exchange his labour without receiving an ample quantity of food in return. Labourers would live in ease and comfort; and would consequently be able to rear a numerous and vigorous offspring.

On the state of this fund, the happiness, or the degree of misery, prevailing among the lower classes of people in every known State, at present chiefly depends. And on this happiness, or degree of misery, depends the increase, stationariness, or decrease of population. (Pop edn1 204–6)

Malthus's account of the practical effects of Godwin's utopian scheme can be set out very simply in terms of the diagrammatic representation of his argument which was suggested above. The abolition of marriage removes the preventive check to population, so the LL schedule will be lowered from $L'L'$ to $L''L''$ in Figure 4.4. At the same time, the abolition of property rights and 'violations' of the harvest of one family by other families in want would 'check the increase of food'. With the rate of increase of food supply reduced to zero, the $D_L D_L$ shedule would fall from $D'_L D'_L$ to $D''_L D''_L$, that is, there would on balance be no net investment, and no increase from year to year in the funds for the maintenance of labour. With a cessation of growth of the capital stock, and at the same time, a more elastic population supply than before at each standard of living, the

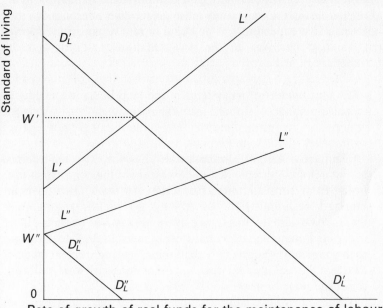

FIGURE 4.4

equilibrium standard of living would fall from $0W'$ to $0W'''$. Godwin's scheme would therefore lead to a great increase in distress and a very large fall in the standard of living of the poorest in the community.

With a restoration of the institution of marriage, together with the obligation on parents to support a family, the population supply schedule would return from $L''L''$ to $L'L'$. With the restoration of property rights and capitalist institutions, capital accumulation would resume and the D_LD_L schedule would shift back up from $D_L''D_L''$ to $D_L'D_L'$ to restore a wage of $0W'$. Malthus says this very clearly where he points out in the quoted passage that, when the fund for the maintenance of labour is 'increasing fast', 'Labourers would live in ease and comfort.' Their standard of living would be 'much larger' where property rights and capitalist institutions were leading to rapid growth of the capital stock, than in Godwin's Utopia where capital was stagnant and births unrestrained.

Malthus's use of his theory of population to answer Godwin was the first application he had in mind, and his belief that Godwin's ideal world was unachievable provided some of the stimulus to write the *Essay on Population*. A similar argument can, of course, be used to show that *any* legislation of any kind to improve the standard of living of the poorest in the community must have similar effects. It can thus be argued that expenditure of any kind to relieve poverty will lower the standard of living of the poor. Malthus first attacked the Elizabethan Poor Law:

> The radical defect of all systems of the kind is that of tending to increase population without increasing the means for its support, and by thus depressing the condition of those that are not relieved by parishes to create more poor...
>
> The famous 43rd of Elizabeth which has been so often referred to and admired, enacts, that the overseers of the poor, 'shall take order from time to time...for setting to work...such persons married or unmarried, as having no means to maintain them...And also to raise, weekly or otherwise, by taxation of every inhabitant, and every occupier of lands in the said parish (in such competent sums as they shall think fit) a convenient stock of flax, hemp, wool, thread, iron, and other necessary ware and stuff, to set the poor to work.'
>
> What is this but saying that the funds for the maintenance of labour in this country may be increased at will, and without limit, by a *fiat* of government, or an assessment of the overseers. Strictly

speaking, this clause is as arrogant and as absurd as if it had enacted that two ears of wheat should in future grow where only one had grown before. Canute, when he commanded the waves not to wet his princely foot, did not in reality assume a greater power over the laws of nature. (Pop edn3 ii.177–9)

During the Napoleonic wars, support for the poor was extended to the point where the wages of all workers were made up to a subsistence minimum through outdoor relief, that is, they received support in their own homes and not in workhouses. Wages were simply made up to the minimum standard, and work was if necessary provided in the manner indicated above. According to Malthus, writing in 1806 in the third edition of his *Essay on Population*, as many as one-half of all workers were receiving some measure of financial relief (Pop edn3 ii.394), and a French *Comité de Mendicité* described the British system of poor relief as 'England's most devouring political plague' (Pop edn3 ii.394[E]). Malthus set out his objections to the system very fully:

The poor laws of England tend to depress the general condition of the poor in these two ways. Their first obvious tendency is to increase population without increasing the food for its support. A poor man may marry with little or no prospect of being able to support a family without parish assistance. They may be said therefore, to create the poor which they maintain; and as the provisions of the country must, in consequence of the increased population, be distributed to every man in smaller proportions, it is evident that the labour of those who are not supported by parish assistance will purchase a smaller quantity of provisions than before, and consequently more of them must be driven to apply for assistance.

Secondly, the quantity of provisions consumed in workhouses, upon a part of the society that cannot in general be considered as the most valuable part, diminishes the shares that would other-wise belong to more industrious and more worthy members (Pop edn3 ii.172)

Poor relief thus increases the numbers of poor, because of its effect on population, and simultaneously depresses the incomes of others:

The greatest sufferers in the scarcity were undoubtedly the classes immediately above the poor; and these were in the most marked manner depressed by the excessive bounties given to those below them. Almost all poverty is relative...This distribution by giving to the poorer classes a command of food, so much greater than that to which their degree of skill and industry entitled them, in the actual circumstances of the country, diminished exactly in the same proportion that command over the necessaries of life, which the classes above them, by their superior skill and industry, would naturally possess (Pop edn3 ii.156–7)

There is worse to come. Not only will population grow as a result of the manner and level of poor relief, and the better off be dragged down to the standard of living of the poorest, but the taxation necessary to finance relief will slow down the rate of growth of the funds for the maintenance of labour which will further depress living standards:

the competition [from the subsidised poor] is supported by a great bounty, by which means, notwithstanding very inferior skill and industry on the part of his competitors, the independent workman may be undersold, and unjustly excluded from the market. He himself perhaps is made to contribute to this competition against his own earnings, and the funds for the maintenance of labour are thus turned from the support of a trade which yields a proper profit, to one which cannot maintain itself without a bounty. It should be observed in general that when a fund for the maintenance of labour is raised by assessment, the greatest part of it is not a new capital brought into trade, but an old one, which before was much more profitably employed, turned into a new channel. The farmer pays to the poor's rates for the encouragement of a bad and unprofitable manufacture, what he would have employed on his land with infinitely more advantage to his country. In the one case, the funds for the maintenance of labour are daily diminished; in the other, daily increased. And this obvious tendency of assessments for the employment of the poor, to decrease the real funds for the maintenance of labour in any country, aggravates the absurdity of supposing that it is in the power of a government to find employment for all its subjects, however fast they may increase. (Pop edn3 ii.186–7)

In terms of the diagram that has been used to represent Malthus's

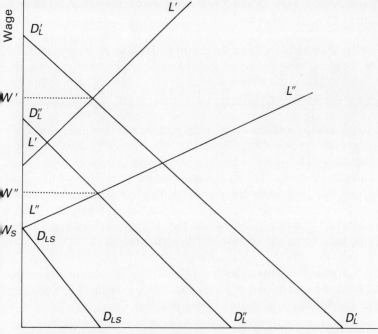

FIGURE 4.5

argument, poor relief weakens the preventive check on population, which lowers the *LL* schedule to *L"L"* in Figure 4.5, and makes this more elastic since support is greater for a large than for a small family. At the same time, the taxation of producers to finance poor relief lowers the rate of growth of the funds for the maintenance of labour from $D_L'D_L'$ to $D_L''D_L''$. This lowers the wage from $0W'$ to $0W''$, and the wage will, of course, fall right down to the subsistence wage $0W_s$ if the growth of subsistence funds halts altogether so that the D_LD_L schedule falls to $D_{LS}D_{LS}$. Malthus was convinced that, from reasoning like that represented in the diagram, the standard of living of the poor must fall considerably as a result of all attempts to relieve poverty:

> I feel persuaded, that if the poor laws had never existed in this
> country, though there might have been a few more instances of
> very severe distress, the aggregate mass of happiness among the

common people would have been much greater than it is at present. (Pop edn3 ii.177)

Moreover, pushed far enough, taxation to relieve poverty would drag the standard of living of all down to the level of the poorest. He actually said that the effects of a tax on the rich of eighteen shillings in the pound would be that:

no possible sacrifices of the rich, particularly in money, could for any time prevent the recurrence of distress among the lower members of society, who ever they were. Great changes might indeed be made. The rich might become poor, and some of the poor rich; but while the present proportion between population and food continues, a part of society must necessarily find it difficult to support a family, and this difficulty will naturally fall on the least fortunate members. (Pop edn3 ii.152)

Even a radical reorganisation of production so that this consisted solely of those subsistence goods best able to support life would not alter the fundamental nature of the problem:

there is nothing perhaps more improbable, or more out of the reach of any government to effect, than the direction of the industry of its subjects in such a manner as to produce the greatest quantity of human sustenance that the earth could bear. It evidently could not be done without the most complete violation of the law of property, from which every thing that is valuable to man has hitherto arisen. Such is the disposition to marry, particularly in very young people, that if the difficulties of providing for a family were entirely removed, very few would remain single at twenty-two. But what statesman or rational government could propose, that all animal food should be prohibited, that no horses should be used for business or pleasure, that all the people should live upon potatoes, and that the whole industry of the nation should be exerted in the production of them, except what was necessary for the mere necessaries of cloathing and houses. Could such a revolution be effected, would it be desirable; particularly as in a few years, notwithstanding all these exertions, want, with less resource than ever, would inevitably recur. (Pop edn3 ii.180–1)

It will be evident that Malthus was convinced that his theory of population had implications which produced a very strong case against any scheme of any kind to relieve poverty and economic distress. However, his argument was a long-term one, as he himself recognised:

> we should always bear in mind that no experiment respecting a provision for the poor can be said to be complete till succeeding generations have arisen. I doubt if there ever has been an instance of any thing like a liberal institution for the poor which did not succeed on its first establishment, however it might have failed afterwards. (Pop edn3 ii.540–1)

In spite of the reluctance which is usually felt to accept arguments which are so long-term in their effects, Malthus's analysis of the effects of attempts to relieve poverty became nineteenth-century conventional wisdom.[5] It influenced the 1834 Poor Law which restricted relief to those living in workhouses and these were made deliberately uncomfortable in the extreme so that no one would be lightly encouraged to have large families from the knowledge that they could eventually rely on support. Britain's failure to provide any significant food for Ireland during the famines of the 1840s also owed much to the belief that keeping Ireland fed was potentially an open-ended commitment which would in the end drag English living standards down to the Irish level.

ARE MALTHUS'S CONCLUSIONS INESCAPABLE?

The living standards of the poorest have grown in many countries of the world to levels that Malthus would have considered unimaginable. Does this mean that his theory was fundamentally mistaken, and that any suffering of the poor that followed from the adoption of policies based on his analysis resulted from gross errors? It is arguably contraception, and rapid technical progress in agriculture and industry which have removed Malthus's trap in many countries – but have they?

Malthus certainly totally failed to foresee the near universal use of contraceptives in many of the world's economies. Francis Place was prosecuted for advocating the use of a contraceptive device in 1822,[6] and Malthus himself, where he discusses Condorcet's utopian scheme for the perfectibility of man, remarks:

Mr. Condorcet's picture of what may be expected to happen when the number of men shall surpass the means of their subsistence, is justly drawn...

He then proceeds to remove the difficulty in a manner, which I profess not to understand. Having observed, that the ridiculous prejudices of superstition, would by that time have ceased to throw over morals, a corrupt and degrading austerity, he alludes, either to a promiscuous concubinage, which would prevent breeding, or to something else as unnatural. To remove the difficulty in this way, will, surely, in the opinion of most men, be, to destroy that virtue, and purity of manners, which the advocates of equality, and of the perfectibility of man, profess to be the end and object of their views. (Pop edn1 152–4)

Malthus was therefore aware of contraception, but he assumed incorrectly that it would be considered unacceptable by whole societies. But even the countries like the United States where the use of contraceptives is all but universal still have very rapid population growth. The United States population does not double in twenty-five years, but it doubles in less than sixty. West European populations mostly double in substantially less than a century. The growth of population is still geometric. Most adults marry, and average family size, despite contraception, provides far more than the two children who themselves marry that are needed to maintain a stable population. Malthus's failure to foresee the near-universal use of contraception in some societies therefore only marginally affects the force of his analysis. One need merely restate him to say that most will marry and *wish to have* families of a size which will inevitably produce geometric population growth to appreciate that one of his laws has every claim to universality. What of the other law, that food supply grows only arithmetically.

There are increasing or at worst constant returns in industry, and some of the relief of individual countries from the pressures he describes has been due to industrial expansion, and the export of manufactures to pay for imported food, which has been readily available from the world's relatively underpopulated continents. Malthus was fully aware of these possibilities, and he devoted one or two chapters of each edition of the *Essay of Population* to the effects of industrialisation, and whether this could relieve particular countries from the effects of the population pressures he described.

In the first edition of 1798, he argued that manufacturing could actually reduce the availability of food; and that it could be beneficial to the working class to produce food unprofitably rather than manufactures at a profit:

> I should differ from Dr. Adam Smith...where he seems to consider every increase of the revenue or stock of a society, as an increase of the funds for the maintenance of labour, and consequently, as tending always to ameliorate the condition of the poor.
>
> The fine silks and cottons, the laces, and other ornamental luxuries, of a rich country, may contribute very considerably to augment the exchangeable value of its annual produce; yet they contribute but in a very small degree, to augment the mass of happiness in the society: and it appears to me, that it is with some view to the real utility of the produce, that we ought to estimate the productiveness, or unproductiveness of different sorts of labour. (Pop edn1 328–30)

> Suppose, that two hundred thousand men, who are now employed in producing manufactures, that only tend to gratify the vanity of a few rich people, were to be employed upon some barren and uncultivated lands, and to produce only half the quantity of food that they themselves consumed; they would be still, more productive labourers with regard to the state, than they were before; though their labour, so far from affording a rent to a third person, would but half replace the provisions used in obtaining the produce. In their former employment, they consumed a certain portion of the food of the country, and left in return, some silks and laces. In their latter employment, they consumed the same quantity of food, and left in return, provision for a hundred thousand men. There can be little doubt, which of the two legacies would be the most really beneficial to the country; and it will, I think, be allowed, that the wealth which supported the two hundred thousand men, while they were producing silks and laces, would have been more usefully employed in supporting them, while they were producing the additional quantity of food.

> A capital employed upon land, may be unproductive to the individual that employs it, and yet be highly productive to the society. A capital employed in trade on the contrary, may be highly productive to the individual, and yet be almost totally unproductive to the society (Pop edn1 332–3)

Here Malthus does not merely take the view that profitable manufactures will provide no relief from population pressures, through commerce. He even prefers to reduce a society's total investible surplus, through the encouragement of loss making agriculture, rather than to increase it through profitable manufactures. He ignores the effects on the rate of growth of food supply of the extra taxes needed to finance two hundred thousand men in agriculture who produce only enough food to feed a hundred thousand. His argument at this stage can be represented by the diagrams set out earlier, with the vertical axis showing the standard of living in terms of food alone, and the horizontal axis, the rate of growth of output of food, instead of the rate of growth of subsistence funds. Food output is all that is relevant in the first edition, and even this is curiously uninfluenced by the economy's aggregate capital stock.

By the time Malthus published the third edition of the *Essay on Population* in 1806, he was clear that it was the *surplus produce of England* that was vital; but he wrote as if this was derived wholly from agriculture. Indeed it has been pointed out that Malthus was to all intents a Physiocrat in the second and third editions,[7] and the following passage would have delighted Quesnay or the elder Mirabeau:

> the position of the Economists will always remain true, that the surplus produce of the cultivators is the great fund which ultimately pays all those who are not employed upon the land. Throughout the whole world the number of manufacturers, of proprietors, and of persons engaged in the various civil and military professions, must be exactly proportioned to this surplus produce, and cannot in the nature of things increase beyond it. If the earth had been so niggardly of her produce as to oblige all her inhabitants to labour for it, no manufacturers or idle persons could ever have existed. But her first intercourse with man was a voluntary present, not very large indeed, but sufficient as a fund for his subsistence, till by the proper exercise of his faculties he could procure a greater. In proportion as the labour and ingenuity of man exercised upon the land, have increased this surplus produce, leisure has been given to a greater number of persons to employ themselves in all the inventions which embellish civilized life. And though, in its turn, the desire to profit by these inventions has greatly contributed to stimulate the cultivators to increase their surplus produce; yet the order of precedence is clearly the surplus produce; because the

funds for the subsistence of the manufacturer must be advanced to him before he can complete his work: and if we were to imagine, that we could command this surplus produce, whenever we willed it, by forcing manufactures, we should be quickly admonished of our gross errour, by the inadequate support which the workman would receive, in spite of any rise that might take place in his nominal wages. (Pop edn3 ii.208–10)

In a further passage, Malthus does recognise that a nation can derive its wealth 'principally from manufactures and commerce', but he only sees this as possible for an 'ephemeral' period:

According to the systems of the Economists, manufactures are an object on which revenue is spent, and not any part of the revenue itself.* But though from this description of manufactures, and the epithet sterile sometimes applied to them, they seem rather to be degraded by the terms of the Economists, it is a very great errour to suppose that their system is really unfavourable to them. On the contrary, I am disposed to believe, that it is the only system by which commerce and manufactures can prevail to a very great extent, without bringing with them at the same time the seeds of their own ruin. Before the late revolution in Holland, the high price of the necessaries of life had destroyed many of its manufactures. Monopolies are always subject to be broken; and even the advantage of capital and machinery, which may yield extraordinary profits for a time, is liable to be greatly lessened by the competition of other nations. In the history of the world, the nations whose wealth has been derived principally from manufactures and commerce, have been perfectly ephemeral beings, compared with those, the basis of whose wealth has been agriculture. It is in the nature of things that a state which subsists upon a revenue furnished by other countries, must be infinitely more exposed to all the accidents of time and chance, than one which produces its own. (Pop edn3 ii.211–12)

* Even upon this system there is one point of view in which manufactures appear greatly to add to the riches of a state. The use of a revenue, according to the Economists, is to be spent; and a great part of it will of course be spent in manufactures. But if by the judicious employment of manufacturing capital, these commodities grow considerably cheaper, the surplus produce becomes proportionably of so much greater value, and the real revenue of the nation is virtually increased...

Malthus spelt out these objections to a dependence on imported food in the fifth edition of the *Essay on Population*, which he published in 1817. First, a nation dependent on imported food and raw materials cannot exist unless it can obtain these from abroad, so its very existence depends on other countries, and *a fortiori* its growth which will end *if foreigners cease to expand*:

> if food and raw materials were denied to a nation merely manufacturing, it is obvious that it could not longer exist. But not only does the absolute existence of such a nation, on an extreme supposition, depend upon its foreign commerce, but its progress in wealth must be almost entirely measured by the progress and demand of the countries which deal with it. However skilful, industrious and saving such a nation might be, if its customers, from indolence and want of accumulation, would not or could not take off a yearly increasing value of its commodities, the effects of its skill and machinery would be but of very short duration.
> (Pop edn5 ii.408–9)

If the country's overseas customers for manufactures stagnated, it could, of course, keep up its growth to some extent by cutting the relative prices of its exports, but demand might be inelastic, in which case cutting the prices of manufactures would not purchase extra food:

> unless...an increase of wealth and demand were produced in the surrounding countries, the increasing ingenuity and exertions of the manufacturing and commercial state would be lost in continually falling prices. It would not only be obliged, as its skill and capital increased, to give a larger quantity of manufactured produce for the raw produce which it received in return; but it might be unable, even with the temptation of reduced prices, to stimulate its customers to such purchases as would allow of an increasing importation of food and raw materials; and without such an increasing importation, it is quite obvious that the population must become stationary. (Pop edn5 ii.409–10)

A further possible source of stagnation is that the country's competitive edge in manufacturing would be lost as other countries industrialised:

> advantages which depend exclusively upon capital and skill, and

the present possession of particular channels of commerce, cannot in their nature be permanent. We know how difficult it is to confine improvements in machinery to a single spot; we know that it is the constant object, both of individuals and countries, to increase their capital; and we know, from the past history of commercial states, that the channels of trade are not unfrequently taking a different direction. It is unreasonable therefore to expect that any one country, merely by the force of skill and capital, should remain in possession of markets uninterrupted by foreign competition. But, when a powerful foreign competition takes place, the exportable commodities of the country in question must soon fall to prices which will essentially reduce profits; and the fall of profits will diminish both the power and the will to save. Under these circumstances the accumulation of capital will be slow, and the demand for labour proportionably slow, till it comes nearly to a stand; while, perhaps, the new competitors, either by raising their own raw materials or by some other advantages, may still be increasing their capitals and population with some degree of rapidity. (Pop edn5 ii.403–4)

Stagnation, however caused, will reduce wages to the level appropriate to zero population growth in the diagrams, for a lack of growth of the food available to support labour will eventually reduce the rate of growth of subsistence funds to zero. Hence a reliance on imported manufactures can be extremely damaging to the standard of living of the working class:

Universally it may be observed, that if, from any cause or causes whatever, the funds for the maintenance of labour in any country cease to be progressive, the effective demand for labour will also cease to be progressive; and wages will be reduced to that sum, which, under the existing prices of provisions, and the existing habits of the people, will just keep up, and no more than keep up, a stationary population. A state so circumstanced is under a moral impossibility of increasing, whatever may be the plenty of corn, or however high may be the profits of stock in other countries. It may indeed at a subsequent period, and under new circumstances, begin to increase again. If by some happy invention in mechanics, the discovery of some new channel of trade, or an unusual increase of agricultural wealth and population in the surrounding countries, its exports, of whatever kind, were to become unusually in demand, it might again import an increasing quantity of corn, and might again increase its population. (Pop edn5 ii.418–19)

For Malthus, the risks involved in a reliance on imported manufactures were just too great. There are echoes in recent British experience of several of his worries: a loss of technological leadership, the effects on exports and living standards of slow growth in the rest of the world, and a price inelastic demand for exports. But it has taken a long time for the difficulties he predicted to emerge. It must be remembered that Malthus's long periods are extremely long. In 1806 he wrote:

> There has never yet been an instance in history, of a large nation continuing with undiminished vigour, to support four or five millions of its people on imported corn; nor do I believe that there ever will be such an instance in future. England is, undoubtedly, from her insular situation, and commanding navy, the most likely to form an exception to this rule; but in spite even of the peculiar advantages of England, it appears to me clear that if she continue yearly to increase her importations of corn, she cannot ultimately escape that decline which seems to be the natural and necessary consequence of excessive commercial wealth. I am not now speaking of the next twenty or thirty years, but of the next two or three hundred. And though we are little in the habit of looking so far forwards, yet it may be questioned, whether we are not bound in duty to make some exertions to avoid a system which must necessarily terminate in the weakness and decline of our posterity. (Pop edn3 ii.275–6)

Malthus wrote this passage with its reference to 'a commanding navy' in the year after Trafalgar. Only somewhat over half of his 'two or three hundred years' have passed, and some of his concern about the dangers of dependence on vital imports with a consequent balance of payments constraint on growth is beginning to sound disturbingly relevant. He recommended for Britain the maintenance of continuing self-sufficiency in food, in which case its growth in output and living standards would be independent of any vicissitudes of the international environment:

> A country with resources in land...if its industry, ingenuity and economy increase, its wealth and population will increase, what-

ever may be the situation and conduct of the nations with which it trades. When its manufacturing capital becomes redundant, and manufactured commodities are too cheap, it will have no occasion to wait for the increasing raw products of its neighbours. The transfer of its own redundant capital to its own land will raise fresh products, against which its manufactures may be exchanged, and by the double operation of diminishing comparatively the supply, and increasing the demand, enhance their price. A similar operation, when raw produce is too abundant, will restore the level between the profits of agriculture and manufactures. And upon the same principle the stock of the country will be distributed through its various and distant provinces, according to the advantages presented by each situation for the employment, either of agricultural or manufacturing capital.

A country, in which in this manner agriculture, manufactures, and commerce, and all the different parts of a large territory, act and re-act upon each other in turn, might evidently go on increasing in riches and strength, although surrounded by Bishop Berkely's wall of brass. (Pop edn5 ii.426–7)

Agricultural self-sufficiency, and balanced growth of industry, agriculture and the services were Malthus's policy recommendations in a series of publications. In 1817 when he published the above passage, he considered it vital that Britain should continue to tax imported corn to maintain agricultural self-sufficiency, and he published two earlier pamphlets in defence of the corn laws.[8] In 1820 in the deep agricultural depression which followed the Napoleonic wars, he analysed the causes of a deficiency of effective demand in his *Principles of Political Economy*, and as will be shown in the next chapter, a balanced growth of industry, agriculture and the services proved to be central to his solution to that problem. The above passage summarises, magnificently, his policy advice. It was his view that with agricultural expansion, together with the availability of manufactures to provide motivation for the agriculturalists, supply could actually create its own demand. Malthus otherwise considered Say's Law erroneous: but expanding food output would expand population, which would in turn ensure that there was in due course a growing market for food.

Therefore, with the best advice that he could offer, the rate of growth of *domestic* food supply set the ultimate limit to population growth. In the century and a half since his death domestic food supply has in fact risen in Western Europe (and also of course in the underpopulated continents) at rates which have far exceeded population growth. The growth of French, German and Italian living standards has not depended on imported food, and these countries have, in effect, followed Malthus's strategy. The result has greatly exceeded his expectations. His view that *ex ante* population growth must outpace food supply to a point where *positive* checks are part of the process whereby population and food grow in line with each other has just not been borne out by events. Domestic food supply has grown geometrically and not arithmetically.

In his view, improvements in agriculture can occur continuously – that is evident from several passages in the *Essay on Population*[9] – and he made it very clear in his *Principles of Political Economy* that the rate of improvement depends partly on the motivations which can be offered to the agriculturalists and this line of argument will be developed in the next chapter. These include, in particular, profitability and the availability of manufactures on which their incomes can be spent.[10] These favourable factors have been far stronger than he anticipated, and agricultural output has advanced far more rapidly in most of Europe than in the thousand years prior to 1798, on which he necessarily based his analysis.

Agricultural output has outpaced population more easily because the preventive check to this has grown in importance and effectiveness in modern societies. He anticipated that an increasing availability of manufactures to the working class in a society with free political institutions and capitalist property rights would strengthen the preventive check. With the smaller families which have resulted from the strong preventive check, European populations have doubled in fifty to one hundred years and not in twenty-five, and population growth has been limited to this rate without significant recourse after around 1880 to positive checks among the poor. It has only required a rate of growth of agricultural output of 2 per cent per annum to significantly outpace such slower *ex ante* rates of population growth, and agricultural output has comfortably grown somewhat faster than this.

What France, Germany, Italy and the other West European economies have achieved, others can too, so it may be that all countries can escape Malthus's trap. Most countries have the potential to cut *ex ante* population growth to less than 2 per cent per annum through the preventive check, and it is not difficult to raise agricultural output as fast as this. Hunger can therefore be gradually removed without continuing recourse to the food surpluses of the world's underpopulated continents. Most of densely populated Europe has managed to achieve high living standards for all, without North American and Australian food. The underpopulated continents are indeed irrelevant to a long-term solution to Malthus's problem for as he pointed out, they cannot remain underpopulated indefinitely. Population in the continents where 'a great degree of knowledge and industry' would have the opportunity to operate 'at once upon rich unappropriated soil' would increase 'with such extraordinary rapidity that the advantage could not last long' (Pop edn3 i.9). North American and Australian populations have indeed been growing far faster than in Europe, and thinking in Malthus's two or three hundred year periods, Europe and Asia will have to rely increasingly on their own domestic agriculture. But, with an adequate preventive check, relatively little will be asked of European farmers in relation to what they have recently achieved.

So was Malthus wrong? He considered continuing 2 per cent agricultural growth unachievable. He can be allowed the last word:

> if any person will take the trouble to make the calculation, he will see that if the necessaries of life could be obtained without limit, and the number of people could be doubled every twenty-five years, the population which might have been produced from a single pair since the Christian aera, would have been sufficient, not only to fill the earth quite full of people, so that four should stand in every square yard, but to fill all the planets of our solar system in the same way, and not only them, but all the planets revolving round the stars which are visible to the naked eye, supposing each of them to be a sun, and to have as many planets belonging to it as our sun has. Under this law of population, which, excessive as it may appear when stated in this way, is, I firmly believe, best suited to the nature and situation of man, it is quite obvious that some limit to the production of food, or some other of the necessaries of life, must exist. (Pr edn1 227–8)

That final proposition of Malthus's of 1820 is unchallengeable. 'Some limit to the production of food, *or some other of the necessaries of life*' must indeed exist. The production functions are *bounded* at some point due to physical space limitations,[11] so even 1 per cent population growth will be more than the environment can accommodate if it continues indefinitely.

5 Malthus's Theory of Effective Demand and Growth

In 1820 when he published his *Principles of Political Economy* Malthus – with David Ricardo, the subject of the next chapter – was one of England's two most distinguished and highly regarded political economists. The *Essay on Population* had run through five editions and become part of the conventional wisdom, and Malthus had also published important pamphlets and become a principal reviewer for the *Edinburgh Review* and subsequently for the more conservative *Quarterly Review*.[1] From this standpoint of high reputation and prestige he attempted to correct the all but universal belief of his contemporaries that effective demand had no influence on output, and that extra thrift always resulted in faster capital accumulation and economic growth. These propositions had originated only from the time of Adam Smith, for the Mercantilists had considered demand extremely important, while the Physiocrats had believed that increasing agricultural investment and a growing demand for food were both indispensable for growth.

Malthus first expressed his doubts about the downgrading of the role of demand in correspondence with Ricardo, during the acute depression with extensive agricultural distress which followed the Napoleonic Wars. It appeared to him that the great fall in unproductive government expenditure after the war had increased the severity of the depression, and that extra government spending on, for instance, public works, and a reduction in thrift by the community as a whole, would restore prosperity. He attempted unsuccessfully to produce a statement of his doubts about Smithian orthodoxy which would convince Ricardo, and in 1820 he endeavoured to convince his contemporaries by setting out a complete theory of growth. In this both effective demand and the supply factors which were predominant in his work on population were vital elements.

His argument was simple and straightforward on the surface but the new principles he propounded and how they were reconcilable with others that he still accepted were difficult to comprehend. The new book's impact on his contemporaries was negligible, and it went unrecognised and ignored until Keynes's essays on Malthus in 1933 and 1935, where he spoke of the 'brilliant intuitions' of Malthus's *Principle of Effective Demand* which he considered more 'far-reaching' than the *Principle of Population*.[2] 'If only Malthus, instead of Ricardo, had been the parent stem from which nineteenth-century economics proceeded, what a much wiser and richer place the world would be today. We have laboriously to re-discover and force through the obscuring envelopes of our misguided education what should never have ceased to be obvious.'[3] Keynes's accolade unleashed a vast twentieth-century literature on how far Malthus had anticipated Keynes, what Malthus's theory of effective demand was if it differed from his, and what its logic amounted to.[4] A very large number of twentieth-century economists have considered that there may be important truths or errors in Malthus's analysis of effective demand, but as Denis O'Brien has remarked 'there are as many secondary interpretations as authors'.[5] There is indeed scarce agreement between any two modern commentators on the fundamental nature of his contribution.

A modern model can indeed be derived from his premises which arrives at some of his most important results. In particular, it can be shown rigorously, following his own assumptions, that growth will be an *impossibility* if saving by landlords is high, while spending by capitalists and the government fails to make an equivalent extra contribution to annual expenditure flows.

In the present chapter, Malthus's argument will be presented in two stages. First, his theory of fluctuations which he published originally in 1798 will be set out. In so far as 'general gluts' are merely the slump in the cycle, they will be fully explained in this first part of the argument which is straightforward and in no way controversial. But it is evident that Malthus believed that something far more profound than the slump of a trade cycle can go wrong with economies:

Production and distribution are the two grand elements of wealth, which, combined in their due proportions, are capable of carrying the riches and population of the earth in no great length of time to the utmost limits of its possible resources; but which taken separately, or combined in undue proportions, produce only, after the lapse of many thousand years, the scanty riches and scanty population, which are at present scattered over the face of the globe. (Pr edn1 426)

Malthus's principle of effective demand must be explained to show how economies can suffer long-term underdevelopment, and it will be shown in the second section of this chapter that the crucial variables which determine profits and effective demand can all too easily get locked into values where growth is a sheer impossibility. The argument will then be stated mathematically in a further section of the chapter, 'A Malthus Growth Model', but its essence will be stated quite simply before this. Finally something will be said about how the explanation of Malthus's theory of effective demand which is presented here differs from previous interpretations.

MALTHUS'S THEORY OF CYCLICAL FLUCTUATIONS

From 1798 onwards in successive editions of the *Essay on Population* Malthus explained how, following any temporary shortage of labour, living conditions would become abnormally prosperous for a time, which would induce unusually rapid population growth. After an interval of eighteen or so years, this would produce an oversupply of labour which would depress living standards again, and this would reduce the rate of population growth until labour again became scarce. In Chapter 4 these continuing fluctuations in the wage and in the rate of population growth were represented by a cobweb diagram – Figure 4.3 on page 117. This showed how there was both an equilibrium rate of population growth, and an equilibrium wage which depended on considerations like the degree of moral restraint in the society in question. At the same time, because adjustment of population to the wage occurred only after a lengthy time-lag, wages and population tended to fluctuate around these equilibrium values.

Malthus went on to argue in the *Principles* of 1820 that his theory of population could be applied in a parallel manner to the growth of the capital stock:

The laws which regulate the rate of profits and the progress of capital, bear a very striking and singular resemblance to the laws which regulate the rate of wages and the progress of population. (Pr edn1 370)

a further proof of a singular resemblance in the laws that regulate the increase of capital and of population, is to be found in the rapidity with which the loss of capital is recovered during a war which does not interrupt commerce. The loans to government convert capital into revenue, and increase demand at the same time that they at first diminish the means of supply. The necessary consequence must be an increase of profits. This naturally increases both the power and the reward of accumulation; and if only the same habits of saving prevail among the capitalists as before, the recovery of the lost stock must be rapid, just for the same kind of reason that the recovery of population is so rapid when, by some cause or other, it has been suddenly destroyed. (Pr edn1 373·4)

If the growth of capital depends on the rate of profit, then the determination of an economy's rate of profit and of its rate of growth of capital can be illustrated with a similar diagram to the one used in Chapter 4 to explain population growth and the wage. In Figure 5.1, KK is a function which relates the supply of capital to the rate of profit and it is similar in principle to LL, the population supply function in Figure 4.3. Capital breeds like labour if the rate of return is sufficiently high in relation to $0r_s$, the 'subsistence minimum' return where the capital stock is constant. $0r_s$ is precisely equivalent to OW_s in Figure 4.5 on page 127, the wage 'required to enable the labourer to maintain a stationary population', and in the second edition of the *Principles of Political Economy* Malthus saw this critical profit rate as perhaps around $6\frac{2}{3}$ per cent when he wrote, 'Nor is it probable that profits would admit of a greater reduction than from $16\frac{2}{3}$ to $6\frac{2}{3}$ before accumulation would be nearly at a stand' (Pr edn2 205). At rates of profit above $6\frac{2}{3}$ per cent, capital will expand, and it will expand faster the higher the rate of profit.

Figure 5.1 is completed with the schedule D_KD_K which shows the potential the economy has to absorb increased capital. A low rate of profit will produce a slow rate of growth of the *supply* of capital (through the schedule KK) but at the same time it will be associated with a high wage and therefore rapid population growth which would

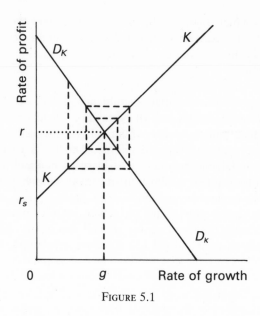

FIGURE 5.1

permit the economy to make use of a rapidly increasing capital stock. The schedule $D_K D_K$ shows the rate of growth of capital which can be absorbed at each rate of profit and this is inferred from the rate of population growth, that is, the growth in the complementary factor of production to labour, at each rate of profit. Where the rate of profit is low, the high opportunity to make use of extra capital as indicated by $D_K D_K$ exceeds the slow increase in the supply of capital as indicated by KK, with the result that the rate of profit will tend to rise. Conversely, where the rate of profit is high and the wage is therefore low, the supply of capital (from KK) increases faster than the economy's ability to make use of it (from $D_K D_K$ – population growth will be slow at the low wage that goes with a high profit rate), and the rate of profit will therefore tend to fall. At a rate of profit of $0r$ capital and labour will both grow at the equilibrium rate of $0g$, and the supply of capital and the economy's ability to absorb it will then both grow at the same rate.

As with population, there will be a lag in the adjustment of the supply of capital to an above-equilibrium rate of profit, so it may take many years for a shortage of capital in relation to the long-term use a society can make of it to be corrected. Similarly it will take several years before a below-equilibrium rate of profit can remove a surplus of capital. The rate of profit and the rate of growth of capital will therefore fluctuate around their equilibrium values in the cobweb manner indicated in Figure 5.1

The schedules LL and D_LD_L of Figure 4.3 and KK and D_KD_K of Figure 5.1 can be stated mathematically, and the equilibrium wage and profit rate, OW and $0r$, are derived simply and straightforwardly from the resulting equations in the mathematical statement of the argument that concludes this chapter. The essential argument is however entirely clear from the two diagrams.

In his last publication, the *Definitions of Political Economy* of 1827, a most interesting and perceptive book which Malthus addressed primarily to his fellow political economists and not to the public at large,[6] he provided an account of self-correcting fluctuations which differs in several interesting ways from the 1798 version of the argument which was quoted in Chapter 4. It is entirely in line with the account of fluctuations provided by the two diagrams:

All the most common causes of an acceleration or retardation in the movements of the great machine of human society, involve variations, and often great variations, in the real wages of labour. Commodities in general, and corn most particularly, are continually rising or falling in money-price, from the state of the supply as compared with the demand, while the money-price of labour remains much more nearly the same. In the case of a rise of corn and commodities, the real wages of common day-labour are necessarily diminished: the labourer obtains a smaller proportion of what he produces; profits necessarily rise; the capitalists have a greater power of commanding labour; more persons are called into full work, and the increased produce which follows, is the natural remedy for that state of the demand and supply, from whatever cause arising, which had occasioned the temporary rise in the money-price of commodities. On the other hand, if corn and other commodities fall in money-price, as compared with the money-price of labour, it is obvious that the day-labourer, who gets employment, will be able to buy more corn with the money which he receives; he obtains a larger proportion of what he produces; profits necessarily fall; the capitalists have a diminished power of commanding labour; fewer persons are fully employed, and the diminished production which follows, is the natural remedy for that state of the demand and supply, from whatever cause arising, which occasioned the temporary fall in the money-price of commodities. The operation of these remedial processes to prevent the continuance of excess or defect, is so much what one should naturally expect, and is so obviously confirmed by general experience, that it is inconceivable that a proposition should have obtained any currency which is founded on a supposed law of demand and supply diametrically opposed to these remedial processes.

It will be recollected, that the question of a glut is exclusively whether it may be general, as well as particular, and not whether it may be permanent as well as temporary. The causes above mentioned act powerfully to prevent the permanence either of glut or scarcity, and to regulate the supply of commodities so as to make them sell at their natural prices. (Def 60–2)

In this 1827 version of the argument the burden of adjustment fall mainly on the rate of capital accumulation, which can be expected to adjust more quickly to the rate of profit than population growth to the wage. The period of the fluctuations may then be less than the sixteen- to eighteen-year gap between generations which had the dominant influence in the 1798 version of the argument.

The two accounts are however essentially the same, and they describe the fluctuations inherent in Figures 4.3 and 5.1. These schedules together with some lagging will produce what Malthus describes: self-correcting fluctuations. It is to be noted that the labour market takes time to clear in both the 1798 and the 1827 accounts of the cycle. In 1798, 'the number of labourers is above the proportion of work in the market' where the wage is high; while in 1827, when 'profits necessarily fall', 'the capitalists have a diminished power of commanding labour; fewer persons are fully employed'. Product markets in contrast clear instantly, but future investment is adversely affected if, as in 'general gluts', they clear at a price which yields a rate of profit which is insufficient to encourage future production (Def 242, 247).

Sowell has seen Malthus's analysis of 'general gluts' in terms of diagrams like these and the economic forces they represent.[7] That this is an important part of the story is evident from the quotation from *Definitions of Political Economy* which describes 'general gluts' entirely in terms of a slump in a self-correcting cycle.

In so far as Malthus saw 'general gluts' in these terms, it is natural that he should have wished to reduce the amplitude and severity of the cycle, especially as this had particularly adverse effects on the working class:

> eight or ten years, recurring not unfrequently, are serious spaces in human life. They amount to a serious sum of happiness or misery, according as they are prosperous or adverse, and leave the country in a very different state at their termination. In prosperous times the mercantile classes often realize fortunes, which go far towards securing them against the future; but unfortunately the working classes, though they share in the general prosperity, do not share so largely as in the general adversity. They may suffer the greatest distress in a period of low wages, but cannot be adequately compensated by a period of high wages. To them fluctuations must always bring more evil than good; and, with a view to the happiness of the great mass of society, it should be our object, as far as possible, to maintain peace, and an equable expenditure. (Pr edn1 521–2)

The severe fall in government expenditure in the transition from war to peace after 1815 produced a sharp fluctuation additional to those which were in any case occurring and so added to the severity of the cycle for a considerable time. Writing in terms of short-period policy prescription – and Keynes insisted that he was the first Cambridge economist[8] – in the slump phase of the cycle in 1820, Malthus argued for extra unproductive consumption, that is, for more government expenditure. Government was responsible for the *extra* severity of the post-1815 slump by increasing expenditure massively during the war and then cutting it back severely after 1815. If government could avoid such severe fluctuations in its own expenditure, the cycle would be less severe, which would above all benefit the working class. Smoothing out the cycle in 1820, that is, maintaining an 'equable expenditure', meant raising unproductive government expenditure because 'An expenditure, which would have absolutely crushed the country in 1770, might be little more than what was necessary to call forth its prodigious powers of production in 1816' (Pr edn1 502). Here Malthus is almost speaking as an early fine-tuner, which was a role that Ricardo neither sought, nor, given the self-correcting mechanisms, considered desirable. As Ricardo said in a letter to Malthus, which has been much quoted:

It appears to me that one great cause of our difference in opinion, on the subjects which we have so often discussed, is that you have always in your mind the immediate and temporary effects of particular changes – whereas I put these immediate and temporary effects quite aside, and fix my whole attention on the permanent state of things which will result from them. Perhaps you estimate these temporary effects too highly, whilst I am too much disposed to undervalue them. (R vii 120)

Malthus was, of course, far more than the first Cambridge demand manager and in the next section his theory of the close interconnection which must exist between effective demand and economic development will be set out.

EFFECTIVE DEMAND AND ECONOMIC DEVELOPMENT

Fortunate economies develop. There are statements by Malthus as early as 1798, on how agricultural techniques and agricultural output will steadily improve over the centuries:

Were a country never to be over-run by a people more advanced in arts, but left to its own natural progress in civilization; from the time that its produce might be considered as an unit, to the time that it might be considered as a million (Pop edn1 138)

Five pages later he used the phrase, 'till the whole earth had been cultivated like a garden'. What determines the rate of improvement? It is clear that he believed that profits and demand play a vital role:

If a great and continued demand should arise among surrounding nations for the raw produce of a particular country, the price of this produce would of course rise considerably; and the expenses of cultivation, rising only slowly and gradually to the same proportion, the price of produce might for a long time keep so much a head, as to give a prodigious stimulus to improvement, and encourage the employment of much capital in bringing fresh land under cultivation, and rendering the old much more productive. (Ess 195–6)

More directly, 'Inventions to save labour seldom take place to any considerable extent, except when there is a decided demand for them' (Pr edn1 401). Conversely, in the absence of demand, productivity can be expected to stagnate or indeed fall:

> the tenant...if there were no foreign vent for the raw produce, and the commodities which contribute to the conveniences and luxuries of life were but little known, would have but small incitement to call forth the resources of his [the landlord's] land, and give encouragement to a rapid increase of population. By employing ten families he might perhaps, owing to the richness of the soil, obtain food for fifty; but he would find no proportionate market for this additional food, and would be soon sensible that he had wasted his time and attention in superintending the labour of so many persons. He would be disposed therefore to employ a smaller number; or if, from motives of humanity, or any other reason, he was induced to keep more than were necessary for the supply of the market, upon the supposition of their being tolerably industrious, he would be quite indifferent to their industry, and his labourers would naturally acquire the most indolent habits. Such habits would naturally be generated both in the masters and servants by such circumstances, and when generated, a considerable time and considerable stimulants are necessary to get rid of them. (Pr edn1 376–7)

Hence, where demand for produce is high, there is a 'prodigious stimulus to improvement', while where it is lacking it is likely that labourers will be allowed to acquire the most indolent habits, and these will be generated 'both in the masters and servants'. Malthus believed that people are not easily motivated to develop their economies, and the range of goods available is an important consideration:

> The greatest of all difficulties in converting uncivilized and thinly peopled countries into civilized and populous ones, is to inspire them with the wants best calculated to excite their exertions in the production of wealth. One of the greatest benefits which foreign commerce confers, and the reason why it has always appeared an almost necessary ingredient in the progress of wealth, is, its tendency to inspire new wants, to form new tastes, and to furnish fresh motives for industry. Even civilized and improved countries cannot afford to lose any of these motives. It is not the most

pleasant employment to spend eight hours a day in a counting-house. Nor will it be submitted to after the common necessaries and conveniences of life are attained, unless adequate motives are presented to the mind of the man of business. Among these motives is undoubtedly the desire of advancing his rank, and contending with the landlords in the enjoyment of leisure, as well as of foreign and domestic luxuries. (Pr edn1 470)

It will already be evident that motivation is central to Malthus's account of economic development. A passage in an important letter to Ricardo underlines the significance of this:

> You constantly say that it is not a question about the motives to produce. Now I have certainly intended to make it amost entirely a question about motives. We see in almost every part of the world vast powers of production which are not put into action, and I explain this phenomenon by saying that from the want of a proper distribution of the actual produce adequate motives are not furnished to continued production. (R ix 10)

In other words, for lack of a market, for lack of 'a proper distribution of the actual produce', underdevelopment continues.

An important point to grasp is that Malthus did not see the level of production as closely connected to quantities of physical inputs. One approach to growth is to ignore motivation and make output solely a function of inputs. A modern production function where output is assumed to be a function of physical capital, labour, natural resources and the state of knowledge is an example. Malthus would have argued that such a production function ignored what mattered no less vitally than the rest – motivation. He could have brought this in by making output a function also of human energy, or more narrowly entrepreneurship (though this would miss the motivation of workers which he also considered vital). Ricardo never perceived the distinction, and it is present in the work of few of today's economists who are mainly content to assume a mechanical connection between output and physical inputs.[9]

Specifically it is evident that in Malthus's view growth depends very much on profitability because it is this that is best calculated to release a society's entrepreneurial energies. The full implications of the assumption that an economy has a rate of technical advance that depends on the incentive to pursue improvements, which in turn depends principally on profitability, will be worked through in the mathematical section of this chapter. It is shown there that a country will have a *potential* rate of growth at full employment which may become faster through time if, as Malthus expected, the proportion of the economy that is subject to agricultural diminishing returns diminishes. It is indeed possible, as Malthus dimly perceived in the later editions of the *Essay on Population*, that with moral restraint – strengthened by an increasing availability of manufactures to the mass of the population – output might begin to grow faster than population to provide an escape from the population trap for a time, until a shortage of physical space per head eventually closed in on a society.[10]

But these happy possibilities from growing profitability and an increasing rate of technical advance can only become manifest if effective demand can grow in line with long-term productive potential. The account of Malthus's analysis of growth which has been presented so far, with self-correcting cycles and the possibility even of a rising rate of growth in industrialising countries, presents a relatively benign view of the world, and it is far from being Malthus's whole view. A major element in his analysis of growth was the role of effective demand in the determination of profits, and how a lack of this must make growth impossible to achieve. His belief that many countries realised none of their growth potential has already been documented. There has been nothing of this kind in the argument so far where cyclical slumps have been the worst that can happen to an economy. There must therefore be more to Malthus's theory of growth, and his account of what actually determines effective demand is what has been missing up to this point.

MALTHUS'S THEORY OF EFFECTIVE DEMAND

The key to Malthus's approach to demand is that a commodity is effectively demanded if it can be sold at a price which covers the necessary costs of production including 'the usual profits upon advances of capital'. A commodity will only be produced if entrepreneurs expect to be able to sell it at a sufficient price:

> If the nature of the object to be obtained requires advances in the shape of capital, as in the vast majority of instances, then by whomsoever this capital is furnished, whether by the labourers

themselves or by others, the commodity will not be produced, unless the estimation in which it is held by the society or its intrinsic value in exchange be such, as not only to replace all the advances of labour and other articles which have been made for its attainment, but likewise to pay the usual profits upon those advances; or, in other words, to command an additional quantity of labour, equal to those profits. (Pr edn2 302)

If profits are adequate in the present, a commodity will continue to be produced for future sale. If profits are insufficient, 'the commodity will not be produced' in future. Profits are therefore crucial because they motivate future production:

By inquiring into the immediate causes of the progress of wealth I clearly mean to inquire mainly into motives. I dont at all wish to deny that some persons or others are entitled to consume all that is produced; but the grand question is whether it is distributed in such a manner between the different parties concerned as to occasion the most effective demand for future produce. (R ix 10)

How must the produce be distributed to motivate future production? A demand for produce from workers alone will not suffice to motivate future production:

And no productive labour will ever be in demand unless the produce when obtained is of greater value than the labour which obtained it. No fresh hands can be employed in any sort of industry merely in consequence of the demand for its produce occasioned by the persons employed. No farmer will take the trouble of superintending the labour of ten additional men merely because his whole produce will then sell in the market at an advanced price just equal to what he had paid his additional labourers. There must be something in the previous state of the demand and supply of the commodity in question, or in its price, antecedent to and independently of the demand occasioned by the new labourers, in order to warrant the employment of an additional number of people in its production. (Pr edn1 348–9)

And

It is indeed most important to observe that no power of consumption on the part of the labouring classes can ever, according to the common motives which influence mankind, alone furnish an encouragement to the employment of capital. As I have before said, nobody will ever employ capital merely for the sake of the demand occasioned by those who work for him. Unless they produce an excess of value above what they consume, which he either wants himself in kind, or which he can advantageously exchange for something which he desires, either for present or future use, it is quite obvious that his capital will not be employed in maintaining them. (Pr edn1 471–2)

From where therefore can adequate demand come to permit the continuing, or better still expanding employment of labour? From the landlords is clearly one possibility:

It may be thought perhaps that the landlords could not fail to supply any deficiency of demand and consumption among the producers, and that between them there would be little chance of any approach towards redundancy of capital. What might be the result of the most favourable distribution of landed property it is not easy to say from experience; but experience certainly tells us that, under the distribution of land which actually takes place in most of the countries in Europe, the demands of the landlords, added to those of the producers, have not always been found sufficient to prevent any difficulty in the employment of capital. (Pr edn1 475)

As for the capitalists, they will be saving rather than consuming, out of a desire to accumulate wealth, so where is sufficient demand to come from?

if the master-producers, from the laudable desire they feel of bettering their condition, and providing for a family, do not consume sufficiently to give an adequate stimulus to the increase of wealth; if the working producers, by increasing their consumption, supposing them to have the means of so doing, would impede the growth of wealth more by diminishing the power of production, than they could encourage it by increasing the demand for produce; and if the expenditure of the landlords, in addition to the expenditure of the two preceding classes, be found insufficient to keep up and increase the value of that which is produced, where are we to look for the consumption required but among the unproductive labourers of Adam Smith?

Every society must have a body of unproductive labourers; as every society, besides the menial servants that are required, must have statesmen to govern it, soldiers to defend it, judges and lawyers to administer justice and protect the rights of individuals, physicians and surgeons to cure diseases and heal wounds, and a body of clergy to instruct the ignorant, and administer the consolations of religion. No civilized state has ever been known to exist without a certain portion of all these classes of society in addition to those who are directly employed in production. To a certain extent therefore they appear to be absolutely necessary. But it is perhaps one of the most important practical questions that can possibly be brought under our view, whether, however necessary and desirable they may be, they must be considered as detracting so much from the material products of a country, and its power of supporting an extended population; or whether they furnish fresh motives to production, and tend to push the wealth of a country farther than it would go without them. (Pr edn1 476–7)

Malthus appears to add the demand for produce by the various classes to see whether in sum there is a sufficient excess over costs of production to produce adequate profits to encourage future production:

There must therefore be a considerable class of persons who have both the will and power to consume more material wealth than they produce, or the mercantile classes could not continue profitably to produce so much more than they consume. In this class the landlords no doubt stand pre-eminent; but if they were not assisted by the great mass of individuals engaged in personal services, whom they maintain, their own consumption would of itself be insufficient to keep up and increase the value of the produce, and enable the increase of its quantity more than to counterbalance the fall of its price. Nor could the capitalists in that case continue with effect the same habits of saving. The deficiency in the value of what they produced would necessarily make them either consume more, or produce less; and when the mere pleasure of present expenditure, without the accompaniments of an improved local situation and an advance in rank, is put in opposition to the continued labour of attending to business during the greatest part of the day, the probability is that a considerable body of them will be induced to prefer the latter alternative, and produce less. But if, in order to balance the demand and supply, a permanent diminution of production takes place, rather than an increase of effective consumption, the whole of the national wealth, which consists of what is produced and consumed, will be decidedly diminished. (Pr edn2 400–1)

Malthus's proposition that insufficient effective demand will produce 'a permanent diminution of production' and a 'decidedly diminished' national wealth appears to rest on a Kalecki-like relationship between a summation of the demand for commodities by the various classes, and the level of commodity production.[11] This relationship can be set out formally to produce Malthus's results.

The total gross incomes received in commodity production, that is, in the 'productive sector' as defined by Malthus, must equal the total *ex post* purchases of domestically produced commodities. Hence

Wages + Profits + Rents ≡ Commodities purchased by productive labour

+ Commodities purchased by unproductive labour in the private sector

+ Commodities purchased by government and with government financed incomes

+ Commidities purchased by capitalists and landlords for private consumption

+ The net increase of the capital stock of the productive sector

+ Exports less imports of commodities

This equation can be simplified:

(i) It can be assumed as is fully implicit in Malthus's work, and indeed in that of Smith and Ricardo, that workers spend their entire incomes on commodities. Hence they don't save and they purchase no services. With this 'classical' assumption, 'Wages' (in commodity production) will equal 'Commodities purchased by productive labour', so these two terms can be cancelled from the equation.

(ii) The total consumption of capitalists and landlords will consist of the physical goods they buy – 'Commodities purchased by capitalists and landlords for private consumption', plus the private services which they purchase. If the private service workers (who derive their entire incomes from this source) buy no services themselves, they will purchase physical commodities with all the money that capitalists and landlords spend on the consumption of private services. Hence, the 'Private consumption (of goods and services) by capitalists and landlords' will equal the sum of, 'Commodities purchased by capitalists and landlords for private consumption' and 'Commodities purchased by unproductive labour in the private sector', and this can be substituted in the equation.

The equation can therefore be rewritten as:

$$
\begin{aligned}
\text{Profits} + \text{Rents} = \; & \text{Private consumption (of goods and services)} \\
& \text{by capitalists and landlords} \\[4pt]
& + \text{Commodities purchased by government} \\
& \quad \text{and with government financed incomes} \\[4pt]
& + \text{Exports less imports of commodities} \\[4pt]
& + \text{The net increase of the capital stock of} \\
& \quad \text{the productive sector}
\end{aligned}
$$

$$(5.1)$$

Now rents will only begin to rise some time *after* farm profits have already risen. In the same way, they will only fall some time after profits fall. As changes in rents are therefore consequential on previous changes in farm profits, it is evident that a rising trend in profits will only be achievable if there is a rising trend in the four items on the right-hand side of this expression, that is, there must be *rising* consumption by landlords, capitalists or the government, or an increase in the trade surplus or in the level of investment. Malthus's argument is even clearer than this, because with his proposition that the theory of capital accumulation is parallel to the theory of population, there will only be a rising trend in investment if there has been some previous expansion of profits. This means that something other than investment must be the first cause of a rising trend in profits, namely growing consumption from private or government financed incomes or an expanding trade surplus.

Similarly, rents will only fall in the short-run after profits have already fallen. The initial fall in profits must be due to a reduction in consumption by capitalists, landlords or the government, or a trade deterioration, and this cut in profits will be followed by a reduction in investment which will reinforce the fall in profits, and produce falling employment if it is sufficiently severe. It must be remembered that investment is quite substantially an advance of wage goods to workers so that they can produce in the following period. If profits are lower in one *year* (the agricultural period) than in the previous one, they will be inadequate in some activities where capitalists will then cease to repeat the production level of the previous year. The above equation and the argument which follows directly from it therefore reproduces much of what Malthus said on effective demand. The influence on profits, effective demand and on future employment of consumption by landlords, capitalists and the government has been very fully documented already. On exports, the following passage may be cited:

It is obvious then that a fall in the value of the precious metals, commencing with a rise in the price of corn, has a strong tendency, while it is going on, to encourage the cultivation of fresh land and the formation of increased rents.

A similar effect would be produced in a country which continued to feed its own people, by a great and increasing demand for its manufactures. These manufactures, if from such a demand the money value of their amount in foreign countries was greatly to increase, would bring back a great increase of money value in return, which increase could not fail to increase the money price of labour and raw produce. The demand for agricultural as well as manufactured produce would thus be augmented (Pr edn2 166)

Perhaps the clearest indication that the relationship set out in the above expression goes to the core of Malthus's argument is the structure of his argument 'On the Progress of Wealth' which is, in effect, the second Part of the *Principles of Political Economy*. After a brief introduction, Section II is entitled, 'Of the Increase of Population considered as a Stimulus to the continued Increase of Wealth', Section III, 'Of Accumulation, or the Saving from Revenue to add to Capital, considered as a Stimulus to the Increase of Wealth', Section IV, 'Of the Fertility of the Soil, considered as a Stimulus to the continued Increase of Wealth', and Section V, 'Of Inventions to save Labour, considered as a Stimulus to the continued Increase of Wealth'. These Sections are all concerned with the supply-side factors which may contribute to growth, and Malthus concludes Section V with the paragraph:

> The three great causes most favourable to production are, accumulation of capital, fertility of soil, and inventions to save labour. They all act in the same direction; and as they all tend to facilitate supply, without reference to demand, it is not probable that they should either separately or conjointly afford an adequate stimulus to the continued increase of wealth. (Pr edn2 360)

These Sections can be likened to the left-hand side of an arch. The top of the arch is Section VI, 'Of the Necessity of a Union of the Powers of Production with the Means of Distribution, in order to ensure a continued Increase of Wealth'. It opens:

> We have seen that the powers of production, to whatever extent they may exist, are not alone sufficient to secure the creation of a proportionate degree of wealth. Something else seems to be necessary in order to call these powers fully into action. This is an effectual and unchecked demand for all that is produced.
> (Pr edn2 361)

The right-hand side of the arch consists of the demand-side factors which contribute to growth: Section VII, 'Of the Distribution occasioned by the Division of landed Property considered as the Means of increasing the exchangeable Value of the whole Produce', and Section VIII, 'Of the Distribution occasioned by Commerce, internal and external, considered as the Means of increasing the exchangeable value of Produce', and Section IX, 'Of the Distribution occasioned by personal services and unproductive Consumers, considered as the Means of increasing the exchangeable Value of the Whole Produce'. These three demand-side headings come close to describing the terms of the right-hand side of equation (5.1).

There, profits are favourably affected by higher consumption by landlords and capitalists, which the break-up of the great estates favours:

> It is physically possible indeed for a nation, with a comparatively small body of very rich proprietors, and a large body of very poor workmen, to push both the produce of the land and manufactures to the greatest extent, that the resources and ingenuity of the country would admit...but, in order to call them forth, we must suppose a passion among the rich for the consumption of manufactures, and the results of productive labour, much more excessive than has ever been witnessed in human society. And the consequence is, that no instance has ever been known of a country which has pushed its natural resources to a great extent, with a small proportionate body of persons of property, however rich and luxurious they might be. Practically it has always been found that the excessive wealth of the few is in no respect equivalent, with regard to effective demand, to the more moderate wealth of the many. A large body of manufacturers and merchants can only find a market for their commodities among a numerous class of consumers above the rank of mere workmen and labourers.
> (Pr edn1 430–1)

Therefore the 'division of landed property,' the subject of one of the three demand-side Sections of Malthus's argument, will undoubtedly raise the consumption of the landlords and capitalists which is one of the three determinants of the change of profits in the equation. The correspondence between the other two, government financed expenditure and exports less imports, and the subjects of the further demand-side Sections of Malthus's argument, namely the influence of unproductive consumption and of commerce, both internal and external, on demand does not require further explanation.

The argument can now move a stage further. Malthus believed that inadequate strength of the demand-side factors could 'produce only, after the lapse of many thousand years, the scanty riches and scanty population, which are at present scattered over the face of the globe'. He believed that, 'without [an easy subdivision of landed property], a country with great natural resources might slumber for ages with an uncultivated soil, and a scanty yet starving population' (Pr edn1 440). A complete account of Malthus's theory of effective demand and growth therefore requires a model where growth will be *an impossibility* if the demand-side factors are too weak.

The need for a significant capitalist class if a society is to achieve economic development provides the clue to Malthus's theory of why some societies stagnate indefinitely. The most direct way of showing how sustained growth will be impossible to achieve in these less fortunate societies is to contrast their investment with their savings potential. The argument is stated rigorously in the next section, but its essence can be outlined very simply. Most of a society's net investments are made by capitalists but saving may come from either capitalists or landlords. Therefore if a society's full potential savings are to be successfully invested, capitalists must be willing to borrow that part of a nation's total income that landlords are prepared to save. If land forms the bulk of wealth and there is no significant capitalist class, landlords' potential saving will find no outlet. Capitalists will be too few to borrow more than a small fraction of what landlords wish to save, and indeed the financial institutions which can enable them to borrow on a substantial scale will only exist in more advanced societies. If investment cannot reach the level of landlords' potential savings, the market demand for farm produce will necessarily have to settle at a level which is so low that the element of landlords' incomes which is received in the form of money is insufficient to incline them to save.

If on the contrary capitalists are numerous and prosperous, these will readily borrow whatever savings landlords make available in addition to reinvesting their own profits. There will then be no fundamental lack of effective demand, though there may of course be temporary deficiencies in the course of the cycle, and there will be no fundamental obstacle to growth in profits and investment of the kind that will be found in economies where a capitalist class is lacking.

The emergence of a significant capitalist class is therefore indispensable for economic development, but this will only materialise if there are adequate incentives to 'spend eight hours a day in a counting-house'. In the absence of luxuries on which higher incomes can be spent and the commercial opportunities that international trade can provide, an economy will merely contain landlords with little incentive to see that their land is farmed efficiently, and workers with no opportunity to better their condition.

Once a significant capitalist class emerges, it is essential that landlords' saving be kept down to a level that capitalists can comfortably borrow. Continual growth requires a willingness by capitalists to borrow that is not swamped by landlords' saving. If landlords' saving potential persistently runs ahead of the borrowing of the capitalist class, effective demand cannot rise, and it is shown in the next section of this chapter (where these crucial interrelationships are set out formally) that this means that profits cannot then increase, with the result that economic development can at no point be sustained.

Malthus had a number of policy suggestions which were actually designed to reduce landlords' savings to a level that capitalists could comfortably borrow. One way of achieving this was actually to increase the money supply which would transfer purchasing power from rentiers to capitalists:

> if such a distribution of the circulating medium were to take place, as to throw the command of the produce of the country chiefly into the hands of the productive classes, – that is, if considerable portions of the currency were taken from the idle, and those who live upon fixed incomes, and transferred to farmers, manufacturers and merchants – the proportion between capital and revenue would be greatly altered to the advantage of capital; and in a short time, the produce of the country would be greatly augmented.
>
> Whenever, in the actual state of things, a fresh issue of notes comes into the hands of those who mean to employ them in the prosecution and extension of a profitable business, a difference in the distribution of the circulating medium takes place, similar in kind to that which has been last supposed...all the industrious classes – all those that sell as well as buy, are, during the progressive rise of prices, making unusual profits; and, even when this progression stops, are left with the command of a greater portion of the annual produce than they possessed previous to the new issues. (Occ 96)

Despite this instance, when a purely monetary expansion raises effective demand by increasing profits relative to rentier incomes, Malthus did not advocate deficit financing. He actually argued that effective demand should be raised through what would nowadays be called a balanced-budget-multiplier expansion, involving the taxing of landlords to finance extra unproductive consumers who would spend what the landlords might partly save. He argued that taxation fell predominantly on rents:

> Though it is by no means true, as stated by the Economists, that all taxes fall on the neat rents of the landlords, yet it is certainly true that they have little power of relieving themselves. It is also true that they possess a fund more disposable, and better adapted for taxation than any other. They are in consequence more frequently taxed, both directly and indirectly. And if they pay, as they certainly do, many of the taxes which fall on the capital of the farmer and the wages of the labourer, as well as those directly imposed on themselves, they must necessarily feel it in the diminution of that portion of the whole produce, which under other circumstances would have fallen to their share. (Pr edn1 204)

The unproductive consumers who are supported by taxation will, by implication, consume more than the landlord taxpayers:

> The effect therefore on national wealth of those classes of unpro- ductive labourers which are supported by taxation, must be very various in different countries, and must depend entirely upon the powers of production, and upon the manner in which the taxes are raised in each country. As great powers of production are neither likely to be called into action, or, when once in action, kept in activity without great consumption, I feel very little doubt that instances have practically occurred of national wealth being greatly stimulated by the consumption of those who have been supported by taxes. (Pr edn1 480–1)

If taxation falls predominantly on the landlords, and greatly reduces their saving without at the same time significantly reducing the real resources of the capitalist class, and Malthus actually indicates that landlords will pay 'many' such taxes as 'fall on the capital of the farmer', an increase in taxation together with a corresponding increase in government expenditure will reduce landlords' saving relative to the investment that capitalists wish to finance, and high enough taxation could presumably eliminate the saving of landlords altogether, which must favour effective demand and its growth.

A further element in the range of policies which is relevant to encouraging the growth of capitalist incomes in relation to rentier incomes of all kinds is of course the break-up of the largest estates into smaller ones, which, as has been shown, Malthus favoured. He argued that the growth of industrial and commercial capital is encouraged by a proliferation of small landowners rather than a handful of great estates:

> The possessor of numerous estates, after he had furnished his mansion or castle splendidly, and provided himself with handsome clothes and handsome carriages, would not change them all every two months, merely because he had the power of doing it. Instead of indulging in such useless and troublesome changes, he would be more likely to keep a number of servants and idle dependants ... Thirty or forty proprietors, with incomes answering to between one thousand and five thousand a year, would create a much more effective demand for wheaten bread, good meat, and manufactured products, than a single proprietor possessing a hundred thousand a year...
>
>   And experience shews us that manufacturing wealth is at once the consequence of a better distribution of property, and the cause of further improvements in such distribution, by the increase in the proportion of the middle classes of society, which the growth of manufacturing and mercantile capital cannot fail to create.
> (Pr edn1 430–1)

A high ratio of capitalist incomes in relation to rentier incomes is essential if stagnation is to be avoided, and it will be evident from the above passages that Malthus himself attached very great importance to this. It was his view that in early nineteenth-century Britain, saving actually did come predominantly from profits, and this is obviously a precondition for growth in the present restatement of his argument. In the early nineteenth century when capital markets were relatively unsophisticated, capitalists could reinvest their saving from their own profits, and some could invest more as a result of fixed interest loans of limited size, but capitalists as a whole could hardly be expected to invest that much more than they saved. It was therefore absolutely essential if a rising trend of profits and investment was to be achieved, that the bulk of rents had to be consumed, either by the landlords themselves, or indirectly through the government.

It might be asked why the self-correcting cycle explained at the start of the chapter should not lift the economy out of a slump, even when landlords' saving was excessive. The problem is that where *ex ante* demand is below *ex ante* supply at the existing price level, prices will fall, and:

> As long as this fall in the money price of produce continues to diminish the power of commanding domestic and foreign labour, a great discouragement to production must obviously continue; and if, after labour has adjusted itself to the new level of prices, the permanent distribution of the produce and the permanent tastes and habits of the people should not be favourable to an adequate degree of consumption, the clearest principles of political economy shew that the profits of stock might be lower for any length of time than the state of the land rendered necessary; and that the check to production might be as permanent as the faulty distribution of the produce and the unfavourable tastes and habits which had occasioned it. (Pr edn1 446–7)

Ought not population growth to be encouraged by the higher real wage that should accompany falling commodity prices and a low rate of profit? Should this not force the wage down and profits up again to produce the recovery phase in the self-correcting cycle that was outlined at the start of the chapter? Malthus thought not, because the real income *of a family*, which is what actually determines population growth, will not be high where effective demand is low:

> There is another cause, besides a change in the habits of the people, which prevents the population of a country from keeping pace with the apparent command of the labourer over the means of subsistence. It sometimes happens that wages are for a time rather higher than they ought to be, in proportion to the demand for labour. This is the most likely to take place when the price of raw produce has fallen in value, so as to diminish the power of the cultivators to employ the same or an increasing number of labourers at the same price. If the fall be considerable, and not made up in value by increase of quantity, so many labourers will be thrown out of work that wages, after a period of great distress, will generally be lowered in proportion. But if the fall be gradual, and partly made up in exchangeable value by increase of quantity, the money wages of labour will not necessarily sink; and the result will be merely a slack demand for labour, not sufficient perhaps to throw the actual labourers out of work, but such as to prevent or

diminish task-work, to check the employment of women and children, and to give but little encouragement to the rising generation of labourers. In this case the quantity of the necessaries of life actually earned by the labourer and his family, may be really less than when, owing to a rise of prices, the daily pay of the labourer will command a smaller quantity of corn. The command of the labouring classes over the necessaries of life, though apparently greater, is really less in the former than in the latter case, and, upon all general principles, ought to produce less effect on the increase of population. (Pr edn1 257–8)

If a labourer commands a peck instead of ¾ of a peck of wheat a day in consequence of a rise of wages occasioned by a demand for labour, it is certain that all labourers may be employed who are willing and able to work, and probably also their wives and children; but if he is able to command this additional quantity of wheat on account of a fall in the price of corn which diminishes the capital of the farmer, the advantage may be more apparent than real, and though labour for some time may not nominally fall, yet as the demand for labour may be stationary, if not retrograde, its current price will not be a certain criterion of what might be earned by the united labours of a large family, or the increased exertions of the head of it in task-work.

It is obvious, therefore, that the same current corn wages will, under different circumstances, have a different effect in the encouragement of population. (Pr edn1 289–90)

In other words, where demand is slack, profits *and the earnings of a family* can be low at the same time, so there will be no encouragement to population. Low effective demand leads to both low profits *and low productivity* – per family – and this in turn leads to slack work through the various incentive effects, and a slower rate of 'improvement' and indeed 'the check to production might be as permanent as the faulty distribution of the produce and the unfavourable tastes and habits which had occasioned it'. An economy can thus be trapped in a situation where effective demand, earnings, incentives, and profits are all low, and there is no way out of this trap apart from a change in the 'faulty distribution of the produce'.

That appears to be Malthus's theory of underdevelopment, and of how an advanced economy can relapse if it oversaves and underspends. If, where effective demand is low, profits are low and the output of a family is also reduced, profits and real incomes per family – which is what determines population – can of course be low at the same time, as Malthus insisted.

It may be added that as rents are fixed in money terms during the ten- to twenty-year period of a typical agricultural lease, the falling farm prices which are a central feature of Malthus's account of the effects of a lack of effective demand may raise money rents relative to farmers' money receipts. Less will then remain to pay wages and profits until leases come up for renewal. A fall in effective demand may then reduce the sum of wages and profits for ten to twenty years, which is therefore another reason why these may both be low at the same time for quite long enough to produce prolonged distress. But can a relatively advanced country like Britain actually relapse to the state of chronic underdevelopment to which Malthus believed that lack of effective demand condemned most of his world?

In the 1820 edition of the *Principles of Political Economy*, he wrote, 'it is obvious that the adoption of parsimonious habits in too great a degree may be accompanied by the most distressing effects at first, and by a marked depression of wealth and population permanently' (Pr edn1 369). In the posthumously published edition of 1836 there is merely, 'a marked depression of wealth and population afterwards' (Pr edn2 326). The account of self-correcting cycles in the *Definitions of Political Economy* of 1827 which has been quoted is not qualified with the reservation that recovery may not occur. On the contrary, he wrote, 'The causes above mentioned act powerfully to prevent the permanence either of glut or scarcity' (Def 62). But the posthumous edition of the *Principles of Political Economy* leaves quite unaltered the statements about the large areas of the world which are underdeveloped for lack of effective demand. It may well be that in 1820 Malthus held the view that an 'impossibility of growth' argument was applicable to Britain. By 1827 he had perhaps become confident that Britain had safely reached the territory of self-correcting cycles, but there were still many countries far less fortunate which could not start to develop because of a 'faulty distribution of their produce'. These had landlords' incomes which were so unequally distributed that the potential savings from rents exceeded what a scarcely emergent capitalist class could be expected to borrow. That arguably is the essence of Malthus's theory of how a lack of effective demand prevented most of the countries in his world from developing their potentially abundant natural resources.

* A MALTHUS GROWTH MODEL

It will now be shown how a simple mathematical restatement of Malthus's theory of effective demand and growth can be set out.

Equations for the functions in the two diagrams (Figures 4.3 and 5.1) which show how the economy's equilibrium wage, its equilibrium rate of profit and its equilibrium rate of growth are determined can be set out simply and straightforwardly.

LL, the population supply function, can be written as:

$$n = \alpha (W - W_s) \tag{5.2}$$

where W is the wage measured in commodities, W_s is the wage where the labour force is constant, n is the rate of growth of the labour force, and α is a positive constant.

KK, the population supply function applied to capital, can be written similarly as:

$$k = \beta (r - r_s) \tag{5.3}$$

where r is the rate of profit, r_s is the rate of profit where the capital stock is constant, k is the rate of growth of the capital stock, and β is a positive constant.

$D_L D_L$ and $D_K D_K$ are derived with the help of the basic relationship:

$$Z(Y/L) = W(1 + r F) \tag{5.4}$$

where Y/L is average output per worker in the commodity-producing sector of the economy, and $(1 - Z)$ is the ratio of rents in total output so that $Z(Y/L)$ is that part of output per worker which is available for wages and profits. If circulating capital to pay wages one period in advance of production were the sole form of capital $Z(Y/L)$ would pay wages of W, plus profits of Wr to compensate capitalists for the need to advance wages, which would come to $W(1 + r)$. If total capital per worker is F times the wage, the capitalists will need to receive WFr, so $Z(Y/L)$ will equal $W(1 + rF)$ as in equation (5.4).

Malthus himself made a similar assumption in response to the problem:

> But it will be asked, how are we to compare the value of the

produce with the labour required to obtain it, when the advances of the capitalist do not consist of labour alone. (Pr edn2 267)

He assumed, neglecting the complications due to the influence of income distribution on the relative value of fixed to circulating capital:

> In cases of this kind, the following very simple mode of proceeding presents itself. It will be allowed that the capitalist generally expects an equal profit upon all the parts of the capital which he advances. Let us suppose that a certain portion of the value of his advances, one-fourth for instance, consists of the wages of im-mediate labour (Pr edn2 267–8).

Malthus then works through a series of examples where the financing of wages paid in advance requires one-quarter of total capital, however wages fluctuate, while fixed capital forms most of the remaining three-quarters. In these examples, he makes assumptions very close to those which lie behind the above formula with $F = 4$, so it does correspond to his own way of setting out the relationship between output per worker, the wage, and the rate of profit.

The schedule $L_D L_D$ which is needed to provide a functional relationship between the wage and the rate of growth of capital for Figure 4.3 can be derived from (5.3) and (5.4):

$$W = \frac{Z(Y/L)}{1 + F(r_s + \dfrac{k}{\beta})} \qquad (5.5)$$

(5.2) and (5.5) together now provide the two schedules of Figure 4.3 which link the wage to the rate of growth. As (5.2) must slope upwards with n, and (5.5) must slope downwards with k, they can only intersect at one rate of growth where $n = k$. It is evident that the equilibrium wage at this rate of growth must lie between a lower limit set by the subsistence wage, W_s (from schedule (5.2)), and an upper limit of:

$$\frac{Z(Y/L)}{1 + Fr_s}$$

derived from (5.5). Hence wages will be higher, *ceteris paribus*, the higher the wage that is needed to keep population constant. 'Moral restraint' will therefore raise the standard of living of the working class as Malthus reiterated on innumerable occasions from 1798 onwards. The equilibrium wage will also vary with Y/L. Higher labour productivity, that is, a higher Y/L, will permit higher profits and therefore faster capital accumulation, which will raise the equilibrium wage. The precise equilibrium values of the wage, the rate of profit and the rate of growth cannot be derived until Malthus's propositions on the influence of effective demand on productivity growth are brought into the argument after the next paragraph, but a certain amount can be inferred from Figure 4.3 alone, together with equations (5.2) and (5.5).

Turning to Figure 5.1 and the determination of the equilibrium rate of profit from the schedules KK and $D_K D_K$, the schedule $D_K D_K$ is derived from (5.2) and (5.4):

$$r = \frac{1}{F} \left(\frac{Z(Y/L)}{W_s + \dfrac{n}{\alpha}} - 1 \right) \tag{5.6}$$

and this must slope downwards with n, while KK slopes upward with k, so again the two schedules can only intersect once where $k = n$. The rate of profit must lie between a lower limit of r_s (from (5.3)) and an upper limit of:

$$\frac{1}{F} \left(\frac{Z(Y/L)}{W_s} - 1 \right)$$

(from (5.6)), so higher output per worker will also influence this favourably.

In Malthus's argument the economy's equilibrium rate of growth where population growth equals the rate of capital accumulation will be strongly influenced by effective demand, because the rate of productivity growth (or the rate of 'improvements') will depend on this. Effective demand in turn will depend on profitability, for the reasons which were outlined in the previous sections. A possible function to show the influence of profitability on technical progress could be written as:

$$a = a_0 + a_1 (r - r_s) \tag{5.7}$$

where a is the rate of technical progress, formulated below as an annual augmentation of a production function, while a_0 and a_1 are the parameters of this technical progress function. This produces the result that the rate of technical progress varies with the rate of profit, which in turn depends on the demand for aggregate output in relation to supply – which was the key factor in motivation as Malthus reiterated. In view of the significance which Malthus also attached to the range of goods available, it should be recognised that a_0 will be higher, the greater the significance of industry and commerce in the total output of the economy.[12] It may suffice to write that:

$$a_0 = f \left(\frac{Y - Y_a + T}{Y} \right) \tag{5.8}$$

$f' > 0$ (subject to the constraint that $Y_a > C_a$)

where Y is total physical output, Y_a is agricultural output and C_a the domestic consumption of food, while T represents international trade. Hence it is assumed, following Malthus's argument, that the rate of technical progress (or the rate of 'improvement' as he would call it), will vary with the proportion of manufacturing output in total output, and with the extent of international trade. The constraint that agricultural output should at least equal domestic consumption is necessary because Malthus was convinced, and reiterated in a series of publications, that great dangers of several kinds were involved in any significant dependence on imported food.[13]

Growth does not depend solely on technical progress: it is also influenced by capital accumulation and the growth of the labour force. As capital–labour substitutability plays a subordinate role in Malthus's various explanations of economic development,[14] a production function which allowed this to have a significant effect on the rate of growth would be misleading. It is more accurate to assume that the growth of Y depends on technical progress – the rate at which 'improvements' are occurring – and on the rate of growth of the labour force, which is interdependent with the rate of growth of the capital stock in the manner set out above. There will, of course, be diminishing returns from the employment of extra labour in agriculture, which is one of Malthus's first and most fundamental propositions. The consequent production function can be written as:

$$Y = \Phi \, e^{at} L^Z \qquad (1 > Z > 0) \tag{5.9}$$

where Φ is a constant, L is labour employed, and Z is less than 1 to an extent which depends on the strength of diminishing returns in agriculture. Z would, of course, equal 1 with constant returns. With competitive factor pricing, which would reflect Malthus's thinking, $(1 - Z)$ will be the share of rents in total commodity output as in equation (5.4). Z will increase over time for two reasons. First Malthus believed that there was a historical tendency for the share of rents to fall in agriculture (Pr edn1 176–7). Second, the share of rents in total output will fall in so far as the share of agriculture falls. Hence, like a_0 from the technical progress function, Z rises through time if $(Y - Y_a)/Y$ rises.

From (5.9) it is possible to obtain a growth equation for each constant value of Z. If g is the rate of growth of commodity output:

$$g = a + Zn \tag{5.10}$$

and equation (5.7) can be used to substitute for a to obtain:

$$g = a_0 + a_1 (r - r_s) + Zn \tag{5.11}$$

Now, $(r - r_s)$ equals k/β from the investment function (5.3) so that:

$$g = a_0 + a_1 \left(\frac{k}{\beta}\right) + Zn \tag{5.12}$$

and in equilibrium growth where output, capital and labour all grow at the same rate:

$$g = k = n = \frac{a_0}{1 - Z - a_1/\beta} \tag{5.13}$$

Thus the economy's equilibrium rate of growth will depend on the coefficients of the technical progress function, a_0 and a_1, and on the coefficient of the investment function, β. It will also depend on the strength of the diminishing returns factors in the productive process, represented by $(1 - Z)$ – which equals the share of rents in total commodity production. If $(1 - Z)$ becomes lower as a result of industrialisation, as well as because of the natural tendency for the share of rents in agricultural output to fall, the economy's equilibrium rate of growth will become faster according to equation (5.13). Industrialisation will also raise the equilibrium rate of growth because there will then be a more favourable production function with a higher a_o in industry, and here Malthus followed Smith. A vital factor is that through its effect on motivation, industrialisation also leads to a faster rate of advance in agricultural productivity.

Provided that $(1 - Z - a_1/\beta)$ remains positive, there will be a steady growth path for each value of Z where output, capital and the labour force can grow in line with each other in the very long run. It was entirely Malthus's view that the strength of diminishing returns in agriculture, and the significance of agriculture in the standard of living of the working class, would ensure that output and the capital stock would not grow faster than the labour force in the very long run. The Malthusian population supply mechanism would always ensure that the growth of the labour force could be expected to catch up with the growth of output if this moved temporarily ahead. There is no doubt, therefore, that in a Malthus growth model, Z is always sufficiently below 1 to keep $(1 - Z - a_1/\beta)$ positive.

With the advantages of hindsight it can now be said that at some point in the eighteenth and nineteenth centuries output and the capital stock started to grow substantially faster than the labour force in some fortunate countries, with the result that these actual economies broke clear of this constraint. In the present model, output, capital and labour simply *cannot* grow in line with each other if $(1 - Z - a_1/\beta)$ once becomes negative, and output and the capital stock can then race ahead of the labour force to produce the strong rising trend in living standards which so many economies have experienced in the past century. Malthus never thought this possible. His own world, and his detailed study of the published evidence from other countries convinced him that capital and output would only grow substantially faster than the labour force in transitory periods while the economy was benefiting from some favourable institutional change. With given institutions and 'habits' economies would settle down to growth rates where *living standards* rose slowly if at all – results entirely compatible with an equation like (5.13).

The equilibrium wage which results from this process is, of course, above subsistence. When equation (5.13) is substituted into the basic population supply and capital supply equations (5.2) and (5.3), to produce expressions for the equilibrium wage and the equilibrium rate of profit in Figures 4.3 and 5.1:

$$W = W_s + \frac{a_0/\alpha}{1 - Z - a_1/\beta} \tag{5.14}$$

and

$$r = r_s + \frac{a_0/\beta}{1 - Z - a_1/\beta} \qquad (5.15)$$

so both the equilibrium wage and the equilibrium rate of profit that the earlier argument produced will be influenced by the strength of the technical progress function. Moreover, if there is a historical tendency for Z and for a_0 to rise with industrialisation, the appropriate steady growth wage and profit rates will rise as the parameters of the model become increasingly favourable.

Equation (5.13) shows the economy's long-term potential rate of growth of supply. It is central to Malthus's argument that the rate of growth of effective demand may fall short of this. The determination of the rate of growth of demand must therefore be explained. It was shown above (equation (5.1) on page 156) that in Malthus's argument:

> Profits + Rents = Private consumption (of goods and services) by capitalists and landlords
>
> + Commodities purchased by government and with government financed incomes
>
> + Exports less imports of commodities
>
> + The net increase of the capital stock of the productive sector

It is clear from the Malthusian investment function (equation (5.3)), that aggregate investment will depend on aggregate profits. If the argument now goes over to period analysis, and, for later simplicity, makes investment depend solely on r, the rate of profit, and no longer on the excess of this over r_s, a required minimum profit rate, the investment function can be written as, $k_t = \beta r_{t-1}$, and since:

$$k = \frac{\text{investment}}{\text{capital}} \quad \text{and} \quad r = \frac{\text{profits}}{\text{capital}}$$

the investment function can be written as:[15]

$$(\text{Investment})_t = \beta (\text{Profits})_{t-1} \qquad 1 > \beta > 0 \qquad (5.16)$$

Moreover, with the assumption of a balanced budget which is justified since Malthus did not advocate deficit financing, and the further assumption that all taxes fall on capitalists and landlords who alone produce a taxable surplus, 'Taxes paid by capitalists and landlords' can be substituted for 'Commodities purchased by government and with government financed incomes', and if it is also assumed for simplicity that imports equal exports, equation (5.1) can be rewritten as:

(Profits − consumption and taxes paid by capitalists)$_t$
+ (Rents − consumption and taxes paid by landlords)$_t$
− β (Profits)$_{t-1}$ = 0

$$(5.17)$$

If s_c is written for the fraction of their pre-tax incomes which capitalists save, and s_r for the fraction of pre-tax rents that landlords save, while P is written for *total profits*, and R for *total rents*, this expression can be rewritten as:

$$s_c P_t + s_r R_t - β P_{t-1} = 0$$

so that

$$\frac{β}{s_c} \left(\frac{P_{t-1}}{P_t} \right) = 1 + \frac{s_r}{s_c} \left(\frac{R_t}{P_t} \right)$$

and since

$$1 + \frac{s_r R_t}{s_c P_t} \quad \text{equals} \quad \frac{\text{total saving}}{\text{saving from profits}}$$

$$\frac{P_t}{P_{t-1}} = \frac{β}{s_c} \left(\frac{\text{saving from profits}}{\text{total saving}} \right) \qquad (5.18)$$

Moreover, it is evident from equation (5.16) that:

$$I_t/I_{t-1} = P_{t-1}/P_{t-2}$$

so that

$$\frac{I_{t+1}}{I_t} = \frac{P_t}{P_{t-1}} = \frac{\beta}{s_c} \left(\frac{\text{saving from profits}}{\text{total saving}} \right)_t \qquad (5.19)$$

The modern economic principle which lies behind this equation is the necessary relationship between saving and investment. To produce stationary demand conditions in a closed economy (and equation (5.19) is derived with that assumption) planned investment must equal planned saving, and this will come about if capitalists who are responsible for all investment decisions plan to invest in excess of their saving, precisely the aggregate amount that landlords save. This will ensue if β/s_c, the ratio of capitalists' investment to capitalists' saving, is precisely equal to the ratio 'total saving/saving from profits', and in this event the right-hand side of equation (5.19) will come to unity which will then produce stationary levels of profits and investment. If β/s_c exceeds 'total saving/saving from profits', capitalists will plan to invest more than they save to an extent greater than that needed to absorb landlords' saving, and demand will in consequence expand. In equation (5.19) the right-hand side will exceed unity where β/s_c exceeds 'total saving/saving from profits', to produce a rising investment and profits trend. Demand will of course contract if β/s_c is less than 'total saving/saving from profits'.

Hence a rising trend in investment, profits and of course effective demand is only a possibility at all if β/s_c, the ratio of the coefficient of capitalists' investment to profits to the coefficient of their savings to profits, exceeds the ratio 'total saving/saving from profits'. With a very small capitalist class in relation to the landlords, or a greater tendency for capitalists to save than to invest, growth will be a sheer impossibility.

To realise a country's full growth potential, it is not of course sufficient that profits and investment achieve a rising trend. The trend must be strong enough to raise profits, investment and demand at a rate at least equal to the economy's long-term growth potential and equation (5.15) showed that the economy's maximum sustainable rate of growth is:

$$\frac{a_0}{1 - Z - a_1/\beta}$$

so there is a final equation which must be fulfilled if this rate of growth is actually to be achievable, that is:

$$\frac{\beta}{s_c} \left(\frac{\text{saving from profits}}{\text{total saving}} \right) - 1 \geq \frac{a_0}{1 - Z - a_1/\beta} \qquad (5.20)$$

The left-hand side of this final equation shows the growth of profits and investment, and this will need to be at least as great as the growth of potential output shown on the right-hand side. An economy will not be prevented from achieving its maximum growth potential in the long-term if the demand-side factors on the left-hand side of this equation are stronger than the supply-side factors on the right. A cycle of the kind set out above will hold down the rate of growth of demand during the slump phase of the cycle, so that over the cycle as a whole, demand on average grows no more rapidly than potential supply.

If, however, the right-hand side of this equation exceeds the left-hand side, effective demand will grow persistently more slowly than the potential rate of growth of supply. There will then be no way in which the country in question can realise its long-term growth potential. It is therefore vital that the left-hand side of equation (5.20) should equal or exceed the right-hand side. This can only occur if there is a capitalist class large enough to allow most saving to come from profits and not from rents.

Equation (5.20) also describes some of the conditions which must be met if the savings propensity is to be optimal when the equation will become an equality. Malthus was himself convinced that there was an optimum savings ratio:[16]

> Adam Smith has stated, that capitals are increased by parsimony, that every frugal man is a public benefactor, and that the increase of wealth depends upon the balance of produce above consumption. That these propositions are true to a great extent is perfectly unquestionable...but it is quite obvious that they are not true to an indefinite extent, and that the principle of saving, pushed to excess, would destroy the motive to production. If every person were satisfied with the simplest food, the poorest clothing, and the meanest houses, it is certain that no other sort of food, clothing, and lodging would be in existence...If consumption exceed production, the capital of the country must be diminished, and its wealth must be gradually destroyed from its want of power to

produce; if production be in a great excess above consumption, the motive to accumulate and produce must cease from the want of will to consume. The two extremes are obvious; and it follows that there must be some intermediate point, though the resources of political economy may not be able to ascertain it, where, taking into consideration both the power to produce and the will to consume, the encouragement to the increase of wealth is the greatest. (Pr edn1 8–9)

With a more sophisticated model a tangency condition would need to be found for the optimum savings ratio, and indeed for the optimum ratio of unproductive consumption which Malthus also presumed to exist (Pr edn1 489–90). With the present elementary restatement where there is no possibility of capital–labour substitution, and no utility function for present and future consumption because Malthus never referred to anything of this kind, there is merely the equality for the optimum savings ratio indicated by equation (5.20).

Malthus, like Keynes, was a Mathematics Wrangler at Cambridge – he was 9th Wrangler in 1788, while Keynes was 12th Wrangler in 1905. For a variety of reasons neither made significant use of mathematics to explain their theories of effective demand, but Keynes's theory has been extensively restated in the language of mathematics by others. It has been shown here that no particular problems arise in presenting a simple mathematical statement of some of Malthus's most fundamental propositions. It goes without saying that he himself would have wished to offer a richer analysis – as he did in plain English. It has not been widely perceived that a logical analytical structure lies behind his prose.

MALTHUS'S THEORY OF EFFECTIVE DEMAND AND THE SECONDARY LITERATURE

In conclusion, there are at least two features of the present restatement of Malthus's argument which may surprise some of those who have studied the literature on his theory of effective demand. The first is the lack of any reference to the rate of interest. There has in fact been no reference to the rate of interest because Malthus himself made none when he was considering these vital matters. Malthus has been criticised for failing to recognise its significance.[17] An investment function which attributed investment to profits was the one on which Malthus focused attention in the early nineteenth century, precisely because this may well have been the appropriate assumption at a time when there were not financial markets in the private sector sufficiently sophisticated to allow *a high fraction* of investment to be financed by borrowing at a competitively determined interest rate. Until 1833 there were even usury laws, though easily evadable ones, which fixed the maximum legal rate of interest at 5 per cent.[18] It is anachronistic to expect Malthus to write as if sophisticated modern capital markets with an equilibrating rate of interest to reconcile the needs of would-be savers and investors was already in existence. There may indeed be economists today who consider Malthus's assumption of profit determined *ex ante* investment more relevant to the determination of the rate of investment than the assumption of an investment function where the rate of interest is especially significant.

A second point of departure from the work of several scholars is the suggestion that Malthus had distinct saving and investment functions, in other words, that there are different functional relationships between investment and profits and saving and profits. It has been argued by several scholars that he assumed that saving and investment were identical.[19] The textual substantiation for this assumption is partly derived from the Section of *Principles of Political Economy* entitled 'Of Accumulation, or the Saving from Revenue to Add to Capital, considered as a Stimulus to the Increase of Wealth'. In this Section he very carefully outlined what the effects would be of a willingness to reinvest substantial *ex ante* savings, but that assumption is almost wholly confined to this Section where reinvestment is an expository assumption.

A further quotation on which weight has been placed in the secondary literature is the italicised passage below.[20] This is from the Section of the *Principles of Political Economy*, 'On Productive and Unproductive Labour' from the Chapter, 'On the Definitions of Wealth and Productive Labour':

> Almost all the lower classes of people of every society are employed in some way or other, and if there were no grounds of distinction in their employments, with reference to their effects on the national wealth, it is difficult to conceive what would be the use of saving from revenue to add to capital, as it would be merely employing one set of people in preference to another, when, according to the hypothesis, there is no essential difference

between them. How then are we to explain the nature of saving, and the different effects of parsimony and extravagance upon the national capital? *No political economist of the present day can by saving mean mere hoarding*; and beyond this contracted and inefficient proceeding, no use of the term, in reference to national wealth, can well be imagined, but that which must arise from a different application of what is saved, founded upon a real distinction between the different kinds of labour which may be maintained by it.

If the labour of menial servants be as productive of wealth as the labour of manufacturers, why should not savings be employed in their maintenance, not only without being dissipated, but with a constant increase of value? But menial servants, lawyers, or physicians, who save from their salaries, are fully aware that their savings would be immediately dissipated again if they were advanced to themselves instead of being employed in the maintenance of persons of a different description. (Pr edn1 32–3)

I am hardly aware how the causes of the increasing riches and prosperity of Europe since the feudal times could be traced, if we were to consider personal services as equally productive of wealth with the labours of merchants and manufactures. (Pr edn1 35)

It will be evident that in this section, Malthus was primarily concerned with the correct borderline between the productive and unproductive sectors of the economy – and its significance – and the reference to hoarding comes in quite incidentally. There is therefore not much weight in the sentence in question to substantiate the interpretation of the secondary literature that Malthus assumed that *ex ante* savings and investment were always identical. As will be shown below, there is in fact very strong evidence that differences between them were central to his argument. This will now be outlined.

First, Malthus distinguishes carefully between the physical capital of a country which is used to earn profits and provide employment, and the physical wealth which is not so used:

Stock is a general term, and may be defined to be all the material possessions of a country, or all its actual wealth, whatever may be its destination; while capital is that particular portion of these possessions, or of this accumulated wealth, which is destined to be employed with a view to profit. They are often, however, used indiscriminately; and perhaps no great error may arise from it; but it may be useful to recollect that all stock is not properly speaking capital, though all capital is stock. (Pr edn1 293)

All *realised* or *ex post* saving must add to stock, but it will not necessarily add to capital. *Ex post* saving and *ex post* capital accumulation are therefore distinct, both practically and theoretically.

Capital accumulation can occur at home or overseas:

the saving from revenue to add to capital, instead of affording the remedy required, would only aggravate the distresses of the capitalists, and fill the stream of capital which was flowing out of the country. (Pr edn1 492)

Hence even that part of *ex post* saving which results in capital accumulation does not necessarily add to the capital of the country which saves. Saving in Britain and investment in Britain – or in any other country – will differ in so far as investment crosses national frontiers, and it can clearly flood out of a country where there is a lack of effective demand and therefore a low rate of profit.[21]

Still more fundamentally, Malthus very clearly distinguishes *ex ante* intentions and *ex post* results. The role of motivation in Malthus's thought has already been discussed. When he says, 'from the want of a proper distribution of the actual produce adequate motives are not furnished to continued production ... I dont at all wish to deny that some persons or others are entitled to consume all that is produced' (R ix 10) he is distinguishing *ex post* saving from *ex ante* investment. The accumulation of property rights over existing produce does not guarantee its reproduction, let alone its expansion. This depends on new *ex ante* decisions to invest which will only be made if profits are sufficiently high:

Unless the estimation in which an object is held, or the value which an individual, or the society places on it when obtained, adequately compensates the sacrifice which has been made to obtain it, such wealth will not be produced in future.

In individual cases, the power of producing particular commodities is called into action, in proportion to the intensity of effectual demand for them; and the greatest stimulus to their increase, independent of improved facilities of production, is a high market price, or an increase of their exchangeable value, before a greater value of capital has been employed upon them.

In the same manner, the greatest stimulus to the continued production of commodities, taken altogether, is an increase in the exchangeable value of the whole mass, before a greater value of capital has been employed upon them. (Pr edn2 361)

There is thus an *ex ante* investment function for the manufacture of each commodity, and for the manufacture of commodities as a whole, and this will be favourably influenced by any rise in prices which results from growing effective demand. Finally:

the labouring classes of society may be thrown out of work in the midst of an abundance of necessaries, if these necessaries are not in the hands of those who are at the same time both able and willing to employ an adequate quantity of labour. (Pr edn1 446)

Thus, falling prices due to weak effective demand will redistribute incomes from profits to rents. That will have no kind of adverse effect on *ex post* saving – there will still be 'an abundance of necessaries' – but it will have a very clear adverse effect on the *ex ante* investment of the next period, because only capitalists are 'able and willing to employ an adequate quantity of labour'.

It is of course the essence of the story that saving and investment are distinct, *ex ante*, and this is something which Malthus fully appreciated and repeatedly said. Moreover, like modern Keynesians, Malthus sometimes correctly equates saving to investment, *ex post*.

Malthus's theory of effective demand is only a part of his total contribution. Like Marx, he was concerned with the laws of motion of societies. This chapter has sought to show that a logically coherent theory of growth and development lies behind the argument of his *Principles of Political Economy*, and it has been seen that this can be set out in elementary mathematics which brings out further elements in Malthus's analysis.

6 Ricardo's Theory of Income Distribution and Growth

It is generally agreed that David Ricardo was the classical economist who came closest to complete logical consistency. His exposition was lucid and he thought with great clarity, so his argument should lend itself most readily to modern restatement. This has been attempted by a number of economists, including in particular Samuelson and Pasinetti who have produced most distinguished modern Ricardian models.[1]

The principal difficulty which stands in the way of twentieth century attempts to restate Ricardo's argument lies in the subtlety and sophistication of his thought. Samuel Hollander has recently demonstrated the extent to which Ricardo anticipated later developments in economics,[2] and any attempt to encapsulate his rich argument in a single chapter is bound to lose some of his insights. It is, however, possible to arrive at most of his principal results with quite a simple modern restatement, and this will be attempted here. Ricardo's basic theory of value and income distribution will be outlined in the first section, and this will be followed by an account of his theory of economic growth. Ricardo's theories of value, distribution and growth will then be applied to the practical problems which especially interested him.

RICARDO'S THEORY OF VALUE AND DISTRIBUTION

The starting point for an understanding of Ricardo's theory of growth

182

and income distribution is his theory of *value* with which his *Principles of Political Economy and Taxation* opens. His most startling proposition is that wage increases do not necessarily raise prices. He suggests an example where a wage increase raises the circulating capital required to produce given quantities of game, fish *and gold* from £200 to £210:

> If the gold mine from which money was obtained were in the same country, in that case, after the rise of wages, £210 might be necessary to be employed, as capital, to obtain the same quantity of metal that £200 obtained before: for the same reason that the hunter and fisherman required £10 in addition to their capitals, the miner would require an equal addition to his. No greater quantity of labour would be required in any of these occupations, but it would be paid for at a higher price, and the same reasons which should make the hunter and fisherman endeavour to raise the value of their game and fish, would cause the owner of the mine to raise the value of his gold. This inducement acting with the same force on all these three occupations, and the relative situation of those engaged in them being the same before and after the rise of wages, the relative value of game, fish, and gold, would continue unaltered. Wages might rise 20 per cent., and profits consequently fall in a greater or less proportion, without occasioning the least alteration in the relative value of these commodities. (R I 55)[3]

Hence the value of fish and game measured in gold, that is, their money prices (provided a country is on a gold standard), will not alter at all in these conditions if wages rise 5 per cent, because this wage increase will raise costs of production in gold mining just as much as in other economic activities. These prices of fish and game which remain constant even when money wages rise, are their *natural* or long-period equilibrium prices. Short-period *market* prices are influenced by temporary discrepancies between demand and supply, but long-period natural prices depend only on the relative costs of manufacturing different commodities, including gold.

The relative value of fish, game and gold and therefore their natural prices measured in gold will, of course, alter if labour productivity rises or falls. If gold is obtained with less labour, the employment of a given number of men will produce more gold than before, and the same quantity of fish and game. Salmon and deer will therefore exchange for more gold than before, and their natural prices measured in gold will rise. Here Ricardo was unknowingly echoing Sir William Petty, the inventor of the term 'Political Arithmetick' to describe economics, who wrote in 1662 (when silver and not gold was the monetary metal in most common use):

> If a man can bring to *London* an ounce of Silver out of the Earth in *Peru*, in the same time that he can produce a bushel of Corn, then one is the natural price of the other; now if by reason of new and more easie Mines a man can get two ounces of Silver as easily as formerly he did one, then Corn will be as cheap at ten shillings the bushel, as it was before at five shillings *caeteris paribus*. (pp. 50–1)

It is important to note that a change in labour productivity in gold mining (or in silver mining if that is the appropriate monetary metal) will cause an alteration in *all* natural prices and not just in those of corn, salmon or deer. If more labour than before is needed to produce a given quantity of gold, all natural prices will fall. If less labour is needed in gold mining, all natural prices will rise.

If in contrast, more or less labour is needed to produce any other commodity, only the natural price of that commodity will be influenced. Thus if more labour is needed to obtain a salmon, only the natural price of salmon will rise.

In the *Principles*, Ricardo decided at an early stage to assume away the first cause of price variation, a change in the value of money due to a change in productivity in gold mining:

> To facilitate, then, the object of this enquiry, although I fully allow that money made of gold is subject to most of the variations of other things, I shall suppose it to be invariable, and therefore all alterations in price to be occasioned by some alteration in the value of the commodity of which I may be speaking. (R I 46)

In consequence, we are left with the simple proposition that all reductions in labour requirements per unit of output will produce a fall in the natural prices of the commodities concerned, while increased labour requirements will lead to higher natural prices:

> If we had then an invariable standard, by which we could measure the variation in other commodities, we should find that the utmost limit to which they could permanently rise, if produced under the circumstances supposed, was proportioned to the additional

quantity of labour required for their production; and that unless more labour were required for their production, they could not rise in any degree whatever. (R I 29)

Unfortunately the situation is not quite as simple as that, because the qualification 'if produced under the conditions supposed' is due to the assumption that game, fish and gold are all produced with equal quantities of capital per worker. Given this, a change in the labour required to produce a unit of output is really the only factor which can alter their relative costs of production. In these conditions, as was clear at the start, a wage increase will have no effect at all on natural prices because it will influence the cost of gold, fish and game equally. The very complicated results which would otherwise follow are carefully stated by Ricardo in his first chapter 'On Value', but very little is made of them afterwards.[4] It will not therefore distort his analysis of growth and income distribution to ignore them in most of the present restatement of his argument, and to assume that gold, fish and game, and indeed all other commodities, are produced with equal capital to labour ratios. The assumption of equal capital to labour ratios in industry and agriculture was not merely one of convenience for Ricardo. He made a speech in the House of Commons on 9 May 1822 which indicates that he believed they were indeed approximately equal. According to the report of his speech that we have:

> He doubted whether the proportion of labour was greater in agriculture than in manufactures. The right way of coming to a sound determination upon that point was, by considering in what the dead capital of both consisted. If he could show that the dead capital in agriculture bore the same proportion to its whole capital, that the dead capital in manufactures did to its whole capital...His learned friend [Mr Brougham]...had said, that almost all the produce of land was made up of labour. His learned friend, however, seemed to have forgotten that there was a great deal of capital in buildings, in horses, in seed in the ground, besides in labour. (R v 177–8)

The use of the description 'dead capital' to refer to material capital half approaches Marx's 'dead labour' to describe this, and it is exceedingly unlikely that Marx had any knowledge of this speech of Ricardo's. With the assumption of equal capital to labour ratios in industry and agriculture which Ricardo makes virtually throughout the *Principles* after the first chapter 'On Value', relative prices are proportional to the labour time required to produce a commodity, which is why Ricardo comes so close to a simple labour theory of value. He actually expresses values in gold produced with unchanging labour productivity, but it is evident from an important passage in the *Principles* that the measurement of values in gold and not in labour is merely an expositional device, because Ricardo indicates that if by some chance productivity in gold mining should double, then the *value* of a unit of gold would be halved (R I 277).

Using the theoretical device of hypothetical gold produced with unchanging labour productivity, some important propositions about the course of price movements in the economy emerge. Thus, if a worker produces M pieces of gold per annum, and Q_m units of manufactures per annum, and capital per worker is the same in gold mining and in manufacturing, these must sell for the same amount in the long run, so that the natural price, and as Ricardo assumes, the value, of a unit of manufactures, will be M/Q_m pieces of gold. As M, the gold produced per annum by a worker is fixed, then the natural prices of manufactures will rise if Q_m has a tendency to fall, while they will fall if, as Ricardo believed to be the case, labour productivity in manufacturing has a long-term tendency to increase:

> The natural price of all commodities, excepting raw produce and labour, has a tendency to fall, in the progress of wealth and population; for though, on one hand, they are enhanced in real value, from the rise in the natural price of the raw material of which they are made, this is more than counterbalanced by the improvements in machinery, by the better division and distribution of labour, and by the increasing skill, both in science and art, of the producers. (R I 93–4)

The statement that the natural price of a unit of manufactures will be M/Q_m abstracts from their raw material content to which Ricardo refers in this passage, but even where this is taken into account, Ricardo evidently considers that Smithian increasing returns in manufacturing, etc., will be sufficiently strong to produce a falling trend in the prices of manufactures. It is certainly correct to assume therefore that Q_m will rise as capital accumulates, and that there will therefore be a falling trend in M/Q_m, the natural price and value of a unit of manufactures.

In agriculture the situation is a little more complex because food can be grown on land of many different qualities which will produce with different levels of labour productivity. Adam Smith made little reference to differences in the fertility of the soil and its influence on agricultural costs of production, but during the Napoleonic wars a high price of food and interruptions to commerce had led to the cultivation of decidedly inferior land. In 1815 a new economic orthodoxy emerged with the near-simultaneous publication of Edward West's *Essay on the Application of Capital to Land,* Malthus's *Inquiry into the Nature and Progress of Rent* and Ricardo's *Essay on the Influence of a Low Price of Corn on the Profits of Stock.*[5] It was agreed by West, Malthus and Ricardo that labour productivity will fall as a society resorts to less fertile and worse located land, and that the marginal land in use will pay no rent. Then, with the assumption that all workers are equally equipped with capital, the employment of a worker on marginal agricultural land which yields only wages and profits must yield precisely the same wages and profits as the employment of a worker in gold mining or manufactures. Hence a worker on marginal agricultural land will produce an annual output which has a value of M pieces of gold, the same value as the result of a year's work in gold mining. If output per worker on the most fertile land is Q_a units of food per annum while output per worker at the margin is θ times that with the best land, an agricultural worker on marginal land will produce only θQ_a units of food per annum. As these sell for M pieces of gold, the natural price of a unit of food will be $M/\theta Q_a$ pieces of gold.

In the course of time, a society is likely to have to resort to inferior land which will lower θ, the ratio of labour productivity on marginal land to that with the most fertile land. This lowering of θ can be expected to produce a rising trend in $M/\theta Q_a$, the natural price of food. As Ricardo put it:

> The most fertile, and most favourably situated, land will be first cultivated, and the exchangeable value of its produce will be adjusted in the same manner as the exchangeable value of all other commodities, by the total quantity of labour necessary in various forms, from first to last, to produce it, and bring it to market. When land of an inferior quality is taken into cultivation, the exchangeable value of raw produce will rise, because more labour is required to produce it. (R ɪ 72)

It is very clear that Ricardo expected $M/\theta Q_a$, the natural price of food, to rise as an economy developed because of a persistent falling trend in θ. He certainly expected some continuing improvement in Q_a, labour productivity with the most fertile land, as a result of agricultural improvements, and it will be evident below that this played a considerable part in his thought, but the vital point is that he expected this to be more than counterbalanced by a historical tendency for θ to fall, with the result that a rising trend in $M/\theta Q_a$ was inevitable.

Ricardo assumed that workers receive a wage that is sufficient to purchase specific quantities of both food and manufactures, and the continual increase in the relative price of food does not, in fact, lead to any change in the physical amounts of food and manufactures purchased:

> The natural price of labour is that price which is necessary to enable the labourers, one with another, to subsist and to perpetuate their race, without either increase or diminution.
>
> The power of the labourer to support himself, and the family which may be necessary to keep up the number of labourers, does not depend on the quantity of money which he may receive for wages, but on the quantity of food, necessaries, and conveniences become essential to him from habit, which that money will purchase. The natural price of labour, therefore, depends on the price of the food, necessaries, and conveniences required for the support of the labourer and his family. With a rise in the price of food and necessaries, the natural price of labour will rise; with the fall in their price, the natural price of labour will fall. (R ɪ 93)

This indicates that the natural wage must be specified as a physical quantity of food, plus a physical quantity of manufactures. If the quantity of food that enters into W_n, the natural wage, is one unit of food written as 1_a units, while the quantity of manufactures is one unit of manufactures written as 1_m, then the quantity of commodities which makes up the natural wage is $1_a + 1_m$. To convert into units of 'value' we must multiply the quantity of food by $M/\theta Q_a$, the natural price of food and the quantity of manufactures by their natural price which is M/Q_m to obtain the expression:

$$W_n = M \left(\frac{1_a}{\theta Q_a} + \frac{1_m}{Q_m} \right) \tag{6.1}$$

Ricardo believed that in a growing economy workers would need to be paid rising money wages because of the continual tendency for θ to fall as less and less fertile land was resorted to:

> It appears, then, that the...increasing difficulty of providing an additional quantity of food with the same proportional quantity of labour, will also raise wages; and therefore if money be of an unvarying value...wages will have a tendency to rise with the progress of wealth and population. (R I 102)

The money wage will of course fall through time if technological improvements in industry and agriculture continuously increase Q_m and Q_a, the productivity of labour in industry and on the best agricultural land, but Ricardo evidently believed that the falling trend in θ would counterbalance this to produce a rising trend in the natural wage, valued in money produced with unchanging productivity.

Profit per worker, P/L, is output per worker less the wage. Since the output of marginal agricultural and industrial workers must each sell for the M pieces of gold that workers in goldmining produce, profit per worker in both agriculture and industry must have a value of M pieces of gold less the wage. Hence, if capital to labour ratios are the same in all sectors, then throughout the economy when workers are paid the natural wage:

$$\frac{P}{L} = M - W_n = M\left(1 - \frac{1_a}{\theta Q_a} - \frac{1_m}{Q_m}\right) \qquad (6.2)$$

It has been shown that 'the increasing difficulty of providing an additional quantity of food' will produce a rising trend in the money value of the natural wage because of its continual tendency to lower θ. The above equation shows that a persistent tendency in the money value of the natural wage to rise must produce a continual fall in profit per worker. The essence of the argument is that since the employer of labour on marginal agricultural land can sell the output of a worker for no more than M pieces of gold, he is bound to earn diminishing profits per worker if he has to pay rising money wages per head. Once it is established that food prices must rise and wages with them because of the need to resort to inferior land, the rising wage trend is established. The falling profits trend follows from the rising wage trend, given the proposition that wage increases cannot be passed on, with which Ricardo's first chapter 'On Value' opens.

This line of argument is clearest when it is applied to agriculture, but it applies equally to manufacturing where the output of a worker is also sold for no more than M pieces of gold, and where wage increases again cannot be passed on. As Ricardo himself wrote:

> Supposing corn and manufactured goods always to sell at the same price, profits would be high or low in proportion as wages were low or high. But suppose corn to rise in price because more labour is necessary to produce it; that cause will not raise the price of manufactured goods in the production of which no additional quantity of labour is required. If, then, wages continued the same, the profits of manufacturers would remain the same; but if, as is absolutely certain, wages should rise with the rise of corn, then their profits would necessarily fall.
>
> If a manufacturer always sold his goods for the same money, for £1,000, for example, his profits would depend on the price of the labour necessary to manufacture those goods. His profits would be less when wages amounted to £800 than when he paid only £600. In proportion then as wages rose, would profits fall. (R I 110–1)

And later he writes:

> Thus in every case, agricultural, as well as manufacturing profits are lowered by a rise in the price of raw produce, if it be accompanied by a rise of wages. (R I 115)

It is therefore wrong to think of the rate of profit as being determined especially in agriculture. Ricardo's argument is that profits will be forced down equally and simultaneously in industry and agriculture by a rise in wages.[6] He only needs to establish that wages will rise in relation to gold, produced with unchanging productivity. That is the vital point.

It is of course essential to the argument that increases in the price of food result in higher wages, when other influences may permit a lowering of wages so that on balance wages do not need to rise. Ricardo was well aware of this:

> It may be said that I have taken it for granted, that money wages would rise with a rise in the price of raw produce, but that this is by no means a necessary consequence, as the labourer may be

contented with fewer enjoyments. It is true that the wages of labour may previously have been at a high level, and that they may bear some reduction. If so, the fall of profits will be checked; but it is impossible to conceive that the money price of wages should fall, or remain stationary with a gradually increasing price of necessaries; and therefore it may be taken for granted that, under ordinary circumstances, no permanent rise takes place in the price of necessaries, without occasioning, or having been preceded by a rise in wages. (R I 118)

Here the wage may 'bear some reduction' because it is temporarily above the natural level so 'the labourer may be contented with fewer enjoyments' but in the long term the effect of a persistent tendency for θ to fall on the money value of the natural wage must be the dominant influence. Perhaps the weakest point in Ricardo's argument is the assumption that even if there is technical progress in agriculture, the relative price of food in relation to labour is still bound to rise. If there is technical progress in agriculture, Q_a, the ratio of agricultural output per worker to the food component of the natural wage, must be rising. Therefore even if θ is falling, $1_a/\theta Q_a$ will not necessarily rise. Ricardo acknowledged that agricultural technical progress would periodically check the tendency for wages to rise and for profits to fall, but insisted that the tendency would still persist. Thus:

The natural tendency of profits then is to fall; for, in the progress of society and wealth, the additional quantity of food required is obtained by the sacrifice of more and more labour. This tendency, this gravitation as it were of profits, is happily checked at repeated intervals by the improvements in machinery, connected with the production of necessaries, as well as by discoveries in the science of agriculture which enable us to relinquish a portion of labour before required, and therefore to lower the price of the prime necessary of the labourer. (R I 120)

It will be evident that the inexorable rise of wages is only 'checked' by agricultural technical progress. There is no hope that technical progress will actually reverse the rise in wages. There is therefore no doubt, that Ricardo was entirely convinced that the long-term effect on the price of food and hence on wages of diminishing agricultural productivity, as inferior land had to be taken into cultivation would

inevitably outweigh any favourable influences from agricultural im
provements and industrial productivity growth.

The formulae presented so far show that money profits per worker
have a continual tendency to fall as the money wage rises, because
the economy is driven to use less and less fertile land, but nothing has
been said yet about the influence of this on the rate of profit on
capital. This is 'profit per worker/capital per worker' and it has been
shown that 'profit per worker' measured in money produced with
unchanging productivity must have a continual tendency to fall. As
'capital per worker' consists quite largely of the wage goods which
make up the natural wage, and the money value of these rises as the
economy is driven to use less and less fertile land, it follows that
'profit per worker/capital per worker' will tend to fall still more
sharply than profit per worker. Diminishing agricultural productivity
simultaneously reduces the money value of 'profit per worker' and
raises the money cost of 'capital per worker' with the result that the
rate of profit on capital is doubly squeezed.

Profits are especially important in Ricardo's analysis because, as
with Smith and Malthus, they provide both the means and the
principal motive for accumulation:

> The farmer and manufacturer can no more live without profit,
> than the labourer without wages. Their motive for accumulation
> will diminish with every diminution of profit, and will cease
> altogether when their profits are so low as not to afford them an
> adequate compensation for their trouble, and the risk which they
> must necessarily encounter in employing their capital product-
> ively. (R I 122)

In this passage Ricardo refers to profits in general as providing the
main means and incentive for accumulation, but in another he refers
specifically to the rate of profit:

> as soon as wages should be equal...to...the whole receipts of the
> farmer, there must be an end of accumulation; for no capital can
> yield any profit whatever, and no additional labour can be
> demanded, and consequently population will have reached its
> highest point. Long indeed before this period, the very low rate of
> profits will have arrested all accumulation, and almost the whole
> produce of the country, after paying the labourers, will be the

property of the owners of land and the receivers of tithes and taxes. (R I 120–1)

It is clearly central to Ricardo's analysis that as an economy develops, wages rise sufficiently to eat into both profits per head (measured in gold produced with unchanging productivity) and into the rate of profit on capital. The fall in profits then reduces the rate of accumulation, and the whole growth process grinds to a halt when profits reach the minimum level where accumulation ceases – the eventual stationary state.

All the time, as the stationary state is approached, agricultural rents rise, because the entire surplus of the productivity of agricultural labour over its productivity on the least fertile land goes to those who own the better land in the form of rent (or, as in the above passage, tithes, if part of the property rights of land belong, in effect, to the Church).

Agricultural rents and their progress through time can indeed be accounted for very simply. Workers each produce Q_a units of food on the most fertile agricultural land, and θQ_a units on the least fertile land in use, and Ricardo, West and Malthus were agreed that all the extra food that resulted from the higher productivity of intra-marginal land would go to landlords in the form of rent. If it did not at first, farmers would compete for the most fertile land, and this would inevitably drive up rents to the point where all land was equally profitable to farmers. This situation would be arrived at when all farmers on land of all fertilities retained θQ_a units of food from the output that each worker produced out of which they had to pay the worker his wage. They paid the balance of food output over θQ_a in rent to their landlords. The θQ_a units of food that farmers retained would, of course, sell for the M pieces of gold that the marginal product of all workers sold for. The landlords who owned the most fertile land would then obtain the Q_a units of food each worker produced, less the θQ_a units that farmers retained, which would leave them with a rent of $(1 - \theta) Q_a$ units of food per worker employed. In his examples in both *An Essay on the Influence of a Low Price of Corn on the Profits of Stock* and in the *Principles* Ricardo invariably assumed an arithmetic rate of decline of productivity from the best land to the worst.[7] With this assumption, the average rent per worker employed on the land will be the average of that on the most fertile land in use, which is $(1 - \theta) Q_a$ units of food, and the least fertile, which yields no rent at all. The average rent yielded per worker employed on all land is therefore $\frac{1}{2}(1 - \theta) Q_a$ units of food, and if the total number of workers employed on the land is L_a, total rents expressed in food, R_a, are,

$$R_a = \frac{1}{2}(1 - \theta) Q_a L_a \tag{6.3}$$

This will rise as the economy develops, both because total agricultural employment, L_a, rises, and because $(1 - \theta) Q_a$, the productivity gap between the most fertile land in use and the least, increases. Indeed, with the present assumption of an arithmetic rate of decline of productivity from the best land to the worst, the productivity gap $(1 - \theta) Q_a$ actually grows at exactly the same rate as L_a, with the result that total rents (which are $\frac{1}{2}L_a$ times the productivity gap) rise twice as fast as L_a, that is:

$$\text{Elasticity of total rents } (R_a) \text{ with respect to agricultural employment} = 2 \tag{6.4}$$

R_a, however, measures rent only in food. As the economy develops the relative price of food rises so that the manufactures and the personal services which rents can purchase will rise considerably faster. Ricardo's unit of value, gold produced with unchanging productivity, will measure purchasing power in terms of all the goods which are produced with unchanging productivity, and also personal services where productivity can be presumed to be constant. In Ricardo's unit of value, total rents, R_v, will be rents measured in food, R_a, times the gold price of a unit of food which is $M/\theta Q_a$ so that

$$R_v = \frac{1}{2}(1 - \theta) \frac{1}{\theta} M L_a \tag{6.5}$$

It will be evident that this rises as the economy develops, because L_a rises, and in addition the continuing fall in θ will doubly raise it, both because it raises $(1 - \theta)$ and because it raises $1/\theta$ to catch the effect of the rise in the relative price of food. The elasticity of R_v, the *value* of rents with respect to total agricultural employment, is in fact $1 + 1/\theta$. This must exceed the elasticity of food rents alone, R_a, with respect to employment which is merely 2. This double effect of declining agricultural productivity on the purchasing power of rents is brought out very clearly by Ricardo:

since the same cause, the difficulty of production, raises the exchangeable value of raw produce, and raises also the proportion of raw produce paid to the landlord for rent, it is obvious that the landlord is doubly benefited by difficulty of production. First he obtains a greater share, and secondly the commodity in which he is paid is of greater value. (R I 83)

This passage refers to the proportion of raw produce which is paid to the landlord while the above expressions refer to the quantity of rent. An expression for the proportion of agricultural output which goes to the landlords, R_a/Y_a, can be obtained very simply, for Y_a will equal average agricultural productivity which is $\frac{1}{2}(1 + \theta) Q_a$, times agricultural employment which is L_a, so that $Y_a = \frac{1}{2}(1 + \theta) Q_a L_a$, and (using (6.3)):

$$\frac{R_a}{Y_a} = \frac{1 - \theta}{1 + \theta} \qquad (6.6)$$

This obviously rises very sharply as a country is obliged to resort to agricultural land of declining fertility. When a country is first settled and uses only its most fertile land, $\theta = 1$, and the share of rent in agricultural output is then zero. When it later has to use land producing only nine-tenths as much per worker as the most fertile land, one-nineteenth of total agricultural output will be paid to the landlords, and if the pressure of population on resources then pushes the society to use land which produces only half as much per head as the most fertile land, one-third of all agricultural output will go to the landlords. The landlords will gain both an increasing share of output and, at the same time, from a continual increase in the purchasing power that agricultural produce commands.

There are two important assumptions in this account of the agricultural sector of the economy which merit attention. The first is the omission of any reference to the intensive margin of cultivation. Ricardo made it very clear in his verbal accounts of the theory of rent that, as the price of food rises, two developments occur. First farmers resort to less fertile land and thus raise the *extensive* margin of cultivation. The effect of this is fully taken into account in the present argument. Secondly however farmers apply more capital to the land already under cultivation, which extends the *intensive* margin of cultivation (R I 71–2). This raises the output of the land already under cultivation, albeit with diminishing returns to successive doses of capital. If this was allowed for, a change in the price of food would lead to an alteration in Q_a, labour productivity with the most fertile land, because it would lead to an alteration in the manner in which this was farmed. This latter effect could be taken into account, and Samuelson (1959) has done so most elegantly, but it immensely complicates the argument. In all his numerical examples Ricardo himself leaves the extra physical output of superior land unaltered when a higher price of food leads to the cultivation of inferior land. It would of course expand if a higher price of food raised both the extensive and the intensive margins of cultivation. This suggests that Ricardo was prepared to work with assumptions similar to those made here, and these do in fact duplicate precisely the assumptions of all his examples.

The second assumption which merits discussion is the premise that the rate of decline of agricultural productivity is *linear* as inferior land is resorted to, so that overall productivity is precisely the average of that with the best land and the worst, as in the above formulae. This, again, is Ricardo's own assumption, and it has the virtue that it allows for variation in the share of rent in total agricultural incomes, which must be right.[8]

The agricultural sector is only part of the Ricardian economy, and since the natural wage consists of one unit of manufactures and one unit of food, the manufacturing sector will need to produce as many units of manufactures for workers as the agricultural sector produces food. This will always be the case if there is no substitution of manufactures for food as relative prices change, but that is indeed what Ricardo assumes in his own specific examples (R I 103–4). Food and the types of manufactures which workers buy are also bought by other classes, and the argument will become intolerably complex if they buy them in different proportions. It will therefore be assumed that the ratio of physical purchases of manufactured necessities to food will be one unit of manufactures to each unit of food for all classes, whether these are used for consumption or as additions to the capital stock. Then, as Y_a, the economy's output of food, is $\frac{1}{2}(1 + \theta)Q_aL_a$, the number of units of necessary manufactures that are produced, Y_m, will also equal $\frac{1}{2}(1 + \theta)Q_aL_a$, and since each worker in manufacturing produces Q_m units, employment in manufacturing, L_m, will be Y_m divided by Q_m, that is:

$$L_m = \tfrac{1}{2}(1 + \theta) \, \frac{Q_a}{Q_m} \, L_a \qquad (6.7)$$

so that L_m/L_a, the ratio of industrial to agricultural employment, equals $\tfrac{1}{2}(1 + \theta) \, (Q_a/Q_m)$. This shows that as the economy has to farm less and less fertile land, and θ therefore falls, the ratio of manufacturing to agricultural employment also falls, and it will fall still more sharply if Q_m has a stronger tendency to rise as a result of industrial increasing returns and technical progress than Q_a. As the economy develops, therefore, an increasing fraction of the labour force will work in agriculture, and a diminishing fraction in the production of manufactured necessities.

The third sector of Ricardo's economy is the one which produces luxuries. A luxury is any good or service which is not bought by workers or used as capital. Because luxuries are not included in the natural wage, the prices and quantities of luxuries which a country produces have no effect at all on the wage measured in gold, so they can have no effect on profits per worker, which must be the M pieces of gold a worker produces in goldmining less the natural wage, throughout the economy. The rate of profit which is 'profit per worker/capital per worker' is also uninfluenced by the prices and quantities of luxuries produced, because this in no way influences capital per worker. The wage, the rate of profit and rents, measured both in food and in Ricardian gold, are all determined entirely in agriculture and the necessity-producing part of industry, because the equations which determine them are all expressed solely in terms of the particular commodities which enter into the natural wage. The proposition that what happens in the production of luxuries has no influence on income distribution, and indeed on growth, in so far as this depends on the rate of profit, is one of Ricardo's most remarkable insights:

It has been my endeavour to shew throughout this work, that the rate of profits can never be increased but by a fall in wages, and that there can be no permanent fall of wages but in consequence of a fall of the necessaries on which wages are expended...The rate of wages would not be affected, although wine, velvets, silks, and other expensive commodities should fall 50 per cent., and consequently profits would continue unaltered. (R I 132)

Luxuries are purchased by both landlords and capitalists, who buy consumer goods like 'wine, velvets and silks', which workers do not buy, and who purchase personal services of many kinds. Ricardo saw rents as the main source of expenditure on luxuries, and the following passage would have delighted François Quesnay, whom Ricardo seems never to have read:

> I estimate as the source from which we derive all we possess the power which the earth has of yielding a surplus produce. In proportion to this power we enjoy leisure for study and the obtaining of that knowledge which gives dignity to life. Without it we could neither possess arts or manufactures, and our whole time would be devoted to procuring food to support a miserable existence. (R ɪɪ 211)

The essence of Ricardo's theory of distribution can now be summarised. As the economy develops the central fact on which attention must be focused is declining marginal agricultural productivity. This raises the cost of labour, which must be supplied with a specific quantity of food, and a continuing rise in wages necessarily squeezes profitability. The other main effect of the continual decline in agricultural productivity is its persistent tendency to raise rents, not merely in terms of food, but still more so when the rising relative price of food is taken into account. Economic development therefore involves a continual shift of economic resources away from capitalists who propel the economy forwards, and towards landlords, who enjoy the fruits of growth without doing anything (in Ricardo's argument) to further it, although they do provide 'leisure for study and the obtaining of that knowledge which gives dignity to life'.

The time has now come to examine the dynamics of Ricardo's theory of economic growth more closely. Up to this point, it has merely been stated that as the economy develops, marginal agricultural productivity must decline, and some of the consequences of this have been set out. Attention may now be focused on the actual rate at which the economy develops, and the precise interconnections between capital accumulation, wages, profits and rents.

RICARDO'S THEORY OF ECONOMIC GROWTH

Ricardo's unit of value, gold produced with unchanging productivity, is ideal for the explanation of relative prices and the influence of these on income distribution, but it is not a satisfactory unit for the measurement of growth in output. Measured in gold, food output increases, both when the price of food rises, and when the quantity of food produced increases. The output of the economy grows however only if a greater quantity of food is produced and not if there is merely an increase in its price. Much of Ricardian scholarship has dealt with this difficulty by representing Ricardo's argument *as if* the non-luxury sector of the economy produced only one commodity, corn. The quantity of corn could therefore be the unit in which output was measured, and an increase in the value of output simply meant that the economy produced more corn. At the same time, if workers consumed only corn, the natural wage could be expressed as a quantity of corn, and profit per worker was simply the excess of marginal corn output per worker over this natural wage. These assumptions produce very simple and elegant restatements of the development of the Ricardian economy (for instance, Pasinetti (1960) and Kaldor (1955–6)), but they suffer from the disadvantage that Ricardo makes innumerable references to the manufacturing sector in the *Principles*, and states even in *An Essay on the Influence of a Low Price of Corn on the Profits of Stock* of 1815, where the possibility that he may have had a 'corn model' in mind is strongest,[9] that:

> If by foreign commerce, or the discovery of machinery, the commodities consumed by the labourer should become much cheaper, wages would fall; and this, as we have before observed, would raise the profits of the farmer, and therefore, all other profits. (R IV 26)

It was therefore always part of Ricardo's argument that necessary manufactures are included in the natural wage, and that technical developments in manufacturing influence wages, profits and the purchasing power of rents.

A method has happily now been discovered of taking almost as much account of the manufacturing sector as Ricardo did, and at the same time attaining all the clarity and simplicity of the 'corn model', which measures the productive inputs and outputs of the economy in terms of a single commodity. Ricardo always described the natural wage as consisting of particular quantities of specific commodities and these do not vary as the relative prices of food and manufactures alter. Hicks (1972) has suggested that this permits a considerable simplification of Ricardo's argument. He had already discovered in *Value and Capital* (1939) that there are two circumstances where a 'basket' of commodities can be analysed as if they are a single commodity. The first is if the relative prices of the commodities in the basket do not change. That in no way fits Ricardo, because in his argument the price of food rises continuously relative to the prices of manufactures. The second circumstance where a collection of commodities is analysable as a single commodity does however fit Ricardo to perfection, and that is where commodities are consumed in fixed proportions. Thus if, as Ricardo suggests in the *Principles*, the natural wage suffices for the purchase of six quarters of wheat a year, and in addition specific quantities of tea, soap, candles, house rent, bacon, cheese, butter, linen, shoes and cloth (R I 103–4), this collection of commodities can be analysed as if it is a single commodity. Because corn, bacon, cheese and butter are produced with diminishing returns, the composite commodity which can be labelled 'necessities' can only be produced with rising real costs as output is expanded. The part of 'necessities' which is manufactured, linen, shoes, cloth, and so on, will be produced in conditions where extra production generally lowers real costs per unit, but as Ricardo says several times, the fact that food output can only be expanded at a rising real cost per unit will exert the dominant influence on the cost of necessities as a whole.

It is therefore possible to reproduce the essence of Ricardo's argument by focusing attention on the sector of the economy where necessities are produced – defining a unit of necessities as the collection of commodities which make up the natural wage. With inputs and outputs in the necessity-producing sector both expressed in the same physical units – the bundle of commodities which make up the natural wage – Ricardo's argument can be restated with clarity and simplicity. It may be added that the fact that the conclusions of the *Essay* of 1815 where references to manufactures are few are so similar to those of the *Principles* of 1817 where manufactures are present throughout is explained as soon as it is recognised that having a unit which includes both manufactures and food, but in fixed proportions, is analytically identical to having a unit which consists solely of food.

If the natural wage is 1 unit of necessities, this unit being the one in which the physical output of the economy is measured, then to parallel the previous statement of Ricardo's theory of value where food and manufactures were distinguished, it can now be assumed that the output of necessities per worker with the best land in the economy is Q units, and that output per worker with marginal land is θQ units. Profits per worker measured in necessities will be the marginal productivity of labour in necessity-production, less the wage. If workers receive the natural wage, profit per worker will be $(\theta Q - 1)$ units of necessities, and this will fall as θ falls. If total capital per worker is K/L units of necessities, then the rate of profit on capital which is 'profits per worker/capital per worker' will equal

$$\frac{\theta Q - 1}{K/L}$$

and this will fall as θ falls.

There is however an important development to this conventional restatement of Ricardo's argument which Hicks and Hollander (1977) and Casarosa (1974, 1978 and 1982) have suggested. If there is a positive rate of profit, that is, if θQ, the marginal productivity of labour in necessity-production, exceeds the wage, then capital will accumulate, and if capital accumulates the demand for labour will be growing. If the demand for labour is expanding, then the wage will exceed the natural rate and Ricardo makes this extremely clear. The natural wage is very specifically what workers must receive if population is to be constant. Like Smith and Malthus, Ricardo believed that workers would receive more than this in conditions where capital and therefore population were expanding:

It is when the market price of labour exceeds its natural price, that the condition of the labourer is flourishing and happy, that he has it in his power to command a greater proportion of the necessaries and enjoyments of life, and therefore to rear a healthy and numerous family: When, however, by the encouragement which high wages give to the increase of population, the number of labourers is increased, wages again fall to their natural price, and indeed from a re-action sometimes fall below it...

Notwithstanding the tendency of wages to conform to their natural rate, their market rate may, in an improving society, for an indefinite period, be constantly above it; for no sooner may the impulse, which an increased capital gives to a new demand for labour be obeyed, than another increase of capital may produce the same effect; and thus, if the increase of capital be gradual and constant, the demand for labour may give a continued stimulus to an increase of people. (R I 94–5)

If population growth depends on the excess of the market wage over the natural wage, as Ricardo here suggests, then during the whole period in which an economy is developing and moving from the point of first settlement to the eventual stationary state, the market wage will mostly be above the natural wage. In the previous account of Ricardo's theory of value and distribution, the fundamental relationships were stated throughout, as Ricardo himself often states them with the wage at its natural level, but it is now evident that in the course of economic development it will often be above it. The previous argument is best seen as comparing a series of situations where population has temporarily adjusted to the capital stock when the wage should actually hit its natural level. But it is evident now that the market wage, which can be written as W units of necessities, is also important in Ricardo's argument. Since the rate of population growth, n, will depend on the excess of the market wage over the natural wage, which is 1 unit of necessities, it can be assumed most simply that $n = \alpha (W - 1)$ where α is a positive constant. This basic population supply equation, which resembles Malthus's and Smith's (and it is algebraically similar to equation (5.2), which explains the determination of population growth in the restatement of Malthus's argument in Chapter 5) can equally be written as an equation to explain the excess of the market wage over the natural wage:

$$W = 1 + \frac{n}{\alpha} \qquad (6.8)$$

That is, the wage (W units of necessities) will exceed the natural wage (1 unit of necessities) to an extent which depends on the rate of population growth.

Ricardo also follows Smith and Malthus in attributing capital accumulation – which determines the rate of growth of demand for population – quite largely to the reinvestment of profits and therefore to the rate of profit on capital. It was shown above that there is a motive for accumulation where the rate of profit is above a certain minimum, and since this motive will diminish with every diminution of profit, it can be inferred that k, the rate of growth of capital, will vary with the excess of the rate of profit over the minimum rate of profit where there is no accumulation. It will obviously simplify the presentation of the argument if the minimum profit at which there is no accumulation can be regarded as a cost, and that procedure which is followed, for instance in Hicks and Hollander (1977), allows accumulation to be attributed directly and simply to profits, since there will then be sufficient motives to encourage accumulation as soon as any net profits are earned. The simplest relationship which can be suggested is that k, the rate of growth of capital, will vary precisely with r, the rate of net profit on capital, that is, that $k = \beta r$, where β is a positive constant, which is also as it happens quite similar to the capital accumulation equation which was used to represent Malthus's argument in Chapter 5 (where it was equation (5.3)). Then:

$$r = \frac{k}{\beta} \qquad\qquad (6.9)$$

As with Malthus, the relationship between capital accumulation and the rate of profit is parallel to that between wages and the rate of population growth. The wage needs to exceed the 'natural' or subsistence wage to an extent which depends on the rate of population growth, while the rate of profit needs to provide both the means and the motivation for capital accumulation. If the wage is at subsistence level and there are no net profits to encourage accumulation, there can be neither capital accumulation nor population growth. This situation will arise when the necessities produced per worker with marginal land, θQ, only just suffice to provide the natural wage, that is, when $\theta Q = 1$. If marginal productivity in necessity-production exceeds 1 unit, then either the wage will be able to exceed the natural wage, in which case the economy will enjoy population growth, or the wage will merely equal the natural wage, and the entire excess of θQ over 1 unit will go to profits and induce maximal capital accumulation. Any excess of marginal productivity in necessity-production over the natural wage will induce population growth in so far as it goes to wages and capital accumulation in so far as it goes to profits.

As the economy develops there will be periods where capital grows faster than labour, and others where population grows faster than the capital stock, but the long-run tendency will be for the labour force and the capital stock to grow broadly in line with each other. If an economy is mechanising and beginning to adopt the large scale use of machinery, this may cause the capital stock to grow faster than employment, and Ricardo took this line of argument directly into account in the third edition of the *Principles* (1821) which contains a chapter 'On Machinery' which will be discussed below. In the earlier chapters of the *Principles* he nevertheless says several times that the long-term tendency is for capital and employment to grow at the same rate, and he says in several places that growth of capital is really the same thing as growth of the labour force. Where capital and labour grow at the same rate, and this is the broad historical tendency in his argument,[10] k the rate of growth of the capital stock will equal n, the rate of growth of the labour force, so some of the potential benefit from any excess of marginal productivity in necessity-production over the natural wage will go to labour in the form of a higher wage than the natural wage in order to induce the appropriate rate of population growth, and some will go to profits in order to induce the appropriate rate of growth of the capital stock.

Formulae for the rates of wages and profits which will induce equal growth rates of capital and labour can be inferred very simply from the relationships which have been set out. The economy's profit per worker will be the excess of marginal productivity in necessity production over the market wage, $(\theta Q - W)$ units, and since r, the rate of profit, is 'profits per worker/capital per worker':

$$r = \frac{\theta Q - W}{K/L} \tag{6.10}$$

If the rate of growth of the labour force is to equal the rate of growth of the capital stock, it follows from (6.8), (6.9) and (6.10) that:

$$k = n = \frac{\theta Q - 1}{\dfrac{1}{\alpha} + \dfrac{1}{\beta}\left(\dfrac{K}{L}\right)} \tag{6.11}$$

This formula shows that where capital per worker is constant there is a particular rate of growth of capital and of population which is directly proportional to the excess of marginal productivity in necessity-production over the natural wage, that is, to $(\theta Q - 1)$. This surplus of θQ over 1 will therefore determine the rate of growth at which capital and labour can grow at the same rate. The surplus will fall as a result of the continuing long-term tendency for θ to fall, and the rate of growth of capital and labour will fall with it until the excess of θQ over 1 falls to zero, when the marginal productivity of labour in necessity-production will no longer be higher than the natural wage.

As the rate of growth falls towards zero, the wage and the rate of profit both fall towards their subsistence rates, and the following relationships show how the wage declines towards 1, and the rate of profit towards zero, as $(\theta Q - 1)$ falls towards zero:

$$W = 1 + \frac{\theta Q - 1}{1 + \dfrac{\alpha}{\beta}\left(\dfrac{K}{L}\right)} \tag{6.12}$$

$$r = \frac{\theta Q - 1}{\dfrac{\beta}{\alpha} + \dfrac{K}{L}} \tag{6.13}$$

It is to be noted that until the stationary state is reached when θQ is 1, both the wage and the rate of profit will exceed their subsistence levels wherever (as will generally be the case) the capital stock and the labour force are both growing, which echoes what Hicks and Hollander and Casarosa have insisted is Ricardo's own theory of wages.[11] In their view *market prices* adjust rapidly to natural prices, but the *market wage* only adjusts *finally* to the natural wage when capital accumulation ceases. Ricardo's own account of what happens to wages as capital accumulates in his chapter 'On Wages' does in fact follow very closely the course indicated by the above relationships. He first explains how a diminishing rate of capital accumulation will produce falling real wages:

> In the natural advance of society, the wages of labour will have a tendency to fall, as far as they are regulated by supply and demand; for the supply of labourers will continue to increase at the same rate, whilst the demand for them will increase at a slower rate. If, for instance, wages were regulated by a yearly increase of capital, at the rate of 2 per cent., they would fall when it accumulated only at the rate of 1½ per cent. They would fall still lower when it increased only at the rate of 1, or ½ per cent., and would continue to do so until the capital became stationary, when

wages also would become stationary, and be only sufficient to keep up the numbers of the actual population. (R I 101)

This statement about the gradual decline of real wages to the natural rate is very clearly brought out by equation (6.12). As capital accumulates, θ falls, and this steadily reduces $(\theta Q - 1)$ towards zero, which reduces wages towards 1, while at the same time the continuing fall in $(\theta Q - 1)$ reduces the rate of capital accumulation. Ricardo continues:

> I say that, under these circumstances, wages would fall, if they were regulated only by the supply and demand of labourers; but we must not forget, that wages are also regulated by the prices of the commodities on which they are expended.
>
> As population increases, these necessaries will be constantly rising in price, because more labour will be necessary to produce them. If, then, the money wages of labour should fall, whilst every commodity on which the wages of labour were expended rose, the labourer would be doubly affected, and would be soon totally deprived of subsistence. Instead, therefore, of the money wages of labour falling, they would rise; but they would not rise sufficiently to enable the labourer to purchase as many comforts and necessaries as he did before the rise in the price of those commodities. (R I 101–2)

Ricardo then works through a series of examples to show how the real wage falls while at the same time the money wage is rising as a result of these two forces, a declining rate of capital accumulation, and a rising price of necessaries, working simultaneously. It has already been shown that the declining real wage is very clearly demonstrated by equation (6.12). That money wages will be rising simultaneously becomes evident if this equation, which expresses the real wage as a quantity of necessities, is restated to express the wage as a quantity of money by multiplying the quantity of necessities by their gold price. This is $M/\theta Q$, since workers equipped with equal capitals may produce either M pieces of gold or θQ units of necessities per annum. Then, rearranging (6.12):

$$W_{v} = \left(\frac{1 + \left(\frac{1}{\theta Q} \right)\left(\frac{\alpha}{\beta} \right)\left(\frac{K}{L} \right)}{1 + \left(\frac{\alpha}{\beta} \right)\left(\frac{K}{L} \right)} \right) M \qquad (6.14)$$

This shows quite unambiguously that W_v, the money wage in Ricardo's unit of value, will rise as a result of a continuing fall in θ as the economy is driven to use less and less fertile land in the production of necessities. It is also, as was emphasised in the first part of this chapter, a central feature of Ricardo's argument that a rising money wage must always produce a declining trend in the rate of profit, and it must have this effect even though real wages are also declining:

> Notwithstanding, then, that the labourer would be really worse paid, yet this increase in his wages would necessarily diminish the profits of the manufacturer; for his goods would sell at no higher price, and yet the expense of producing them would be increased. (R I 102)

The present restatement of Ricardo's argument echoes this surprising result, and it reproduces these very paradoxical propositions about income distribution. In particular, as soon as his full argument where the rate of growth of capital influences the real wage is stated, it emerges very clearly that the real wage and the rate of profit both show a persistent tendency to decline as the economy is forced to resort to inferior land.

Ricardo himself made interpretation difficult for his successors by sometimes stating his argument with the simpler results outlined in the previous section which follow when the wage is actually at its natural level. There are further passages like those quoted above which make it clear that it was an integral part of his complete argument that while capital accumulation was actually proceeding, the market wage would tend to be persistently above the natural wage. It would then fall towards its natural level as resort to inferior land gradually forced the rate of profit and the rate of capital accumulation downwards.[12]

The fact that the economy is driven on to inferior land as capital accumulates means that there is a persistent tendency for output to grow more slowly than the capital stock. This is because the capital to output ratio rises continuously: it always requires K/L units of necessities to equip an extra worker, but the marginal product of that worker will be θQ units of necessities which falls continuously as θ falls. The rate of growth of output will fall short of the rate of growth of the labour force (and the capital stock) to exactly the same extent as the marginal product of labour (θQ) falls short of the average produce of labour (which is $\frac{1}{2}(Q + \theta Q)$ – the average of productivity with the best land and the worst). The elasticity of extra necessity-production with respect to extra capital and labour will equal the ratio of the marginal product of labour to its average product, so that:

$$\text{Elasticity of necessity production with respect to capital and labour} = \frac{2\theta}{1 + \theta} \qquad (6.15)$$

Thus, in a newly settled country where $\theta = 1$, a 1 per cent increase in labour and capital will raise output 1 per cent. As θ falls to nine-tenths it will raise output $^{18}\!/_{19}$ per cent, and it will raise it just $\frac{2}{3}$ per cent if θ subsequently falls to one-half, and by as little as $\frac{1}{2}$ per cent if θ falls to one-third.

While the output of necessities always grows more slowly than capital and employment, rents rise considerably faster. As in the previous section where agriculture was analysed as a separate sector, any excess in necessity-production per worker over that with the least fertile land in use must go to the landlords. Extra productivity in necessity-production is entirely attributable to the influence of superior land on the ease of producing the food component of the necessity basket, and any surplus due to this goes to the landlords. It was shown previously that food rents rise twice as fast as agricultural capital and employment (equation (6.4)), and rents measured in necessities will similarly rise twice as fast as the labour and capital used to produce necessities. Thus, as capital and employment expand, each 1 per cent increase raises the output of necessities less than 1 per cent, indeed by just $2\theta/(1 + \theta)$ per cent, and total rents by a full 2 per cent. The share of rent in output therefore rises sharply and continuously. Landlords receive the fraction of necessity output, $(1 - \theta)/(1 + \theta)$, that they received previously in agriculture (equation (6.6)), and as θ falls this rises sharply until marginal productivity in necessity-production reaches the lowest level that the economy can sustain. This will actually occur when marginal productivity in necessity-production is no more than the natural wage, that is, when $\theta Q = 1$. It follows that the economy will arrive at its eventual stationary state when $\theta = 1/Q$, so that the maximum that the share of rent in necessity production can reach, R/Y max, is:

$$\left(\frac{R}{Y} \right)_{max} = \frac{Q - 1}{Q + 1} \tag{6.16}$$

At the economy's first settlement where there is no gap between the fertility of the best land and of marginal land, rents will be zero, and they will rise gradually to the fraction $(Q - 1)/(Q + 1)$ of total necessity-production as the economy moves on to ever inferior marginal land. Profits and wages will in contrast start high, and at the point of first settlement when $\theta = 1$, capital accumulation will be at its maximum rate of (from (6.11)):

$$\frac{Q - 1}{\dfrac{1}{\alpha} + \dfrac{1}{\beta} \left(\dfrac{K}{L} \right)}$$

and the rate of profit will then be (from (6.13)):

$$\frac{Q - 1}{\dfrac{\beta}{\alpha} + \dfrac{K}{L}}$$

and the wage (from (6.12)):

$$1 + \left(\frac{Q - 1}{1 + \dfrac{\alpha}{\beta} \left(\dfrac{K}{L} \right)} \right)$$

As the stationary state when $\theta = 1/Q$ is approached, accumulation falls towards zero, and with the present reformulation, profits also fall towards zero while wages fall towards their natural level of 1.

The examples of a newly settled country and one in its final stationary state are the easiest ones to set out precisely. In practice the economies in which Ricardo was most interested, and Britain in particular, came between these extremes. It is therefore where θ lies between its initial value of 1 and its final value of $1/Q$ that the most relevant interrelationships of a Ricardian economy are to be found. The account of the Ricardian economy in this intermediate state which has been set out here can be used to provide answers to the practical questions in which Ricardo was especially interested, and which he constructed his theory to elucidate.

THE PRACTICAL IMPLICATIONS OF RICARDO'S THEORY OF GROWTH AND INCOME DISTRIBUTION

The questions which Ricardo especially wished to answer were the following. How will improved methods of cultivation influence the economy, and especially the distribution of incomes? Will any rate of saving be compatible with the full utilisation of the capital stock? How does the size of the national debt and the taxation needed to finance it influence the rate of growth? How could recovery from the post-Napoleonic agricultural depression best be achieved? How will a greater use of machinery influence the development of the economy and the standard of living of the labouring classes? Finally, how would the abolition of the corn laws and consequent free trade in food influence the development of the economy? Ricardo believed that these vital questions could be answered quite straightforwardly with the help of his theory of growth and income distribution.

His analysis of the influence of agricultural improvements will be set out first. According to Ricardo:

> improvements in agriculture are of two kinds: those which increase the productive powers of the land, and those which enable us, by improving our machinery, to obtain its produce with less labour. They both lead to a fall in the price of raw produce; they both affect rent, but they do not affect it equally. (R ı 80)

He goes on to describe the first kind of agricultural improvement in detail:

> The improvements which increase the productive powers of the land, are such as the more skilful rotation of crops, or the better choice of the manure. These improvements absolutely enable us to obtain the same produce from a smaller quantity of land. If, by the introduction of a course of turnips, I can feed my sheep besides

raising my corn, the land on which the sheep were before fed becomes unnecessary, and the same quantity of raw produce is raised by the employment of a less quantity of land. (R I 80)

In terms of the present restatement of Ricardo's argument, it can be assumed that with such 'output-augmenting' improvements, the output of each worker engaged in necessity-production, and of each acre, will rise proportionately by a_f which will be the extent of food or necessity 'output-augmenting technical progress'. This increase in labour productivity in necessity-production will lower the real labour cost of necessities, which will raise the rate of profit and lead to faster accumulation of capital. As Ricardo wrote:

> the improvement in agriculture, or rather in consequence of less labour being bestowed on its production, would naturally lead to increased accumulation; for the profits of stock would be greatly augmented. This accumulation would lead to an increased demand for labour, to higher wages, to an increased population, to a further demand for raw produce, and to increased cultivation. (R I 79)

These are however its long-term effects. Ricardo assumes that the *immediate* impact of an agricultural improvement is to leave the demand for food unaltered because, 'With the same population, and no more, there can be no demand for any additional quantity of corn' (R I 79). Here he is focusing attention on the initial situation immediately upon the increase in agricultural productivity where there is as yet no increase in population, and where the improvement has (apparently) not yet begun to raise the real wage. In this situation workers' demand for corn (necessities in the present restatement) is unaltered, but the supply of necessities would be increased by a_f if the former number of workers and the former acreage of land continued to be used to produce them. In view of this potential excess in the supply of necessities over the immediate demand, Ricardo assumes that some of the agricultural labourers (in the present restatement, some of the workers engaged in necessity-production) and an equivalent fraction of the capital stock would immediately be withdrawn from the land and 'devoted to the production of other commodities desirable to the community' (R I 79). In the present restatement the workers withdrawn from necessity-production produce luxuries instead, though 'other commodities desirable to the community' would include manufactured necessities in a more general restatement of Ricardo's argument.

With the present assumption that the short-term demand for food (necessities) does not change because there has as yet been no change in the labour force or the wage, employment in necessity-production has to fall. If employment was unchanged, necessity-production would actually rise by a_f and it must be ascertained how large a cut in employment is needed to hold the level of output constant. Since the elasticity of necessity-production with respect to employment is $2\theta/(1 + \theta)$ (equation (6.15)), it follows that a proportional fall in employment of $a_f(1 + \theta)/2\theta = a_f(1/2\theta + 1/2)$, is needed to cut necessity-production by a_f and so cancel out the favourable effect on output of the rise in productivity. Hence with Ricardo's assumptions, where the output of food (necessities) is initially held constant, employment in necessity-production falls by $a_f(1/2\theta + 1/2)$, and these workers become available to produce luxuries. Will the extra luxuries go to capitalists or to landlords? The outcome will clearly depend on how output-augmenting agricultural improvements affect rents.

If employment had been held constant, rents would have risen by a_f, for each worker would have produced a_f more necessities, and the differential between the output of the most productive worker and the least would also have risen by a_f. But employment in necessity-production has actually fallen by $a_f(1/2\theta + 1/2)$ and as the elasticity of total rents with respect to employment is 2 (equation (6.4)) this fall in employment reduces rents by $a_f(1/\theta + 1)$. In sum, therefore, rents rise by a_f because each acre produces a_f more necessities, and they then fall by $a_f(1/\theta + 1)$ because agricultural employment falls, so, summing these, rents actually fall by a_f/θ. Hence:

$$\text{The short-term elasticity of total rents with respect to output-augmenting technical process} = -\frac{1}{\theta} \quad (6.17)$$

Thus, where θ equals one-half, 1 per cent output-augmenting technical progress will reduce total rents by 2 per cent, and rents will actually fall by 4 per cent if θ equals one-quarter. As necessity-production is held constant in this immediate response to output-augmenting agricultural technical progress, the share of rent in output falls to exactly the same extent as total rents. The landlords therefore lose equally in absolute terms and as a share of output.

Rents fall because the best land produces a_f more food (necessities) than before, and since the demand for food (necessities) is initially unchanged, society does not need to make use of some of the worst land that it formerly had to cultivate. As total rents depend on the excess of the productivity of the best land in use over the worst and this narrows, total rents fall. As Ricardo put it, 'whatever diminishes the inequality in the produce obtained from successive portions of capital employed on the same or on new land, tends to lower rent; and that whatever increases that inequality, necessarily produces an opposite effect, and tends to raise it' (R I 83). Thus Ricardo arrived at the very startling proposition that whatever eases the problems of feeding the population reduces the incomes of the landlords, while any changes which make this more difficult raise rents. Malthus considered this an extraordinary error:

> Yet it has been said by Mr. Ricardo that, 'the interest of the landlord is always opposed to that of the consumer and the manufacturer,' that is, to all the other orders of the state. To this opinion he has been led, very consistently, by the peculiar view he has taken of rent, which makes him state, that it is for the interest of the landlord that the cost attending the production of corn should be increased, and that improvements in agriculture tend rather to lower than to raise rents. (Pr edn1 205)

Malthus argued that agricultural improvements will always lead to an increased population, and hence to an increased demand for food and eventually to far higher rents than before. That was indeed also Ricardo's view of the *long-term* effects of agricultural improvements, and what he showed in the part of his analysis which has just been restated is merely the *immediate* effects of output-augmenting technical progress. These are immediate effects because he assumed that the labour available for employment and the corn component of the wage were both given. Ricardo's precise reply to the above passage in Malthus's *Principles* is:

> I will only observe here that Mr. Malthus must recollect the qualification which I give to the opinion which he has quoted from my work – I have said that it is only the immediate interest of the landlord which is at variance with improvements in agriculture, and the reduction in the cost of production of corn. Inasmuch as the power of the land, as a machine, is improved, the landlord will

be benefited when it is again called into action; and that it infallibly will be after the population has increased in proportion to the increased facility of producing food. (R II 184–5)

It was shown above that the economy reaches its eventual stationary state when $\theta = 1/Q$, where Q is the ratio of labour productivity in necessity-production with the economy's most fertile land to the natural wage. If this rises from three times to four times the natural wage as a result of output-augmenting technical progress, then the stationary state will only be reached when labour productivity with the worst land falls to one-quarter of its level with the best in place of the former one-third. In consequence, the economy will reach its eventual stationary state later in time, and with a larger population. With more productive land the economy will support more people. It will also have a higher share of rent at the end of the day, for in the eventual stationary state this is $(Q - 1)/(Q + 1)$ (equation (6.16)). Hence, if Q rises from 3 to 4 times the natural wage, the eventual share of rents in necessity-production will rise from ½ to ⅗. Thus in the longest of long runs, output-augmenting technical improvements raise rents. Why did Ricardo focus on their immediate effect, which is to cut rents and raise profits? One possible answer to this question is a most interesting one. On 17 October 1815 he wrote to Malthus:

> but I ask if by any miracle the produce of that land could at once be doubled would rents then continue as high as before, or could they possibly rise? We are speaking of the immediate not the ultimate effects. The improvements in skill and machinery may in 1000 years go to the Landlord but for 900 they will remain with the tenant. (R VI 302)

Clearly Ricardo's long periods are far longer than is often supposed. For this reason he may have preferred to focus attention on the immediate effects of agricultural improvements, and to do this by working out the precise consequences in the simple case where the population and capital stock is fixed in aggregate size, but free to move between the various sectors of the economy – in the present restatement from necessity- to luxury-production. He did this very clearly, and his analysis can be restated to produce his very startling result.

Output-augmenting technical progress was, however, just one of the two kinds of agricultural improvement which he analysed in detail. An alternative type of technical progress has no tendency to lower rents, even in the short run:

> But there are improvements which may lower the relative value of produce without lowering the corn rent...Such improvements do not increase the productive powers of the land; but they enable us to obtain its produce with less labour. They are rather directed to the formation of the capital applied to the land, than to the cultivation of the land itself. Improvements in agricultural implements, such as the plough and the thrashing machine, economy in the use of horses employed in husbandry, and a better knowledge of the veterinary art, are of this nature. Less capital, which is the same thing as less labour, will be employed on the land; but to obtain the same produce, less land cannot be cultivated. Whether improvements of this kind, however, affect corn rent, must depend on the question, whether the difference between the produce obtained by the employment of different portions of capital be increased, stationary, or diminished. (R I 82)

It can be assumed that in this case, the labour (and supporting capital) needed to produce a given level of output on the best and on all other land is diminished by the fraction a_n. Then output per worker on the best land and on all other land is increased by approximately a_n and this can be described as the rate of 'labour-augmenting' technical progress. Output per acre is, however, unaltered, so with Ricardo's assumption that the demand for food (necessities) is immediately unaltered, exactly the same acres, each producing precisely the same quantity of necessities as before, will be in cultivation. There is, therefore, no change whatsoever in the excess output of the best land in use over the worst, so there is no change in θ, and rents measured in necessities will be precisely the same as before. If the output of necessities is maintained in this way, and rents measured in necessities are held constant, a fraction, a_n, of the labour producing necessities (and the accompanying capital) can be released to produce luxuries. Output-augmenting technical progress, in contrast, reduced rents immediately by as much as $1/\theta$ times the rate of technical progress when the output of necessities was held constant. It was remarkably perceptive of Ricardo to set out these two superficially similar kinds of agricultural improvement and to show how they could have such different immediate effects on rent.

Curiously, by the time long run stationary state equilibrium is reached, the impact on rent of output- and labour-augmenting technical progress, which have such distinct immediate effects, becomes identical. Both kinds of technical progress raise the rate of profit (because they raise marginal productivity in necessity-production relative to the wage) and the rate of accumulation, and therefore the demand for necessities and hence their output will grow more quickly through time. It is only immediately when Ricardo assumes that the demand for corn (necessities) is given that rents fall (in the case of output-augmenting technical progress) or else remain unchanged (in the case of labour-augmenting technical progress). As the wage, and with it the demand for necessities, will immediately start to expand as capital accumulates, rents will at once start to rise and continue to until their share of output reaches $(Q - 1)/(Q + 1)$ in the stationary state. Now output- and labour-augmenting technical progress at rates a_f and a_n will raise Q by multiples of $(1 + a_f)$ and $(1 + a_n)$ respectively, so they will raise Q (and therefore the eventual share of rent) equally if they occur at similar rates. Both kinds of agricultural improvement will therefore have the same effect in the end, but if that can take up to a thousand years, Ricardo was right to focus attention on their very different short-term effects.

Agricultural profitability preoccupied Ricardo as both a theoretical and a practical question. The *Principles* appeared in the post-Napoleonic depression when there was great agricultural distress, and this continued until Ricardo's death in 1823. There was therefore inevitably controversy about the applicability of his analysis to the immediate problem of restoring the financial viability of agriculture, and the demand for agricultural labour, to the conditions of relative prosperity which had prevailed during most of the war.

Ricardo's analysis of the conditions which influence the demand for labour was entirely straightforward in the 1817 and 1819 editions of the *Principles*. The wage depends on the demand for labour in relation to the supply, and capital and the demand for labour are virtually synonymous. Hence anything that raises the capital stock will raise the demand for labour and therefore the wage and the standard of living of the working class. Capital accumulation will cease in the end, when the rate of profit falls to the minimum return needed to compensate for risk and minimal entrepreneurial returns. Growth will cease once that point is reached, and the wage falls to the natural rate. However, he believed throughout his life that the eventual stationary state was happily distant. Therefore he was adamant against all criticism, and especially that of Malthus, that extra capital accumulation was bound to relieve the distress of the labouring classes, and that government policy should be designed to assist accumulation in every possible way.

He was never concerned that *ex ante* saving might fail to result in *ex post* investment. In the restatement of his argument presented here, saving and capital accumulation are assumed to derive from profits, and there are many passages in his work, a few of which are quoted above, which suggest that the motive to invest and the funds for investment derive principally from these. There is then no particular difficulty in translating a willingness to save into demand for an increased stock of capital goods, since capitalists are both the economy's savers and the economy's investors. For Ricardo there was no problem whatever. If wages were no higher than the natural rate, profits would inevitably be above the minimum return needed to induce accumulation (provided that the stationary state was distant) so there would be ample means and motivation for accumulation. If, on the contrary, profits were too low to induce accumulation, then wages must be well above the natural rate, so workers would be entitled to demand the goods that capitalists temporarily lacked the means to purchase. In this situation capitalists would lack the motivation to invest, but they would also lack the means to spend, which would temporarily belong to workers. With wages well above the natural rate, they would enjoy a temporary prosperity which would soon raise population and bring wages down again and so restore profitability.[13]

As was shown in Chapter 5, Malthus argued in a stream of letters to Ricardo, and in his own *Principles of Political Economy*, that wages and profits could be low at the same time if effective demand was lacking. A low effective demand would reduce profitability and the demand for labour. With a low demand for labour, earnings per family which depended partly on 'task-work' (that is, piece-rates) and the number of members of the family who worked would both be low. Hence profits and the earnings of a family could both be low at the same time, even though the stationary state was still distant. Moreover, depressed current prices of food would produce actual unemployment if money wages failed to fall in line with prices. If prices fell faster than nominal wages, some workers would be unemployed and face starvation or recourse to the limited welfare provision available in parishes in the early nineteenth century.

Ricardo denied the possibility of sticky money wages, and repeatedly denied that real wages and profits could be low at the same time.

He insisted that they could both be low only in the distant stationary state. So Ricardo saw recovery from the recession as absolutely inevitable, because either high wages or high profits, whichever came first, would lead to better conditions.

What if, as Malthus insisted, depressed agricultural prices put high real incomes into the hands of those who did not by custom invest – the landlords, instead of the capitalist farmers on whom capital accumulation depended? Falling food prices would clearly redistribute real incomes from capitalists to landlords, since money rents could not be expected to fall as quickly as agricultural prices. Ricardo like Malthus believed that saving and investment came primarily from profits, but it in no way worried him that higher real incomes might belong to a class which did not by custom invest:

> there is...no danger that...accumulated capital...would not find employment, or that the commodities which it might be made to produce would not be beneficially sold, so as to afford an adequate profit to the producers. On this part of the subject it is only necessary to add that there would be no necessity for stockholders to become farmers or manufacturers. There are always to be found in a great country, a sufficient number of responsible persons, with the requisite skill, ready to employ the accumulated capital of others, and to pay to them a share of the profits, and which, in all countries, is known by the name of interest for borrowed money. (R IV 179–80)

Ricardo's belief that a lack of effective demand can never lead to a loss of potential output is underpinned by this assumption of an elastic supply of potential entrepreneurs, always ready to convert the savings of *any* class into investment. Malthus believed that entrepreneurs would only appear while capitalists were earning high profits, and he would not have expected an elastic supply of potential entrepreneurs to offer to invest substantial rentier savings at the height of an agricultural depression.

There was however one aspect of the depression that profoundly worried Ricardo. His hope of eventual recovery depended on the existence of a substantial excess of the value of output with marginal agricultural land over the natural wage. If this excess went to labour, it would produce recovery through a larger population, leading in time to a lower wage. If it went to capital there would be immediate recovery in any case. There was, therefore, nothing to worry about provided that $(\theta Q - 1)$ in the present restatement of Ricardo's argument was significantly positive. Now the British government had raised the national debt to £800m by the end of the Napoleonic wars, and debt interest amounted to about £30m in 1815. It has been estimated that the National Income was around £300m in 1815, so the national debt amounted to between two and three times the national income, and debt interest was about 10 per cent of the national income.[14] In so far as the taxes needed to finance this fell on wages, they could in no way depress the natural wage. The food and manufactures workers had to be able to buy to maintain a constant population were given as specific physical quantities. Hence any taxes which apparently fell on workers would have to come ultimately from profits or from rents. If the total taxes which fell on workers and capitalists amounted to a fraction Γ of the natural wage, the excess of marginal necessity production available to them over the natural wage would sink from $(\theta Q - 1)$ to $(\theta Q - \Gamma - 1)$. High taxation therefore brought the stationary state nearer by limiting the possibility of a wage higher than the natural rate, or of a sufficiently high rate of profit to encourage accumulation. Taxation would also cut the rate of profit where capital and labour grow at the same rate from:

$$\frac{\theta Q - 1}{\dfrac{\beta}{\alpha} + \dfrac{K}{L}} \quad \text{to} \quad \frac{\theta Q - \Gamma - 1}{\dfrac{\beta}{\alpha} + \dfrac{K}{L}}$$

and it would cut the rate of growth where $k = n$ from:

$$\frac{\theta Q - 1}{\dfrac{1}{\alpha} + \dfrac{1}{\beta}\left(\dfrac{K}{L}\right)} \quad \text{to} \quad \frac{\theta Q - \Gamma - 1}{\dfrac{1}{\alpha} + \dfrac{1}{\beta}\left(\dfrac{K}{L}\right)}$$

If the surplus of output per worker with marginal land over the natural wage was, say, 20 per cent, a diversion of 10 percentage points to recipients of debt interest via the taxation of wages and profits would cut capital accumulation by one-half, which would considerably slow the rate of recovery of the economy.

About half the chapters of Ricardo's *Principles* are concerned with the incidence of taxation, and he was able to predict this precisely from his complete model of the working of the economy. Two kinds of taxation would fall on neither wages nor profits. First, the taxation of rents would obviously in no way fall on the margin of $(\theta Q - \Gamma - 1)$ which determines the rate of profit and the rate of growth. Secondly, as has already been shown, the taxation of luxuries has no effect on the rate of profit:

> a tax on luxuries would have no other effect than to raise their price. It would fall wholly on the consumer, and could neither increase wages nor lower profits. (R I 243–4)

A luxury is, of course, any commodity which does not enter into the natural wage, and which is not used at any point as a capital good. It then enters in no way into the expression $(\theta Q - \Gamma - 1)$ so it will indeed have no effect on the rate of profit or the rate of growth, or the excess of the market wage over the natural wage. Taxes on necessities will of course be passed on by labour and influence the rate of profit and the rate of growth, as will all the taxes which are levied directly on capital and on labour.

With this framework of analysis, anything which reduced Γ, the total taxes falling on labour and capital, would raise the rate of growth, the rate of profit and the wage (though not necessarily in that order), and postpone arrival at the stationary state. It is no wonder that Ricardo considered Malthus's proposal to raise unproductive expenditure (together with the taxation needed to finance it) in order to increase effective demand an extraordinary fallacy. His notes on the section of Malthus's *Principles* entitled, 'Of the Distribution occasioned by unproductive Consumers, considered as the Means of increasing the exchangeable Value of the whole Produce', includes the comments:

> A body of unproductive labourers are just as necessary and as useful with a view to future production, as a fire, which should consume in the manufacturers warehouse the goods which those unproductive labourers would otherwise consume. (R II 421)

How can unproductive consumption increase profits? Commodities consumed by unproductive consumers are given to them, not sold for an equivalent. They have no price – how can they increase profits?

Mr. Malthus has defined demand to be the will and power to consume. What power has an unproductive consumer? Will the taking 100 pieces of cloth from a clothiers manufactory, and clothing soldiers and sailors with it, add to his profits? Will it stimulate him to produce? – yes, in the same way as a fire would. (R ii 424–5)

How can they by their consumption give value to the results of the national industry? It might as justly be contended that an earthquake which overthrows my house and buries my property, gives value to the national industry. (R ii 436)

Ricardo is nowhere else as scathing as this. His own approach to achieving a post-1815 recovery was the opposite of Malthus's. According to his analysis, taxation needed to be reduced, not increased, and the obvious way to cut public expenditure and taxation was to get rid of debt interest, a mere transfer payment. As a Member of Parliament in 1819, he spoke in favour of a capital levy to repay the national debt on several occasions in the House of Commons. Thus on 9 June 1819:

He would, however, be satisfied to make a sacrifice; the sacrifice would be a temporary one, and with that view he would be willing to give up as large a share of his property as any other individual. By such means ought the evil of the national debt to be met. It was an evil which almost any sacrifice would not be too great to get rid of. It destroyed the equilibrium of prices, occasioned many persons to emigrate to other countries, in order to avoid the burthen of taxation which it entailed, and hung like a mill-stone round the exertion and industry of the country. (R v 21)

On 24 December 1819 he added:

[The corn laws] had tended to raise the price of sustenance, and that had raised the price of labour, which of course diminished the profit on capital. But of all this evil, the national debt, and the consequent amount of taxation, was the great cause. Hence the main object of the legislature should be to provide for the payment of that debt, and that provision should commence its operation as soon as possible. For as this debt was chargeable upon all the capital of the country, it was obvious that any capital which went out of the country was exonerated from that charge, while the capital which remained was of course compelled to pay a greater proportion of debt and taxes. (R v 38)

On 6 March 1823 he was still trying to convince his fellow Members of Parliament:

> He thought a national debt of 800 millions a very serious evil; and he thought so from the heart-burnings which were occasioned by the taxes levied to pay it, which in one year affected one interest, and the next year another interest. Taxation pressed on every interest; and did he not propose to benefit mankind when he said we ought to endeavour to get rid of the debt? By doing this, should we not get rid of the expense of collecting taxes? Should we not get rid of the immorality of smuggling and of the excise laws? By getting rid of smuggling, should we not benefit trade? For all the profit of the smuggler was a tax on the whole community.
> (R v 268)

Ricardo had proposed a capital levy over five years, equivalent to the whole national debt. He believed that this would not depress the prices of capital assets and land:

> With respect to the objection, that the effect...would be to bring so much land into the market, that purchasers could not be found for such a glut, the answer was, that the stockholder would be eager to employ his money, as he received it, either in the purchase of land, or in loans to the farmer or landowner, by which the latter might be enabled to become the purchaser. (R v 34–5)

Nor would this vast capital levy reduce the true personal wealth of individuals. Ricardo had already explained in the *Principles* that at, for instance, an interest rate of 5 per cent, a perpetual obligation to pay taxes of £100 was equivalent to a debt of £2 000, so a capitalist who had £2 000 levied upon him as his share of a national debt repayment programme could reasonably incur a private debt of up to £2 000 to meet it provided his taxes were reduced by at least £100 per annum, as they certainly should be (R I 247–8).

   The logic of Ricardo's analysis is clear, and in the twentieth century it has actually been rediscovered and reiterated by Robert Barro (1974). The desirability of repaying the national debt follows naturally from his economic theory of the detailed interconnections of the economy, but the boldness of the proposal left his contemporaries breathless. Mr Alexander Baring, speaking immediately after Ricardo's 1823 speech from which a passage is quoted above, said he had never listened to one which led to 'so singular a conclusion'. It was 'the plan of a man who might calculate well and read deeply, but who had not studied mankind' (R v 270). Lord Brougham wrote in his posthumous sketch of Ricardo in Parliament:

> When he propounded, as the best way of extricating us from our financial embarrassments, that the capital of the country should be taxed 700 or 800 millions, and the debt at once paid off, and defended this scheme upon the twofold ground, that what a debtor owes is always to be deducted from his property and regarded as belonging to his creditors, and that the expense of managing the debt and raising the revenue to pay the interest would be a large saving to the nation, he assumed as true two undeniable facts, but he drew a practical inference not more startling at its first statement than inadmissable when closely examined upon the clearest grounds of both expediency and justice. (R v xxxiii)

Ricardo's proposal was ignored by his contemporaries, but the national debt was not allowed to rise further after 1819 (when it reached a peak of £844m) so it fell regularly as a ratio of the national income. From 1819 to 1914 the national income rose from about £300m to about £2 200m while the national debt fell from £844m to £620m – an enormous relative reduction,[15] which may well have owed something to the economic arguments which Ricardo was one of the first to put forward. The reduction in the ratio of the national debt to the national income which occurred in the century after his death would have pleased him, but it was far slower than he would have wished.

Ricardo's contemporaries must have found his analysis of the effects of the introduction of machinery just as startling and unexpected as his proposal to repay the national debt. On 30 May 1823 it is recorded that in the House of Commons:

> Mr. Ricardo said, his proposition was, not that the use of machinery was prejudicial to persons employed in one particular manufacture, but to the working classes generally. It was the means of throwing additional labour into the market, and thus the demand for labour, generally, was diminished. (R v 303)

By 1820 Ricardo had read a brilliant book by John Barton, which convinced him that machinery could reduce the demand for labour.

As Barton wrote in 1817:

> It does not seem that every accession of capital necessarily sets in motion an additional quantity of labour. Let us suppose a case. – A manufacturer possesses a capital of £1,000, which he employs in maintaining twenty weavers, paying them £50 per annum each. His capital is suddenly increased to £2,000. With double means he does however hire double the number of workmen, but lays out £1,500 in erecting machinery, by the help of which five men are enabled to perform the same quantity of work as twenty did before. Are there not then fifteen men discharged in consequence of the manufacturer having increased his capital?
>
> But does not the construction and repair of machinery employ a number of hands? – Undoubtedly – As in this case a sum of £1,500 was expended, it may be supposed to have given employment to thirty men for a year, at £50 each. If calculated to last fifteen years (and machinery seldom wears out sooner) then thirty workmen might always supply fifteen manufacturers, with these machines; – therefore each manufacturer may be said constantly to employ two. – Imagine also that one man is always employed in the necessary repairs. We have then five weavers, and three machine makers, where there were before twenty weavers...
>
> The demand for labour depends then on the increase of circulating, and not of fixed capital. Were it true that the proportion between these two sorts of capital is the same at all times, and in all countries, then indeed it follows that the number of labourers employed is in proportion to the wealth of the state. But such a position has not the semblance of probability. As arts are cultivated, and civilization is extended, fixed capital bears a larger and larger proportion to circulating capital. The amount of fixed capital employed in the production of a piece of British muslin is at least a hundred, probably a thousand times greater than that employed in the production of a similar piece of Indian muslin. – And the proportion of circulating capital employed is a hundred or a thousand times less. It is easy to conceive that under certain circumstances, the whole of the annual savings of an industrious people might be added to fixed capital, in which case they would have no effect in increasing the demand for labour. (pp. 15–17)

Ricardo quoted the last of these three paragraphs in the third edition of the *Principles* which he published in 1821, and he proposed an example extremely similar to Barton's where the construction of a machine involved the conversion of circulating capital into fixed capital, and as with Barton, the demand for labour depended only upon circulating capital. The construction of machinery reduced the quantity of circulating capital, and so the demand for labour.

In Ricardo's example a capitalist has a capital valued at £20 000 which is initially £13 000 circulating and £7 000 fixed. The profit to the capitalist is £2 000, which is entirely consumed, so no growth of capital is occurring. In a particular year he converts £7 500 of the circulating capital into fixed capital by employing some of his workers to construct a machine instead of producing provisions. In consequence in the following year his total capital is still £20 000 but his fixed capital is up from £7 000 to £14 500 as a result of the construction of the machine, while his circulating capital is down from £13 000 to £5 500. Ricardo concludes that in this case, where there is no net accumulation of capital, the capitalist's 'means of employing labour would be reduced in the proportion of £13 000 to £5 500, and, consequently, all the labour which was before employed by £7 500, would become redundant' (R I 389). Surprisingly, as he seems in such close agreement with Barton, he supplements his quotation from him with the qualification:

> It is not easy, I think, to conceive that under any circumstances, an increase of capital should not be followed by an increased demand for labour; the most that can be said is, that the demand will be in a diminishing ratio. (R I 396)

That conclusion can in fact be arrived at entirely straightforwardly from the logic of Ricardo's argument. Up to this point in the present restatement, the influence of the accumulation process upon K/L, capital per worker measured in necessities, has been neglected, and the time has now come to remove this deficiency. It is simplest to assume that $K/L = F(K_c/L)$, where K_c/L is circulating capital per worker measured in necessities, while F is the ratio of total capital to circulating capital. If L is the total labour force, and K the total capital stock, it follows that:

$$L = \frac{K}{F\left(\dfrac{K_c}{L}\right)} \qquad (6.18)$$

Thus L, the total labour force, will grow at the same rate as K, the total capital stock, if K_c/L, circulating capital per worker, is constant, and if F, the ratio of total capital to circulating capital, is also constant. Therefore, the labour force will grow in line with the capital stock provided that its growth does not actually initiate a rising trend in circulating capital per worker, or a tendency towards mechanisation which continuously raises F by raising fixed capital relative to circulating capital. Throughout most of his analysis Ricardo does not bring rising circulating capital per worker or a rising ratio of fixed to circulating capital into the argument. On the contrary, he says several times that an increase in capital and a consequent increase in employment are equivalent.[16] There are however passages in the third edition of the *Principles* which make it clear that by 1821 this was merely a simplifying assumption.

It was shown in the first part of this chapter that as capital accumulates there is a continuing tendency for inferior land to be resorted to, and that even with Ricardo's more sophisticated assumptions about wages, this always produces a tendency for money wages to rise. This continual rise in money wages then produces the celebrated 'Ricardo effect'. As the money wage rises, the cost of labour rises relative to the cost of constructing a machine. If a single machine-making worker produces Q_k physical units of machinery, these will always have the same value as the M pieces of gold that a goldminer produces if there are equal capital to labour ratios in machine-making and goldmining. Hence a unit of machinery will sell for M/Q_k pieces of gold, whatever happens to money wages. In Ricardo's words, 'We see then that machines would not rise in price, in consequence of a rise of wages' (R I 41). This sentence was inserted into the third edition of the *Principles* – the one which for the first time included the chapter 'On Machinery'. Ricardo then added the following extremely important footnote:

> We here see why it is that old countries are constantly impelled to employ machinery, and new countries to employ labour. With every difficulty of providing for the maintenance of men, labour necessarily rises, and with every rise in the price of labour, new temptations are offered to the use of machinery. This difficulty of providing for the maintenance of men is in constant operation in old countries, in new ones a very great increase in the population may take place without the least rise in the wages of labour.
> (R I 41)

In the new machinery chapter itself there is a similar passage:

> In America and many other countries, where the food of man is
> easily provided, there is not nearly such great temptation to
> employ machinery as in England, where food is high, and costs
> much labour for its production. The same cause that raises labour,
> does not raise the value of machines, and, therefore, with every
> augmentation of capital, a greater proportion of it is employed on
> machinery. (R I 395)

There are, therefore, important passages inserted into the third
edition of the *Principles* which argue that the adoption of machinery
is an integral part of the growth process itself, and not the result of a
series of chance events. As capital accumulates and employment rises
and the economy is forced on to inferior land, money wages are
driven up relative to the cost of machinery, which leads to mechanisation that raises F, the ratio of total capital to circulating capital. The
result is that employment will not necessarily grow as fast as the
capital stock, and this follows quite clearly from equation (6.18),
from which the following expression can readily be derived:

$$\text{Elasticity of } L \text{ with respect to } K = \frac{1}{1 + \text{Elasticity of } F \text{ with respect to } L + \text{Elasticity of } K_c/L \text{ with respect to } L} \quad (6.19)$$

Labour growth will raise F continuously through the 'Ricardo effect',
which will ensure that the elasticity of F with respect to L will always
be positive. But the elasticity of K_c/L with respect of L will tend to be
negative because of the falling trend in the real wage as the stationary
state is approached, which will slowly reduce circulating capital per
worker measured in necessities. The elasticity of L with respect to K
will only be less than 1 in so far as the tendency of F to rise with
employment is stronger than the tendency of K_c/L to fall with this.
Clearly it sometimes will be, and over such periods the strength of the
trend towards mechanisation will cause employment to grow more
slowly than the *total* capital stock.

Could capital accumulation actually produce a decline in employment as a result of the machinery effect? The answer to that question
is an unequivocal 'no'. It is labour growth itself which forces a society

on to ever less fertile land. It is this that raises money wages in relation to the cost of machinery, which then causes capitalists to substitute machinery for labour and so raise F. Hence the process of mechanisation will only get under way at all while employment is growing. There must, therefore, be growing employment to set off the process which leads to the adoption of machinery. That most plausibly is why Ricardo was adamant that an increase in capital would always lead to some increase in the demand for labour. If there was no mechanisation, capital and labour could grow in line with each other, while if there was mechanisation, this was occurring mainly because the labour force was growing and forcing the economy on to inferior land, which pushed up wages and made the use of machinery increasingly attractive.

There is a clear contrast between the continuing trends of growing economies, where capital accumulation together with an endogenous tendency towards mechanisation is inevitably associated with growing employment, and the one-off effects of the adoption of machinery by a particular employer. A single capitalist may clearly cut the employment he provides, as in Barton's example and Ricardo's own. Even in this case, however, favourable long-term effects on employment must follow in the end. Ricardo assumed that his capitalist would have the same money profits of £2 000 after he had constructed his machine, but since this must reduce the cost and price of what he produces, 'it could not fail to follow from the reduction in the price of commodities consequent on the introduction of machinery, that with the same wants he would have increased means of saving – increased facility of transferring revenue into capital. But with every increase of capital he would employ more labourers' (R I 390). There will then be favourable long-term effects on employment if the adoption of machinery raises profits and some of these extra profits are reinvested:

> I have before observed, too, that the increase of net incomes, estimated in commodities, which is always the consequence of improved machinery, will lead to new savings and accumulations. These savings, it must be remembered are annual, and must soon create a fund, much greater than the gross revenue, originally lost by the discovery of the machine, when the demand for labour will be as great as before, and the situation of the people will be still further improved by the increased savings which the increased net revenue will still enable them to make. (R I 396)

Thus, in spite of adverse short-term effects which lower the rate of growth of the demand for labour, and reduce demand absolutely in particular industries and occupations, Ricardo was convinced that the introduction of machinery must have favourable effects on the demand for labour in the end.

There were attempts in Parliament to protect workers from the short-run adverse effects. On 30 May 1823 Mr Attwood presented a petition from the manual weavers of Stockport complaining of 'certain improvements in machinery, the effect of which had been to reduce the quantity of employment of those who wove by hand, and which threatened to leave a large population without any means whatever of support'. Ricardo's reaction is interesting:

> it was evident, that the extensive use of machinery, by throwing a large portion of labour into the market, while, on the other hand, there might not be a corresponding increase of demand for it, must, in some degree, operate prejudicially to the working classes. But still he would not tolerate any law to prevent the use of machinery. The question was, – if they gave up a system which enabled them to undersell in the foreign market, would other nations refrain from pursuing it? Certainly not. They were therefore bound, for their own interest, to continue it. (R v 302–3)

International considerations, therefore, made it imperative that full advantage be taken of machinery. Ricardo had already explained this very clearly in the machinery chapter in the 1821 edition of the *Principles*:

> The employment of machinery could never be safely discouraged in a State, for if a capital is not allowed to get the greatest net revenue that the use of machinery will afford here, it will be carried abroad, and this must be a much more serious discouragement to the demand for labour, than the most extensive employment of machinery; for, while a capital is employed in this country, it must create a demand for some labour; machinery cannot be worked without the assistance of men, it cannot be made but with the contribution of their labour. By investing part of a capital in improved machinery, there will be a diminution in the progressive demand for labour; by exporting it to another country, the demand will be wholly annihilated. (R i 396–7)

In fact international trade has vital effects on Ricardo's whole argument. Machinery could only have temporary adverse effects on workers' living standards because in time its favourable effects on accumulation would restore a rising trend in the demand for labour, but there was one development which could make long-term growth an impossibility – diminishing agricultural efficiency, the centrepiece of Ricardo's analysis. However the obstacles to growth that this presented were all avoidable. The corn laws taxed imported food heavily and it was this that brought the eventual stationary state closer by throwing the need to feed a growing population *on to British marginal land*. It goes without saying that Ricardo sought the abolition of the corn laws, because if they went, only world-wide diminishing returns could bring the stationary state nearer, and these were so distant that he did not even trouble to mention them when he set out how international trade could make indefinite growth a possibility:[17]

> A real rise of wages is necessarily followed by a real fall of profits, and, therefore, when the land of a country is brought to the highest state of cultivation, – when more labour employed upon it will not yield in return more food than what is necessary to support the labourer so employed, that country is come to the limit of its increase both of capital and population.
>
> The richest country in Europe is yet far distant from that degree of improvement, but if any had arrived at it, by the aid of foreign commerce, even such a country could go on for an indefinite time increasing in wealth and population, for the only obstacle to this increase would be the scarcity, and consequent high value, of food and other raw produce. Let these be supplied from abroad in exchange for manufactured goods, and it is difficult to say where the limit is at which you would cease to accumulate wealth and to derive profit from its employment. (R IV 179)

The abolition of the corn laws and the repayment of the national debt were therefore the two major policy proposals which followed from his analysis. Debt interest and other government expenditure, with the consequent need to levy high taxation, could bring growth prematurely to a halt. The need to grow extra food at home could also do this. If an elastic supply of food could be obtained from overseas in exchange for manufactures, the rate of profit would suffer no tendency to fall. Ricardo concluded that the British economy could have a remarkable future if only the debt burden could be removed and the corn laws abolished. He put this succinctly in an important speech in the House of Commons on 16 May 1822, about a year before his death:

> Of all the evils complained of, he was still disposed to think the corn laws the worst. He conceived that were the corn laws once got rid of, and our general policy in these subjects thoroughly revised, this would be the cheapest country in the world; and that, instead of our complaining that capital was withdrawn from us, we should find that capital would come hither from all corners of the civilized world. Indeed, such a result must be certain, if we could once reduce the national debt – a reduction, which, although by many considered to be impracticable, he considered by no means to be so. That great debt might be reduced by a fair contribution of all sorts of property – he meant, that, by the united contribution of the mercantile, the landed, and he would add, the funded interest, the national debt might be certainly got rid of. If this were done, and if the government would pursue a right course of policy as to the corn laws, England would be the cheapest country in which a man could live; and it would rise to a state of prosperity, in regard to population and riches, of which, perhaps, the imaginations of hon. gentlemen could at present form no idea. (R v 187–8)

This is remarkable analysis. Who else was so optimistic in 1822? The corn laws were of course abolished in 1846, and debt interest fell steadily from 10 per cent of the national income in 1815 to less than 1 per cent in 1914, and the remarkable growth that he predicted occurred.

In addition to his successes in both prediction and policy advice, Ricardo is supremely the economist's economist. He never hesitated to go where his logic took him, however astonishing the result. He constructed an economic model of the working of the economy which showed that wage increases were as likely to reduce prices as to raise them, that output-augmenting agricultural improvements would reduce rents, that the installation of machinery was contrary to the interests of the working class, that agricultural profitability could be raised by allowing in free imports of food, and that a national debt almost three times as large as the national income could and should be repaid within five years. He was extremely influential despite the astonishment of some of his contemporaries at these propositions.

How influential is naturally a matter of controversy, but many who voted to abolish the corn laws in 1846 must have learned that this was correct policy from financial writers who had themselves been influenced by Ricardo's logic. His success as a practical economist therefore by no means ended with the £800000 he made for his family, and left, naturally enough, almost wholly invested in land.[18] In today's world he would be appalled by the effect of Britain's entry into the European Economic Community on the cost of food, and therefore, he would surmise, on the rate of profit. He would also be appalled by workers' efforts to prevent the efficient use of machinery which foreign workers use so effectively in competition against them. Even today, we ignore Ricardo at our peril.

7 Marx's Theory of Exploitation

Many would consider Marx's contribution to economics a very small part of his total achievement. As Machiavelli has remarked:

> Of all men who have been eulogised, those deserve it most who have been the authors and founders of religions; next come such as have established republics or kingdoms.[1]

In addition to all that, Marx was the last great classical economist. As with so much of his thought, the importance of his economic analysis was scarcely recognised at first. For thirty years he and John Stuart Mill produced their vastly different analyses of similar problems in the same city, but Mill was all but unaware of Marx's existence in London. By the time Alfred Marshall published his *Principles of Economics* in 1890 Marx had found his way into the index: 'Marx, Karl, his misunderstanding of Ricardo; circular reasoning in arguments of; his definitions of capital; borrowings by, from earlier works'. Keynes, in his *The General Theory of Employment, Interest and Money*, refers to the 'underworlds of Karl Marx, Silvio Gesell or Major Douglas'.[2] After the Second World War Marx emerged from the 'underworld' in Britain and the United States and since then a vast literature on the interpretation, reinterpretation and modern significance of his analysis, including important contributions by Morishima, Samuelson and Joan Robinson, has appeared in English.[3] His economics was of course taken seriously in the non-English speaking world as soon as it appeared.

It is important to recognise that much of Marx's devastatingly influential economic analysis followed directly from that of his great predecessors. As will soon become evident, he followed Quesnay, Smith, Malthus and Ricardo in dividing the economy into productive and unproductive sectors. As in their analysis, the surplus of the productive sector, which virtually disappeared from economics after Marx, is the source of capital accumulation and the principal determinant of growth. As with his classical predecessors, population has the potential to grow rapidly at a miserable wage. The proposition that the rate of profit has a long-run tendency to fall is one of the most striking elements in Marx's predictions for the future of capitalism, but Smith and Ricardo before him predicted a continuing fall in the profit rate, though for different reasons.

Marx also had no monopoly of the belief that workers are exploited by the owners of capital and land. Over a century before the publication of *Capital*, Adam Smith, then a forty-year-old Professor of Moral Philosophy, wrote in an early draft for *The Wealth of Nations:*

> In a civilized society the poor provide both for themselves and for the enormous luxury of their superiors. The rent which goes to support the vanity of the slothful landlord is all earned by the industry of the peasant...Among savages, on the contrary, every individual enjoys the whole produce of his own industry.

Smith went on, no less strikingly:

> In a society of an hundred thousand families, there will perhaps be one hundred who don't labour at all, and who yet, either by violence or by the more orderly oppression of law, employ a greater part of the labour of the society than any other ten thousand in it. The division of what remains, too, after this enormous defalcation, is by no means made in proportion to the labour of each individual. On the contrary those who labour most get least. (Jur 563–4)

But Smith did not go on to develop a *theory* of exploitation, and by the time he published *The Wealth of Nations* at the age of fifty-three he appreciated that capital accumulation originates from the supluses obtained from the output of productive labour, and that this can continuously raise the demand for labour and offer the principal hope of higher wages. By 1776 he therefore saw some (though by no means complete) harmony of interests between workers and other classes where, in his 1763 manuscript, he saw the exploitation of one class by others.

A vital factor which prevented Marx from following Smith in the more benign view that capitalists and workers both gain from higher profits in so far as these lead to faster capital accumulation, was the fundamental line of argument he developed – echoing Ricardo's machinery chapter – that capital accumulation can destroy as many jobs as it creates, so that the re-investment of profits will not have long-term favourable effects on wages. Therefore, while the young Marx, like Smith at first, believed that workers were exploited by other classes, he found no reason to modify that opinion in his mature published work. On the contrary, he thought through and published his important and influential theory of exploitation.

THE THEORY OF EXPLOITATION

The starting point for an understanding of this is to examine the ways in which an embryo capitalist, Mr Moneybags as Marx calls him, can become rich. Suppose he comes to market with £100 of money, buys commodities of some sort with this, and then manages to sell them for £110. In Marx's terms he has started with money, M, changed this into commodities, Q, and then sold these for M' of money. This sequence can be written as $M - Q - M'$ and since M' exceeds M by £10, Mr Moneybags has gained £10. He is satisfactorily on the way to becoming richer, but he has also been very fortunate, for other capitalists must have sold to him commodities for £100 and then discovered that it cost £110 to buy back the same commodities, or alternatively, that for the £100 obtained from selling the first commodities, less can be bought back. Alongside the sequence:

$$M - Q - M'$$

of the first capitalist, other capitalists will have sold commodities, Q, for money, M, and then used this to buy commodities, Q', to produce the sequence:

$$Q - M - Q'$$

where Q' must be less than Q to precisely the extent that M' exceeds M. The two sequences are equivalent because each time one capitalist trades commodities for money, another is trading money for commodities. Hence, wherever M is written for one capitalist, Q must be written for another, and vice versa.

If Mr Moneybags has gained £10 from his $M - Q - M'$, the other capitalists must have lost the very same £10 in their $Q - M - Q'$. Capitalists who bring money and commodities to the marketplace are therefore collectively playing what is nowadays called a zero-sum game in that, for every capitalist who comes out of any subsequent transactions with a profit, others must lose equivalently. The possible sequences are complex, but as Marx puts the crux of the argument:

> A may be clever enough to get the advantage of B or C without their being able to retaliate. A sells wine worth £40 to B, and obtains from him in exchange corn to the value of £50. A has converted his £40 into £50, has made more money out of less, and has converted his commodities into capital. Let us examine this a little more closely. Before the exchange we had £40 worth of wine in the hands of A, and £50 worth of corn in those of B, a total value of £90. After the exchange we have still the same total value of £90. The value in circulation has not increased by one iota, it is only distributed differently between A and B. What is a loss of value to B is surplus-value to A; what is 'minus' to one is 'plus' to the other. The same change would have taken place, if A, without the formality of an exchange, had directly stolen the £10 from B. The sum of the values in circulation can clearly not be augmented by any change in their distribution, any more than the quantity of the precious metals in a country by a Jew selling a Queen Anne's farthing for a guinea. The capitalist class, as a whole, in any country, cannot over-reach themselves. (Cap i.160)

Clearly capitalists as a whole who trade money for commodities and vice versa can neither gain nor lose, but must take from the market exactly what they collectively put into it. The growing wealth of the capitalist class as a whole is therefore in no way explained by what occurs in the marketplace. So how is Mr Moneybags to become rich? He has to make use of markets, because he will certainly need them if he is to change what he starts with into more money, but he apparently cannot expect to make money in markets:

> Our friend, Moneybags, who as yet is only an embryo capitalist, must buy his commodities at their value, must sell them at their value, and yet at the end of the process must withdraw more value from circulation than he threw into it at starting. His development

into a full-grown capitalist must take place, both within the sphere of circulation and without it. These are the conditions of the problem. (Cap i.163)

The solution to the problem is that Mr Moneybags must purchase 'labour-power', or 'the aggregate of those mental and physical capabilities existing in a human being, which he exercises whenever he produces a use-value of any description' (Cap i.164). Provided that Mr Moneybags lives in a society where workers actually own their potential labour power, and are free to market it for finite periods, capitalists can expect to be able to persistently purchase it at a discount which allows them to earn profits. They cannot earn profits by buying and selling physical commodities, because as has been shown there must be losses to some capitalists wherever there are profits to others. But capitalists can buy labour-power at its *value in exchange* – the market price of labour – and use it in a production process to obtain its *value in use*, which as Marx explains will often be much higher.

The value of labour-power that capitalists have to pay for – its value in exchange –

is determined, as in the case of every other commodity, by the labour-time necessary for the production, and consequently also the reproduction, of this special article...

If the owner of labour-power works to-day, to-morrow he must again be able to repeat the same process in the same conditions as regards health and strength. His means of subsistence must therefore be sufficient to maintain him in his normal state as a labouring individual. His natural wants, such as food, clothing, fuel, and housing, vary according to the climatic and other physical conditions of his country. On the other hand, the number and extent of his so-called necessary wants, as also the modes of satisfying them, are themselves the product of historical develop-ment, and depend therefore to a great extent on the degree of civilisation of a country, more particularly on the conditions under which, and consequently on the habits and degree of comfort in which, the class of free labourers has been formed. In contradis-tinction therefore to the case of other commodities, there enters into the determination of the value of labour-power a historical and moral element. Nevertheless, in a given country, at a given period, the average quantity of the means of subsistence necessary for the labourer is practically known.

The owner of labour-power is mortal. If then his appearance in the market is to be continuous, and the continuous conversion of money into capital assumes this, the seller of labour-power must perpetuate himself, 'in the way that every living individual perpetuates himself, by procreation'. The labour-power withdrawn from the market by wear and tear and death, must be continually replaced by, at the very least, an equal amount of fresh labour-power. Hence the sum of the means of subsistence necessary for the production of labour-power must include the means necessary for the labourer's substitutes, i.e., his children, in order that this race of peculiar commodity-owners may perpetuate its appearance in the market. (Cap i.167–8)

It is to be noted that the exchange value of labour-power, that is, the wage that workers are actually paid, has both a physiological and a social element. The wage is not just the quantity of commodities needed to keep a worker and his family alive to produce more workers in the next generation. The wage also depends on the 'degree of civilisation of a country' and on the 'habits and degree of comfort in which the class of free labourers has been formed', but as Marx argues, 'in a given country, at a given period, the average quantity of the means of subsistence necessary for the labourer is practically known'. When Mr Moneybags pays his workers enough money to buy this quantity of commodities, he purchases their labour-power and obtains the full use of this:

> The seller of labour-power, like the seller of any other commodity, realises its exchange-value, and parts with its use-value. He cannot take the one without giving the other. The use-value of labour-power, or in other words, labour, belongs just as little to its seller, as the use-value of oil after it has been sold belongs to the dealer who has sold it. The owner of the money has paid the value of a day's labour-power; his, therefore, is the use of it for a day; a day's labour belongs to him. (Cap i.188)

All the commodities that the labour-power produces in a day therefore belong to Mr Moneybags, because labour-power's *value in use* has contributed to their manufacture, but workers only need to be paid enough to buy the commodities that correspond to its *value in exchange*. Thus, 'the value of labour-power, and the value which that labour-power creates in the labour-process, are two entirely different magnitudes; and this difference of the two values was what the capitalist had in view, when he was purchasing the labour-power' (Cap i.188). If, for instance, labour's value in use is twice its value in exchange, one could say that half the working day is devoted to the manufacture of commodities for the worker's own consumption, while the goods the worker produces in the remaining hours of the day will belong to the capitalist who has bought his labour-power. The worker therefore works half a day for himself and half a day for the capitalist who employs him. 'The circumstance, that on the one hand the daily sustenance of labour-power costs only half a day's labour, while on the other hand the very same labour-power can work during a whole day, that consequently the value which its use during one day creates, is double what he pays for that use, this circumstance is, without doubt, a piece of good luck for the buyer, but by no means an injury to the seller' (Cap i.188).

Marx's argument can be set out formally. A capitalist with a money capital of M buys commodities with this to produce the previous sequence, $M - Q$. The commodities the capitalist buys are 'means of production', Q_K, that is, physical commodities such as machinery and raw materials which are used up in the process of production, and 'labour-power', Q_L, and $Q = Q_K + Q_L$. This initial purchase of commodities can be written as, $M - Q(=Q_K + Q_L)$. The capitalist then uses $(Q_K + Q_L)$ in a production process to manufacture commodities Q' which he sells for M'. The complete sequence can be written out as:

$$M - Q(= Q_K + Q_L)...\text{production process}...Q' - M'$$

In the previous sequence where only the trading of commodities was involved, whenever a particular capitalist made a profit from the sequence, $M - Q - M'$, the capitalist class as a whole could not make money, because there was necessarily the counterpart sequence for other capitalists of $Q - M - Q'$, who lost whatever the first capitalist gained. However, as there is now a production process, M' can exceed M for the capitalist class as a whole, because Q', the products which emerge from production, can be sold for more than the Q (that is, means of production and labour-power) that manufacturing them costs. Let M' exceed M by m, and let Q' exceed Q by q. Then:

$$M - Q(= Q_K + Q_L) -...\text{production process}...$$
$$-Q'(= Q + q) - M'(= M + m)$$

m is the profit that results from the production process expressed in money, and q is the gain in commodities which is obtained by the capitalist class. During the production process capital which costs Q (equalling $Q_K + Q_L$) becomes worth $Q + q$. Is it the Q_K element of capital, the means of production, or the Q_L element, the labour-power, that produces the extra q and m, or is it the two together?

To answer this fundamental question, consider first the simplest possible case of a 'corn-model' where Q_K consists entirely of seed-corn, which is then used together with Q_L of labour-power to produce a corn harvest of Q'. The Q_K of corn that goes into the production process as a means of production can be regarded as equivalent to Q_K of the corn which emerges after the harvest: according to Marx identical physical goods held before and after production cannot have different values. These identical quantitites of corn can be deducted from both the capital which goes into production (so that this is expressed net of seed-corn) and from the eventual harvest (so that this too is expressed net of the seed-corn needed to produce it). Then the capital needed to produce the net harvest is Q_L, labour-power alone, and the harvest is $(Q' - Q_K)$ which can be written as $(Q_L + q)$ since $Q' = Q_K + Q_L + q$. Hence, expressed net of seed-corn, a capitalist uses a capital of Q_L to produce a harvest of $Q_L + q$. The gain of q that results from production therefore depends entirely on the rate at which labour-power is paid. If labour-power is paid the entire harvest net of seed-corn of $Q_L + q$, there will be no profit for the capitalists. If labour-power can be bought more cheaply than this, profits will emerge. The productivity of labour power (that is, its *value in use*) relative to the cost of labour-power (its *value in exchange*) is therefore the key factor which determines profitability.

The argument has so far been set out with 'corn-model' assumptions. In reality the means of production, Q_K, and the food and manufactures which emerge from the production process to make up Q' will mostly be different commodities. However, any trading of means of production for final products will follow the zero-sum-game rules of simple commodity exchange. The capitalist class as a whole will no more be able to become rich by trading means of production for final products, than by trading commodities for other commodities, or commodities for money. An individual capitalist will be able to make money both as a result of paying less for labour-power than its value in use, and from a rise in prices of his final products in relation to the costs of his previously purchased means of production. But all capitalists obviously cannot obtain real surpluses by selling their final products at prices which have risen in relation to the prices of means of production. That could only occur if the producers of means of production suffered persistent relative price reductions in relation to those who produce final products, and competition would prevent this (Cap i.158–9). For the capitalist class as a whole, therefore, only the underpayment of labour-power will produce profits, because other capitalists holding commodities or money whose relative prices fall will necessarily lose whatever one capitalist gains from fortunate relative price changes. For the capitalist class as a whole, all commodity exchanges, including inter-temporal exchanges, will follow zero-sum-game rules in the manner that has been set out. For the capitalist class as a whole, therefore, the sequence derived with corn-model rules is valid, even though it is invalid for individual capitalists. For the capitalist class as a whole, a value equivalent to the total means of production, Q_K, can be deducted from total output, Q', to show that the employment of labour-power adds a value of $(Q' - Q_K)$ to the means of production. Profits are then obtained to the extent that labour-power can be bought for less than $(Q' - Q_K)$.

The wage bargain and the extent to which labour can be paid less than the value in use of labour-power is, therefore, the central factor which determines the share of profits in the total value that is added to the means of production. Mr Moneybags will become rich to the extent that he can underpay labour-power, which is all that workers have available for sale in a capitalist economy:

> He, who before was the money-owner, now strides in front as capitalist; the possessor of labour-power follows as his labourer. The one with an air of importance, smirking, intent on business; the other, timid and holding back, like one who is bringing his own hide to market and has nothing to expect but – a hiding. (Cap i.172)

In 1867 Marx clearly believed that the worker with only labour-power to sell, and the absolute need to sell it because starvation was the alternative, was bound to be massively exploited. Capitalists could in effect *coerce* workers to accept employment on terms dictated by their need to survive.[4]

It is of course only where material commodities are produced, that is, in industry and agriculture, that a surplus is obtainable through the underpayment of labour in the manner which has been set out. Marx therefore echoes his predecessors in believing that the economy has a productive sector which generates a surplus, and an unproductive sector which does not. With his theory the surplus arises in so far as the workers who manufacture *material commodities* are underpaid, and the surplus takes the form of commodities produced by workers, which belong to the capitalists who acquire the use of their labour-power at a favourable price. Workers who provide services for capitalists will be equally underpaid, and the capitalists in the service sector will also obtain profits by underpaying labour, but no material surplus is generated there. The capitalists in the service industries will therefore have to obtain an appropriate share of the economy's original and true surplus which is generated in industry and agriculture.[5]

Marx's formula for the 'rate of exploitation' in industry and agriculture follows directly from the argument which has been set out. The total output of material commodities has been written down so far as Q' or as $Q_K + Q_L + q$. Output is the sum of material capital inputs, that is, Q_K, which is that part of the means of production which is actually absorbed into products (which equals the total machinery and materials which capitalists make use of, less what remains that they can still use in the next period), and Q_L, the labour-power purchased and, in addition to these, q, the surplus value or profit that is obtained through the use of capital. Hence output is means of production absorbed, plus labour-power purchased, plus surplus-value. Marx invents a new terminology to describe the two kinds of capital input, once he has demonstrated that surplus-value is entirely derived from the underpayment of labour power in industry and agriculture:

> That part of capital then, which is represented by the means of production, by the raw material, auxiliary material and the instruments of labour, does not, in the process of production, undergo any quantitative alteration of value, I therefore call it the constant part of capital, or, more shortly, *constant capital*.
>
> On the other hand, that part of capital, represented by labour-

power, does, in the process of production, undergo an alteration of value. It both reproduces the equivalent of its own value, and also produces an excess, a surplus-value, which may itself vary, may be more or less according to circumstances. This part of capital is continually being transformed from a constant into a variable magnitude. I therefore call it the variable part of capital, or, shortly, *variable capital*. (Cap i.202)

C can be written for the *total* stock of constant capital or the total means of production that capitalists require in order to produce, and V for the *total* variable capital, or their *total* expenditure on labour-power, and S for *total* surplus-value.

Total output, hitherto $Q' = Q_K + Q_L + q$, can then be written as $\Pi C + V + S$, where Π is the fraction of the total stock of means of production which is absorbed into final outputs as raw materials and through the depreciation of machinery each year. Marx departed from conventional terminology by using the term *variable capital* to refer to that part of capital from which (in his argument) all profits originate, and *rate of exploitation* to describe S/V, the ratio of the fruits of exploitation to the wage bill.

Marx's economic units can be defined in a way which highlights the principal elements in his theory of exploitation. If V and S are measured in hours of labour and not quantities of commodities, it can be supposed that $V + S$ hours of labour time (of standard efficiency) are combined with ΠC units of physical means of production in a production process to manufacture final products of $\Pi C + V + S$ units. Workers receive V of the $V + S$ units of net output that result from human exertion, while the capitalist class receives the remaining S units. It can then be said that workers are only paid for V of the $V + S$ hours that they labour. The V hours in which they work for themselves provide the socially determined standard of living which ensures the reproduction of the working class: the remaining S hours provide surplus goods for the capitalists. S/V, the rate of exploitation, can then be regarded as the ratio, 'surplus labour/necessary labour'.

Clearly, if V and S are measured in hours of labour time, C must also be measured in these units. If the workers who manufacture means of production work with the same physical capital per head as those who manufacture finished goods of every kind, an hour of labour time will always lead to the production of goods which sell for the same sum of money. Goods can then be valued either in money, or in the man hours needed to produce them, without in any way affecting *relative* quantities. This echoes Ricardo's analysis where measured outputs are proportional to the labour time required to produce an article wherever capital per worker is the same.[6] Marx found it especially illuminating to *value C, V* and *S* in hours of labour time, because this made *S/V*, the rate of exploitation, 'surplus labour/necessary labour', which at once focused attention on what he regarded as a central factor in income distribution – the length of the working day.[7]

THE SIGNIFICANCE OF THE LENGTH OF THE WORKING DAY

Suppose that the goods required to provide the price of labour in exchange, that is, what workers need to be paid, can be produced in just six hours a day. Then if the working day is six hours, *S* will be zero, *S/V* will be zero and the rate of exploitation will be nil. If, in contrast, the length of the working day is nine hours, and labour productivity is unaffected by this lengthening of the working day, workers will work three hours a day to produce surplus-value and six hours a day to produce the goods they need to buy back themselves to maintain the standard of living of the working class at the socially necessary level, so 'surplus labour/necessary labour' will be 'three hours/six hours' and the rate of exploitation will be 50 per cent. If the working day is lengthened to twelve hours, 'surplus labour/necessary labour', will become 'six hours/six hours' and the rate of exploitation will be 100 per cent. A major factor influencing the rate of exploitation is, therefore, the socially determined length of the working day. There was much Victorian debate on this, and legislation to limit the length of the working day was controversial and to an extent effective. That is probably why Marx put so much emphasis on the length of the working day as a factor influencing income distribution. With the assumption that extra hours of work always raise the total amount produced, capitalists who seek to maximise the rate of exploitation can be assumed to devote much energy to lengthening the working day to the greatest possible extent. Any lengthening of the working day in no way raises the incomes of workers (which are determined entirely by the factors which determine necessary working time) and go entirely to raise surplus working time and therefore the rate of exploitation. Hence any lengthening of the working day benefits only capitalists and costs workers the time and the loss of health due to prolonged labour.

It is only in capitalism, where workers have only their labour-power to sell, that the entire extra output that results from a longer working day goes to the employer, while nothing extra goes to the workers who labour for longer hours. With the introduction of machinery in the early years of the Industrial Revolution, the incentive to capitalists to prolong the working day became especially great, as did their power to prolong it. Marx pointed out that in 1833 British parliamentary legislation had reduced the working day for children aged 13 to 18 years to a maximum of twelve hours a day, which happened to be the hours of work in the 'Ideal Workhouse', the 'House of Terror' of 1770. In other words, hours that were seen as punishing in 1770 had become less than the norm by 1833 (Cap i.263). In a powerful passage, Marx wrote:

> the capitalist employment of machinery, on the one hand, supplies new and powerful motives to an excessive lengthening of the working-day, and radically changes, as well the methods of labour, as also the character of the social working organism, in such a manner as to break down all opposition to this tendency, on the other hand it produces, partly by opening out to the capitalist new strata of the working-class, previously inaccessible to him, partly by setting free the labourers it supplants, a surplus working population, which is compelled to submit to the dictation of capital. Hence that remarkable phenomenon in the history of Modern Industry, that machinery sweeps away every moral and natural restriction on the length of the working-day. Hence, too, the economic paradox, that the most powerful instrument for shortening labour-time, becomes the most unfailing means for placing every moment of the labourer's time and that of his family, at the disposal of the capitalist for the purpose of expanding the value of his capital. 'If', dreamed Aristotle, the greatest thinker of antiquity, 'if every tool, when summoned, or even of its own accord, could do the work that befits it,...if the weavers' shuttles were to weave of themselves, then there would be no need either of apprentices for the master workers, or of slaves for the lords.' And Antipatros, a Greek poet of the time of Cicero, hailed the invention of the water-wheel for grinding corn, an invention that is the elementary form of all machinery, as the giver of freedom to female slaves, and the bringer back of the golden age. Oh! those

heathens! They understood...nothing of Political Economy and Christianity. They did not, for example, comprehend that machinery is the surest means of lengthening the working day. They perhaps excused the slavery of one on the ground that it was a means to the full development of another. But to preach slavery of the masses, in order that a few crude and half-educated parvenus, might become, 'eminent spinners', 'extensive sausage-makers', and 'influential shoe-black dealers', to do this, they lacked the bump of Christianity. (Cap i.384–5)

Marx believed that the conflict between labour and capital which establishes the length of the working day is one of the principal ways in which the outcome of the class struggle determines income distribution:

The history of the regulation of the working-day in certain branches of production, and the struggle still going on in others in regard to this regulation, prove conclusively that the isolated labourer, the labourer as 'free' vendor of his labour-power, when capitalist production has once attained a certain stage, succumbs without any power of resistence. The creation of a normal working-day is, therefore, the product of a protracted civil war, more or less dissembled, between the capitalist class and the working-class. (Cap i.283)

In *Wages, Prices and Profit* which Marx wrote in 1865, two years before the publication of the first volume of *Capital*, he said:

As to the *limitation of the working day* in England, as in all other countries, it has never been settled except by *legislative interference*. Without the working men's continuous pressure from without that interference would never have taken place. (WPP 73)

He also wrote in an important passage:

The fixation of its [the maximum rate of profit's] actual degree is only settled by the continuous struggle between capital and labour, the capitalist constantly tending to reduce wages to their physical minimum, and to extend the working day to its physical maximum, while the working man constantly presses in the opposite direction.

The matter resolves itself into a question of the respective powers of the combatants. (WPP 72–3)

These passages begin to indicate how Marx's theory of income distribution breaks out of the boundaries of what is conventionally regarded as economics, and seeks to take into account a wide range of factors coming within the general heading of 'class power', including in this naturally the power of the respective classes to pass and implement legislation. Making the length of the working day a centrepiece of the argument brings these political and social factors quite naturally to the forefront.

The length of the working day is not, of course, the sole influence on the rate of exploitation. The ratio, 'surplus labour/necessary labour', is also influenced by the number of members of a family who work. If women and children work as well as men, this will not increase the total 'necessary labour' of the family as a whole, the hours of work needed to provide the subsistence goods required by that family for the conventional standard of living of the society in question. Hence all the extra hours provided by wives and children will add to 'surplus labour':

> The value of labour-power was determined, not only by the labour-time necessary to maintain the individual adult labourer, but also by that necessary to maintain his family. Machinery, by throwing every member of that family on to the labour-market, spreads the value of the man's labour-power over his whole family. It thus depreciates his labour-power. To purchase the labour-power of a family of four workers may, perhaps, cost more than it formerly did to purchase the labour-power of the head of the family, but, in return, four days' labour takes the place of one, and their price falls in proportion to the excess of the surplus-labour of four over the surplus-labour of one. In order that the family may live, four people must now, not only labour, but expend surplus-labour for the capitalist. (Cap i.373)

Thus if it has become conventional that four members of a family work, the capitalist will find that their combined labour 'may, perhaps, cost more than it formerly did to purchase the labour-power of the head of the family' but it will not cost that much more. The combined family will receive just enough to ensure that there will be future generations supported at the conventional standard of living, so the head of the family himself will find that he is paid very much less than the amount needed to maintain his family. The price of his labour falls 'in proportion to the excess of the surplus-labour of four over the surplus-labour of one', and the family will only have enough to live at the conventional standard if four members of it do indeed work. Therefore, as with a lengthening of conventional hours of work which raises profits without raising wages, creating conditions where wives and children work raises surplus value without significantly increasing family living standards. Legislation to limit child labour and the hours worked by women therefore directly influences income distribution by reducing the ratio, 'surplus labour/necessary labour', in just the same way as legislation to limit adult hours of work. The aggregate hours a family works is only one of the factors which influence income distribution. Marx made it very clear that both an increase in hours of work and an increase in 'the intensity of labour' will raise the rate of surplus-value:

> Our analysis of absolute surplus-value had reference primarily to the extension or duration of labour, its intensity being assumed as given...It is self-evident, that in proportion as the use of machinery spreads, and the experience of a special class of workmen habituated to machinery accumulates, the rapidity and intensity of labour increase as a natural consequence. (Cap i.385–6)

> Increased productiveness and greater intensity of labour, both have a like effect. They both augment the mass of articles produced in a given time. Both, therefore, shorten that portion of the working-day which the labourer needs to produce his means of subsistence or their equivalent. (Cap i.496)

If the commodities which make up the exchange value of labour-power can be produced in four hours a day instead of six as a result of an increase in the intensity of labour, or an increase in productivity due to improved methods of production, while hours of work continue to be twelve, the rate of exploitation will rise from 'six hours/six hours' to 'eight hours/four hours', that is, from 100 to 200 per cent. A reduction in the hours needed to manufacture wage goods which results from an increase in productivity due to either improved methods of production or an increase in the intensity of labour raises what Marx calls 'relative surplus-value':

The surplus-value produced by prolongation of the working-day, I call *absolute surplus-value*. On the other hand, the surplus-value arising from the curtailment of the necessary labour-time, and from the corresponding alteration in the respective lengths of the two components of the working-day, I call *relative surplus-value*. (Cap i.299)

Increases in labour productivity therefore create *relative* surplus-value by reducing the labour time needed to produce necessities, and therefore the exchange value of labour-power. Marx makes it very clear that it is only productivity growth in the manufacture of necessities and of means of production which will have this effect:

In order to effect a fall in the value of labour-power, the increase in the productiveness of labour must seize upon those branches of industry, whose products determine the value of labour-power, and consequently either belong to the class of customary means of subsistence, or are capable of supplying the place of those means. But the value of a commodity is determined, not only by the quantity of labour which the labourer directly bestows upon that commodity, but also by the labour contained in the means of production. For instance, the value of a pair of boots depends, not only on the cobbler's labour, but also on the value of the leather, wax, thread, &c. Hence, a fall in the value of labour-power is also brought about by an increase in the productiveness of labour, and by a corresponding cheapening of commodities in those industries which supply the instruments of labour and the raw material, that form the material elements of the constant capital required for producing the necessaries of life. But an increase in the productiveness of labour in those branches of industry which supply neither the necessaries of life, nor the means of production for such necessaries, leaves the value of labour-power undisturbed. (Cap i.299)

Marx echoes Ricardo in this dichotomy between productivity growth in industries which produce wage goods and means of production and therefore influence income distribution, and productivity growth in the industries which produce luxuries that leave income distribution unaltered.[8]

Continual growth in labour productivity plays a central role in Marx's argument. Necessities are produced more and more efficiently, so they are produced in fewer hours, with the result that there is a strong rising trend in relative surplus-value. Marx echoed Smith's well-known propositions about the division of labour. With co-operation between workers in the process of production, tasks can be shared out so that each worker specialises in the performance of just one operation, 'Consequently, he takes less time in doing it, than the artificer who performs a whole series of operations in succession... Moreover, when once this fractional work is established as the exclusive function of one person, the methods it employs become perfected. The workman's continued repetition of the same simple act, and the concentration of his attention on it, teach him by experience how to attain the desired effect with the minimum of exertion' (Cap i.321). Moreover, workers are allocated to the operations they are especially likely to perform comparatively well: 'After Manufacture has once separated, made independent, and isolated the various operations, the labourers are divided, classified, and grouped according to their predominating qualities' (Cap i.330). By concentrating on one task, workers spend less time passing from job to job: 'An artificer, who performs one after another the various fractional operations in the production of a finished article, must at one time change his place, at another his tools. The transition from one operation to another interrupts the flow of his labour, and creates, so to say, gaps in his working-day' (Cap i.322). The specialisation of workers in particular tasks leads to the development of tools designed specifically to make their performance more efficient, 'so soon as the different operations of a labour-process are disconnected the one from the other, and each fractional operation acquires in the hands of the detail labourer a suitable and peculiar form, alterations become necessary in the implements that previously served more than one purpose...The manufacturing period simplifies, improves, and multiplies the implements of labour, by adapting them to the exclusively special functions of each detail labourer' (Cap i.323).

Up to this point Marx is merely repeating Smith's account of the immense gains from the division of labour, which was set out in Chapter 3, but *Capital* was published almost a century after *The Wealth of Nations* and in that time there were enormous developments in the use and extent of machinery which are reflected in the argument:

A real machinery system...a chain of machines of various kinds, the one supplementing the other...The special tools of the various detail workmen, such as those of the beaters, combers, spinners, &c., in the woollen manufacture, are now transformed into the tools of specialised machines, each machine constituting a special organ, with a special function, in the system...

A system of machinery, whether it reposes on the mere co-operation of similar machines, as in weaving, or on a combination of different machines, as in spinning, constitutes in itself a huge automaton, whenever it is driven by a self-acting prime mover...

An organised system of machines, to which motion is communicated by the transmitting mechanism from a central automaton, is the most developed form of production by machinery. Here we have, in the place of the isolated machine, a mechanical monster whose body fills whole factories, and whose demon power, at first veiled under the slow and measured motions of his giant limbs, at length breaks out into the fast and furious whirl of his countless working organs. (Cap i.358–61)

These developments in some industries lead to similar developments in others:

A radical change in the mode of production in one sphere of industry involves a similar change in other spheres...the revolution in the modes of production of industry and agriculture made necessary a revolution in the general conditions of the social process of production, i.e., in the means of communication and of transport...[these] gradually adapted to the modes of production of mechanical industry, by the creation of a system of river steamers, railways, ocean steamers, and telegraphs. But the huge masses of iron that had now to be forged, to be welded, to be cut, to be bored, and to be shaped, demanded, on their part, cyclopean machines...If we now fix our attention on that portion of the machinery employed in the construction of machines, which constitutes the operating tool, we find the manual implements re-appearing, but on a cyclopean scale. (Cap i.362–4)

Naturally, these developments immensely increase labour productivity. Marx updates Smith's famous pin factory:

According to Adam Smith, 10 men, in his day, made in co-operation, over 48,000 needles a-day. On the other hand, a single needle-machine makes 145,000 in a working-day of 11 hours. One woman or one girl superintends four such machines, and so produces near upon 600,000 needles in a day, and upwards of 3,000,000 in a week. (Cap i.432)

Marx gives other examples of enormous increases in productivity as a result of developments involving the division of labour and the use of ever improving machinery. Using mule spindles, 150 hours of labour convert 366 pounds of cotton into yarn. With hand spinning wheels, 27 000 hours of labour were needed to achieve this. With machine printing, 'a single machine prints, with the aid of one man or boy, as much calico of four colours in one hour, as it formerly took 200 men to do'. Eli Whitney's cotton gin allows one negress to clean as much cotton in a day as formerly took 100 days (Cap i.369). 'The first steel-pens were supplied by the handicraft system, in the year 1820, at £7 4s. the gross; in 1830 they were supplied by manufacture at 8s., and today the factory system supplies them to the trade at from 2s. to 6d. the gross' (Cap i.433).

These developments lead to enormous increases in the surplus-value that goes to capitalists:

> The immediate result of machinery is to augment surplus-value and the mass of products in which surplus-value is embodied. And, as the substances consumed by the capitalists and their dependants become more plentiful, so too do these orders of society...A larger portion of the produce of society is changed into surplus-produce, and a larger part of the surplus-produce is supplied for consumption in a multiplicity of refined shapes. In other words, the production of luxuries increases. (Cap i.419)

All this underlines that as the economy develops, there is a persistent trend for commodities, including those that enter into costs of production, to become cheaper. This reduces the time needed to produce the means of production and subsistence goods for the workers, and so increases the time that workers have available to labour for the capitalists who employ them. That is inevitable unless hours of work fall exactly in proportion to any rise in labour productivity, and it has been shown that Marx considered this extremely unlikely. If anything, he believed that mechanisation would give capitalists strong inducements to lengthen hours of work, and in the early stages of industrialisation they often succeeded in this. If hours of work are lengthened from 10 to 12 in a period in which growing productivity cuts necessary labour from six hours to four, the ratio 'surplus labour/necessary labour' will of course be doubly raised. Surplus labour will rise from four to eight hours while necessary labour falls *from six to four hours*, with the result that the rate of exploitation rises from 'four hours/six hours' to 'eight hours/four hours', or from 66⅔ to 200 per cent. The growth in labour productivity or the increase in relative surplus-value, taken by itself, raises the rate of exploitation from 'four hours/six hours' to 'six hours/four hours', or from 66⅔ to 150 per cent. The increase in hours of work leading to an increase in absolute surplus-value, taken by itself, raises the rate of exploitation from 'four hours/six hours' to 'six hours/six hours', or from 66⅔ to 100 per cent. The two together raise the rate of exploitation from 66⅔ to 200 per cent.

THE TENDENCY OF INCREASING MECHANISATION TO CREATE A RESERVE ARMY OF SURPLUS POPULATION

A continuous fall in the proportion of output which goes to the working class – as the rate of exploitation rises – is not the sole trend which follows from the continual mechanisation of a capitalist economy that is unfortunate for labour. There is a second tendency, to which Marx attached great significance, which has overwhelmingly important consequences. Mechanisation and the division of labour lead to immense increases in the means of production which each labourer works up into final products. The capitalists lay out constant capital of *c per worker*, that is, means of production of *c*, and variable capital or purchases of labour-power of *v per worker*, and Marx considered a rising trend in *c/v* which he described as 'the organic composition of capital', inevitable:

> the degree of productivity of labour, in a given society, is expressed in the relative extent of the means of production that one labourer, during a given time, with the same tension of labour-power, turns into products. The mass of the means of production which he thus transforms, increases with the productiveness of his labour. But those means of production play a double part. The increase of some is a consequence, that of the others a condition of the increasing productivity of labour. E.g.,

with the division of labour in manufacture, and with the use of machinery, more raw material is worked up in the same time, and, therefore, a greater mass of raw material and auxiliary substances enter into the labour-process. That is the consequence of the increasing productivity of labour. On the other hand, the mass of machinery, beasts of burden, mineral manures, drain-pipes, &c., is a condition of the increasing productivity of labour. So also is it with the means of production concentrated in buildings, furnaces, means of transport, &c. But whether condition or consequence, the growing extent of the means of production, as compared with the labour-power incorporated with them, is an expression of the growing productiveness of labour...

This change in the technical composition of capital, this growth in the mass of means of production, as compared with the mass of the labour-power that vivifies them, is reflected again in its value-composition, by the increase of the constant constituent of capital at the expense of its variable constituent. There may be, e.g., originally 50 per cent. of a capital laid out in means of production, and 50 per cent. in labour-power; later on, with the development of the productivity of labour, 80 per cent. in means of production, 20 per cent. in labour-power, and so on. This law of the progressive increase in constant capital, in proportion to the variable, is confirmed at every step (as already shown) by the comparative analysis of the prices of commodities, whether we compare different economic epochs or different nations in the same epoch. The relative magnitude of the element of price, which represents the value of the means of production only, or the constant part of capital consumed, is in direct, the relative magnitude of the other element of price that pays labour (the variable part of capital) is in inverse proportion to the advance of accumulation. (Cap i.583–4)

It is not surprising that Marx argues that capital per worker must rise massively as the economy develops and becomes increasingly mechanised. Adam Smith foreshadowed Marx with his statement that, as the division of labour advanced, the employment of an equal number of workers would require 'an equal stock of provisions, and a greater stock of materials and tools than what would have been necessary in a ruder state' (WN 277). That is, in effect, Marx's rising c/v ratio. The further propositions that Marx derives from the conviction that the organic and technical composition of capital must rise are of fundamental importance.

Marx uses these trends to challenge the view of his predecessors that capital accumulation must ultimately produce a significant increase in the demand for labour, and therefore in the standard of living of the working class. It was shown in Chapter 6 how Barton, and following him Ricardo, were the first economists to argue that mechanisation and capital accumulation could reduce the demand for labour, but Ricardo saw this as at worst a possible once-for-all adverse effect. The installation of machinery could convert circulating capital into fixed capital, and since only extra circulating capital represents an increase in wage goods, mechanisation cuts the supply of wage goods in the first instance, and therefore the demand for labour. But the higher rate of profit that results from machinery then leads to faster capital accumulation, including the accumulation of wage goods, so in due course the demand for labour becomes higher than it otherwise would have been. Mechanisation therefore raises the standard of living of the working class in the end, even though it reduces it at first. But Ricardo's assumption is that there is a single change of technique from manual production to machine production. There is thus a once-for-all rise in the capital to labour ratio after which there is no further increase, and consequently a once-for-all fall in the demand for labour upon the adoption of machinery, after which there is no further reduction from this cause.

Marx argues in contrast that the rise in the capital to labour ratio is continuous, that mechanisation rises all the time with the division of labour. The application of improving machinery to the various parts of the productive process goes on without significant interruption. Productivity therefore keeps on rising and capital to labour ratios keep on growing. If Ricardo is right to argue that each increase in fixed capital per worker reduces the demand for labour, a continuing increase in capital per worker will continuously reduce the demand for labour. Ricardo's machinery effect was therefore not just a once-for-all effect. It would continue indefinitely, so that mechanisation would all the time reduce the demand for labour, with the result that the working class would at no point reap long-term benefits from capital accumulation.

The working class does of course benefit from capital accumulation during periods where there is no change in the technique of production, so that capital accumulates with an unchanging c/v ratio, and therefore with no growth in its technical and organic composition. Marx fully recognises this:

> If we suppose that, all other circumstances remaining the same, the composition of capital also remains constant (i.e., that a definite mass of means of production constantly needs the same mass of labour-power to set it in motion), then the demand for labour and the subsistence-fund of the labourers clearly increase in the same proportion as the capital, and the more rapidly, the more rapidly the capital increases. Since the capital produces yearly a surplus-value, of which one part is yearly added to the original capital; since this increment itself grows yearly along with the augmentation of the capital already functioning; since lastly, under special stimulus to enrichment, such as the opening of new markets, or of new spheres for the outlay of capital in consequence of newly developed social wants, &c., the scale of accumulation may be suddenly extended, merely by a change in the division of the surplus-value or surplus-product into capital and revenue, the requirements of accumulating capital may exceed the increase of labour-power or of the number of labourers; the demand for labourers may exceed the supply, and therefore, wages may rise. This must, indeed, ultimately be the case if the conditions supposed above continue. For since in each year more labourers are employed than in its predecessor, sooner or later a point must be reached, at which the requirements of accumulation begin to surpass the customary supply of labour, and, therefore, a rise of wages takes place. (Cap i.575)

This traditional analysis of the favourable effects of capital accumulation on the demand for labour and on wages depends of course on the assumption of a constant technical and organic composition of capital. But, as Marx states several times, 'with every advance in the use of machinery, the constant component of capital, that part which consists of machinery, raw material, &c., increases, while the variable component, the part laid out in labour-power, decreases' (Cap i.423). Marx sets out the implications of this for employment:

> With the advance of accumulation, therefore, the proportion of constant to variable capital changes. If it was originally say 1:1, it now becomes successively 2:1, 3:1, 4:1, 5:1, 7:1, &c., so that, as the capital increases, instead of ½ of its total value, only ⅓, ¼, ⅕,

⅙, ⅛, &c., is transformed into labour-power, and, on the other hand, ⅔, ¾, ⅘, ⅚, ⅞, into means of production. Since the demand for labour is determined not by the amount of capital as a whole, but by its variable constituent alone, that demand falls progressively with the increase of the total capital, instead of, as previously assumed, rising in proportion to it. It falls relatively to the magnitude of the total capital, and at an accelerated rate, as this magnitude increases. With the growth of the total capital, its variable constituent or the labour incorporated in it, also does increase, but in a constantly diminishing proportion. The intermediate pauses are shortened, in which accumulation works as simple extension of production, on a given technical basis...This accelerated relative diminution of the variable constituent, that goes along with the accelerated increase of the total capital, and moves more rapidly than this increase, takes the inverse form, at the other pole, of an apparently absolute increase of the labouring population, an increase always moving more rapidly than that of the variable capital or the means of employment. But in fact, it is capitalistic accumulation itself that constantly produces, and produces in the direct ratio of its own energy and extent, a relatively redundant population of labourers, i.e., a population of greater extent than suffices for the average needs of the self-expansion of capital, and therefore a surplus-population. (Cap i.589–90)

In this important passage, Marx says that the demand for labour 'does increase, but in a constantly diminishing proportion', and at a slower rate than the increase in the working population. Marx's argument is therefore that the demand for labour can run ahead of the supply in periods where the organic composition of capital is constant, but where organic composition increases as it will more and more of the time as the use of machinery is extended, the labour force increases faster than the demand for labour, to produce Marx's celebrated 'reserve army of the unemployed'. This emerges increasingly as the economy mechanises:

With the magnitude of social capital already functioning, and the degree of its increase, with the extension of the scale of production, and the mass of the labourers set in motion, with the development of the productiveness of their labour, with the greater breadth and fulness of all sources of wealth, there is also an extension of the scale on which greater attraction of labourers by capital is accompanied by their great repulsion; the rapidity of the change in the organic composition of capital, and in its technical form increases, and an increasing number of spheres of production becomes involved in this change, now simultaneously, now alternately. The labouring population therefore produces, along with the accumulation of capital produced by it, the means by which it itself is made relatively superfluous, is turned into a relative surplus-population; and it does this to an always increasing extent. (Cap i.591)

The reserve army plays a fundamental role in the development of capitalism:

But if a surplus labouring population is a necessary product of accumulation or of the development of wealth on a capitalist basis, this surplus-population becomes, conversely, the lever of capitalist accumulation...The mass of social wealth, overflowing with the advance of accumulation, and transformable into additional capital, thrusts itself frantically into old branches of production, whose market suddenly expands, or into newly formed branches, such as railways, &c., the need for which grows out of the development of the old ones. In all such cases, there must be the possibility of throwing great masses of men suddenly on the decisive points without injury to the scale of production in other spheres. Overpopulation supplies these masses. The course characteristic of modern industry, viz., a decennial cycle (interrupted by smaller oscillations), of periods of average activity, production at high pressure, crisis and stagnation, depends on the constant formation, the greater or less absorption, and the re-formation of the industrial reserve army or surplus-population. (Cap i.592–3)

The reserve army which is created in the periods where the organic and technical composition of capital rises, and then diminished in periods in which accumulation continues with a near to constant organic composition has important effects on the rate of exploitation. The basic prediction of a continuous rising trend in the organic and technical composition of capital ensures that the long-term demand for labour will grow more slowly than the potential growth of population. It is shown in Chapter 8 below that this result is confirmed by a simple mathematical restatement of Marx's argument. There is therefore no long-term upward pressure on wages from growth in the demand for labour. But in addition to this:

> The industrial reserve army, during the periods of stagnation and average prosperity, weighs down the active labour-army; during the periods of over-production and paroxysm, it holds its pretensions in check. Relative surplus-population is therefore the pivot upon which the law of the demand and supply of labour works. It confines the field of action of this law within the limits absolutely convenient to the activity of exploitation and to the domination of capital. (Cap i.598)

The presence of the reserve army of labour allows the capitalist class to raise the rate of exploitation by raising both the intensity of work of the employed part of the labour force, and also hours of work. Hence the rising trend in the organic and technical composition of capital damages the standard of living of the working class, both by greatly reducing the trend rate of growth of demand for labour, and also by weakening the bargaining power of those workers fortunate enough to have jobs. These trends will all, of course, increasingly *alienate* workers from any personal acceptance of their role in the production process and in the society which makes use of them and gives them so little in exchange.[9]

The way of dealing with the situation which seems obvious to Marx is the setting up of trade unions to organise planned co-operation between the employed and the unemployed:

> As soon, therefore, as the labourers learn the secret, how it comes to pass that in the same measure as they work more, as they produce more wealth for others, and as the productive power of their labour increases, so in the same measure even their function as a means of the self-expansion of capital becomes more and more precarious for them; as soon as they discover that the degree of intensity of the competition among themselves depends wholly on the pressure of the relative surplus-population; as soon as, by Trades' Unions, &c., they try to organise a regular co-operation between employed and unemployed in order to destroy or to weaken the ruinous effects of this natural law of capitalistic production on their class, so soon capital and its sycophant, Political Economy, cry out at the infringement of the 'eternal' and so to say 'sacred' law of supply and demand. (Cap i.599)

In the absence of successful trade union action a low rate of growth of demand for labour due to the persistent trend towards capital deepening, and the competition of the unemployed who undermine the bargaining power of the employed, will perpetuate a high and rising rate of exploitation of labour, and a miserable standard of living for the working class. But, because the rate of exploitation depends partly on 'the respective powers of the combatants' united union action can improve the situation of the working class. In its absence workers have little to hope for.

In Marx's analysis class power influences wages in a way which had no parallel in the work of his great predecessors. In Ricardo, for instance, wages could never rise in the presence of a reserve army of the unemployed, because these would relentlessly depress the standard of living of those at work until the labour market cleared. In Marx, however, the extent to which the competition of the unemployed undermines the wages of the employed actually becomes one of the principal questions on which income distribution turns. If, as a result of the formation of trade unions, which were just beginning to exercise occasional influence at the time Marx wrote, the employed and the unemployed co-operated to an extent, then the conventional standard of living of the employed could be raised above the market clearing wage. Moreover, this higher wage would not necessarily be eliminated by subsequent population growth as his predecessors assumed, because this would only depress wages in so far as the unemployed competed away the extra incomes of the employed. As the growth of population depends in turn on the incomes of both the employed and the unemployed, higher wages alone will not encourage this to soar in the way that his predecessors supposed. The factors which influence wages are therefore less inextricably linked to those which determine population growth,[10] and that is one reason why Marx was able to be contemptuous of Malthus's theory of population.[11] According to Marx, those at work can be paid for more hours and therefore suffer less exploitation, provided that the unemployed co-operate sufficiently with the employed to prevent a subsequent collapse of wages when unemployment grows. The ratio of wages to profits can therefore be influenced to an extent by what actually happens in the course of wage bargaining, which was not the case with the wage theories of his predecessors.

THE COMPLICATIONS DUE TO NON-UNIFORM CAPITAL TO LABOUR RATIOS

Marx's framework for the analysis of income distribution, with its central result that 'profits/wages' equal 'surplus labour/necessary labour', is an ideal one for the analysis of how class power influences income distribution, but it suffers from an obvious difficulty. As soon as there is any departure from the assumption that all workers use the same amount of constant capital, profits cease to be directly related to labour time throughout the economy. Suppose variable capital per worker is 100_v in two industries which initially provide equal employment, while constant capital per worker is 300_c in one and 500_c in the other. With necessary labour of eight hours in a working day of twelve hours, the rate of exploitation will be 'four hours/eight hours' in both industries, and their surplus-value per worker will therefore be $\frac{1}{2} \times 100_v = 50_s$. If the rate of profit is the ratio of surplus-value to total capital, this will be $50_s/(100_v + 300_c) = 12\frac{1}{2}$ per cent in the low capital intensive industry, and $50_s/(100_v + 500_c) = 8\frac{1}{3}$ per cent in the high capital intensive one. If a discrepancy of profit rates like this actually emerged at any point, capitalists would leave the high capital intensive industry and enter the low capital intensive one until the market rate of profit became the same in both, and Marx entirely accepted that in a competitive capitalist economy, actual market prices or 'prices of production', would depart from labour values until the rate of profit was the same in each industry (sphere of production).[12] As capitalists leave the high capital intensive industry its 'prices of production' will rise relative to its costs of production, while the competition of extra capitalists in the other industry will reduce its 'prices of production' until the two rates of profit are the same. It can be supposed, to follow Marx, that surplus-value per worker will still average 50_s in the two industries taken together when the rate of profit is equalised between them, and that average capital per worker will still be $100_v + 400_c = 500$. In that case, the rate of profit in the two industries taken together and in each industry separately will be $50_s/(100_v + 400_c) = 10$ per cent. If profits per worker in the low capital intensive industry fall from 50_s to 40_s, its rate of profit will become $40_s/(100_v + 300_c) = 10$ per cent, and if profits per worker rise to 60_s in the high capital intensive industry, its rate of profit will increase to $60_s/(100_v + 500_c) = 10$ per cent.

With this *transformation* of labour values into prices of production, the rate of exploitation will appear to be $40_s/100_v = 40$ per cent in the low capital intensive industry, and $60_s/100_v = 60$ per cent in the high capital intensive one, but there is no difference in their conditions of exploitation. One industry simply uses more constant capital per worker, and with ordinary competition between capitalists, this must attract more profit per worker. Hence at the industry level, profits are in part a return to extra constant capital, so they are not wholly explained by the conditions of exploitation. And that is not all: before the transformation of labour values into prices both industries produced a net output per worker of $100_v + 50_s = 150$, but at their prices of production, net output per worker is $100_v + 40_s = 140$ in one industry and $100_v + 60_s = 160$ in the other. Hence extra constant capital per worker raises net value-added per worker when this is measured at market prices, so constant capital does more than merely pass its own value into final outputs. It adds an increment to measured outputs, which is received as higher profits per worker in capital intensive industries.

This brief summary of what occurs when labour values are transformed into prices follows Marx, and it suffers from a weakness in his presentation that only *final* prices have been modified. *Input prices* of machinery and raw materials will also differ from labour values. If their prices have to be raised or lowered in relation to labour values to equate profit rates, the two industries will no longer use constant capitals per worker of precisely 300_c and 500_c. If all prices have to be transformed in a world where capital intensities and production processes differ, complex mathematical problems will need to be solved before formulae can be derived to transform a value system reflecting labour inputs alone into a price system where the rate of profit is equal in all activities. This can be done,[13] but why is it necessary to have a labour accounting system at all if so much trouble is involved in transforming its relative values into the market prices of a competitive capitalist economy?

The merit of the labour accounting system is that it is the ideal one for presenting the consequences of Marx's fundamental insights into income distribution. His principal hypothesis was that the owners of capital have the power to coerce workers to labour longer and more intensively than the satisfaction of their own needs conceivably requires. Marx also believed that the competitive wages and prices of nineteenth-century capitalism obscured that reality. In nineteenth-century England workers were mostly entirely free to sell their labour in the best market they could find, and the coercions of feudalism or slavery which clearly made exploitation possible were in no way to be found. Companies mostly faced strong competition, which limited the prices they could charge. Superficial observers who confined their attention to the seeming realities of competitive wages and prices would find it difficult to perceive that coercion might still underpin the labour market, but once attention is focused instead on the determination of the length of the working day, the possibility that labour is being exploited re-emerges. Having set out what he considered the true laws of income distribution, and expressed them in the language of valuation in labour time, Marx then had to transform these fundamental values into what he considered the far less illuminating values of real world capitalism's competitive market prices, in order to show that valuation in labour time was not describing a different world remote from experience. It was instead an attempt to penetrate more deeply into what was happening in the real world. As two modern scholars have remarked, 'Marx's account of the formation of a general rate of profit in competition, his transformation procedure, is precisely the transition from the "inner but concealed essential pattern" to "the pattern of economic relations as seen on the surface".'[14]

That is why it is more illuminating to present Marx's theory of exploitation in the language of labour time.[15] It is however also necessary to know that hypotheses expressed in labour time are still meaningful when they are applied to a market economy. There is indeed a forceful line of argument which suggests that the difficulties involved in transforming Marx's labour values into market prices are merely technical, and of the kind that many companies nowadays continually need to solve.

To see this as simply and clearly as possible, a capitalist economy can be thought of as *a single giant firm*. Within that firm goods are produced for both workers and capitalists. The proportion of their labour time which workers devote to producing goods for themselves will go a long way towards the explanation of the ratio of total wages to net output in this single firm economy. The ratio of net profits to wages will actually equal, 'surplus labour/necessary labour', if the constant capital per worker which is required to produce workers' consumer goods is on average the same as that required to produce the goods that capitalists buy for consumption.[16] If workers' consumer goods are produced with, on average, less capital intensive technologies, 'goods produced for capitalists/goods produced for workers', measured at market prices, will come to more than 'surplus labour/necessary labour', and vice versa.[17] The ratio, 'surplus labour/

necessary labour' can explain the ratio, 'goods produced for capitalists/goods produced for workers', once this complication is allowed for, and also the ratio, 'profits/wages', measured at competitive market prices. Within the single capitalist firm, that is, in the capitalist economy as a whole, goods manufactured in one department are frequently needed as inputs in other departments: capital goods of many kinds assist in the production of each consumer good. Wherever goods are transferred beteen departments, transfer prices are needed for internal accounting reasons, to allow each department to show the same rate of profit on its total activities. The firm's accountants will need to solve the problem of calculating these, and nowadays computers could doubtless be programmed (perhaps even with the help of some of the mathematical solutions to 'the transformation problem' which have been derived) to estimate the price-system which equates the rate of profit in each process of a complex technology. But the exact derivation of this set of transfer prices is an accounting problem and the details of the solution are not especially interesting.

What is provocative of thought is Marx's proposition that the ratio of net profits to wages is quite largely explained by the ratio, 'surplus labour/necessary labour', in the firm as a whole, that is, in a complete capitalist economy, or indeed in world capitalism as a whole. He believed that mankind lived in a world where technical developments had a persistent tendency to raise the demand for labour more slowly than the growth of populations, with the result that labour scarcities would only pull up real wages for a few years at a time. At the time he wrote, the influence of the capitalist class on legislation and on law enforcement appeared to be pervasive in the countries he examined, while the persistence of a reserve army of the unemployed made it difficult for the working class to exercise countervailing power by forming effective unions. The result was that workers could be made to work long hours, and such increases in real wages as occurred appeared to be far below increases in productivity. In consequence, rising productivity was benefiting capitalists far more than workers, and according to Marx's analysis, it was the power of the capitalist class to influence hours of work and indeed the conditions of exploitation as a whole that made this inevitable.

8 Marx's Theory of the Declining Rate of Profit and the Collapse of Capitalism

Marx believed that the technical advances which offered workers so little would in the end prove equally disappointing to the capitalists. Production would become increasingly concentrated into a handful of giant companies, so that the beneficiaries of capitalism would not be numerous. Moreover, the technological trends that he extrapolated from his own century indicated that growing capital intensification would force down the rate of profit that even these companies could earn until they failed to be financially viable. Alternatively, capitalism might collapse because an impoverished working class could provide no market for their vast potential output. It is remarkable that Marx could predict a dismal economic future for *both workers and capitalists* in the face of rapid and continuous technical advance.

Marx's premises were not in fact markedly different from those of his predecessors, but he pushed trends which Smith and Ricardo were aware of to their logical limits. Smith, for instance, opened *The Wealth of Nations* with an account of the immense benefits mankind could derive from the division of labour. Marx noted that this could also be expected to lead to an increasing monopolisation of production by the diminishing number of companies able to take full advantage of the economies of large scale production. The increasing mechanisation associated with continuous extensions of the division of labour would continually raise the minimum capital a capitalist needed to command in order to compete with other capitalists:

An increased number of labourers under the control of one capitalist is the natural starting-point, as well of co-operation generally, as of manufacture in particular. But the division of labour in manufacture makes this increase in the number of workmen a technical necessity. The minimum number that any given capitalist is bound to employ is here prescribed by the previously established division of labour. On the other hand, the advantages of further division are obtainable only by adding to the number of workmen, and this can be done only by adding multiples of the various detail groups. But an increase in the variable component of the capital employed necessitates an increase in its constant component, too, in the workshops, implements, &c., and in particular, in the raw material, the call for which grows quicker than the number of workmen. The quantity of it consumed in a given time, by a given amount of labour, increases in the same ratio as does the productive power of that labour in consequence of its division. Hence, it is a law, based on the very nature of manufacture, that the minimum amount of capital, which is bound to be in the hands of each capitalist, must keep increasing (Cap i.339–40)

As mechanisation develops this continuing increase in minimum capital requirements leads to waves of bankruptcies as small businesses become unable to compete with larger ones. Businesses based on handicraft production cannot compete with factory production methods, and then small-scale factories are themselves bankrupted by the larger concentrations of capital which can alone take full advantage of the opportunities which open up as technology advances:

> [The attraction of capitals] does not mean that simple concentration of the means of production and of the command over labour, which is identical with accumulation. It is concentration of capitals already formed, destruction of their individual independence, expropriation of capitalist by capitalist, transformation of many small into few large capitals...Capital grows in one place to a huge mass in a single hand, because it has in another place been lost by many...
>
> The battle of competition is fought by cheapening of commodities. The cheapness of commodities depends, *caeteris paribus*, on the productiveness of labour, and this again on the scale of

production. Therefore, the large capitals beat the smaller. It will further be remembered that, with the development of the capitalist mode of production, there is an increase in the minimum amount of individual capital necessary to carry on a business under its normal conditions. The smaller capitals, therefore, crowd into spheres of production which Modern Industry has only sporadically or incompletely got hold of. Here competition rages in direct proportion to the number, and in inverse proportion to the magnitudes, of the antagonistic capitals. It always ends in the ruin of many small capitalists, whose capitals partly pass into the hands of their conquerors, partly vanish. Apart from this, with capitalist production an altogether new force comes into play – the credit system, which in its first stages furtively creeps in as the humble assistant of accumulation, drawing into the hands of individual or associated capitalists, by invisible threads, the money resources which lie scattered, over the surface of society, in larger or smaller amounts; but it soon becomes a new and terrible weapon in the battle of competition and is finally transformed into an enormous social mechanism for the centralisation of capitals. (Cap i.586–7)

The result of all this is that Mr Moneybags, Marx's embryo would-be capitalist, will have to be very fortunate to survive in competition with those who have access to vast capitals, assisted by the financial capitalists who control the banking and credit system. The trend will be towards concentration, centralisation and monopolisation with the result that a small number of extremely powerful and wealthy capitalist companies will emerge and dominate an increasing fraction of production. The capitalists who actually come to benefit from these trends will not be numerous. Most of the smaller capitalists will be swallowed by the larger, either through 'the violent method of annexation', or by 'the smoother process of organising joint-stock companies' (Cap i.588). The great technological advances which occur will therefore benefit only a small fraction of the population.[1]

Even the economic progress of the giant companies which come to dominate industry and commerce is by no means satisfactory. Marx does not, in fact, expect them to exploit their monopoly power by raising prices so far in relation to costs that they earn higher profits than firms in industries where the tendencies towards monopolisation are less pronounced. Marx never departs from the assumption that competition will tend to equalise profit rates throughout the economy. He does however expect companies in general, the monopolised and the rest, to achieve an ever-rising rate of exploitation of the labour they employ, and the ratio, 'surplus labour/necessary labour', should increase continuously for all the reasons set out in the previous chapter. However, the rate of profit which they can earn on their capital, which is surplus-value per worker, s, divided by constant plus variable capital per worker, $c + v$, is quite another matter. The ever-rising organic composition of capital, that is, the ever-rising c/v ratio, which is central to Marx's analysis of capitalism, can produce a falling trend in $s/(c + v)$, even though s/v keeps moving upwards. The rate of profit, $s/(c + v)$, can be written as $(s/v)/(1 + c/v)$, and it is obvious that a rising organic composition of capital which will continuously raise c/v can counteract or more than counteract any possible increase in s/v.

Marx argues that the tendency for $(1 + c/v)$ to rise will in the end be stronger than the tendency of s/v to rise, so that there will be an eventual secular fall in the rate of profit. He states first, entirely correctly, that if c/v rises while s/v is constant, the rate of profit must fall:

> If it is further assumed that this gradual change in the composition of capital is not confined only to individual spheres of production, but that it occurs more or less in all, or at least in the key spheres of production, so that it involves changes in the average organic composition of the total capital of a certain society, then the gradual growth of constant capital in relation to variable capital must necessarily lead to *a gradual fall of the general rate of profit*, so long as the rate of surplus-value, or the intensity of exploitation of labour by capital, remain the same. Now we have seen that it is a law of capitalist production that its development is attended by a relative decrease of variable in relation to constant capital. (Cap iii.212)

That statement, of course, says no more than that $(s/v)/(1 + c/v)$, the rate of profit, must decline if s/v, the rate of exploitation is constant, while c/v rises because of the law that capitalist production 'is attended by a relative decrease of variable in relation to constant capital'. Marx goes on to make an assertion which is far stronger:

> [Capitalist production] produces a progressive relative decrease of the variable capital as compared to the constant capital, and consequently a continuously rising organic composition of the total

capital. The immediate result of this is that the rate of surplus-value, at the same, or even a rising, degree of labour exploitation, is represented by a continually falling general rate of profit. (Cap iii.212–13)

Here it is asserted that $(s/v)/(1 + c/v)$ will fall, even if s/v is 'rising', so here Marx is presuming that the tendency for $(1 + c/v)$ to rise is greater than the tendency for s/v to rise. There are general reasons why he appears to believe this, but the proposition is not demonstrably based on evidence in the way that his other fundamental theorems are.

Marx recognises that this 'law' is weaker than some of his others by emphasising that it is no more than a *tendency*, and by following his chapter 'The Law as Such' with another headed 'Counteracting Influences'. These include sudden sharp increases in s/v through extra intensification of labour which temporarily offset the influence of a rising c/v on $(s/v)/(1 + c/v)$. International trade may also open up opportunities to raise s/v through competition with overseas capitalists who use greatly inferior technologies. Advances in productivity in the manufacture of means of production may postpone inevitable increases in c/v by allowing capitalists to raise the technical composition of capital without their having to raise the relative money cost of constant capital commensurately. But these are all temporary offsets to the inevitable tendency for $(1 + c/v)$ to rise faster than s/v. Why was this in any way an inevitable tendency?

Marx may have had the underlying belief that the long-term tendency for the rate of exploitation to rise was a weaker one than the largely technological tendency for the composition of capital to rise. The working class might, for instance, have the power to resist further increases in the rate of exploitation beyond a certain point, by, for example, preventing further increases in hours of work, and there is after all a physical limit to these, as Marx indicated:

Two labourers, each working 12 hours daily, cannot produce the same mass of surplus-value as 24 who work only 2 hours, even if they could live on air and hence did not have to work for themselves at all. In this respect, then, the compensation of the reduced number of labourers by intensifying the degree of exploitation has certain insurmountable limits. (Cap iii.247)

Two workers can be exploited for twelve hours each and no more, therefore, for simple physical reasons. If there is an upper limit to the intensity of labour, a maximum is set to the surplus labour which can be extracted from a worker, apart from the relative surplus labour that results from a cheapening of the means of production. Marx on occasion actually accepts that workers may sometimes share in the benefits from productivity growth.[2] It will be shown below that some increase in wages with productivity growth is, in fact, essential to the underlying logic of his argument, but suppose for the time being that hours of work are at a maximum, that intensity of labour is at a maximum, and that productivity growth increases in equal proportions what capitalists and workers receive. Then the rate of exploitation, s/v, will be at a maximum and it will increase no further. If, at the same time, $(1 + c/v)$ continues to rise, and Marx insists that it will, then $(s/v)/(1 + c/v)$ will necessarily have a persistent tendency to decline. That is probably a central feature of Marx's argument. There are obstacles to an unlimited increase in s/v, such as that hours of work and the intensity of labour may already be at an upper limit, while capitalists may not in fact enjoy the full fruits of technical progress. There is in contrast no limit to the persistent tendency of c to rise in relation to v, so $(1 + c/v)$ will rise indefinitely. Once it is accepted that there is a certain upward stickiness to s/v, there is a limit to the surplus-value measured in labour, or in hours of work that capitalists can extract. In a significant passage, Marx shows that this is indeed an important element in his argument:

> the compensation of a decrease in the number of labourers employed, or of the amount of variable capital advanced, by a rise in the rate of surplus-value, or by the lengthening of the working-day, has impassable limits. Whatever the value of labour-power may be, whether the working-time necessary for the maintenance of the labourer is 2 or 10 hours, the total value that a labourer can produce, day in, day out, is always less than the value in which 24 hours of labour are embodied...The absolute limit of the average working-day – this being by nature always less than 24 hours – sets an absolute limit to the compensation of a reduction of variable capital by a higher rate of surplus-value, or of the decrease of the number of labourers exploited by a higher degree of exploitation of labour-power. (Cap i.289)

If that is accepted, surplus-value reaches an upper limit of $s_{max}L$ where s_{max} is the maximum surplus hours of work per labourer, and L

is the employed labour force. As total capital is $(c + v)L$ and this will go on growing indefinitely, total capital is bound to grow in relation to maximum surplus-value to produce, in the end at any rate, a declining rate of profit. That is the essence of Marx's argument.[3] He speaks several times of the proposition that unpaid living labour of sL depends on the finite labour force actually in employment, which will grow slowly, if at all, because the demand for labour will grow more slowly through time for the reasons outlined in the previous chapter, while s may after a time come near to its upper limit of s_{max}. The dead labour which makes up cL will, in contrast, continue to grow, with the result that $(c + v)L$ is far more elastic upwards than $s_{max}L$, to produce the persistent tendency for the rate of profit when s is at its maximum, which can be written as $(s_{max}L)/(c + v)L$, to decline (Cap iii.215–16 and 218–19).

There is a truistic demonstration (not directly derivable from Marx's actual statements) of a necessary tendency for the rate of profit to fall if the particular trends he describes are pushed to their absolute limits. The rate of profit, $s/(c + v)$, can be written as $s/(s + v)$ times $(s + v)/(c + v)$. Now suppose that the rate of exploitation rises entirely without limit, so that s/v asymptotically approaches infinity. In that event $s/(s + v)$ will tend to unity. The highest value $s/(s + v)$ can possibly reach is 1, however high s becomes in relation to v. In contrast, $(s + v)/(c + v)$, which equals 'value-added / total capital', can fall asymptotically towards zero as total capital rises steadily in relation to what it produces. Hence as Marx's long-term trends move towards their absolute limits, so that $s/(s + v)$ rises gradually towards 1, while $(s + v)/(c + v)$ falls towards 0, their multiple, $s/(c + v)$, will necessarily fall towards zero. The rate of profit will therefore fall in the end.[4] It is, in fact, possible to establish Marx's result of an inevitable eventual decline in the rate of profit with a very simple mathematical restatement of his argument, and this will be outlined in the next section. It will be shown there that his conviction that the rate of profit will inevitably fall in economies with strong increasing returns, a rising rate of exploitation, and a growing organic composition of capital was well founded, even though he did not demonstrate the proposition decisively himself.

He certainly believed he had said enough to demonstrate the inevitability of an eventual decline in the rate of profit, and he claimed a major discovery:

Simple as this law appears from the foregoing statements, all of political economy has so far had little success in discovering it...Since this law is of great importance to capitalist production, it may be said to be a mystery whose solution has been the goal of all political economy since Adam Smith. (Cap iii.213)

He went on to use the 'law' to show just why it would make capitalism untenable, even for the handful of giant companies which would in the end emerge to dominate industry and commerce as a result of the monopolising effects of increasing returns. Up to now in the present restatement of his argument, these companies have been the sole beneficiaries of the inevitable trends of capitalism. These have failed to benefit the working class because of the inevitable decline in the rate of growth of demand for labour, which produces the reserve army of labour discussed in the previous chapter. At the same time the great majority of capitalists have been reduced to the standard of living of the proletariat, because of the inevitable tendency for their businesses to be bankrupted in the process of the continuing concentration of production. That leaves only the large monopolistic companies as potential beneficiaries, and it appeared to Marx that even they must suffer in the end from the inevitable decline in the rate of profit. Why should this be fatal to them when Smith and Ricardo also predicted an inevitable decline in the rate of profit without ever envisaging such disastrous consequences as Marx?

The difficulties which result from the declining rate of profit centre on what Marx called the problem of 'realising' surplus-value:

As soon as all the surplus-labour it was possible to squeeze out has been embodied in commodities, surplus-value has been produced. But this production of surplus-value completes but the first act of the capitalist process of production – the direct production process. Capital has absorbed so and so much unpaid labour. With the development of the process, which expresses itself in a drop in the rate of profit, the mass of surplus-value thus produced swells to immense dimensions. Now comes the second act of the process. The entire mass of commodities i.e., the total product, including the portion which replaces the constant and variable capital, and that representing surplus-value, must be sold. If this is not done, or done only in part, or only at prices below the prices of production, the labourer has been indeed exploited, but his exploitation is not realised as such for the capitalist, and this can be bound up with a total or partial failure to realise the surplus-value pressed out of him, indeed even with the partial or total loss of the capital. The conditions of direct exploitation, and those of realising it, are not identical. They diverge not only in place and time, but also logically. The first are only limited by the productive power of society, the latter by the proportional relation of the various branches of production and the consumer power of society. But this last-named is not determined either by the absolute productive power, or by the absolute consumer power, but by the consumer power based on antagonistic conditions of distribution, which reduce the consumption of the bulk of society to a minimum varying within more or less narrow limits. (Cap iii.244)

The total surplus-value that capitalists produce will only be *realised* when they receive total sales revenues sufficient to cover their total wage bill (their expenditure on variable capital), the depreciation of constant capital, and the total surplus-value they have managed to produce by exploiting labour. They will receive revenue from three sources, from workers who buy necessary consumer goods, from capitalists who use some surplus-value to buy luxury consumer goods, and from capitalists who purchase means of production to maintain and expand the capital stock. Marx sets out these important interrelationships in his celebrated 'reproduction scheme', but the principal implications this has for the problem of realising the full surplus-value that results from exploitation can be explained very simply.[5]

If the rate of exploitation rises to, say, 200 per cent as capitalism develops, then only one-third of output (net of the depreciation of constant capital) will be bought by workers spending their wages on necessities (Marx speaks above of how the consumption of the bulk of society is reduced 'to a minimum') and two-thirds of net output will need to be sold to capitalists for their luxury consumption and for accumulation. It is only if capitalists buy as much as two-thirds of net output from each other that they will *realise* a rate of surplus value of 200 per cent. Marx says several times that Malthus was right to emphasise that capitalists cannot realise profits by merely selling necessities to workers, because this does no more than return to them costs that the capitalist class has already incurred (TSV iii.39–51).

In Marx's actual examples, capitalists spend a fixed fraction of their incomes on luxury consumption, and this fraction is set at one-half in the extended reproduction scheme (Cap ii.511). In that case capitalists will first sell output to workers equivalent to V, the *total* variable capital they have used up in production. Second, they will sell luxury consumer goods to the capitalist class for ½S, that is, for half the *total* surplus-value that results from the exploitation of labour-power. Third, they can be expected to sell sufficient goods to cover the depreciation of constant capital. Thus while their output net of depreciation needs to be sold for their total wage-bill plus total surplus-value, or for $V + S$, sales for necessary and luxury consumption can be expected to bring in only $V + ½S$. To realise their full surplus-value of S, they will need to sell a further ½S to other capitalists, and this will need to be used to extend the net capital stock. If capitalists spend less than this on accumulation, they will receive back an insufficient sum of money to restore their wage costs and to convert their surplus-value into realisable wealth. Hence if S/V, the rate of exploitation, is 10 per cent, out of every 110 units of net output produced (which will divide into 100_v and 10_s) 100_v will be purchased for workers' consumption, 5_s for luxury consumption, and 5_s will need to be purchased for net accumulation. If S/V is 50 per cent, of each 150 units produced (dividing into 100_v and 50_s), 100_v will be consumed by workers, 25_s by capitalists, and 25_s will need to be purchased for net accumulation: while when the rate of exploitation becomes 200 per cent, of every 300 units produced (100_v and 200_s), 100_v will be purchased by workers, 100_s as luxuries by capitalists, and 100_s will need to be purchased for accumulation. The fraction of output which capitalists need to purchase for accumulation if surplus-value is to be realised will therefore rise from 5/110, that is, from 4.54 per cent when the rate of exploitation is 10 per cent, to 25/150, that is, to 16.67 per cent when it becomes 50 per cent, and 100/300, that is, to 33.33 per cent when it reaches 200 per cent. In general, the fraction $s_c[S/(S + V)]$ of net output (where s_c is the proportion of profits which capitalists fail to consume, that is, which they save) will need to be purchased for accumulation, and this obviously rises continuously as S increases in relation to V. Will capitalists, in fact, be prepared to purchase this ever rising share of net output for accumulation once the rate of profit begins to fall continuously?

According to Marx, capitalists are overwhelmingly motivated to accumulate. 'Accumulate, accumulate! That is Moses and the prophets!' (*Cap* i.558). But a falling rate of profit will undermine accumulation: 'the rate of profit, being the goad of capitalist production (just as self-expansion of capital is its only purpose), its fall checks the formation of new independent capitals and thus appears as a threat to the development of the capitalist production process. It breeds over-production, speculation, crises, and surplus-capital alongside surplus-population' (Cap iii.241–2). Moreover, 'The rate of profit, i.e., the relative increment of capital, is above all important to all new offshoots of capital seeking to find an independent place for themselves. And as soon as formation of capital were to fall into the hands of a few established big capitals, for which the mass of profit compensates for the falling rate of profit, the vital flame of production would be altogether extinguished. It would die out. The rate of profit is the motive power of capitalist production' (Cap iii.259).

The problem for capitalism is then that, as the rate of exploitation rises, an ever increasing fraction of output has to be devoted to accumulation if the high surplus-value created is to be realised, but the rate of profit provides the principal motive for accumulation and this will be falling. Hence the incentive to invest and innovate will be falling at the very time that a capitalist economy needs an ever growing share of investment. According to Marx, the inevitable consequence is that:

> a rift must continually ensue between the limited dimensions of consumption under capitalism and a production which forever tends to exceed this immanent barrier. (Cap iii.256)

More generally:

> the more productiveness develops, the more it finds itself at variance with the narrow basis on which the conditions of consumption rest. It is no contradiction at all on this self-contradictory basis that there should be an excess of capital simultaneously with a growing surplus of population. For while a combination of these two would, indeed, increase the mass of produced surplus-value, it would at the same time intensify the contradiction between the conditions under which this surplus-value is produced and those under which it is realised. (Cap iii.245)

When the periodic and ever deepening crises occur, a failure of effective demand to allow potential surplus-value to be realised produces sharp falls in money prices with important implications:

> Part of the commodities on the market can complete their process of circulation and reproduction only through an immense contraction of their prices, hence through a depreciation of the capital

which they represent. The elements of fixed capital are depreciated to a greater or lesser degree in just the same way. It must be added that definite, presupposed, price relations govern the process of reproduction, so that the latter is halted and thrown into confusion by a general drop in prices. This confusion and stagnation paralyses the function of money as a medium of payment, whose development is geared to the development of capital and is based on those presupposed price relations. The chain of payment obligations due at specific dates is broken in a hundred places. The confusion is augmented by the attendant collapse of the credit system, which develops simultaneously with capital, and leads to violent and acute crises, to sudden and forcible depreciations, to the actual stagnation and disruption of the process of reproduction, and thus to a real falling off in reproduction. (Cap iii.254)

Marx emphasised the role of money in economic crises:

It is a basic principle of capitalist production that money, as an independent form of value, stands in opposition to commodities, or that exchange-value must assume an independent form in money; and this is only possible when a definite commodity becomes the material whose value becomes a measure of all other commodities, so that it thus becomes the general commodity, the commodity *par excellence* – as distinguished from all other commodities. This must manifest itself in two respects, particularly among capitalistically developed nations, which to a large extent replace money, on the one hand, by credit operations, and on the other by credit-money. In times of a squeeze, when credit contracts or ceases entirely, money suddenly stands as the only means of payment and true existence of value in absolute opposition to all other commodities. Hence the universal depreciation of commodities, the difficulty or even impossibility of transforming them into money, i.e., into their own purely fantastic form. Secondly, however, credit-money itself is only money to the extent that it absolutely takes the place of actual money to the amount of its nominal value. With a drain on gold its convertibility, i.e., its identity with actual gold becomes problematic. Hence coercive measures, raising the rate of interest, etc., for the purpose of safeguarding the conditions of this convertibility. This can be carried more or less to extremes by mistaken legislation, based on false theories of money and enforced upon the nation by the interests of the money-dealers...A depreciation of credit-money (not to mention, incidentally, a purely imaginary loss of its character as money) would unsettle all existing relations. Therefore, the value of commodities is sacrificed for the purpose of safeguarding the fantastic and independent existence of this value in money. As money-value, it is secure only as long as money is secure. For a few millions in money, many millions in commodities must therefore be sacrificed. (Cap iii.516)

As the rate of profit falls, the crises due to a failure to realise surplus-value which have these disastrous monetary effects become deeper and deeper. The development of capitalism is undermined because, 'the rate of profit, the stimulating principle of capitalist production, the fundamental premise and driving force of accumulation' is 'endangered by the development of production itself' (Cap iii.259). If the development of production did indeed involve inevitable capital deepening and therefore a declining rate of profit and a declining rate of growth of employment, as well as a need for an ever growing share of investment if there were to be sufficient aggregate demand, then capitalism truly could not continue indefinitely. These particular trends which Marx considered inevitable and inescapable would steadily diminish the numbers of those who stood to gain from the continuation of capitalism, while even the apparent beneficiaries would increasingly suffer from the deepening crises. All this would happen because capitalists are merely motivated to expand capital:

The *real barrier* of capitalist production is *capital itself*. It is that capital and its self-expansion appear as the starting and the closing point, the motive and the purpose of production; that production is only production for *capital* and not vice versa, the means of production are not mere means for a constant expansion of the living process of the *society* of producers. The limits within which the preservation and self-expansion of the value of capital resting on the expropriation and pauperisation of the great mass of producers can alone move – these limits come continually into conflict with the methods of production employed by capital for its purposes, which drive towards unlimited extension of production, towards production as an end in itself (Cap iii.250)

Because capitalism is solely concerned with the expansion of capital, and not at all with 'the society of producers', its political foundations will be steadily undermined. The surviving capitalists will moreover acquire social power that they are unfitted and indeed unwilling to exercise, so power will inevitably pass from those who merely own the means of production:

> We have seen that the growing accumulation of capital implies its growing concentration. Thus grows the power of capital, the alienation of the conditions of social production personified in the capitalist from the real producers. Capital comes more and more to the fore as a social power whose agent is the capitalist. This social power no longer stands in any possible relation to that which the labour of a single individual can create. It becomes an alienated, independent, social power, which stands opposed to society as an object, and as an object that is the capitalist's source of power. The contradiction between the general social power into which capital develops, on the one hand, and the private power of the individual capitalists over these social conditions of production, on the other, becomes ever more irreconcilable, and yet contains the solution of the problem, because it implies at the same time the transformation of the conditions of production into general, common, social, conditions. (Cap iii.264)

The actual revolution in which power passes to the working class will, of course, partly result from the increasing numerical weakness of the capitalists, and also because workers will become more and more aware how crushing capitalism is to those with only their labour to sell:

> Along with the constantly diminishing number of the magnates of capital, who usurp and monopolise all advantages of this process of transformation, grows the mass of misery, oppression, slavery, degradation, exploitation; but with this too grows the revolt of the working-class, a class always increasing in numbers, and disciplined, united, organised by the very mechanism of the process of capitalist production itself. The monopoly of capital becomes a fetter upon the mode of production, which has sprung up and flourished along with, and under it. Centralisation of the means of production and socialisation of labour at last reach a point where they become incompatible with their capitalist integument. This integument is burst asunder. The knell of capitalist private property sounds. The expropriators are expropriated. (Cap i.715)

A final comment on the lack of long-term viability of capitalism comes when Marx extrapolates the trend of a falling rate of growth of employment into the future:

> A development of productive forces which would diminish the absolute number of labourers, i.e., enable the entire nation to accomplish its total production in a shorter time span, would cause a revolution, because it would put the bulk of the population out of the running. This is another manifestation of the specific barrier of capitalist production, showing also that capitalist production is by no means an absolute form for the development of the productive forces and for the creation of wealth, but rather that at a certain point it comes into collision with this development...The limit of capitalist production is the excess time of the labourers. The absolute spare time gained by society does not concern it. (Cap iii.263–4)

A continual growth in production while the bulk of the population was 'out of the running' could hardly continue. The spare time potentially available from growing productivity and a falling demand for labour would have to become a benefit and not a sentence to penury and starvation for more and more people. A reorganisation of society into one where an opportunity for growing leisure was compatible with full employment and falling hours of work would become inevitable, and the new society would not be capitalist, if this was bound to produce intensive work for some and unemployment for the rest, together with deepening financial crises and an ever diminishing fraction of the population which actually gained from capitalism.

Marx's prediction that the continuation of capitalism must inevitably lead to this sorry state of affairs rested on his conviction that there were inevitable trends which must after a time produce a declining tendency in the rate of profit, and a continual fall in the rate of growth of demand for labour. In the next section it will be shown that these must indeed occur in an economy where technology develops in the way that Marx assumed.

Marx's assumptions about inevitable developments in technology were by no means out of the ordinary. In almost every case they echoed the assumptions of one or more of his great predecessors.

*A DEMONSTRATION OF THE TENDENCY OF THE RATE OF PROFIT AND THE RATE OF GROWTH OF EMPLOYMENT TO DECLINE – WITH MARX'S TECHNOLOGICAL ASSUMPTIONS

It is in fact possible to establish several of Marx's principal results with a very straightforward mathematical restatement of his argument, but before this is set out, something must be said about the units in which the argument will be stated. Marx expressed his theory of exploitation in units of labour time, but as with the restatement of Ricardo's argument in Chapter 6, output and growth are most conveniently measured in physical units. It is inconvenient to measure economic growth in labour units of value because a doubling of physical output per worker with unchanged hours of work would show up as a zero rate of growth in the *value* of the output of a worker. Marx himself used labour units of value in his celebrated 'Reproduction on an Extended Scale' in the second volume of *Capital*, where he outlined some of the detailed interrelationships of a growing economy, but there is no productivity growth in the reproduction schemes. Output grows only as a result of rising employment and not at all as a consequence of capital deepening. The reproduction schemes therefore fall short of explaining the fundamental contradictions of capitalism which are set out in the third volume of *Capital*. There it is a rising organic composition of capital and productivity growth which produce a declining rate of profit and a growing reserve army of labour, and in addition a realisation problem of increasing difficulty which in the end renders capitalism unviable. Because of the change in labour productivity which occurs throughout these processes, physical units of output and not labour units are the ideal ones in which to restate Marx's argument.

Such measurement of output in physical terms need involve no departure from the essentials of Marx's theory of exploitation. With the assumption that constant capital per worker, c, variable capital per worker, v, and surplus-value per worker, s, all measured in physical units of output, are uniform throughout the economy, aggregation problems are avoided, and the explanation of the falling rate of profit, etc., is greatly simplified. At the same time, c/v, the uniform organic and technical composition of capital, s/v, the uniform rate of exploitation, and $s/(c + v)$, the uniform rate of profit, will still be determined by the full range of factors with which the argument of Chapter 7 was concerned.

It is very clear that Marx believed that once an economy moves forward from handicraft production, output per worker will grow continuously as a result of increasing mechanisation and the advantages which can be derived from the division of labour. He believed firmly that means of production needed to be increased faster than output in order to obtain the continual advances in productivity that are mainly derived from the increasing returns that follow from the division of labour. These general assumptions about the development of technology can be represented by the two fundamental equations which are set out below. First, to show that there will be increasing mechanisation as output expands:

$$k_m = Hg \quad (H > 1) \tag{8.1}$$

where k_m is the rate of growth of the means of production, while g is the rate of growth of output and H is a constant which exceeds unity. This equation reflects Marx's belief that the way in which industrial output advances once capitalism begins to emerge is through, on balance, faster increases in constant capital than in output.[6] With the above equation, means of production have to be increased H times as fast as output, and the assumption that H exceeds 1 reflects Marx's belief that the organic and technical composition of capital will have a continual tendency to rise, which is not, in practice, influenced by what happens to relative factor prices, for Marx does not refer to the influence of these upon c/v.

How much extra labour, if any, will the economy require as output increases, and how will labour requirements be influenced by Marx's strong belief in the continual productivity advantages to be derived from the division of labour? The simplest possible assumption which can be made is that there is a linear relationship between the growth of labour requirements, means of production and output, namely:

$$n = Bg - Ak_m \tag{8.2}$$

where n is the rate of growth of the required labour force, while A and B are constants. If there were constant returns to scale, A would have to equal $(B - 1)$ in this equation so that, rearranging:

$$g = \frac{1}{B} n + \left(1 - \frac{1}{B}\right)k_m \tag{8.3}$$

With this equation, where $(B - 1)$ has been substituted for A in equation (8.2), a 5 per cent rate of growth of means of production and of labour would produce a 5 per cent rate of growth of output, that is, $g = 0.05$ if $k_m = n = 0.05$. Now to echo Marx's assumptions, more than this constant returns effect from increases in factor supplies is required, and this is achieved if $(ZB - 1)$ is substituted for A in equation (8.2) with Z exceeding 1, that is:

$$n = Bg - (ZB - 1)k_m$$

$$g = \frac{1}{B} n + \left(Z - \frac{1}{B}\right)k_m \qquad (Z > 1) \tag{8.4}$$

Here a 5 per cent rate of growth of means of production and of labour would produce a $5Z$ per cent rate of growth of output, that is, $g = 0.05Z$ if $k_m = n = 0.05$ so that, if $Z = 1.2$, output would grow 6 per cent if capital and labour grew at a rate of 5 per cent. Equation (8.4) therefore reproduces the effect of increasing returns which was so significant in Marx's writings. There is, however, an important respect in which equation (8.4) does not yet reflect Marx's assumptions about technology: it admits the possibility of a myriad of ways in which an economy could benefit from increasing returns to scale. Thus capital could increase far faster than labour, or labour far faster than capital, and equation (8.4), which is derived from the linear labour requirements equation (8.2), would show the economy still able to derive benefits from the underlying assumption of increasing returns, on which a Z exceeding 1 depends.

Equation (8.4) thus describes many possible ways in which an economy could achieve higher productivity. There is, however, only one way in which an economy can raise productivity if Marx is right to believe that the ratio of constant to variable capital and hence the capital to output ratio (under most assumptions) must rise continuously if the particular techniques of production which permit continual productivity growth are to be attained. The economy must, in fact, satisfy the assumptions underlying equation (8.1) which imposes a rising capital to output ratio, as well as the increasing returns labour requirements equation from which equation (8.4) is derived. The simultaneous satisfaction of both these sets of technical

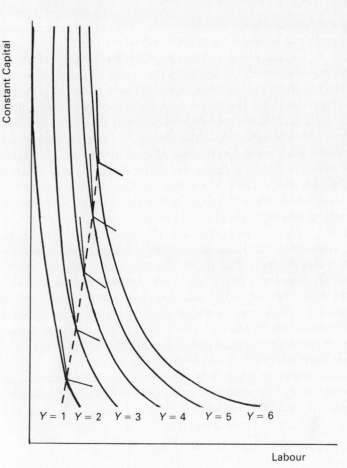

FIGURE 8.1

conditions is illustrated in Figure 8.1. Here there are isoquants which show how, starting from $Y = 1$ (an output of 1), an output of 2 can be attained with all the combinations of labour and capital illustrated by the $Y = 2$ isoquant, an output of 3 at any point on the $Y = 3$ isoquant, and so on. These isoquants are drawn using equation (8.4) with the assumption that $Z = 1.2$, i.e. that a 10 per cent increase in both labour and constant capital would raise output 12 per cent, and that $B = 1\frac{1}{3}$, that is (from equation (8.4)) that in the absence of capital accumulation a $1\frac{1}{3}$ per cent increase in labour would be needed to raise output 1 per cent. The assumption of increasing returns is shown in the familiar way by the compression of the successive isoquants, so that the gap between $Y = 6$ and $Y = 5$ is less than that between $Y = 5$ and $Y = 4$, and so on. A Marx economy has to adopt the successive technologies which are linked by the dotted line, and these show the effect of stipulating that the economy also follows the course set out in equation (8.1). The dotted lines are drawn on the assumption that $H = 1\frac{1}{3}$, that is, that means of production have to be increased one and one-third times as fast as output. A Marx economy can only benefit from the opportunities offered by increasing returns if it follows a particular path like this dotted line. That it is constrained to this path is illustrated by the superimposition of a series of square-shaped isoquants at the points where the dotted line (equation 8.1)) and the isoquants permitting substitution (equation (8.4)) intersect. These square-shaped isoquants represent the true technological opportunities which are open to the economy, and they show that, over an extremely wide range of factor prices, these techniques will be the successive ones which will be adopted as the economy expands. The purpose of equation (8.4) which permits substitution between labour and capital was to enable us to arrive at a true representation of Marx's technological assumptions (in conjunction with equation (8.1)) and this is provided by the square-shaped isoquants indicated on the diagram.

These unique production opportunities are, of course, derived most readily by combining equations (8.1) and (8.4) mathematically, and this yields the following:

$$g - n = \{(BZ - 1) - \frac{1}{H}(B - 1)\}k_m \tag{8.5}$$

$$g = \frac{1}{H} k_m \tag{8.6}$$

$$n = \{1 - B(Z - \frac{1}{H})\}k_m \tag{8.7}$$

Thus $(g - n)$, the rate of growth of productivity, g, the rate of growth of output, and n, the rate of growth of employment, are each multiples of k_m, the rate of growth of the means of production, and the parameters H, Z, and B. Thus there will be no growth at all in output, productivity or employment, in the absence of accumulation of the means of production. This is right because there are no references in *Capital* to an annual rate of technical progress which accrues whether or not there is capital accumulation. There is no justification for technical progress which occurs independently of accumulation in Marx's extensive writings on the development of technology and the explanation of productivity growth.[7] Marx's position instead echoes Smith's, that productivity advances as a result of the division of labour, which can only be extended further as capital and output are expanded. Equation (8.5) permits no productivity growth at all in conventional neoclassical equilibrium growth with constant returns to scale, that is, with $Z = 1$; and with a constant capital to output ratio, that is, with $H = 1$. If however there are increasing returns or the capital to output ratio is rising, then productivity will expand at a rate which depends on the rate of growth of the means of production, and if, for instance, $Z = 1\frac{1}{6}$ (that is, a 6 per cent increase in all factor inputs would raise output 7 per cent) and $H = 1\frac{1}{2}$, that is, means of production are increased one and a half times as fast as output, and $B = 1\frac{1}{3}$, that is, a $1\frac{1}{3}$ per cent increase in labour is needed to raise output 1 per cent, then $(g - n) = \frac{1}{3}k_m$. Therefore, with these assumptions, productivity would grow one-third as fast as the means of production. Productivity would of course grow faster if increasing returns were stronger, or the capital to output ratio increased more rapidly. With these assumptions however, a 6 per cent rate of growth of the means of production would permit sufficient further benefits from the division of labour, and from rising capital intensity, to raise labour productivity 2 per cent per annum.

Equation (8.6) which is merely a restatement of equation (8.1) shows how output rises more slowly than the means of production to an extent which depends only on H, and if this is $1\frac{1}{2}$, output grows two-thirds as fast as the means of production, so that it grows at 4 per cent per annum if constant capital grows at 6 per cent per annum.

Equation (8.7) is the interesting and important equation which links the rate of growth of employment to the rate of growth of constant capital. A positive rate of growth of constant capital is bound to produce growth in output and labour productivity, but it will not necessarily produce any growth in employment. It follows from equation (8.7) that:

$$\frac{d\,n}{d\,k_m} \gtreqless 0 \text{ where } \frac{1}{B} \gtreqless Z - \frac{1}{H} \tag{8.8}$$

In other words, employment will grow as constant capital expands if

$1/B$ exceeds $(Z - 1/H)$ and employment will actually decline as constant capital expands if $(Z - 1/H)$ exceeds $1/B$. Now on a conventional neoclassical steady growth path, $Z = 1$, and $H = 1$ so that $(Z - 1/H) = 0$, and this cannot possibly exceed $1/B$ which must always be positive (since it is the inverse of the amount of labour needed to raise output 1 per cent in the absence of capital accumulation). If however there are increasing returns, and there is a rising trend in the capital to output ratio, $(Z - 1/H)$ can be quite significantly positive, and even large enough to exceed $1/B$. For instance, if $B = 1\frac{1}{3}$ so that $1/B = \frac{3}{4}$, $(Z - 1/H)$ would exceed this if Z exceeded $1\frac{1}{4}$ when H equalled 2, if Z exceeded $1\frac{5}{12}$ when H equalled $1\frac{1}{2}$, and if Z exceeded $1\frac{1}{2}$ when H equalled $1\frac{1}{3}$. These combinations of increasing returns and a rising capital to output ratio would all suffice to reverse the proposition that capital accumulation creates jobs. It will be evident that if the tendency towards increasing returns is strong, and means of production have to be increased considerably faster than output, these in combination can produce a situation where the faster capital accumulates, the greater the number of jobs which will be destroyed. Several previous restatements of Marx's analysis have rested on constant returns assumptions,[8] and have, therefore, failed to derive as an integral part of the argument a reserve army of labour which extra capital accumulation will not remove.

The reserve army would, of course, reach chronic proportions if the demand for labour actually started to fall at any point. Marx did not believe that that situation had been reached in his lifetime apart from agriculture. His position was rather that the rate of growth of employment was far less than the rate of growth of capital, and that it had a tendency to decline. If, for instance, in equation (8.7), $Z = 1\frac{1}{6}$, which suggests a relatively modest increasing returns effect, $H = 1\frac{1}{2}$, which again suggests a relatively modest tendency for means of production to grow faster than output, and $B = 1\frac{1}{3}$, the rate of growth of employment will equal $\frac{1}{3}k_m$ so that employment will grow at a rate of 2 per cent per annum when the means of production grow at a rate of 6 per cent. That kind of result would reflect Marx's thinking more closely than an actually negative relationship between employment and the rate of capital accumulation.

Marx did however believe that the rate of growth of employment, while positive, had a tendency to fall. Equation (8.7) shows it falling if H has a tendency to rise, if Z has a tendency to rise, or if k_m has a tendency to fall. Marx did not speak of a tendency for the force of increasing returns to become continually stronger, but there are passages compatible with a rising tendency in H. For instance, in the passages already quoted: 'the rapidity of the change in the organic composition of capital, and in its technical form increases, and an increasing number of spheres of production becomes involved in this change', and 'With the growth of the total capital, its variable constituent or the labour incorporated in it, also does increase, but in a constantly diminishing proportion. The intermediate pauses are shortened, in which accumulation works as simple extension of production, on a given technical basis' (Cap i.590–1). It would be in line with these passages to assume that H may have a tendency to rise which, through equation (8.7), would gradually reduce the rate of growth of employment associated with any given rate of growth of constant capital. Thus if $Z = 1\frac{1}{6}$ and $B = 1\frac{1}{3}$, employment will grow one-third as fast as constant capital when $H = 1\frac{1}{2}$, one-ninth as fast if H rises to 2, and it will actually start to decline as constant capital increases once H reaches $2\frac{2}{5}$. A tendency for H to rise would therefore help to produce the result which Marx predicted, that a steady rate of growth of means of production would be associated with a declining rate of growth of employment, and if H went on increasing, that employment would in due course actually decline.

The most direct reason to expect a fall in the rate of growth of employment is, however, because of the tendency of the rate of profit to decline, which is the centrepiece of Marx's predictions. If the rate of profit declines, capital accumulation, which is financed from profits, will decline with it, and as the rate of growth of constant capital declines, equation (8.7) indicates that the growth of employment will decline correspondingly. In his illustrative examples, Marx assumed that a fixed fraction of *total* surplus value, S, will not be consumed by the capitalist class, and this fraction, s_c, will be the proportion of surplus-value which is available for accumulation. If all the surplus-value available for accumulation is added to the capital stock:

$$\text{net increase in capital} = s_c \times \text{surplus-value}$$

so that:

$$\frac{\text{net increase in capital}}{\text{total capital}} = s_c \times \frac{\text{surplus-value}}{\text{total capital}}.$$

Since

net increase in capital
------------------------- is k, the rate of growth
        total capital   of *total* capital,

while

surplus-value
------------- is r, the rate of profit:
total capital

$$k = s_c r \qquad (8.9)$$

Hence if s_c, the proportion of surplus value available for accumulation, is constant, the economy's potential rate of growth of total capital, constant and variable together, will vary directly with the rate of profit. If Marx was correct in believing that the rate of profit will have an inevitable tendency to fall, then the rate of growth of total capital will fall correspondingly. In equation (8.7), the rate of growth of employment depends upon k_m, the rate of growth of *constant* capital, and of course on H, Z and B. It has been explained that if k_m, Z and B are constant while H has a tendency to rise, the rate of growth of employment will have a tendency to fall. It is now evident that k, the rate of growth of *total* capital, will fall to the extent that the rate of profit falls, and if total capital grows more slowly, k_m will also grow more slowly (though not in proportion with k). If k_m has a tendency to fall with the falling rate of profit, and at the same time H has a tendency to rise, equation (8.7) shows that the rate of growth of employment will doubly fall. It is therefore vital to determine whether Marx's law of the tendency of the rate of profit to decline is well founded. If it is, the tendency for employment to grow more and more slowly and in the end to decline will be firmly established.

Marx believed that the rate of profit would have an inevitable tendency to fall because he envisaged that constant capital per worker would grow sufficiently in relation to output per worker to bring about this result, despite a simultaneous upward trend in labour productivity as a result of the division of labour and increasing mechanisation. To reflect these insights, it will be assumed, first, that as output increases (at a rate which it is at no point necessary to specify) constant capital has to be increased H times as fast as output, where H exceeds 1, and second that variable capital has to be increased only U times as fast as output where U is less than 1. The ratio of the rate of increase of variable capital to the rate of growth of output, U, will be less than 1 because as output per worker increases, wages per head rise considerably more slowly if at all.

To state these assumptions precisely, if the economy's total constant capital is C_o when the economy's total output is 1 (defined as above net of the depreciation of constant capital), it will have to be increased to $C_o e^{Hx}$ by the time total net output reaches e^x. At the same time, if total variable capital is V_o when the economy's total output is 1, it will equal $V_o e^{Ux}$ by the time total output has risen to e^x. It follows from these assumptions and definitions that total surplus-value, S, which is net output less variable capital, will amount to $e^x - V_o e^{Ux}$ when output is e^x. The rate of exploitation is total surplus-value divided by total variable capital, so that:

$$\text{rate of exploitation} = \frac{S}{V} = \frac{1}{V_o} e^{(1 - U)x} - 1$$

The rate of profit, r is total surplus-value divided by total capital (the sum of constant and variable capital) which is $C_o e^{Hx}$ plus $V_o e^{Ux}$ when output is e^x. Hence:

$$\text{rate of profit} = r = \frac{\dfrac{1}{V_o} e^{(1 - U)x} - 1}{\dfrac{C_o}{V_o} e^{(H - U)x} + 1} \tag{8.10}$$

As x rises, output, constant capital and variable capital all rise simultaneously, and r will increase for so long as the numerator of the right hand side of this equation, $(1/V_o)e^{(1 - U)x} - 1$, rises at a faster proportional rate (with respect to x) than the denominator which is $(C_o/V_o)e^{(H - U)x} + 1$. It can easily be shown that the numerator will rise faster for so long as:

$$1 + \frac{\text{net output}}{\text{constant capital}}$$

exceeds $(H - 1)/(1 - U)$ times the rate of exploitation, that the numerator will rise exactly as fast as the denominator so that the rate of profit is at a maximum where these are equal, and that the numerator will grow more slowly than the denominator to produce a falling rate of profit, once

$$1 + \frac{\text{net output}}{\text{constant capital}}$$

becomes less than $(H - 1)/(1 - U)$ times the rate of exploitation. It is therefore possible to write:[9]

> r will rise or fall as output increases depending on whether

$$1 + \frac{\text{net output}}{\text{constant capital}} \gtreqless \frac{H - 1}{1 - U} \times \text{rate of exploitation} \quad (8.11)$$

As labour productivity rises just above the level where capitalist exploitation is first possible,

$$1 + \frac{\text{net output}}{\text{constant capital}}$$

is bound to exceed 1, while $(H - 1)/(1 - U)$ times the 'rate of exploitation' will only just exceed zero, because the rate of exploitation then only just exceeds zero. At that point the left-hand side of equation (8.11) is bound to exceed the right-hand side with the result that it is quite clear that the rate of profit must be rising. As output expands, the left-hand side, $1 +$ (net output/constant capital), must fall because of the assumption that constant capital always rises faster than output, while the right-hand side, $(H - 1)/(1 - U)$ times the rate of exploitation, is bound to rise because the assumption that the wage bill always rises more slowly than output entails an ever rising rate of exploitation. As the left-hand side falls indefinitely, while the right-hand side rises indefinitely, the left-hand side is bound to fall to equality with the right-hand side, and they can only become equal once. The rate of profit rises for so long as the left-hand side is higher than the right-hand side, it reaches its maximum when these are equal and it falls continuously as the left-hand side falls below the right-hand side. All that is necessary to arrive at the result that the rate of profit rises at first, reaches a maximum, and then falls indefinitely, is that constant capital grows faster than output as this expands, while at the same time the wage bill grows more slowly than output. There must also be stability in H and in U.

An indefinite number of examples could be constructed to illustrate how, as output expands, the rate of profit rises, reaches a maximum, and then declines. A typical example is set out in Table 8.1. Here the economy achieves a sufficient level of productivity to cover the subsistence wage once its net output reaches 100_{v+s}, and exploitation therefore becomes a possibility once output exceeds 100_{v+s}. It is assumed that constant capital needs to be increased one-and-one-half times as fast as output, that is, that $H = 1\frac{1}{2}$ and that the total wage-bill rises half as fast as output, that is, $U = \frac{1}{2}$. When output is 100_{v+s} a constant capital of 80_c is needed to produce this, so by the time output has risen by a factor of $2^2 = 4$ from 100_{v+s} to 400_{v+s}, constant capital will have had to rise by a factor of $2^3 = 8$ from 80_c to 640_c. The wage bill which rises half as fast as output will at the same time rise by a factor of 2 from 100_v to 200_v in the period in which output rises by a factor of 2^2 and constant capital by a factor of 2^3. The various values of constant capital and the total wage bill as net output rises from 100_{v+s} to 110_{v+s}, 150_{v+s}, 200_{v+s}, 400_{v+s}, 625_{v+s}, 1000_{v+s}, 2000_{v+s}, and 5000_{v+s} are set out in Table 8.1, and this also shows total surplus value (S), the rate of exploitation (S/V) and the rate of profit $S/(C + V)$. According to equation (8.11) the latter reaches its maximum where:

$$1 + \frac{\text{net output}}{\text{constant capital}} = \frac{H - 1}{1 - U} \times \text{rate of exploitation}$$

In Table 8.1, $(H - 1)/(1 - U) = 1$, so the rate of profit attains its maximum where $1 + [(V + S)/C] = S/V$. This occurs where net output is 625_{v+s} when constant capital is 1250_c so that $1 + [(V + S)/C] = 1.5$; and since surplus-value is then 375_s and the wage-bill 250_v, S/V is also 1.5. The condition that the rate of profit is at a maximum as set out in equation (8.11) is therefore satisfied when constant capital is 1250_c. At that point the rate of profit does indeed reach a maximum of 25 per cent.

While the rate of profit falls in Table 8.1 once net output exceeds 625.0_{v+s}, it is a well-known weakness in Marx's argument that individual profit-maximising capitalists do not necessarily have an incentive to raise the scale of production of their own factories beyond their rate of profit-maximising size. In Table 8.1 variable capital rises half as fast as output. This could mean that wages per

TABLE 8.1   Capital output and profits where the wage-bill rises half as fast as net output; while constant capital increases one-and-a-half times as fast as net output

Constant capital C	Net output V + S	Variable capital V	Surplus value S	Rate of exploitation S/V	Rate of profit S/(C + V)
80.0	100	100	0	0	0
92.3	110	104.9	5.1	4.9%	2.6%
147.0	150	122.5	27.5	22.4%	10.2%
226.3	200	141.4	58.6	41.4%	15.9%
640.0	400	200.0	200.0	100.0%	23.8%
1 235.06	620.01	249.0	371.01	149.0%	24.9997%
1 250.0	625.0	250.0	375.0	150.0%	25.0%
1 265.06	630.01	251.0	379.01	151.0%	24.9997%
2 529.8	1 000	316.2	683.8	216.3%	24.0%
7 155.4	2 000	447.2	1 552.8	347.2%	20.4%
28 284.3	5 000	707.1	4 292.9	607.1%	14.8%

Since $H = 1\frac{1}{2}$ and $U = \frac{1}{2}$, $C = 80 \times \{(\frac{V + S}{100})\}^{1\frac{1}{2}}$

and $V = 100 \times \{(\frac{V + S}{100}\}^{\frac{1}{2}}$

The remaining columns can be estimated for each value of $(V + S)$ by simple arithmetic once C and V are known.

head are constant, and that the labour force grows half as fast as output, or that the labour force is constant and that wages per head grow half as fast as output – or any permutation of these with the product of the wage and the labour force growing half as fast as output. In Table 8.2 it is supposed that the wage is constant, and that the entire growth of variable capital indicated in Table 8.1 therefore corresponds to growth in employment. If the labour force is 250 at the point in Table 8.1 where the rate of profit is maximum and total variable capital is 250_v as in the table, the wage per head is then 1.0_v while net output per worker is 2.5_{v+s} and constant capital per head is 5.0_c. In Table 8.2 it is supposed that the wage remains equal to 1.0_v. Therefore, by the time net output reaches 2000_{v+s} and variable capital reaches 447.2_v, total employment must have risen from 250 to 447.2, which means (using Table 8.1) that constant capital per head will have risen to $7155.4_c/447.2 = 16.0_c$, and output per head to $2000_{v+s}/447.2 = 4.472_{v+s}$. The implications of a level of employment

TABLE 8.2   What happens when variable capital per worker (the wage) does
not rise, so that the labour force is 447.2 when net output is 2000_{v+s} if it was
250 when net output was 625_{v+s} in Table 8.1

Constant capital per worker	*Net output per worker*	*Variable capital per worker*	*Surplus value per worker*	*Rate of profit*
5.0_c	2.5_{v+s}	1.0_v	1.5_s	25.0%
16.0_c	4.472_{v+s}	1.0_v	3.472_s	20.4%

of 447.2 at the time that net output is supposedly 2000_{v+s} are set out
in Table 8.2.

If some capitalists are astute enough to maintain the technique of
production and the plant size that produce a rate of profit of 25 per
cent, they will outperform those who raise constant capital per
worker in the ratio of 5_c to 16_c, and output per worker in the ratio of
2.5_{v+s} to 4.472_{v+s} indicated in the table. The increase in plant size
involved in raising productivity from 2.5_{v+s} to 4.472_{v+s} is not
economically correct under the rules of capitalism, because it will
reduce the rate of profit earned from 25.0 per cent to 20.4 per cent,
even though the wage is unchanged at 1.0_v. Capitalists who expand
by simply multiplying units of low productivity plant offering an
output per worker of a mere 2.5_{v+s} would be able to supply the
market and continue to earn 25 per cent on their capital, so that is
what would happen in a competitive capitalist system. If the wage
sticks at 1.0_v, the rate of profit will stick at 25 per cent as most
capitalists avoid the error of further capital deepening, and comfortably outcompete any capitalists so unwise as to raise the technical and
organic composition of capital beyond the point where the rate of
profit is maximum.

Marx says several times in plain words that capitalists have to raise
the technical and organic composition of capital once some capitalists
begin to do this, or be driven out of business. For instance:

No capitalist ever voluntarily introduces a new method of production, no matter how much more productive it may be, and how
much it may increase the rate of surplus-value, so long as it
reduces the rate of profit. Yet every such new method of production cheapens the commodities. Hence, the capitalist sells them
originally above their prices of production, or, perhaps, above

their value. He pockets the difference between their costs of production and the market-prices of the same commodities produced at higher costs of production. He can do this, because the average labour time required socially for the production of these latter commodities is higher than the labour-time required for the new methods of production. His method of production stands above the social average. But competition makes it general and subject to the general law. There follows a fall in the rate of profit – perhaps first in this sphere of production, and eventually it achieves a balance with the rest. (Cap iii. 264–5)

This just will not happen in the conditions set out in Table 8.2 where the wage (measured in physical products) remains at 1.0_v, however much labour productivity rises. Any capitalists who raised constant capital per worker in the ratio of 5_c to 16_c indicated in Table 8.2 would suffer a fall in their rate of profit, so they would not rationally adopt the more capital intensive techniques involved. As Samuelson pointed out in 1957, a logically coherent account of Marx's law of the declining rate of profit does entail that wages per head rise to some extent with growing labour productivity:

we should note a contradiction in Marx's thinking that analysts have pointed out. Along with the 'law of the falling rate of profit', Marxian economists often speak of the 'law of the falling (or constant) real wage of labour'. Some Marxians have even thought that the important fruit of *Capital's* peculiar definitions has been this law of the 'immiserisation' of the working classes, with the rich getting richer the poor poorer, and with nothing to be done about it until capitalism becomes so senile and cycle-ridden as to lead inevitably to a revolutionary transformation into socialism or communism. The facts of economic history have, of course, not dealt kindly with this law. And Marx himself did not adhere to it at all times. But he perhaps didn't fully realize the inconsistency of his two inevitable laws. As Joan Robinson points out: 'Marx can only demonstrate a falling tendency in profits by abandoning his argument that real wages tend to be constant'[10] (pp. 892–3).

Faced with two contradictory dogmas, what are we to do?...of course, we jettison one (at least!) of the dogmas. Which one? I nominate the law of the declining (or constant) real wage for the junk pile, and note with interest that modern Marxians increasingly turn to that part of the sacred writings more consistent with last century's tremendous rise in workers' real wage rates. (p. 895)

Four years later Okishio showed, naturally enough, that with the real wage fixed, a very wide range of technological improvements must raise the rate of profit.[11] Since it is impossible to make complete logical sense of Marx's argument with the assumption that the real wage is constant, it has to be assumed that this rises to some extent with labour productivity (though, of course, at a slower rate). That will occur if either the socially determined element in the standard of living of the working class has a rising trend, or alternatively if the bargaining power of labour is such that a fraction of the gain in labour productivity which results from increases in capital per worker goes to labour. The effect of this assumption is illustrated in Table 8.3, where in contrast to Table 8.2, it is now assumed that half the increase in the total wage-bill raises wages per head, while the remaining half goes to pay extra workers. Returning to the two examples from Table 8.1 of levels of net output of 625_{v+s} and 2000_{v+s}, when output is 625_{v+s} the wage-bill of 250_v pays 250 workers a wage of 1.0_v each. When it is 2000_{v+s} the total wage-bill of 447.2_v is 78.9 per cent higher and it is now assumed that wages per head are 33.7 per cent higher at 1.337_v and the labour force is also 33.7 per cent higher at $250 \times 1.337 = 334$ workers. With the labour force at 334 in the situation set out in Table 8.1 where net output is 2000_{v+s}, constant capital per worker is $7,155.4_c/334 = 21.423_c$, while output per worker is $2000_{v+s}/334 = 5.988_{v+s}$.

The progression to a more capital intensive technology is now

TABLE 8.3 What happens when variable capital per worker (the wage) rises at the same rate as the labour force while net output rises from 625_{v+s} to 2000_{v+s} in Table 8.1

Constant capital per worker	Net output per worker	Variable capital per worker	Surplus value per worker	Rate of profit
5.0_c	2.5_{v+s}	1.0_v	1.5_s	25.0%
21.423_c	5.988_{v+s}	1.337_v	4.651_s	20.4%

For comparison: the effect of continuing to use the less capital intensive technology when the wage is 1.337_v

5.0_c	2.5_{v+s}	1.337_v	1.163_s	18.4%

logically possible, because if some capitalists raise productivity in the manner indicated in Table 8.3, and at the same time the wage rises from 1.0_v to 1.337_v, the rate of profit of those who stick to the former technology but have to pay this new and higher wage will fall from 25 per cent to 18.4 per cent. The rate of profit of those who advance their scale of production and mechanise will in contrast fall only from 25 per cent to 20.4 per cent. Those who expand their scale of production, and advance the capital to output ratio at the same time will, therefore, outcompete those who maintain an unchanged technology, and fail to raise the organic and technical composition of their capital. It is, therefore, with the assumptions of Table 8.3 where there is some continuing rise in wages per head as productivity rises, though the wage-bill still rises far more slowly than output, that Marx's results are precisely reproduced. Individual entrepreneurs raise their scale of production, which raises labour productivity. The rate of profit earnable with the previous technology then falls as soon as wages adjust upwards by a fraction of the increase in labour productivity, until the new technology and scale of production is indeed the most profitable one.

That comes as close to Marx's own argument as set out in the previous quotation as it is possible to get. It will be seen that with ordinary capitalist incentives, the successive adoption of techniques of production which in the end offer lower rates of profit becomes inevitable, whatever the initial technical conditions, so long as constant capital has to be increased faster than output. The one difference between the present restatement and Marx's own analysis is that there must be some advance of wages with labour productivity, but wages can advance very much less than productivity and still produce the result of an inevitable tendency in the rate of profit to decline.[12]

As Marx perceived, this inevitable tendency towards decline in the rate of profit has important implications for the rate of growth of employment. Capital accumulation is due to the reinvestment of profits, and if a fixed fraction of net profits of $(1 - s_c)$ is consumed by the capitalist class, the fraction s_c will be available for net investment. Equation (8.9) shows that k, the rate of growth of the *total* capital stock will equal $s_c r$ if all the profits available for investment are in fact reinvested. The economy's potential rate of growth of capital is therefore proportional to the rate of profit, and if this falls, so will the rate of growth of capital, and therefore the rate of growth of employment also in so far as this depends on capital accumulation.

The equation derived earlier which linked employment to capital accumulation (8.7) made this depend on k_m, the rate of growth of constant capital, while it is k, the rate of growth of *total* capital, which is directly related to the rate of profit. It is therefore necessary to determine what rate of growth of constant capital will be associated with each rate of growth of the total capital stock. The relationship between the rate of growth of constant capital and the rate of growth of the total capital stock can in fact be derived straightforwardly.

Since $K = K_m + K_v$ where K is the total stock, K_m is constant capital and K_v is variable capital:

$$k = \left(\frac{C/V}{C/V + 1} \right) k_m + \left(\frac{1}{C/V + 1} \right) k_v \tag{8.12}$$

where C/V is the ratio of *total* constant to *total* variable capital, that is, the organic composition of capital, while k_m and k_v are the rates of growth of constant and variable capital. Because constant capital grows H times as fast as net output, while output grows $1/U$ times as fast as variable capital, constant capital grows H/U times as fast as variable capital so that:

$$k_m = \frac{H}{U} k_v \tag{8.13}$$

Equation (8.13) can be used to substitute for k_v and k_m in equation (8.12) to produce equations for both k_m and k_v in terms of k:

$$k_m = \left(\frac{C/V + 1}{C/V + U/H} \right) k \tag{8.14}$$

$$k_v = \left(\frac{V/C + 1}{V/C + H/U} \right) k \tag{8.15}$$

Equation (8.13) shows that if H and U are constant, and H exceeds 1 while U is less than 1, as must always be the case in a Marx growth model, the rate of growth of constant capital will always be a fixed multiple of the rate of growth of variable capital. In Marx's own scheme for extended reproduction, there is no allowance for an ever rising organic composition of capital. In consequence growth proceeds with the proportions between the sectors of the economy which eventually allow Department I, which manufactures means of production, and Department II, which manufactures necessary consumer goods, to grow at the same rate. Equation (8.13) shows that once the effects of a rising organic composition of capital are allowed for, the output of Department I will always have to grow H/U times as fast as the output of Department II, and with equal capital intensities in the two Departments, the capital stock of Department I will have to grow H/U times as fast as the capital stock of Department II to achieve this result. This would have to be allowed for in a more complex scheme of extended reproduction than Marx's. With the previous examples where $H = 1\frac{1}{2}$ and $U = \frac{1}{2}$, Department I would have to grow three times as fast as Department II.

As the ratio of k_v to k_m is always less than 1, the rate of growth of variable capital is bound to be less than that of the total capital stock, and it is also evident that this must be the case from equation (8.15). Similarly, the rate of growth of constant capital must exceed that of the total capital stock and (8.14) shows this unambiguously. Equation (8.14) also shows that as the organic composition of capital rises, the proportional excess of the rate of growth of constant capital over the rate of growth of the total capital stock diminishes. If, for instance, $H = 1\frac{1}{2}$ and $U = \frac{1}{2}$, equation (8.14) will become:

$$k_m = \left(\frac{C/V + 1}{C/V + \frac{1}{3}} \right) k$$

so that the rate of growth of constant capital will be $1.5k$ when $C/V = 1$, $1\frac{2}{7}k$ when $C/V = 2$, $1\frac{1}{5}k$ when $C/V = 3$, and $1\frac{1}{8}k$ when $C/V = 5$. The rate of growth of constant capital thus falls asymptotically towards equality with the rate of growth of the total capital stock as the organic composition of capital rises.

When equation (8.9) is used to substitute for k in equation (8.14):

$$k_m = s_c r \left(\frac{C/V + 1}{C/V + U/H} \right) \tag{8.16}$$

which shows how the rate of growth of constant capital falls with the rate of profit. Equation (8.7) linked the rate of growth of employment to the rate of growth of constant capital, and when this is used to substitute for k_m in equation (8.16):

$$n = s_c r \left(\frac{C/V + 1}{C/V + U/H} \right) \left[1 - B \left(Z - \frac{1}{H} \right) \right] \tag{8.17}$$

·If, for instance, $H = 1\frac{1}{2}$, $U = \frac{1}{2}$, and $B = 1\frac{1}{2}$, and $Z = 1\frac{1}{5}$:

$$n = \frac{1}{5}s_c r\left(\frac{C/V + 1}{C/V + \frac{1}{3}}\right)$$

This equation predicts that in these assumed conditions, the rate of growth of employment will fall asymptotically towards $\frac{1}{5}s_c r$ as the organic composition of capital rises. A rising organic composition of capital in fact doubly reduces the rate of growth of employment. First, as soon as the rising C/V ratio starts to reduce the rate of profit, it reduces the rate of growth of the total capital stock (which equals $s_c r$) at the same proportional rate, as a result of the assumption that a constant fraction of profits is available for investment. Additionally, as C/V rises, the expression:

$$\frac{C/V + 1}{C/V + \frac{1}{3}}$$

falls asymptotically towards 1, and this shows how the increase in constant capital requirements per worker relative to variable capital reduces the rate of growth of employment by increasing the cost of equipping extra workers.

Because the rate of growth of employment falls faster than the rate of profit as the organic composition of capital rises, it must reach its maximum earlier than the rate of profit. The rate of growth of constant capital (on which the power to equip extra workers depends) actually reaches its maximum when:[13]

$$\frac{C \text{ (rate of exploitation)}}{C/V + U/H} = \frac{1 - U}{H - U} \tag{8.18}$$

The rise in the rate of growth of employment to a maximum and its subsequent fall as the organic composition of capital rises is illustrated in Table 8.4, which is based on the same assumptions as Table 8.1 where $H = 1\frac{1}{2}$ and $U = \frac{1}{2}$. The rate of profit reaches its maximum of 25 per cent when $C/V = 5$ and total variable capital reaches 250_v. If s_c, the proportion of surplus-value available for accumulation, is constant at $\frac{1}{3}$, the rate of growth of constant capital reaches its maximum of 9.5119035 per cent per annum considerably earlier when C/V equals only 3.8376 and total variable capital is just 219.02_v.[14]

Table 8.4 also follows the present example by having $B = 1\frac{1}{2}$ and Z $1\frac{1}{5}$, and in that event employment grows one-fifth as fast as constant capital to produce the result that the rate of growth of employment reaches its maximum rate of 1.9023807 per cent per annum when C/V $= 3.8376$ and total variable capital $= 219.02_v$.

The fall in the rate of growth of employment while the organic composition of capital rises from 3.8376, where the rate of growth of employment is maximum, to 5.00, where the rate of profit is maximum, is in fact negligible. During this period, the influence of the still-rising rate of profit favours the growth of employment, while the rising organic composition of capital, which reduces k_m in relation to k, causes employment to grow more slowly. There is therefore only a slight *net* reduction in the rate of growth of employment until the rate of profit actually starts to fall. Once this occurs, the falling rate of profit reduces the rate of growth of the total capital stock, and the rising organic composition of capital reduces k_m still faster, so these effects reinforce each other to doubly reduce the rate of growth of employment. That the rate of growth of employment will clearly fall once the rate of profit starts to fall is entirely in line with Marx's own argument, as he reiterated that the fall in the rate of profit and

TABLE 8.4 Capital per worker, the rate of profit and the rate of growth c employment where one-third of surplus-value is accumulated

Constant capital C	Variable capital V	Organic composition C/V	Rate of profit r	Growth of capital k	Growth of constant capital k_m	Growth of employment n
80.0	100.0	0.80	0	0	0	0
92.3	104.9	0.88	2.59%	0.86%	1.34%	0.27%
147.0	122.5	1.20	10.20%	3.40%	4.88%	0.98%
226.3	141.4	1.60	15.94%	5.31%	7.15%	1.43%
640.0	200.0	3.20	23.81%	7.94%	9.44%	1.89%
839.72490	218.95205	3.8352000	24.601268%	8.2004226%	9.5119027%	1.9023805%
840.51325	219.02055	3.8375999	24.603222%	8.2010739%	9.5119035%	1.9023807%
841.30185	219.08902	3.8400001	24.605170%	8.2017233%	9.5119028%	1.9023806%
1250.0	250.0	5.00	25.00%	8.33%	9.38%	1.88%
2529.8	316.2	8.00	24.03%	8.01%	8.65%	1.73%
7155.4	447.2	16.00	20.42%	6.81%	7.09%	1.42%
28284.3	707.1	40.00	14.81%	4.94%	5.02%	1.00%

Note: C, V, C/V and r are calculated as in Table 8.1. With $s_c = \frac{1}{3}$, $k = \frac{1}{3}r$ (from equation (8.9)), and k_m can be calculated from this, using (8.14) with $U = \frac{1}{2}$ and $H = 1\frac{1}{2}$. n derivable from k_m using (8.7), and it is $\frac{1}{5}k_m$ where $B = 1\frac{1}{2}$, $Z = 1\frac{1}{5}$ and $H = 1\frac{1}{2}$.

the fall in the rate of growth of employment which he predicted are part of the same dynamic process. For instance:

> It therefore follows of itself from the nature of the capitalist process of accumulation, which is but one facet of the capitalist production process, that the increased mass of means of production that is to be converted into capital always finds a correspondingly increased, even excessive, exploitable worker population. As the process of production and accumulation advances therefore, the mass of available and appropriated surplus-labour, and hence the absolute mass of profit appropriated by the social capital, *must* grow. Along with the volume, however, the same laws of production and accumulation increase also the value of the constant capital in a mounting progression more rapidly than that of the variable part of capital, invested as it is in living labour. Hence, the same laws produce for the social capital a growing absolute mass of profit, and a falling rate of profit. (Cap iii.218–19)

And again:

> Thus, the same development of the social productiveness of labour expresses itself with the progress of capitalist production on the one hand in a tendency of the rate of profit to fall progressively and, on the other, in a progressive growth of the absolute mass of the appropriated surplus-value, or profit; so that on the whole a relative decrease of variable capital and profit is accompanied by an absolute increase of both. This two-fold effect, as we have seen, can express itself only in a growth of the total capital at a pace more rapid than that at which the rate of profit falls. For an absolutely increased variable capital to be employed in a capital of higher composition, or one in which the constant capital has increased relatively more, the total capital must not only grow proportionately to its higher composition, but still more rapidly. It follows, then, that as the capitalist mode of production develops, an ever larger quantity of capital is required to employ the same, let alone an increased, amount of labour-power. Thus, on a capitalist foundation, the increasing productiveness of labour necessarily and permanently creates a seeming over-population of labouring people. (Cap iii.223)

Blaug (1960) has argued that it is somewhat astonishing that capitalists should continuously raise constant relative to variable capital, that is, that they should continually substitute capital for labour, in a situation where labour is cheap and increasingly redundant. It was shown above that there is no hint of a neoclassical production function permitting substitution between labour and capital in Marx's analysis of the factors which determine capital intensity, and the composition of capital rises continually because this is the sole way in which the benefits of higher productivity can be attained. This then produces the double effect of a declining rate of profit and a growing reserve army of labour.

Table 8.4 sets out just one example of how these tendencies which Marx predicted are produced with the present mathematical restatement of his argument. Innumerable other examples could be worked through with the same general result of an eventually declining rate of profit, and starting sooner, a declining rate of growth of employment. The table uses assumed values for H, Z and B which produce a positive association between the growth of means of production and employment (and the relationship between these is set out in equation (8.7)). If H, Z and B were such that extra means of production reduced employment, the pattern of Table 8.4 of a rate of growth of employment that rose and then fell would not be followed and equation (8.18), which shows the conditions where the rate of growth of the means of production reaches a maximum, would show, at that point, the situation where the rate of growth of employment reached a *minimum*. But in that event employment would increase at no stage in the development of a capitalist economy, and Marx was not as pessimistic as that, so it can safely be assumed that H, Z and B will combine to produce a positive association between accumulation and employment as in Table 8.4.

Marx was however a little more pessimistic about the employment-creating capacity of capitalism than the mathematical restatement illustrated in Table 8.4. That never produces a decline in employment, but it was shown above that Marx believed that there *could* in the end be decline. Table 8.4 is derived on the assumption of a constant H, that is, a constant ratio of the increase in the means of production to the increase in total output. This had to be assumed constant to permit the derivation of the formulae, including those for the conditions where the rate of profit is maximum. It was indicated earlier however, that if H has a long-run tendency to rise, and Marx believed that it had, then a rate of capital accumulation which produces increasing employment during one historical period could produce declining employment in a later one. That would accentuate all the adverse trends in the rate of profit and in employment which have been set out.

SOME CONCLUDING COMMENTS

There was a vast accumulation of means of production in the century prior to 1867 when Marx published the first volume of *Capital*. The evolution of technology from handicraft to factory production increased constant capital massively, and since this started low in relation to output, it must have risen far faster than output from 1750 to 1867. There have not been satisfactory attempts to measure the increase in the capital to output ratio during the British Industrial Revolution, but it must have risen very sharply indeed. Productivity and employment rose at the same time. There were, moreover, large increases in the capital to labour ratio in agriculture, and these greatly increased agricultural productivity, and as Marx indicated, reduced the demand for agricultural labour, which provided much of the reserve army that industry required. It is also overwhelmingly clear that the share of industrial profits grew sharply in the century prior to the publication of *Capital*. This is obvious if the profits derived from the handicraft methods of production prevailing in the early eighteenth century are contrasted with the non-farm profits of 30 per cent of the gross domestic product which British capital received in 1873, the nearest date to 1867 for which satisfactory data are available.[15] Property owners received a further 13 per cent of the gross domestic product in the form of farm profits and rents. There was a rising trend in wages after about 1850 – whether the real wage rose before this is controversial – but there must have been a far faster rise in profits than in wages to produce the 43 per cent share of domestic property income in the gross domestic product of 1873.

In the century prior to the publication of *Capital* there were therefore very plausibly a rising technical and organic composition of capital, and a rising rate of exploitation. Few modern economists have been so fortunate as to find premises so closely in accord with the broad facts of a previous century of economic development.

There was of course no falling rate of profit from 1750 to 1867, but Marx's argument does not require one. The rate of profit rises before it falls. The switch from handicraft to factory production involved an increase in the rate of exploitation which raised profits per worker considerably faster than capital per worker, and so produced an initial rising trend in the rate of profit as in the above tables. There was at the same time an initial rising trend in the rate of growth of industrial employment. Marx's argument was that if the organic and technical composition of capital continued to rise indefinitely, and he thought they would (on the basis of a proof by induction from the evidence of over a century of technological development in several countries), then their adverse effect on the rate of profit would eventually outweigh the favourable effects of a rising rate of exploitation. He took it for granted that the need to increase means of production faster than output would continue indefinitely, because he saw this as fundamental to the process by which productivity advanced. Here he was mistaken, but it is understandable that like most economists before and since he was content to base his predictions on the extrapolation of the experience of a century or more into the future.

The work of Matthews, Feinstein and Odling-Smee on the measurement of the growth of capital and output in Britain from 1856 to 1973 is the most professional to date, and they find that the ratio of the domestic British capital stock to the gross domestic product, measured at constant prices, averaged 4.0 in 1856–73, 4.1 in 1873–1913, 4.8 in 1924–37 when the level of output was depressed as a result of generally weak effective demand and 4.1 in 1951–73.[16] Capital as they measure it is approximately equivalent to Marx's constant capital or means of production, and if the constant capital to output ratio was actually 4.0 when Marx wrote the first volume of *Capital* and 4.1 a century later, constant capital and output have grown at almost precisely the same rate over that period. In the United States it appears that output has actually been growing faster than the capital stock in the twentieth century.[17] In terms of the mathematical statement of Marx's argument in this chapter, the British data indicate that H may have been close to unity in the century since the publication of *Capital*.

It is only of course if H exceeds 1, that is, if constant capital grows faster than output, that extra capital accumulation may fail to raise the demand for labour. If constant capital actually grows at the same rate as output, Marx's argument that capital accumulation may fail to produce a sufficient growth in the demand for labour to create enough new employment opportunities to match the growth of population collapses. Marx himself acknowledged that at a constant organic composition of capital (which is not quite the same thing as a constant capital to output ratio – but the two trends are closely related),[18] extra accumulation would raise employment and wages.[19] There will also, of course, be no declining trend in the rate of profit from an ever growing organic composition of capital if output grows as fast as constant capital.

All are nowadays aware that technical progress may involve increases *or reductions* in the capital to output ratio. Up to 1867 there must have been increases most of the time. Since then the British capital to output ratio has apparently been very nearly constant. What if there should on balance be increases again from 1973 to 2073? Could that not produce results like those that Marx predicted? He worked out the consequences of a particular direction of technological development, believing it to be the only possible one. But is it an impossible one? Will the demand for labour cease to grow if the change in the capital to output ratio now resumes the course that Marx predicted. The capital to output ratio has risen significantly since 1973 in most OECD countries. What if there is more of the same in the coming decades?

Capitalism has now developed a new defence against Marx's trends. With the great rise in real wages which occurred in the period in which the capital to output ratio has been constant, the standard of living of the working class has come to include a considerable quantity of personal services. In North America employment to provide services accounts for almost two-thirds of total employment, while industry, agriculture and mining between them account for little more than one-third. In Western Europe the service sector now provides almost 55 per cent of total employment. In so far as the high North American standard of living consists of food and manufactured goods, only one-third of the labour force needs to be employed *directly* to provide these. This is precisely the kind of trend that Marx predicted, but it has not condemned the remaining two-thirds to unemployment and destitution. In his time it could reasonably be argued that personal services were luxuries which would only be demanded by the recipients of profits and rents, but today the service sector of the economy also provides a wide range of *necessities for the working class*.

Some services are provided with the aid of technological methods which, to an extent, resemble those of modern industry. Supermarkets in retail distribution where there have been strong trends towards rising productivity and a concentration of sales into fewer chains of shops is an obvious example. There are other service activities where there are not significant economies of large scale production, and where there have not been strong trends towards rising capital intensity. Any increase in demand for these services is bound to provide growing employment opportunities. In economies where 60 to 70 per cent of the labour force is employed in the service sector, extra output and capital accumulation in the economy as a whole is bound to increase the demand for the labour intensive services and therefore for the employment they provide, even if jobs are at the same time being lost in industry and agriculture. Therefore, even if future technical developments in industry and agriculture take precisely the form that Marx predicted, in which case Marxist growth theory would provide a valid explanation of de-industrialisation, the labour force would increasingly obtain employment in the labour intensive services, which use technologies that often resemble those of the handicrafts from which the whole process of industrialisation began. So Marx's theory of the tendency of the rate of profit and the growth of employment to decline can make little sense to economists today. His proposition that wages will rise less than productivity, if at all, is still more irrelevant to an understanding of how modern economies develop. Mainstream economics therefore almost wholly ignores Marx's explanations and predictions of the broad historical tendencies.

A few interesting propositions have been derived from modifications to his argument. Fellner, for instance, has shown that the rate of profit can fall, and wages fail to rise at the same time, if there are natural resource constraints which continually raise the prices of raw materials relative to manufactures.[20] This is true enough but diminishing returns in primary production played no part in Marx's own analysis. They of course played a fundamental role in Ricardo's, and there is no difficulty in predicting a declining real wage and a declining rate of profit, however favourable the conditions of production in industry, with Ricardo's assumption of strong diminishing returns in agriculture, which obviously stands for all primary production including, today, oil.

Marx's argument commands far more attention when it is applied to the century and a half prior to the publication of *Capital*. He kept close to known facts and his propositions derive from them. That is why historians, and especially economic historians, take his analysis very seriously indeed. Many disagree with him, but where they present well-argued accounts of the Industrial Revolution and its aftermath which differ from the Marxist one, they have to present a documented case against the Marxist interpretation of these events.[21] Marxist history and Marxist economic history is now very much part of the mainstream of scholarship. In contrast, Marx's analysis of the laws which influence the development of economies receives little or no attention from economists. They have appeared a complete irrelevance to most because they are so much at variance with what has happened since 1867. Are economists in fact right to pay such scant regard to the economics of *Capital*? Marx predicted deepening crises and a declining rate or profit. Are there not deepening crises, and is not the rate of profit falling?

The crises, in so far as their explanation is Keynesian, depend on repeated failures of effective demand to keep pace with the growth of productive capacity. Marx called such difficulties a failure to realise surplus-value, and he said a little about the nature and implications of the realisation problem. Keynes and the economists who followed him have set all this out in very great detail, and with a rigour which Marx never attempted.[22] What he said about the realisation problem (which echoes the previous analyses of Quesnay and Malthus) will seem wholly sensible to many today, but there is not very much of it. This was not an element of *Capital* which he worked through fully and completely, and what he had to say made little impact until Keynes rediscovered the same lines of argument, and set them out in a way which convinced his contemporaries.

As for the fall in the rate of profit in the twentieth century, this has not been falling as a result of a rising organic composition of capital. The composition of capital has not been rising. The explanation of the twentieth-century fall in the rate of profit can therefore have nothing to do with Marx's. The rate of profit has fallen while the share of wages and salaries in the national income has been rising, and therefore there has been a falling rate of exploitation. Marx never predicted this. Nevertheless a case can be made that his method of analysis is central to an explanation of the fall in the rate and share of profits which appears to be occurring, and his theory of exploitation which was the concern of the previous chapter may well have much to contribute to an understanding of what is occurring in the second half of the twentieth century.

Marx analysed the determination of the share of profits in terms of relative class power. As was argued in Chapter 7, at the time that Marx wrote, capitalists could pass and enforce legislation to limit the power and indeed the very existence of trade unions. At the same time there were few laws to limit or constrain the profit maximising behaviour of capitalists: just a few which were passed with great difficulty to limit the hours of employment of women and children. Employers were wholly free to combine, without government attempts to control them, to fix prices in relation to wages and to limit wages, and they could dismiss workers at will and without compensation. In the absence of welfare provision for the unemployed, mere survival dictated that workers sell their labour-power on the best terms they could get. Many capitalists, in contrast, could survive financially without workers for months or even years. Capital therefore had the power to coerce labour, and some see in this the most fundamental of all the conditions that permit exploitation.[23]

In the late twentieth century, in contrast, legislation has been passed in many countries which sets virtually no limits to the exercise of union power, while at the same time capitalists can only dismiss workers if they pay considerable compensation. Capitalists are forbidden to combine to fix prices as a result of legislation which is often enforced. Such laws as exist to limit the exercise of union power are, in contrast, often not enforced because governments believe that they cannot or should not use a degree of force against strikers which would have been imposed as a matter of course (to contain riots) in the nineteenth century. Still more fundamentally, welfare provisions are such that it is an open question whether workers can live without companies for longer than companies can survive without workers. Capital therefore now lacks the power to coerce labour.

Someone who has learned from Marx would say, and rightly, that these changes are partly due to an increase in the power of the working class and a decline in the power of the capitalist class. The rate of exploitation has in consequence fallen, which has raised the share of wages and salaries in the national income and reduced the share of profits – and indeed the rate of profit. A reader of Marx would think it right to take all the factors which influence income distribution into account, including in particular the decline in the power of capital *to coerce* labour, and the underlying reasons why the power of business interests to pass laws *and have them enforced* has declined. An economist who has learned nothing from Marx can all too easily fall into the trap of attempting to explain changes in income distribution by assuming a theoretical world where there is no institutional change, and where workers and those who control corporations are equally free to act to maximise their utilities in an unchanging legal and institutional environment.

Marx provided a richer analysis. His predictions about the nature and direction of technical change and what followed from this may have been quite largely mistaken, but his attempt to explain income distribution as a consequence of relative class power will always deserve close attention.

9 The Classical Theory of Economic Growth

Within six years of publication, half the citations that there will ever be to a modern economics article will already have appeared.[1] After that, with a few notable exceptions, references rapidly cease. That puts the achievement of Quesnay, Smith, Malthus, Ricardo and Marx into perspective, for after one or two hundred years their economics is still very much alive, and a good deal of it is still as controversial as when it first appeared.

That is not the case with Quesnay, who is still as he was in the eighteenth century, an economist's economist. There is however no need to spell out the significance of Smith for the radical Right which has achieved office in Britain and in North America in the 1980s, that of Malthus for those who are increasingly concerned by the prospect of ecological disaster, that of Ricardo as the inspirer of the flourishing neo-Ricardian school, and of Marx for the radical Left. Their continuing influence is a testimonial to the richness of their thought. Each generation of scholars manages to bring out the elements of their work which modern economics has managed to develop. Thus the revival of growth theory by Harrod and Domar led a generation of scholars to attribute Harrod-neutral technical progress to Marx. Before that, modern scholars lacked the techniques to come to terms in any significant way with Marx's analysis of growth. Kaldor's preoccupation with increasing returns in the 1960s has shown a new generation of scholars how this may be modelled, and that has allowed this element in the work of Smith and Marx, which was always central to their argument, to be represented.

Anyone who has attempted to come to terms with the great books the classical economists wrote will appreciate how immensely vast and complex any attempt to produce the full richness of their argument in the language of modern scholarship is bound to be. Hollander has managed to give an account of the range, the diversity and the logical rigour of Smith and Ricardo, and he has done this entirely non-mathematically.[2] But nowadays it is customary to state economic propositions in algebra as well as in words so that fellow scholars can grasp *precisely* what a new contribution amounts to. If Smith, Malthus, Ricardo and Marx had had to do this (Quesnay would have welcomed the challenge – after devoting his 60s to economics, he attempted to square the circle in his 70s),[3] they would have had to omit between one-half and three-quarters of what they considered important. What remained would now be far better understood and one would venture to guess much less read. It is an error to assume that a logically clear and developed argument from the limited range of premises which even a good mathematician can handle, will necessarily say more than a less developed statement which takes a wider range of considerations into account. A book of the latter kind can be entirely worthless, but of the thousands which are written the few that survive the test of continuing interest after one or two centuries have a remarkable amount to contribute.

There is also an economic model of growth which can be set out in the modern way in the work of Quesnay, Smith, Malthus, Ricardo and Marx, and it has been the object of this book to rediscover it and reproduce it. There is much more, very much more, but the growth model has been the specific objective. The principal proposition on which this is based is, at its simplest, that only some economic activities generate a surplus. The reinvestment of that surplus is the main influence on the rate of economic growth. At the same time, the enjoyment of the surplus becomes the principal source of high personal incomes and of government tax revenues. This is so obvious that it is difficult to believe that the financial advisers of governments ever failed to understand it. There was, however, little economic writing which attempted to explain the full interconnections between industry, agriculture, commerce and the tax revenues on which government depends until the seventeenth century. Finley has suggested that the subtle and sophisticated interrelationships which challenge the intellect did not emerge until economies had become quite fully monetised.[4] Before that, decisions taken in one part of an economy will have had an essentially administrative influence on the rest. Economic pamphleteering certainly only began to break out on a significant scale in seventeenth- and eighteenth-century Europe, and two examples from the work of respected authors show that there was no general awareness before Quesnay of the connection between surplus-generation, government revenues and growth.

Davenant, publishing in London in 1699, divided the population into those who were increasing and those who were decreasing the wealth of the kingdom, and argued that it was the surplus of the former class that provided the revenues which employed the latter. He published a *Tableau* which listed those who were increasing wealth as the nobility, the Church, officers in the Army and Navy, and city merchants.[5] The country's labourers and simple soldiers and sailors were dependent for their employment on the revenues of the nobility, etc. It is not surprising that with this framework of analysis, a loss of money revenues to other countries was expected to cause destitution, while a mercantilist defence of domestic revenues was expected to raise employment for the mass of common labourers. It did not occur to Davenant and his contemporaries that it was the labourers who supported the nobility.

In mid-eighteenth-century France, Victor Riqueti, Marquis de Mirabeau, made the important advance of attributing wealth to population, with the result that he saw a country's ordinary labourers as the source of production and tax revenues. His *L'Ami des Hommes* was a populationist tract which analysed the growth of wealth in terms of the encouragement of population growth.[6] The book was immensely successful and it established Mirabeau's fame as an enlightened aristocrat who himself became known as 'L'ami des hommes'. In 1757 he met Madame de Pompadour's doctor for the first time in an entresol in Versailles. At that time Quesnay had only published one article on economics, the essay *'Fermiers'* in the *Encyclopedia*. Mirabeau wrote an account of the meeting in a letter to Rousseau ten years later:

> I had...reasoned in this way [in *L'Ami des Hommes*]: Wealth is the fruit which comes from the land for the use of men; the labour of man alone possesses the capacity to increase wealth. Thus the more men there are, the more labour will there be; the more labour there is, the more wealth there will be. The way to achieve prosperity is therefore: (1) to increase men; (2) through these men, to increase productive labour; (3) through this labour, to increase wealth. In this position I felt myself invulnerable, and I gaudily decorated my political edifice with marriages, sumptuary laws, and the rest, just as I wanted to. Never did Goliath go into

battle with as much confidence as I did when I sought out a man who, I had been informed, had written on the margin of my book these insolent words: 'The child has been suckled on bad milk; the force of his temperament often puts him right so far as results are concerned, but he understands nothing as to principles.' My critic did not beat about the bush with me, and told me quite plainly that I had put the cart before the horse, and that Cantillon, as a teacher of the public, was nothing but a fool. This blasphemy made me regard as a fool the one who uttered it, but, reflecting that in every dispute the exchange of opinions usually proceeds by way of retaliation, I restrained myself, broke off the conversation, and, fortunately for me, returned in the evening to ask questions after thinking things over. It was then that Goliath's head was cloven asunder. My man asked me to do the same honour to men as is done to sheep, since anyone who wants to increase his flock begins by increasing his grazing-land. I replied to him that sheep were a secondary cause in abundance, whereas man was the primary cause in the creation of fruits. He started to laugh, and asked me to explain myself better and to tell him if man, when he arrived on the earth, had brought bread in his pocket to enable him to live until the time when the land, having been prepared, sown, covered with ripe crops, reaped, threshed, etc., could feed him. I was caught: one had either to imagine that man had licked his paws for 18 months, as the bear does during the winter in his lair, or to maintain that this creator of fruits had found some when he arrived which he had never sown. He then asked me to have the kindness to allow all the subsequent population to share the same benefit, because otherwise they too could not exist.[7]

Eagly has attributed to Quesnay the invention of the concept of *capital*,[8] and it is evident that in this reported conversation it was the need to have agricultural capital as a precondition for the survival and growth of population that devastated Mirabeau's populationism. Mirabeau went on to collaborate with Quesnay after this reported conversation, and the fifth, sixth and seventh volumes of *L'Ami des Hommes* which were added to the original four in 1758, 1759 and 1760 were written jointly by Quesnay and Mirabeau and contain the famous '*Tableau Economique avec ses Explications*' which provides one of the fullest and most detailed accounts of the *Tableau* which Quesnay invented in 1758. Mirabeau has remarked that before he met Quesnay he was 'no more an economist than his cat'.[9]

Quesnay went on to publish the original account of the classical theory of economic growth, the subject of the first two chapters of this book. In his version only agriculture and other primary production produced an investable surplus. In so far as that surplus accrued to the farmer, growth in the agricultural capital stock occurred, because farmers automatically reinvested any excess income that came their way. If the farmers merely received the normal income of their class, they maintained capital and the level of output constant, and if they received less than this, they had to sell off or consume some of their capital with the result that output declined. There were two circumstances in which part of the society's net product could go to farmers rather than to the landlords who normally received it. First, if demand for food grew from period to period (which would occur if the society's propensity to consume food exceeded the fraction needed to produce stable demand in the *Tableau*) farmers' incomes would rise during the nine years that should elapse before agricultural leases came up for renewal. During that period farmers would increase their capital and so produce growth in the economy. Secondly, if the argument applied to American and not to French farmers, there would be no rents to absorb the net product, so this could all be invested by farmers to produce about ten times the European rate of growth.

The government could, of course, prevent growth and indeed produce decline in output by taxing away what farmers needed to preserve in order to maintain a constant level of output. If that occurred, it would not merely produce poor farmers, but a poor aristocracy and a poor King and collapsing government finances. Quesnay and Mirabeau were aware of the political instability of the French monarchy and the precarious economic foundations on which it rested. In a famous letter to Mirabeau which began by explaining details of the newly invented *Tableau*, Madame de Pompadour's doctor wrote at the end:

> In your last letter you say truly that the efforts of individuals are very unfruitful; but we must not lose heart, for the appalling crisis will come, and it will be necessary to have recourse to medical knowledge.[10]

The final collapse of the finances of the French monarchy which was followed by the summoning of the *Etats Généraux* and the Revolution occurred thirty years after that letter, and in the meantime a succession of Finance Ministers endeavoured to arrest the collapse. A near-Physiocrat, Turgot, was indeed Finance Minister from 1764 to 1770, and he attempted to apply much of the logic of Quesnay's theory.[11] Lengthening agricultural leases was an obviously desirable microeconomic reform. What would now be called the macroeconomic element of the solution involved raising the price of food relative to wages to make farmers richer and the population of Paris poorer. In time the rich farmers would expand output and spend part of the surplus they obtained on manufactures so that all would gain. A final vignette on the failure of the policy of raising the price of bread in the short-term is Bachaumont's account in 1771 of, 'some common people ready to smash the bust of that man [Quesnay] on hearing that he was the cause of the current dearness of grain through the false theories and the baneful influence which he had had on government'.[12]

It fell to Smith to make a number of corrections to Quesnay's argument which greatly increased its practicality and accessibility. Smith regarded Quesnay as his greatest predecessor,[13] and a vital element of *The Wealth of Nations* is his development of Quesnay's version of the classical theory of economic growth. Before his visit to Paris in 1765–6 when he resided there continuously for nine months, Smith did not refer – for instance, in his lectures to Glasgow students – to the distinction between productive and unproductive labour. There is no awareness that growth is significantly influenced by the extent to which the surplus of the productive exceeds the consumption of the unproductive, and the frugal man only became a public benefactor in 1776.[14]

Much of the argument of *The Wealth of Nations* had been thought through before then. *The Theory of Moral Sentiments* has the hidden hand and a full development of the argument that the pursuit of individual self-interest benefits all. It is perhaps a contrast between dour Glasgow and Paris that led Smith to assert that those who build prisons are directed by 'a juster spirit of patriotism' than those who build palaces, while Quesnay included 'the beautification of the Kingdom' among the economic objectives which governments should pursue.[15] Smith's account of the benefits societies can derive from the division of labour was first written out in the 1750s, and the advantages of trade were explained in detail in the Glasgow lectures. But there is no account before his visit to France of how the rate of capital accumulation is determined and therefore of what allows the benefits from the division of labour to be exploited in some societies and not others.

Once Smith had absorbed what the Physiocrats had to say, he was able to provide the complete account of how economies develop which became *The Wealth of Nations*. This removes a major weakness in Quesnay's argument which Voltaire had ridiculed devastatingly in *L'Homme aux Quarante Ecus* which he published in 1768. The man with an income of 40 crowns or 120 livres, the average French family income of 1768, derived this entirely from the rent of a piece of land from which he could pay only 12 livres taxation and survive. The government however published new edicts which, after a preamble which pointed out that only land should be taxed because everything comes from the land, stipulated that 'The man of forty crowns' should now pay twenty in taxation. As he leaves his plot of land in despair he meets a merchant who used to be poorer than he is, but is now driving a six horse carriage, with six liveried servants to whom he pays 240 livres each, and a mistress to whom he gives 120 000 livres every six months. He assumes that his acquaintance is also having to pay half his income to Versailles:

> I contribute to the needs of the state. Don't make me laugh, I have inherited my wealth from an uncle who made eight millions in Cadiz and Surat; I have not an inch of land; all my wealth is in bills of exchange and contracts; I need owe nothing to the state; it is for you who are a landed seigneur to give half of your subsistence. Don't you see that if the Minister of Finance tried to get some support for the country from me, he would be an imbecile who could not calculate? For everything comes from the soil; money and bills are only means of exchange; instead of writing on a card, a hundred bushels of wheat, a hundred cows, a thousand sheep and two hundred bags of oats, I use pieces of money which represent these lowly products. If, after charging the single tax on these provisions, they still came to me for money, don't you see that that would be a double tax? that it would be to ask for the same thing twice? My uncle sold your wheat for two millions and cloth made from your silk in Cadiz for two millions; he made over 100 per cent from this business. You will appreciate that this profit was made from the soil which was already taxed, that he bought ten sous of wheat from you and resold them for more than 50 francs in Mexico, and all expenses paid, he came back with eight millions.
>
> You will feel truly that it would be a terrible injustice to ask him for a few pennies on the ten sous that he gave you. If twenty nephews like me each had uncles who made eight millions in

Mexico, Buenos Aires, Lima, Surat or Pondicherry and each gave the state just 200,000 francs at times when the country was in desperate need, that would produce four millions; how dreadful. Pay, my friend, you who enjoy in peace a clear revenue of forty crowns. Serve your country well, and come and eat sometimes with my servants. (pp. 205–6[E])

The Physiocrats were of course wide open to this assault. It was patently obvious that there were large and growing commercial fortunes, while Quesnay was insisting that merchants ought not to be producing taxable surpluses. Individual merchants could obviously make profits to balance the losses of their less successful rivals, but any surplus that merchants achieved in the aggregate were simply the result of local monopoly power, which should not exist. Industrial fortunes which were less in evidence in the France of the 1760s were also only explicable as a consequence of monopoly power. Profits as a return to capital are not to be found in Quesnay's analysis, and Smith's division (which followed Turgot's) of incomes into wages, profits and rents is a major advance. Profits, appropriately defined, are of course a clear surplus which can be accumulated or consumed by the capitalists who obtain them, or by government and its servants. Since profits are obtainable in agriculture, industry or commerce, these are all part of the productive sector in Smith's analysis, and he repeats several times that farmers, manufacturers and merchants are productive. Quesnay's division between agriculture and the rest sharply contradicted the perceptions of the economically aware. Smith's distinction between economic activities which yield profits and rent, and those which do not, was entirely in line with what men of affairs considered sensible.

To Smith, accumulation therefore depended on that part of the output of agriculture, industry and commerce which was surplus to the consumption of the productive and the unproductive. Smith believed that the desire to accumulate wealth by the productive and by landlords who would on balance wish the power and wealth of their families to grow, should ensure that the surplus of the productive sector would not be consumed in its entirety in so far as the decisions to consume rested with its owners. But government consumed without producing, so it was perfectly possible that public consumption could destroy capital faster than the desire for family betterment in the private sector could advance it. That appeared entirely sensible analysis to Smith's eighteenth-century readers.

Quesnay's belief that a preference for manufactures over food could also produce economic decline in no way corresponded to what the educated and the powerful believed, and it was based on the false premise that only agriculture could provide an investable surplus.

Smith's other great advance over Quesnay was his immense simplification of the analysis. The Physiocrats were able to assert the conditions where accumulation would occur, and to publish sequences of *Tableaux* to illustrate growth or decline, but the precise explanation of these *Tableaux* was incomprehensible to all but a handful of initiates, and even they differed on the details. There was, therefore, no possibility that the governing classes would understand the precise reasoning of the Physiocrats. They could hire Physiocrats: Catherine the Great paid Mercier de la Rivière travelling expenses of 12 000 livres to come to St Petersburg,[16] and a near-Physiocrat might achieve brief political power like Turgot, but there was no possibility of educating a whole class to an understanding of the new economics. The problem which led to extreme complexity with Quesnay's model was that it was what Hicks has described as a fixprice model.[17] When the *Tableau* is in equilibrium, and that is the only situation the Physiocrats analysed at all carefully, the prices of food, manufactures, exports, imports and so on, all have to be fixed at precisely the level which persuades producers to keep output constant, and the input-output relations of the *Tableau* then require that the supply and demand of each product in home and overseas markets balances at those prices. That involves a complex set of equations, and they are, in fact, so complex that only some of them are shown in the various explanations of the *Tableau* which the Physiocrats published, which is why their published writings had to be taken so largely on trust. They could not be understood in the absence of the oral tradition from which Smith benefited in 1765–6. With the economy's equilibrium stationary state relationships so difficult to grasp, there was no hope at all of a clear analysis of the behaviour of the economy in disequilibrium. The published sequences of *Tableaux* in disequilibrium only relax one of the equilibrium conditions at a time, and set out the effects of disequilibrium in an arbitrary manner.

It was a great advance by Smith to go over to flexprice analysis. With supply and demand able to re-allocate production between industry, agriculture and commerce, and between exports and home production, the economy was far more capable of adjustment. Smith's economy could respond to imbalances between demand and supply in any sector by lifting prices relative to costs where there was excess demand, and depressing them where there was excess supply, which then produced the market economy's familiar supply responses. The hidden hand was far less in evidence in France where regulation interfered much more with the pattern of production than in eighteenth-century England.[18] For whatever reason, Smith had no need to concern himself with the relationship between the reciprocal demands and supplies of food and manufactures at home and overseas, because the market would ensure that the proportions supplied would come into line with demand. He had no need to concern himself with the balance between exports and imports because Hume had shown him (but apparently not Quesnay) how the relative price levels of different countries would adjust to produce balance of payments equilibrium via international money flows.[19] Finally, Smith was satisfied that saving in any sector of the economy would lead to accumulation because, in his competitive system, money and physical capital could move freely between the sectors so that profits earned in industry could expand agriculture or commerce, if that was where a society was willing to spend more. The assumption that capital would never be idle ensured that extra saving *anywhere* would always lead to extra investment somewhere.

All this meant that there was far less to prevent growth in *The Wealth of Nations* than in the Physiocratic models. Only excess government expenditure which absorbed more than the surplus of the productive sector, and so rendered accumulation impossible, or government regulation, or a failure to sustain property rights could prevent the market from solving one or more of the many problems it was required to solve.[20] Smith's simple statements that all that was profitable was productive, and that too much government expenditure or interference could prevent the conversion of the potential surpluses of the productive into the extra capital that was necessary for growth, were comprehensible to all, and sufficiently plausible to the economically literate to remain utterly orthodox until 1936.

Smith's explanation of accumulation was both simpler and more accurate than Quesnay's. His analysis of the benefits from accumulation was in addition far richer. Quesnay did not spell out the manner in which accumulation raised the standard of living of the mass of the population by raising the demand for labour relative to the supply. His detailed analysis of stationary state equilibrium relationships precluded comparisons between the wage in periods where there was disequilibrium because the capital stock was growing, and disequilibrium because it was declining. Smith in contrast made the rate of capital accumulation the main determinant of the real wage. This was to become a central element in the classical theory of growth in the work of Malthus and Ricardo. Smith also improved greatly on Quesnay's analysis by bringing out the technological advantages of industrialisation. It was not merely that industry was as productive as agriculture because both were profitable. Industry benefited from increasing returns while agriculture did not, so the fundamental hope of raising living standards for the mass of the people lay in taking advantage of the opportunities for raising productivity that industry provided. That this also required accumulation which depended on the reinvestment of the surplus of the productive sector, and not its consumption by government, tied together Smith's new contributions, and those he had found and improved on in the work of his great predecessor.

Smith's version of the classical theory of economic growth was not entirely optimistic: he had a few references to the tendency of the rate of profit to fall to a minimum, when growth would cease. That the rate of profit should have a long-term tendency to decline became a central thread in the classical economics that came after Smith, and Malthus, Ricardo and Marx had far clearer reasons for expecting this. Smith was after all optimistic about costs of production in industry, and he believed that labour productivity in the production of corn would be stable. However this stability of labour productivity was only obtainable by using an increasing ratio of farm capital and especially cattle to labour. If output per worker is stable, while capital per worker has a persistent tendency to rise, the profit per unit of capital that farmers can obtain will quite plausibly have the persistent tendency to fall that Smith envisaged. The Physiocrats had denied the existence of diminishing returns in agriculture, but it emerged that Mirabeau had to spend much of his fortune to improve the gritty soil in his estate of *la Rocheguyon* so that it could become as fertile as the best land in the kingdom, to fit the theory that fertile land was not scarce. His French contemporaries laughed at the eccentricity of the theory, and the expense he was willing to undertake to prove it true.[21] Smith's argument that there were constant costs in agriculture was a subtler one. There are diminishing returns as inferior land is resorted to, since new colonies earn the highest returns with the land that is first cultivated,[22] but this tendency is compensated by the use of more farm capital per worker so that labour productivity keeps up. The rate of profit declines, however, because labour productivity is only being held up at increasing cost to the farmer. But Smith only hints at this, and scholars have had to look hard to find such diminishing returns in agriculture as there are in *The Wealth of Nations*.

Malthus believed that Smith had failed to take the overwhelmingly important influence of diminishing returns in agriculture adequately into account, and this was the starting point of his theory of population and all that followed from it. The first chapter that Malthus ever penned is dominated by agricultural diminishing returns and many of the thousands of pages he published after 1798 are pervaded by them. As he also believed that there were specific requirements of food per head which must be met before population can exist or grow, diminishing returns in agriculture became one of the most important, if not *the* most important constraint on growth in his argument.

Malthus therefore criticised Smith for placing industry on a par with agriculture and arguing that growth could be achieved through either agricultural or industrial expansion. To Malthus agricultural output was the prime mover of growth, because without food there could not be population, and food output could only be expanded with diminishing returns and at a sharply rising real cost. Hence Malthus had much in common with the Physiocrats. There are many passages in his writings which could have been written equally by Quesnay. Strangely there is no evidence that Malthus ever read Quesnay or even Mirabeau. Smith's assault on the errors of the Physiocrats was so successful that Malthus apparently believed their errors were so great that it was unnecessary to read them: he at no point cited or quoted directly from Quesnay. McCulloch read the Physiocrats with some thoroughness,[23] and Brougham makes a precise citation in an *Edinburgh Review* article of 1804,[24] but there is astonishingly no evidence that the two leading English political economists of the early nineteenth century, Malthus and Ricardo, felt any temptation or obligation to read their recent French predecessors. They must have believed that to consider manufacturing sterile was an error of such magnitude that nothing worthwhile could possibly remain.

Malthus, therefore, in virtually complete ignorance of the similar analysis published only thirty or forty years previously, proceeded to set out a Physiocrat analysis with the modification that there were diminishing and not constant returns in agriculture. As food was the only input needed to support population, the growth of agricultural output determined the rate of growth of population. Given this, population growth would accelerate if profitable manufacturers were replaced by loss-making agricultural employment, and that is precisely what Malthus said in 1798, accusing Smith at the same time of the error of preferring profitable manufactures to an unprofitable agriculture.[25] Malthus did not stick persistently to this stark analysis where only food production mattered and manufacturers were an irrelevance so far as the support of population was concerned, but he all but returned to it in the final editions of the *Essay on Population*. In 1817 he was explaining how unreliable export markets for manufactures were likely to prove in the long term for a variety of reasons, and that home grown food was the only secure foundation for the lasting support of a population.[26]

But growth would not be ensured by a large physical surplus of food over the consumption needed by those who worked in agriculture. In the post-war slump after 1815 Malthus began to argue that the food surplus also had to be in demand, which meant that there had to be non-agriculturalists prepared to pay for it. Otherwise there might be a large potential physical surplus which would sell for no more than it cost its cultivators. Agriculturalists would then lack any incentive to expand or even to maintain output. This would bring population growth to a halt and lead to stagnant production. That there always needed to be effective demand for food was an important and controversial innovation by Malthus.

Manufacturing began to play a vital role in Malthus's argument at this point, because he began to see that the sale of food to manufacturers would help to keep up its price, and give agriculturalists incentives to produce more food. They would be able to sell it at high prices to manufacturers, while the availability of manufactures would provide powerful incentives to farmers and farm labourers to use their energies to raise production. Manufactures therefore became important to Malthus, not because they were a necessary input for the production process, but because of their effect on reciprocal demand and the price of food, and on the incentives to release the energies latent in human beings that many societies failed to provide an outlet for.

The reciprocal demands of farmers for manufactures and of manufacturers for farm produce were of course set out in detail in Quesnay's *Tableau*, but it is very much part of the history of economic thought that the same propositions need to be discovered again and again. This is because many economists have always been convinced that their subject is advancing so rapidly that there is no need to read their predecessors.

Malthus's postulate that the prices of food and manufactures both had to be high enough in relation to their costs to provide incentives for the maintenance of output meant that, like Quesnay, his was essentially a fixprice theory. There is a particular price level of food (and manufactures) in relation to their costs of production where output will be constant, and a higher one where it will expand. There are particular reciprocal demands of manufacturers for food and of farmers for manufactures which will sustain these prices. Moreover, since government expenditure is spent on both food and manufactures while the taxation which finances it reduces the supply of both, this can be too low or too high to sustain the prices which are needed for growth. In an analysis of such complexity, there is, as with Quesnay's similar analysis, a great deal that can go wrong and so interrupt the growth process.

Despite these complications, there is a central thread to Malthus's version of the classical theory of economic growth which he persisted with throughout his life. The growth of domestic food output determines the long-term rate of growth of population since the use of imported food to support extra people will not last. The growth of food output is in turn constrained by persistent diminishing returns in agriculture, and by the multiplicity of possible ways in which there may be insufficient effective demand for food to encourage farmers to expand production. Malthus's ideal is a self-sufficient agriculture coupled with a large enough industrial sector to create reciprocal demand and incentives to produce. At the same time the mainly public sector which produces unproductive public services has to be large enough to sustain effective demand, but not so large that it diverts resources away from the agricultural and industrial investment that is needed to achieve the rate of growth made possible by the increase of effective demand. There will be precise proportions between industry, agriculture and unproductive employment which set this three-sector fixprice model on to a viable expansion path. Malthus believed that there were particular proportions between the sectors which would produce the maximum possible rate of growth, the 'elevation at which the projectile will go the farthest',[27] but he was of course incapable in 1820 of working out the conditions which would produce the optimum ratios. He nevertheless saw the problem of maximising the rate of growth in terms of discovering what they were, and so striking the right balance between agriculture, industry and public expenditure. He also wished to discover the optimum balance between accumulation and unproductive consumption, in order to create the strongest possible incentives to expand production

– and above all the output of food because this was the ultimate determinant of growth.

Because there was in his view an optimum savings ratio, Malthus, unlike Smith, was not prepared to say that extra saving would at once lead to more growth. If the savings ratio was above the optimum, less saving and more public expenditure would raise the rate of growth. The fact that his policy conclusions were not clearly deducible from his theory, since he was unable to set this out as a soluble optimisation problem, meant that he had nothing precise to offer his contemporaries. He could only make a series of policy recommendations which depended on which side of the various optima he believed Britain was at in particular periods, and this naturally seemed inconsistent to many. Smith and Ricardo, in contrast, always had precise advice to offer which was clearly inferable from their published work.

One reason why Ricardo was able to arrive at clearer and sharper results which were readily comprehensible to his contemporaries, was that he followed Smith in assuming that the market would take care of the balance between agriculture and industry, and between exports and imports. The incentive to individual capitalists to produce whatever was most in demand would suffice to keep the growth of agricultural and industrial output in line with the home and international demand for each. This meant that, like Smith, he could focus attention on the economy's single productive sector without having to worry about the proportions between its components. The fact that his analysis was essentially flexprice made this possible. With only the productive sector as a whole to consider, he was able to arrive at a clear account of the conditions where growth would be maximised. Malthus in contrast with his multi-sector assumptions could only say that future generations of economists might understand how to answer the important questions.

Ricardo followed Malthus in attaching very great significance to the influence of diminishing returns in agriculture. Because Smith assumed constant costs, marginal land yielded wages, profits and rent. David Hume had written to Smith as early as April 1776, within weeks of the publication of the first edition of *The Wealth of Nations*, 'I cannot think, that the Rent of Farms makes any part of the Price of the Produce, but that the Price is determined altogether by the Quantity and the Demand.'[28] Hume died within months of writing that letter and it was not until 1815 that Ricardo (together with Malthus and West) appreciated that with the assumption of agricultural diminishing returns, marginal food output would yield only wages and profits, which made a clear and simple analysis of income distribution possible. Ricardo began by setting out the argument *as if* the entire productive sector could be represented by a number of farmers who grew corn. If workers consumed only corn, the inputs and outputs of the productive sector could be expressed in the same physical units, and this expositional device – and it was no more than an expositional device: Ricardo departed from it in footnotes – allowed him to arrive at very sharp results. The excess of corn output per worker over the corn a worker had to be paid determined profits per worker, while the rate of profit on capital was this corn profit divided by the corn needed to employ a worker. As agricultural diminishing returns gradually reduced corn output per worker relative to the corn a worker had to be paid, the corn-surplus per worker inevitably fell, and the rate of profit with it. Since investment and capital accumulation depended on the rate of profit, the falling rate of profit would also lead to a falling rate of growth. On this analysis, anything which raised productivity on the margin of corn production would raise the rate of profit and the rate of growth, while anything that reduced productivity would have the opposite effect. At the same time, anything which made it cheaper to employ labour in corn production would raise accumulation and growth. Thus all agricultural improvements would raise the rate of profit and the rate of growth. At the same time, any change in commercial policy which allowed corn to be obtained more cheaply from overseas would raise the rate of profit and the rate of growth, by allowing the economy to avoid the use of the low-productivity land that would otherwise need to be used. Any taxation of any kind which fell on marginal corn production was bound to reduce the rate of profit (after tax) and therefore the rate of growth, because it was bound to reduce the investable surplus of corn output over the wage.

The policy conclusions which followed from this analysis were therefore that in order to maximise growth, taxation should be minimised, corn should be freely importable, and there should be the greatest possible incentives to achieve agricultural improvements. Malthus supported only the latter.

In the *Principles of Political Economy and Taxation* of 1817 Ricardo was able to arrive at essentially the same results with assumptions which were less restrictive. Workers consumed both food and manufactures, and the productive sector produced both food and manufactures. The device that enabled Ricardo to arrive at the same conclusions with these more general assumptions was the supposition that, at any one time, workers consume 'corn-and-manufactures' in fixed proportions. 'Corn-and-manufactures' were then in effect a single commodity and could be analysed as such, as Hicks has shown.[29] Like corn itself in the earlier analysis, the output of 'corn-and-manufactures' could only be expanded with diminishing returns, and profit per worker was the excess of 'corn-and-manufactures' produced per worker over the 'corn-and-manufactures' a worker purchased with his wage. The rate of profit was again simply this surplus over the 'corn-and-manufactures' needed to employ a worker. Therefore anything that reduced the cost of 'corn-and manufactures', including industrial and agricultural innovations, raised the rate of profit and the rate of growth, while anything which made these more expensive, including taxation and interference with trade, reduced profits and growth. The conclusions were therefore the same as those with the earlier argument, where everything could be expressed in terms of corn alone. That argument was therefore extremely robust since the more general and far fuller analysis of the *Principles* left its main conclusions intact.

It is not surprising that it was Ricardo's modifications to Smith's analysis and not Malthus's which carried the day, and influenced what economists and the politically aware believed for several generations.[30] He arrived at clear conclusions while Malthus did not. His argument always called for lower public expenditure and taxation while Malthus's only sometimes did. His argument always called for freer trade, while Malthus sometimes favoured freer trade and sometimes not. And provided that the market could do the work demanded of it, Ricardo's argument was essentially correct. If resources could move freely from agriculture to industry and vice versa, any overexpansion of one or the other could easily be corrected. It was unnecessary to discover the correct theoretical proportions between them. Provided that food and manufactures could be exchanged freely on world markets, then again a country could only gain by exporting manufactures and importing food more cheaply than it could produce food at the margin. That would reduce the domestic market cost of 'corn-and-manufactures' and so raise the rate of profit and the rate of growth. Finally, provided that a surplus obtained in one section could be lent through the market to capitalists willing to use it in another, it simply did not matter where surpluses originated. They did not need to accrue to the capitalists on whom all depended. They could be lent to capitalists whatever their origin.

Ricardo, with a personal capital of only £800, had had the service of the dead read over him (because he married a gentile) when he was twenty-one, and left seven manors to his descendants,[31] one of which Gatcombe Park, is now a Royal Residence. He undoubtedly had to rely on borrowed money at the start of his career and he made remarkable use of it. Because Ricardo believed that any surplus was bound to be lent and invested, surplus maximisation would always lead to growth maximisation as with Smith.

Ricardo therefore incorporated diminishing returns in agriculture into Smith's flexprice analysis, worked out its effects rigorously, and followed Smith in arriving at simple and utterly comprehensible policy conclusions. All surpluses in the production of food and manufactures would lead to growth if they were reinvested, and they would undoubtedly be reinvested to the extent that they were not consumed by the unproductive. At the same time, anything that raised efficiency or made it possible to employ workers more effectively, or cheaply, including cheap food imports, would raise the rate of surplus and the rate of growth. Agricultural diminishing returns would reinforce the tendency for the rate of profit to decline, which Smith discovered, but technical progress in agriculture and industry could make the rate of decline extremely slow.

There was just one qualification to this simple and straightforward analysis. Machinery would reduce costs of production and therefore it would make the rate of profit and the rate of growth higher than it otherwise would have been, like any other innovation in the production of necessities. It would, however, at the same time increase the total capital needed to employ a worker. It might therefore at the same time raise the rate of profit and the rate of growth, but reduce the rate of growth of employment, and make workers worse off than they otherwise would have been. Mechanisation would not therefore necessarily benefit the workers who made up the bulk of the population. This new line of analysis, which Ricardo only discovered in the last years of his life, did not lead him to modify any of his main policy conclusions. He believed that the machinery would be used by foreign producers in any case, so it would be still worse for the standard of living of British workers if it was not brought into use in England. Also, the faster rate of capital accumulation which would follow mechanisation, would produce a faster rate of increase in the demand for labour. Hence, even though mechanisation might reduce the demand for labour in the first instance, its faster rate of growth subsequently would eventually make it higher than it otherwise would have been. Ricardo therefore had no doubt that mechanisation would maximise the *long-term* demand for labour as well as growth.

The first dark echo of Ricardo's machinery analysis came in the Irish famine of the 1840s which John Stuart Mill analysed in precisely the terms of the machinery chapter in his *Principles of Political Economy*.[32] Mill showed that an agricultural improvement which raised capital per worker would have precisely the same effect on the demand for labour as industrial mechanisation, namely it would raise the rate of profit, but reduce the demand for labour in the short term. Mill went on to say:

> The remarkable decrease which has lately attracted notice in the gross produce of Irish agriculture, is, to all appearance, partly attributable to the diversion of land from maintaining human labourers to feeding cattle; and it could not have taken place without the removal of a large part of the Irish population by emigration or death. We have thus...recent instances, in which what was regarded as an agricultural improvement, has diminished the power of the country to support its population. (p. 95)

Ricardo's machinery argument did indeed apply to Ireland and the Irish famine as Mill perceived. The failure of the potato crop raised the wage that capitalists had to pay in Ireland. At the former wage workers could be expected to live largely off potatoes. After the failure of the potato crop they had to be able to afford dearer food. That rise in wages persuaded capitalists to prefer a more capital intensive agriculture, which required more farm animals and fewer workers. A switch to farm animals, like a switch to machinery, reduced the number of workers employed relative to the capital stock. Hence the evictions and the starvation which continued long after the potato crop failed. Before the welfare state, machinery often killed, and Mill remembered and reminds us that in the nineteenth century as in the sixteenth, sheep and indeed cattle were 'the devourers of men'.[33] In England in 1581 as in Ireland three hundred years later, 'wheare XL persons had theire lyvinges, nowe one man and his shepard hathe all'.[34]

Ricardo believed that this once-for-all tendency of mechanisation to reduce the demand for labour in relation to the capital stock would be followed by faster growth in employment (from that reduced level) as the higher rate of profit led to a faster increase in the capital stock. Marx denied this. He did not see why increasing mechanisation should not continue indefinitely, so that there would be a continual tendency for the demand for labour to fall in relation to the capital stock. In Ricardo's time a very small fraction of the total capital stock consisted of machinery, so mechanisation could be seen as a rare event which would involve relatively few workers.[35] Agricultural technical progress involving increasing mechanisation on the land was in turn a slow process and it took one or more centuries to alter methods of farming throughout a country. Ricardo did not therefore envisage continuing mechanisation involving whole populations which would prevent the overall demand for labour from expanding. By the time the argument reached Marx, over one-third of the labour force was employed in what is nowadays defined as industry.[36] By 1867 therefore when Marx published the first volume of *Capital*, it made perfectly good sense to argue as he did that mechanisation could continue indefinitely and actually prevent the demand for labour from increasing.

That development of Ricardo's final element of the classical theory of economic growth transformed the argument. With Quesnay, Smith, Malthus and Ricardo a larger surplus which was then invested benefited workers, the government, and of course the capitalists who invested. With Marx's development of the machinery argument, the investment of the surplus no longer benefited workers. The extra returns that followed from an increase in the capital stock benefited only capitalists, landlords, and the government, which was assumed to act entirely in the interests of those who received the economy's surplus. This gave those who received the surplus vast resources to purchase political influence – including the financing of vulgar economics which taught that the *status quo* was the best of all possible worlds.

Marx also modified the argument of his predecessors on the origin of the surplus and its growth through time. The theory of exploitation which he invented attributed the entire surplus to the underpayment of labour in the production of investable commodities. This meant that surpluses could be obtained through the exploitation of labour in industry and agriculture but not in commerce. Commerce produced no investable commodities so it could not add to a country's investable surplus. Workers in commerce were indeed underpaid like those in industry and agriculture. Marx insisted that a state education in the commercially useful languages would cheapen multilingual clerks and so raise the profits of their employers and reduce their wages – only commercially useless educational expenditures could be guaranteed not to depress the wages of the skilled.[37] This has its echoes in modern Marxist educational theory, but it is itself an echo of Smith who pointed out that the subsidised education of the clergy led to very low incomes for curates (WN 146–8). However, while workers in commerce were underpaid, commercial capital was unproductive, so it had to obtain a share of the surplus that the underpayment of labour extracted in industry and agriculture. The profits of commerce therefore had to be abstracted from the true investable surplus which originated in industry and agriculture, where workers actually produced investable commodities and were paid substantially less than they produced. There is therefore a departure from Smith and Ricardo, who designated all activities which produce profits as productive. To Marx, commercial profits appeared to make financial activities productive to those who did not perceive the underlying realities, but this was an illusion. True surplus production had to involve the extraction of a surplus from commodity production. Quesnay had insisted that, despite appearances, only agriculture was productive. Marx followed him in seeking to look under the appearances, and he came out with the answer that the origin of the surplus lay in the production of physical commodities by labour which was underpaid.

This attribution of the surplus to the excess of output over wages in industry and agriculture does not involve a very great *practical* departure from the work of his predecessors. Whatever the philosophical principles involved in the theory of value, Ricardo and Smith agreed that the excess of industrial and agricultural output over the wage formed the bulk of an economy's investable surplus. Omitting commercial profits is no more than a modification of detail.

Marx's important corrections to the classical theory of growth continued with the assumption that increasing returns predominated over diminishing returns in industry and agriculture taken together. They were pervasive in industry and this sufficed to dominate any tendency that agricultural diminishing returns might have to raise the real cost of employing labour. That assumption, which reflected the growing importance of industry relative to agriculture which had emerged by 1867, exploded Ricardo's theory of income distribution. Marx's alternative theory had a rising share of profits in output as the economy expanded. Productivity in industry and agriculture could be expected to rise continuously because of the influence of increasing returns in manufacturing, while the wage would fail to keep pace because continuing mechanisation would all the time restrict the demand for labour in relation to the supply. However, because of increasing mechanisation, the rate of profit on capital would in the end begin to fall. It has been widely shown that this conclusion is far from clear and its demonstration requires mathematics and particular technological assumptions. Ricardo's version of the classical argument has a far clearer explanation of the tendency of the rate of profit to decline. Its decline does depend on the influence of significant diminishing returns in primary production, but these have been important during much of the past thousand years, and they may well become important again. Marx's argument would have the rate of profit decline, despite increasing returns, through a continual increase in mechanisation of a kind that has not yet produced a declining rate of profit over any prolonged period.

In Marx's argument, growth depends on the investment of the surplus. This will be a growing share of output because of the tendency of the share of profits to rise, but the incentive to invest will diminish if the rate of profit tends to fall. This establishes a distinct possibility that the investment needed to produce the demand that allows potential surplus-value to be realised will not in fact materialise, or it may only follow profits upwards erratically to produce severe cycles. Marx followed Quesnay and Malthus in setting out a multi-sector account of the proportions of a growing economy. His sectors produce wage goods, means of production and luxuries, and as with his predecessors, very precise conditions must hold if the demand for the output of each sector is to grow in line with what it supplies at a uniform rate of profit. As with Quesnay and Malthus, the need for demand and supply to grow at the same rate, when prices are set to produce a uniform economy-wide rate of profit, amounts to the assumption of a fixprice economy. That sets very precise conditions which have to be fulfilled before there can be growth. Smith attempted to answer the resulting worries of the Physiocrats by insisting that it did not matter which sectors expanded in the first instance, since relative price flexibility would curb the growth of any sector which overexpanded, and stimulate the growth of any sector which lagged behind. Ricardo responded to Malthus's worries in the same way. Marx's fixprice assumptions again pose problems which price flexibility largely remove. But if there were indeed a continual increase in saving from profits, and a decline in the rate of profit, a lack of inducement to invest on an adequate scale which no degree of price flexibility could correct would in the end emerge. If Marx's assumptions about technology were ever correct, his belief that there would then be contradictions in capitalism, which would in the end prevent it from reinvesting the surplus that the exploitation of labour provided, would be well founded.

The alternation of fixprice and flexprice analysis continued after Marx. The great late-nineteenth-century neoclassicals made flexprice assumptions which removed many of the possible causes of interruption to the growth process and then, faced by the massive unemployment of the 1930s, Keynes returned to fixprice assumptions. The two kinds of model are therefore both very much alive as they have been since the late eighteenth century.[38] It has been shown that the classical theory of growth can be presented with either kind of assumption, and that its practitioners alternated between the automatic equilibrating effect of flexprice assumptions, and the challenge to correct resource allocation posed by the need to price to produce a uniform rate of return in each sector.

There are some characteristics of the classical theory of economic growth which all its practitioners were agreed on, which have now all but disappeared from economics. There is first the insistence that only some economic activities are surplus producing, and that government, capital investment, and luxury consumption depend entirely on the surplus.

For Quesnay the surplus was the excess of agricultural output over wages and farmers' necessary costs. For Smith and Ricardo, it was the excess of output over wages in industry, agriculture and commerce. For Marx it was the excess of output over wages in industry and agriculture alone. Economists ceased to think in these terms after Marx. Indeed it began to be argued as early as the 1820s that industry, agriculture and commerce had no particular primacy over the non-commercial services. Many services provided by government and by entertainers are productive in that they have all kinds of favourable indirect effects on the productivity of industry, agriculture and commerce. As McCulloch argued in 1825 in an assault on Smith's version of the distinction between productive and unproductive labour:

The whole of Dr Smith's reasoning proceeds on a false hypothesis. He has made a distinction where there is none, and where it is not in the nature of things there can be any. The end of all human exertion is the same – that is, to increase the sum of necessaries, comforts, and enjoyments; and it must be left to the judgement of every one to determine what proportion of these comforts he will have in the shape of menial services, and what in the shape of material products. (p. 407)

The manufacturer is *not* a producer of matter, but of *utility* only. And is it not obvious that the labour of the menial servant is also productive of utility? (p. 406)

Most modern economists would undoubtedly applaud these passages, but McCulloch went on to say:

An occupation may be futile and trifling to the last degree without being unproductive. We are entitled to affirm, at once, that an individual who employs himself an hour a day in blowing bubbles or building houses of cards, is engaged in a futile employment; but we are not, without further inquiry, entitled to affirm that it is unproductive. This will depend on a contingency: The employment will be as unproductive as it is frivolous, if it does not stimulate the individual to make any greater exertion during the remaining twenty-three hours of the twenty-four than he did previously: But if, in order to indemnify himself for the time that is thus spent, he produces as many useful and desirable commodities during the period he can still devote to that purpose as he previously produced, the employment will *not* be unproductive: And if the desire to indulge in it leads him to produce more commodities than he did before, it will be positively productive. (p. 409)

Malthus leapt on this extraordinary statement:

But it is difficult to say what may not be called wealth, or what labour may not be called productive, in Mr. Macculloch's nomenclature. According to his view of the subject, any sort of exertion, or any sort of consumption which tends, however *indirectly*, to encourage production, ought to be denominated productive; and before we venture to call the most trivial sort of exercise or amusement, such as blowing bubbles, or building houses of cards unproductive, we must wait to see whether the person so employed does not work the harder for it afterwards. But, not to mention the impossibility of any, the most useful classification, if such doctrines were admitted, and we were required to wait the result in each particular case, and make exceptions accordingly, I will venture to affirm, that if we once break down the distinction between the labour which is so directly productive of wealth as to be estimated in the value of the object produced, and the labour or exertion, which is so indirectly a cause of wealth, that its effect is incapable of definite estimation, we must necessarily introduce the greatest confusion into the science of political economy, and render the causes of the wealth of nations inexplicable. (Def 96–7)

Building houses of cards and blowing soap bubbles has naturally failed to find its way into twentieth-century economists' measures of output – they fail to produce money incomes for those who build or blow – but otherwise Malthus's plea for the maintenance of the distinction between productive and unproductive labour has failed. A modern economy's national income accounts sum all legally earned incomes (and the undistributed income of companies) to obtain an estimate of the nation's total output. There is no distinction between the incomes of those who produce investable output and those who do not, and there is no recognition that some activities which produce income are more capable of supporting government services or capital investment than others. Nor perhaps should there be a distinction between productive and unproductive labour which is anything like Smith's. The opera dancers and singers whom he deemed unproductive, not to mention the hundreds of thousands of servants in today's restaurants and hotels, can all earn foreign currency which can be used to purchase foreign machinery of the most advanced technical kind if that is what a country requires for growth. The surplus earning power of an opera house or a hotel are as capable of contributing to the financing of a welfare state as factories and farms.

This is not, however, the case with the unmarketed services provided by government itself which cannot be used to provide the resources for investment, imports, or a still larger welfare state. A case can therefore be argued for still drawing a line between those activities which can provide a surplus that can be invested or used to provide the real resources that government requires, and those that cannot. That line would place agriculture, industry and the entire private sector (and not merely commerce) in the surplus-producing sector, and the provision of unmarketed government services into the surplus-using sector. That is however a recent echo of classical growth theory.[39] In general the division of the economy into surplus-producing and surplus-using sectors disappeared in the late nineteenth century from all but the Marxist economic literature.

A second element in classical growth theory which has all but disappeared is the assumption that non-wage incomes provide the principal resources for government and for capital investment. All the classical economists saw wages as necessary costs of production which were almost wholly consumed. Almost all investment and government expenditure therefore had to be financed from profits and rent. There was no essential difference in Quesnay or in the corn model simplification of Ricardo between the wages which workers had to be paid and the food which had to be fed to labouring cattle, for instance oxen. In each case food was fed in advance to creatures who worked to provide more food than they originally consumed. With cattle the resources available for other uses are obviously the food they produce less the food they consume: there is no possibility that the food they consume can itself be taxed. Government and capital accumulation can obviously only be supported from the surplus of their output over the food which they themselves require.

There was however increasing deviation from the 1750s onwards between the analysis that was appropriate for labouring cattle and for farm labourers. Smith, Ricardo, Malthus and Marx made it increasingly clear that there was a strong social element in the real wage, and that wages would rise substantially above physical subsistence as labourers developed a taste for what previous generations had considered luxuries. Anything that entered their standard of living to the point where they would expect to continue to buy it even though they had a wife and children to support, and would refrain from marrying if they *expected* to have to do without it in consequence, became part of the natural wage according to Smith, Ricardo, Malthus and Marx. However, while the increasing inclusion of luxury commodities in the real wage separated this more and more from the subsistence of labouring animals, it did not alter the theoretical supposition that the wage was untaxable. If workers expected to be able to purchase shoes, silk stockings, meat, beer and white bread, and would refrain from marriage if that threatened to reduce them to potatoes, taxation which threatened to reduce them to potatoes would equally hold back the growth of population, produce labour scarcities, and so force up wages to a level where workers could again afford their white bread, meat and beer. Taxation would therefore fall entirely on profits and rent in the long run, even though wages were substantially above animal subsistence levels. It was therefore not the lowness of the real wage that made this untaxable, but the classical population mechanism. So long as the growth of population was sensitive to the real wage, as all the classical economists before Marx assumed, this could not be forced below the level where population growth would keep in line with the labour requirements of the capital stock.

The interrelationship between population growth and the real wage must have broken down (if it ever existed) in the late eighteenth and early nineteenth century in much of Europe and the whole of North America. The demand for labour grew faster than the supply at a given wage, despite Marx's analysis, with the result that wages were pulled up continually in relation to the level necessary to sustain an adequate rate of population growth. In consequence, workers began to receive incomes that were substantially higher than those needed to produce a modestly expanding population. Their incomes therefore began to contain an element which was saveable and taxable, and investment and government consumption came to be financeable to an increasing extent from workers' incomes. The classical view that only profits and rents provide the resources for government expenditure and accumulation therefore became increasingly obsolete. Modern economists have shown that the proportion of income which it is rational for an individual worker to save (in the absence of state pensions) is independent of the absolute level of income, since provision for old age is rational at all income levels.[40] That is one reason why so high a fraction of a modern economy's total saving comes from workers and salary earners. The taxes which finance government have also been paid to an increasing extent by workers, including even those with substantially below-average incomes. Any particular identification of the finance of government and of capital accumulation with profits and rents is therefore now quite largely out of date.

There would still be a close connection between profits and growth if company investment in the private sector came predominantly from profits. Ricardo had already decided in 1820 that transferring very large sums to fundholders, as a result of the repayment of the national debt which he favoured, would not diminish investment, because potential new entrepreneurs could always be found who would borrow whatever the fundholders chose to save.[41] Limited liability, which became possible in Britain in the mid-nineteenth century, made the passage of financial resources to would-be entrepreneurs who lacked capital still easier. Malthus and Marx continued to identify investment with the reinvestment of profits, but the link between profits and investment necessarily weakened as financial markets became increasingly sophisticated. There are nevertheless still entrepreneurs and those who lend to them who are risk averse, and this may be especially the case with some smaller firms; investment funds for such companies are most securely found through the classical mechanism of reinvesting profits. Constraints on increasing borrowing faster than the rate at which profits are growing may prevent some larger companies from raising investment faster than the rate of growth of aggregate profits.[42] Statisticians have, however, failed to find close links between investment and profits in modern economies,[43] which suggests that profit levels have more than sufficed to allow most companies to borrow as much as they wished, and still keep within prudent borrowing limits. If profits had persistently acted as a constraint on growth, investment would have moved up and down with profits and that has not occurred. Obviously if profits were lower in some future period, investment might be limited to those profits plus prudent borrowing, and the level of aggregate profits could then act as a constraint on growth in the manner that some of the classical economists predicted, but there is no convincing evidence that that situation has yet been reached in any modern economy.

There are therefore several reasons why the classical theory of economic growth has become obsolete. The division of the economy into a productive sector which produces a surplus and an unproductive one which does not has become unfashionable. The vastly faster increase in capital than in population has pulled wages up to the point where they include a taxable and investable surplus which has become far greater in the aggregate than that obtainable from profits and rents. The growing sophistication of capital markets has weakened the link between profits and investment. It is therefore widely agreed that growth no longer depends on the existence of a surplus over wages in *one* particular sector of the economy.

But there are not logical weaknesses in the classical theory of economic growth, and like all good economics, it is valid where its assumptions hold. Moreover, as Hicks has recently reminded us, economic theories which become obsolete for one generation can recover their validity for a later one if underlying conditions move in their favour.[44] Are there possible developments to modern economies whch could restore the validity of the growth theory of Quesnay, Smith, Malthus, Ricardo and Marx? There are several possible ways in which this could occur, and three in particular.

The wage used to be untaxable because of the classical population supply mechanism. That meant that the finance of government had to be derived from profits and rent. This population supply mechanism is now generally regarded as obsolete, but sufficiently powerful trade unions which seek to preserve the real level of workers' private consumption, however high taxes become, can have precisely the same effect. If workers have the power to pass on extra taxation beyond a certain point, any extra growth of government expenditure can only occur at the expense of luxury consumption by non-workers, or of capital investment, or of the balance of payments.[45] That essentially is what Smith might have said.

We have happily lived through two centuries where diminishing returns in primary production have been kept at bay, and the relative prices of food and raw materials have not risen in relation to the cost of manufactures. But that may not last. If population presses against the world's capacity to supply food or energy or mere living space in the next centuries, the relative prices of primary products will begin to rise and perhaps quite sharply. If workers manage to maintain their living standards, or to almost maintain them, the rise in the real cost of food and energy will be paid essentially from profits. That is what Ricardo would have said, and the high incomes which holders of scarce oil reserves are already enjoying is no more than a particular example of his theory that the owners of scarce natural resources will receive rents which rise sharply as economies develop.

Finally, it is possible that the nature of capital will alter. At the beginning of the present story it was stores of food and seed-corn and horses and ploughs. In the nineteenth century it became machines crowded into factories. The horses and ploughs and the Victorian factories needed the co-operation of millions of workers. What if the next generation of capital acquires the characteristics of the robot? It would not be especially surprising if developments in the electronic control of machinery made it possible to produce mobile machines which would carry out *all* the tasks a weakly educated labourer can perform at a cost below that of the expensive food and manufactured luxuries which workers are nowadays paid.

Robots would then produce more cheaply than unskilled labourers in all the very many tasks for which such workers are now needed. If that occurred, economic growth could continue, but market mechanisms would allocate none of the benefits to the bulk of the population. That is what Marx would have said.

The classical theory of economic growth may therefore enjoy several revivals in the centuries to come.

Notes

1 François Quesnay's *Tableau Economique*

1. Leontief (1941) p. 9.
2. Schumpeter (1943) p. 22.
3. Marx, TSV i. 344.
4. See Samuelson (1962) pp. 3–4.
5. See Hecht (1958).
6. This is the view of Salleron, the editor of *François Quesnay et la Physiocratie* (1958) p. 687[E].
7. Weulersse (1910a) p. 96 [E].
8. Quesnay assumes a system of crop rotation where the land is ploughed but left fallow in the year before it is sown with corn. This was widely used in the eighteenth century (see Slicher van Bath (1963) pp. 59, 244–5).
9. Cf. the much less detailed comparisons in Fitzherbert (1534) folio 6: 'Whither is better a plow of horses, or a plow of oxen.'
10. In addition to the annual and original advances of the farmers, landlords' advances (*avances foncières*) to make the land fit for farming are also needed. These are hardly ever mentioned by Quesnay himself, but they play a considerable part in the work of later Physiocratic writers; L'Abbé Baudeau (1770) in particular saw rent as partly a return on the *avances foncières* of the landlords.
11. In the '*Explication du Tableau Economique*' of 1759, annual advances are said to be 1050 million livres and original advances 4333 million livres (Tab edn 3 v and viii) while in the '*Analyse de la formule arithmétique du Tableau Economique*' of 1766 original advances are said to be five times annual advances (Q 795).
12. See R ii 237–8.
13. See, for instance, Q 479, Tab edn 3 20 and Q 713–19, where it is argued that a rate of return of 150 per cent on annual agricultural advances is earned in England.
14. Cantillon (1755) p. 83.

15. It is interesting that Meek has suggested that 'In particular, a number of the problems of interpretation which have subsequently arisen are cleared up in the seventh chapter [of *Philosophie Rurale*] which seems to have been largely written by Quesnay himself and which has been unduly neglected by most modern interpreters' (1962) p. 278.

16. Tab edn 3 viii–ix. The annual advances of the 'sterile' sector are said to be 525 million livres, and the original advances for 'tools, machines, mills, forges, and other works, etc.' 2000 million livres. This has even led Eagly (1969) to reconstruct Quesnay's argument with a sterile sector that produces the fixed capital for *both* sectors. See also Eagly (1974) ch. 2.

17. See Tab edn 3 10 [M]. 'The daily wage of a labourer is fixed on the basis of the price of corn, and amounts to a twentieth of the price of one *setier*.'

18. See Fox-Genovese (1976) for a rich and detailed analysis of the underlying political philosophy and property rights which led to the emergence of Physiocracy in mid eighteenth century France.

19. From a letter to Damilaville on 16 October 1767 (see G. Weulersse, (1910b) vol. i, p. 147 [E]). Voltaire's common ground with the Physiocrats was limited. See pp. 316–17 in Chapter 9.

20. Woog (1950) sets out Quesnay's reasons why industry is dependent on agriculture very clearly on pp. 20–1.

21. See Cantillon (1755) chs XII–XVI. Quesnay knew the book, and quotes from it in '*Grains*' (1757) (Q 482–3).

22. What happens to the money that is retained until the end of the circulation process will become evident when the full *Tableau* is explained.

23. Figure 1.2 is derived from Diagram (1.1) in Hishiyama (1960). The totals are derived in each case by summing two geometric progressions. The left-hand column, for instance, can be written as $[(Rq + Rq^2 (1 - q) + Rq^3 (1 - q)^2)...] + [Rq (1 - q) + Rq^2 (1 - q)^2 + Rq^3 (1 - q)^3)...]$. The formulae can be checked against the totals in AH in Part vi, *Tableau* on p. 192. Eagly (1969) has also set out the multiplier effects of the circulation of the revenue very clearly.

24. See Foley (1973).

25. 'Thus the total money stock of an agricultural nation is only about equal to the net product or annual revenue of its landed property, for when it stands in this proportion it is more than sufficient for the nation's use' (Tab edn 3 17 [M]). See also Tab edn 3 ix and AH vi, 165 and 226.

26. See note 43 below. Woog (1950) pp. 72–83 has suggested that the sterile class holds its advances in the form of money, but this would make the money supply exceed total revenue, which would contradict Quesnay's several statements that it equals this.

27. In view of some of these difficulties and others, Samuelson (1982) has thought it appropriate to substitute a radically different model under the title, 'Quesnay's "Tableau Economique" as a Theorist would Formulate it Today'. He assumes that only land is scarce, when in Quesnay's work it is agricultural capital and not land which is the scarce factor. He has a section entitled, 'The Chimera of the Zig-Zags' when his model has no zig-zags of Quesnay's kind because agriculturists consume no manufac-

tures, with the result that expenditure flows do not criss-cross between the sectors as farmers buy manufactures from industrialists who then spend a fraction of the extra revenues thus received on food. It goes without saying that Samuelson's model has the elegance and clarity of twentieth-century economics at its best, but it describes an economy which has only the slightest correspondence to the one that Quesnay envisaged (see pp. 343–4, note 8, for an especially odd result of Samuelson's model).

28. See note 43 below.

29. Weulersse (1910b), vol. i, p. 86.

30. It is highly probable that Quesnay was author and not just part author of the passages in *Philosophie Rurale* where the new *Tableau* is set up, and where sequences of *Tableaux* are used to show growth or decline when its equilibrium is disturbed. This can be inferred: (i) because the passages in question are stylistically Quesnay and not Mirabeau; (ii) Quesnay wrote to Mirabeau of a passage he had drafted for *Philosophie Rurale*, 'This spiritual chemistry demands more from the readers than arithmetical hieroglyphs, which displease you more than them' (Weulersse (1910a) p. 81 [E]), which clearly indicates that Quesnay may have taken more interest in the calculations than Mirabeau, and these are almost all based on the manipulation of *Tableaux*. R. L. Meek has also drawn attention to Mirabeau's self-confessed dislike of calculation to attribute authorship of an important section of *Philosophie Rurale* to Quesnay (Meek (1962) p. 38); (iii) the author of '(*Premier*) *problème economique*' of 1766, and this is undoubtedly Quesnay, at several points describes increases in an unorthodox way: an increase of 20 per cent is described as an increase of one-sixth throughout the article. The identical unorthodoxy is to be found in an important passage containing sequences of *Tableaux* in PR ii. 184–5 and 188.

31. PR ii. 162 [E]. Figure 1.4 is based on the diagram on p. 175 of vol. ii.

32. The theory clearly requires that where rates of return are substantially less than 100 per cent, there are sufficient 'rich' farmers who hold and spend money during the 'winter'. Otherwise the economy will contain regions where money hardly circulates, and monetisation will be confined to the areas where landlords congregate and spend their revenues – these being insufficient to circulate money universally. This would limit the applicability of the *Tableau* in obvious ways.

33. The rule that must be followed to produce this result is to make the advances of the sterile sector one-quarter of the sum of annual agricultural advances and rents, as in the original *Tableau*. Only this makes the reproduction of the original *Tableau* possible. The rule is stated in PR i. 124, and again in i. 328.

34. Q 793–812. It is translated in Meek (1962) pp. 150–67 with one omission.

35. Phillips (1955). See also Barna (1975) for an input-output table based on the 1758–9 version of the *Tableau*.

36. It is presumably assumed that interest is earned to replace original advances which are five times annual advances in the 1766 version, at a rate of 10 per cent per annum.

37. There is a very extensive literature on the expenditure flows indicated on the diagram, and the major controversies are very comprehensively outlined and discussed in Woog (1950), pp. 38–72. However, the only explanation that will work where the rate of return on annual agricultural advances differs from 100 per cent (and none of the ones Woog refers to will) is the one set out in *Philosophie Rurale*, so it must be assumed that this also applies to the final version of the *Tableau*.

38. Smith might have carried the argument an interesting stage further and said that the *larger* industrial sector associated with a more efficient agriculture would also produce more efficiently because the division of labour could be further extended in industry; and this leads directly to the proposition that England should be more efficient in industry than France (given the greater profitability of its agriculture) in the conditions of 1766–76.

39. See Meek (1962), pp. 282–3. Spengler (1945b) following Baudeau (1770) suggests that the final *Tableau* understates the total output of the sterile class because it does not include the products that the sterile class manufactures for itself. Thus he believes that the total wages of the industrial class should equal $\frac{1}{2}A (1 + r)$ and not the $\frac{1}{4}A (1 + r)$ indicated in Table 1.2. They can then spend $\frac{1}{4}A (1 + r)$ on food for their own consumption as Quesnay says, and supply themselves with equivalent manufactures without needing to trade. However, the Baudeau-Spengler argument makes industrial wages twice the industrial sector's raw material costs, and it is clearly stated in each of Quesnay's accounts of the *Tableau* that wages are one-half and not two-thirds of the industrial sector's costs, so it is unlikely that this solution is the one he had in mind. Moreover, their solution makes industrial wages as great as agricultural wages where r is 100 per cent, and the industrial wage bill is substantially smaller than the agricultural wherever Quesnay refers to this relationship.

40. According to Table 1.2, exports plus the advances of the sterile class, which equal exports plus its raw material purchases, total $\frac{3}{8}A (1 + r)$ or $\frac{3}{8} \times$ (agricultural advances + revenues). In chapter 7 of *Philosophie Rurale*, annual agricultural advances total 1 921 000 000 livres, and revenues total 2 001 000 000 livres (Q 710), so $\frac{3}{8} \times$ (agricultural advances + revenues) equals 1 470 750 000 livres.

41. In Table 1.2 the ratio of trade to agricultural output is $(1 + r)/(12 + 8r)$, agricultural output totalling wages *plus* rents *plus* interest where the cost of agricultural raw materials used in agriculture is disregarded as in the case in question. This comes to 13/144 where r, the rate of return on advances, is 30 per cent.

42. It is to be noted that Quesnay always assumes that workers and landlords have the same propensity to consume 'food'.

43. Quesnay's precise assumption in his '*Explication*' to the 3rd edition of 1759 is: 'Circulation brings 600 livres to the sterile expenditure class, from which 300 livres have to be kept back for the *annual advances*, which leaves 300 livres for wages' (Tab edn 3. iii [M]). It is evident from this that the sterile sector buys the next period's advances after the circulation of the revenue is completed. Moreover, in the above quota-

tion, wage goods are distinguished from the advances of the sterile sector, so these must, strictly speaking, be raw materials – and this is Quesnay's precise assumption in the later versions of the *Tableau* (see Q 712 and 795). He is not, however, consistent on this point in his explanation of the *Tableau* of 1759 where the advances of the sterile class are sometimes said to include subsistence goods and there is no specific statement about the amount it spends on raw materials, which can only be inferred from the above quotation.

44. International trade is one of the activities of the sterile sector, so it buys the goods that are exported as one of its own inputs, and the economy's imports are sold together with its own products via the *Tableau's* zigzags.

45. The actual level of expenditure on animal feeding stuffs and other agricultural raw materials, M_a, is of course irrelevant to the *Tableau's* interrelationships because these are wholly produced and consumed in the same sector. For this reason they do not enter the basic equations that determine the model and this can be in equilibrium with M_a at any level.

2 QUESNAY'S THEORY OF ECONOMIC GROWTH

1. See Tutain (1963) and Dupâquier (1968).

2. See Hufton (1974)

3. These are '*(Premier) problème economique*' (1766); and '*Second problème economique*' (1767). These are translated into English with the omission of one passage in Meek (1962) pp.168–202.

4. See p. 341, note 30. Sequences of *Tableaux* are to be found in PR i.405–11; ii. 179–98, 298–325 and 354–75; iii. 33–53.

5. *Tableaux* in disequilibrium are to be found in AH vi 192, 204, 214 and 254.

6. Accounts of the effect of this on growth are to be found in PR iii. 33–53, and AH vi. 192–202.

7. The expenditure flows of the original *Tableau* on which Table 2.1 is based are explained in general terms in pp. 21–5, while the precise equations are set out in pp. 34–7.

8. In his reformulation of Quesnay's *Tableau*, Samuelson (1982) arrives at the result that a reduction in landlords' propensity to consume food and a corresponding increase in their propensity to consume manufactures 'must lead to a new long-run equilibirum with *increased* labour population, all of which goes into manufacturing' (pp. 53–4). He arrives at this extraordinarily un-Quesnayian result by making the Ricardian assumption that the marginal productivity of labour in agriculture varies inversely with employment, and the still more modern assumption (which Ricardo never made) that agricultural workers are paid their full marginal product. These anachronistic assumptions then go on to produce the result that the fall in food output which immediately follows a reduction in the demand for food raises the marginal product of farm labourers and therefore their wages, and this then raises the population through the classical population supply mechanism. Population then

grows until employment in agriculture is restored, while employment in industry will of course be permanently higher. Hufton's (1974) French peasantry, who starved to death when the demand for agricultural output fell, would have been delighted if their living standards had risen instead as Samuelson insists, and he does insist. 'In the rockbottom Physiocratic model adumbrated here, the effect of the specified change in tastes is clear. And its correct description seems not to have been achieved by Quesnay and Mirabeau or, according to my best recollection, by any of the commentators on them' (p. 53). Indeed not.

9. If annual agricultural advances are initially A, so that rents, R, are also initially A, the financial surplus of the agricultural sector in Table 2.1 will be the $A [(2q - q^2)/(1 - q + q^2)]$ it receives from the circulation of the revenue, *plus* half the receipts of the sterile sector, that is, $\frac{1}{2}A [(1 - q^2)/(1 - q + q^2)]$ for sales of raw materials, *minus* $(1 - q) \times A [(2q - q^2)/(1 - q + q^2)]$ for purchases of manufactures *minus* R (which equals A) for the payment of rent, and this comes to $A [(2q + q^2 - 2q^3 - 1)/(2 - 2q + 2q^2)]$. If half of this is added to the next period's advances, these grow from A at a rate of $[(2q + q^2 - 2q^3 - 1)/(4 - 4q + 4q^2)]$. (2.1) is arrived at by substituting $(0.5 + d)$ for q in this expression.

10. The rates of growth and decline that are arrived at in *Philosophie Rurale* (iii. 33–53) as a result of a q of 0.6 and 0.4 are rather different from those produced by the above formula, but the précis *Tableau* is used there, despite the fact that this gives answers which differ from those of the original *Tableau's* zigzags where q does not equal one-half. Hishiyama (1960) arrives at a different result by simply assuming that the total at the foot of the advances column in the original *Tableau* will always be precisely the following year's advances, which fails to take the full financial transactions of the agricultural class into account.

11. See Quesnay's '*Second problème economique*' (1767); PR i.393–411, and ii.298–325 the first passage is from chapter 7 (which Quesnay definitely drafted); and AH vi.204–11 and 254–70.

12. The expenditure flows of the final version of the *Tableau* on which Table 2.3 is based were explained in detail in pp. 29–31.

13. See Quesnay's '*(Premier) problème economique*'; and '*Progression de la réparation de l'agriculture par l'abolissement des causes de son dépérissement*' (PR ii. 354–78).

14. See Weulersse (1910b) vol. I, pp. 111–19, 154–5, 180–5, 199–212 and 223–6, and in addition *Livre Quatre*, '*La Réalisation du Programme Physiocratique*'.

15. Meek (1962) p. 38.

16. It is assumed for simplicity that farmers' transactions with the industrial sector just balance, to bring out the principal effects of the higher rate of return in agriculture as sharply as possible.

17. See p.39.

18. PR ii, table opposite page 366 (translated in Meek (1962), p. 145), which shows the 'PROGRESSION' of the Cultivators' Profit' from 1761 to 1770 on the assumption that four-fifths of the 'increase in the net product' is added to 'original advances' and one-fifth to annual advances.

19. See Q 795. See p. 8 for a more detailed account of requirements for

annual advances and original advances in Quesnay's argument.

20. Translating this formula into the concepts of modern economics, r/F is the rate of return on *total* farm capital, so the rate of growth of agricultural capital is assumed to equal the rate of profit that results from agricultural investment, plus a further term in d which depends on whether demand trends favour agriculture relative to other sectors. Leaving aside the term that depends on d, the formula simply states that the rate of growth equals the rate of profit, which is what modern theory would say if all profits are reinvested once the subsistence needs of farmers have been met as Quesnay assumes, and provided that the constraint which Quesnay explicitly recognises does not limit growth to some lower rate.

21. See Turgot (1770), section LX, p.152.

22. Stewart (1793), p. 304

23. Gray (1972), pp. 499–500.

3 ADAM SMITH'S THEORY OF ECONOMIC GROWTH

1. See, for instance, Hahn and Matthews (1964) who survey the modern growth theory published prior to 1964.

2. See Arrow (1962)

3. The dichotomy between Smith's arguments that point to indefinite progress as a result of increasing returns, and those that point to an eventual stationary state, is very clearly brought out in an unpublished paper by Dr R. N. Ghosh.

4. Spengler (1959) has emphasised the importance of this in an article which provides a comprehensive account of the many different factors which influence growth in Smith's argument.

5. See Hollander (1973) pp. 208–12, for a similar account of the relationship between employment and technical progress in *The Wealth of Nations*.

6. This also implies that a 1 per cent increase in output might be associated with an increase in labour productivity of ½ per cent, implying what would now be called a Verdoorn coefficient of 0.50 in the long run. It is interesting to note that this is close to the Verdoorn coefficient Kaldor (1966) found for the industry of developed economies in 1954–64.

7. It may not be possible to use *fixed* capital at a profit at any reasonable set of factor prices if demand is insufficient, but this difficulty, which is one of those that make Keynesian unemployment possible, was not noticed by Smith, and it may well have had little importance in the eighteenth century.

8. In modern theory an important echo of Smith's distinction is to be found in Piero Sraffa's (1960) classically based argument where goods (and presumably services) that are used as factors of production and those that are bought by workers influence the prices of other goods, the wage, the rate of profit, etc.; while goods (and presumably services) that are solely consumed by non-workers do not.

9. It is clear that James Mill (1808) ch. 6 thoroughly understood this line of argument. Thus, 'We perceive, therefore, that there are two species of consumption; which are so far from being the same, that the one is more properly the very reverse of the other. The one is an absolute destruction of property, and is consumption properly so called; the other is a consumption for the sake of reproduction' (p. 69).

10. See Hartwell (1976) pp. 39–40 for a succinct and stimulating summary of the propositions that, with an appropriate constitution 'which guarantees liberty, property, and contract, and which carefully defines and limits the role of government', individual self-interest will suffice to produce growth – provided that government expenditure is contained.

11. See pp. 332–5 below.

12. How difficult it is to return to Smith's assumptions is illustrated by Barkai (1969) whose stimulating modern restatement of Smith's theory of growth has distinct saving and investment functions, where planned investment depends on the rate of profit and planned saving on thriftiness conditions. In consequence he believes that Smith needs an 'extreme' version of Say's law to achieve $I = S$.

13. See Hollander (1973) pp. 188–204, for a possible explanation of this.

14. Spengler (1959) p. 7, has noted the importance of this line of argument in *The Wealth of Nations*.

15. See Hollander (1973) pp. 157–8.

16. Blaug (1978) pp. 45–6, points out that wages may rise continuously in Smith's argument where the demand for labour grows faster than the supply.

17. It might be thought that the increased subdivision of labour would reduce the relative prices of all manufactured goods, but in a 'few' cases the unfavourable effects of rising raw material costs outweigh the favourable effects of increasing returns in the manufacturing process (see WN 260).

18. Equation (3.1) can be written as $(Y/L_p) = J L_p^{Z-1}$, and this produces the schedule, AB of Figure 3.1, that is, a rising straight line (on a double log scale) with a slope of $(Z - 1)$.

19. See Hicks (1965) ch. 4.

20. In Adelman's interesting restatement of Smith's theory of growth (1962) ch. 3 increasing returns together with capital accumulation always produce a falling marginal capital-output ratio. She arrives at this result because she does not allow for the need for increasing raw materials, etc., per worker, as capital accumulates.

21. It is to be noted that Z will exceed 1 to a greater extent than before if increasing returns are stronger in a fixed capital model (and fixed capital certainly plays a substantial part in Smith's account of increasing returns in industry), but a higher Z would have no effect on the basic form of equation (3.2).

22. $K_{f,t+1} - K_{f,t} = GL^H{}_{t+1} - GL^H{}_t = GL^H{}_t[(1 + n)^H - 1] = nHGL^H{}_t$ since n will be small in a single period. Now $K_{f,t}$ can be written for $G L^H{}_t$ and $E (K_{c,t+1} - K_{c,t})/K_{c,t}$ for n (from (3.7) using the period form of this equation which is legitimate where n is small).

23. Ricardo's objection to the argument will become evident in Chapter 6. Hollander (1973) pp. 195 and 280–7, has also suggested that this part of Smith's argument is 'unsound'. He has, however, seen the argument as the purely static one that the employment of capital in agriculture produces an *immediately higher level* of employment, and this only follows if capital costs per worker are lower in agriculture, which is not clear. He does not mention Smith's dynamic argument that agriculture produces a faster *rate of growth* of employment, as in North America, and therefore a level of employment that rapidly becomes higher.

24. Thweatt (1957) shows a continuous increase in the rate of profit as capital accumulates, and following Schumpeter, he describes Smith's growth model as a 'hitchless' one. His diagrammatic representation clearly fails to take the factors which produce a declining rate of profit in *The Wealth of Nations* into account. Lowe (1954) mentions one of these in the article on which Thweatt's lucid diagram is based, but he says that a Smithian economy will move forward in 'dynamic equilibrium' in the absence of 'disturbances from without'. See also Lowe (1975).

25. Cf. Kaldor (1972).

4 MALTHUS'S THEORY OF POPULATION GROWTH

1. See pp. 10, 86 above.

2. See Styles (1761) and Price (1769), (1771), (1772), (1773) and (1783). It was from the fourth edition of the *Observations on Reversionary Payments* of 1783 that Malthus quoted, so that is presumably the edition in which he first found this evidence.

3. Cf. the fundamentally similar diagrammatic representation of Malthus's theory of population growth in Sowell (1963). J. F. Wright used a similar diagram in an unpublished paper on Malthus which he presented in 1962. Two of the insights of this paper are published in Wright (1965). There are similar diagrams in Levy (1976). In the present book the schedules are drawn arbitrarily as straight lines. There is, of course, no reason why the relationships they represent should be linear and whether they are or not has no effect on the argument.

4. Malthus was also replying to propositions published in *The Enquirer, Reflections on Education, Manners and Literature*, which Godwin published in 1797.

5. Petersen (1979) gives an admirable account of the contemporary controversies that Malthus's theory of population aroused, and of how effectively he disposed of the various attempts at refutation with the result that by 1834 his thesis and its social implications was virtually unchallenged. Petersen also provides an illuminating account of the extent to which Malthus's demography anticipates modern demography. James (1979) also gives a most interesting account of contemporary reactions to the various editions of the *Essay on Population*.

6. Place (1822).

7. See Semmel (1965). There is no direct reference by Malthus to any of Quesnay's writings at any point, and it can be inferred that his acquaintance with the actual writings of the Physiocrats, was slight.
8. Malthus, (1814) and (1815a).
9. See, for instance, Pop edn1 138 and 143.
10. This line of argument is developed very fully in Spengler (1945a).
11. Boulding (1955) outlines some interesting mathematical developments of Malthus's argument, and suggests that the ultimate constraint on population is only food in the case of 'skinny' creatures (for instance, coyotes, deer and alley cats). In the case of 'plump' creatures (for instance, robins and domestic cats) the constraint on population is more likely to be the space available.

5 MALTHUS'S THEORY OF EFFECTIVE DEMAND AND GROWTH

1. See Semmel (1963) for an account of Malthus's contributions to the *Edinburgh* and *Quarterly Reviews*, and for an edition of the articles.
2. Keynes (1935) p. 107.
3. Keynes (1933) pp. 100–1.
4. See, for instance, Black (1967), Blaug (1958), Corry (1959), Eagly (1974), Gordon and Jilek (1965), Hollander (1962 and 1969), Lambert (1956 and 1966), Link (1959), O'Leary (1942 and 1943), Skinner (1969), Sowell (1963 and 1972), Spengler (1945a), and Vatter (1959).
5. O'Brien (1975) p. 238.
6. James (1979) in her excellent biography of Malthus underrates the clarity and penetration of this book when she writes of his chapter on Samuel Bailey's *Dissertation on Value* (1825), 'It is painful to read, for one gets the impression that Malthus is trying to defend the whole political economy of a bygone age' (p. 410). *The Definitions* arguably contains some of Malthus's sharpest economic analysis.
7. Sowell (1963 and 1972).
8. Keynes (1933).
9. The work of Leibenstein (summarised in 1980) comes closest to recognising the modern significance of 'human energy' in the production function, which is an important element in X-efficiency. The significance of motivation in Malthus's *Principles* is stressed in Wright (1965).
10. See p. 139.
11. Cf. Kalecki (1954) ch. 3. Link (1959) has derived a similar interpretation from these passages.
12. The important role that manufacturing and commerce play in providing the incentives that lead to growth and development is emphasised in Spengler (1945a), and also in Wright (1965).
13. See in particular Malthus (1815a) and Pop edn5 Book III, chs 9–12, and Pr edn1 217–25.
14. However, see Pr edn1 261–5 and 301–8, for two quite full and detailed statements of the scope for capital–labour substitutability, and its influence on income distribution.

15. In this equation, and in those that follow, profits need to be defined gross of tax, because they are gross of tax in equation (5.1), which is based on the necessary identity between the income categories and expenditure flows. β, the coefficient of the investment function in equation (5.16), therefore relates investment to the *gross of tax* profits of the previous period. Hence β will depend on the rate at which profits are taxed as well as on the willingness of entrepreneurs to invest. It has been seen that Malthus believed taxation fell largely on rents, directly or indirectly, so β will be only slightly influenced by profits taxation. The predominant influence must be entrepreneurial willingness to invest and reinvest.
16. Lange (1938) discusses the role of the optimum savings ratio in Malthus's work.
17. See, for instance, Corry (1959) p. 722.
18. See Clapham (1926) pp. 347–9.
19. See, for instance, Blaug (1958) pp. 86–8 and Corry (1959) pp. 719–21.
20. See, for instance, Blaug (1958) p. 86, and Robbins (1958) p. 248.
21. See also the reference to an international flight of capital due to low profits in, 'Six letters from Malthus to Pierre Prévost' (Zinke (1942)). Hollander (1969) argues that Malthus's saving and investment functions are distinct, and cites the letters to Prévost and other evidence to point to the significance of overseas investment in a situation where domestic investment is unprofitable.

6 RICARDO'S THEORY OF INCOME DISTRIBUTION AND GROWTH

1. See Samuelson (1959) and Pasinetti (1960).
2. See Hollander (1979).
3. This very clear paragraph is to be found only in the first and second editions of the *Principles*.
4. The main effect of departing from the assumption of equal capital to labour ratios in the production of all commodities is the following: if gold is produced with more capital per worker than other commodities, labour costs will constitute a lower fraction of the cost of gold than of those commodities, so a wage increase will reduce the relative cost of gold. It will, therefore, raise the money prices of those commodities 'which had less fixed capital employed upon them than the medium in which price was estimated' while 'all those which had more, would positively fall in price when wages rose' (R I 46).
5. Sraffa has shown from publishers' advertisements that Malthus's pamphlet was first advertised on 3 February 1815, West's on 13 February and Ricardo's on 24 February (R IV 4–5).
6. Hollander (1979) and Rankin (1980) have argued strongly that Ricardo's is a general equilibrium argument involving the simultaneous determination of profits in industry and agriculture, and not the initial determination of the rate of profit in agriculture alone, with competition then forcing manufacturers to accept this agricultural profit rate.
7. See the arithmetical examples in R IV 17, and ch. 2 of the *Principles*.

8. Some of the secondary literature assumes that the production function in agriculture is Cobb–Douglas (for instance, Brems (1970)), so that doubling agricultural inputs other than land raises output 2^Z times. With this assumption the share of rents in agricultural output is always $(1 - Z)$ so that Ricardo's 'principal problem in Political Economy', 'the proportions of the whole produce of the earth which will be allotted to each of these classes' (R I 5) must be answered with, 'the share of rents is always $(1 - Z)$ because we have assumed it so'.

9. It was originally suggested by Sraffa (1951) that the *Essay* of 1815 was based on a 'corn model'. This suggestion has been supported by, for instance, Eatwell (1975) and disputed by Hollander (1975).

10. In a full and complete statement of Ricardo's argument, there would be two qualifications to the proposition that capital and labour tend to grow at similar long-term rates. It will be shown below that as the economy moves towards the eventual stationary state, the money wage (measured in gold produced with unchanging productivity) tends to rise, while the real wage (measured in necessities) tends to fall. The rising trend in the money wage makes mechanisation increasingly attractive, and this element in Ricardo's argument, which will be explained on pp. 226–8 causes capital to grow faster than labour, as has already been remarked. The falling trend in the real wage produces a contrary effect, for wage goods made available in advance of production form a considerable fraction of capital per worker, and the capital stock therefore needs to grow less rapidly than the labour force while the real wage is falling (see Casarosa (1982) for an account of some of the very important implications of this). As these two complicating effects pull in opposite directions, capital and labour may indeed grow at rather similar rates as Ricardo frequently remarks.

11. Hicks and Hollander (1977) and Casarosa (1974, 1978 and 1982) have published important restatements of Ricardo's theory of growth and income distribution, where the market wage exceeds the natural wage while capital accumulation is continuing. Caravale and Tosato (1980) have developed an interesting 'Ricardian' growth model where the natural wage is redefined as any constant wage where the rate of growth of the labour force equals the rate of growth of the capital stock.

12. There has been very considerable controversy in the secondary literature because Ricardo sometimes very clearly states his arguments in terms of the simple conclusions that follow where the wage is at its natural rate and all prices are long-period equilibrium ones, while at other times he shows such sophisticated awareness of the full complexities that follow from a more general analysis that a case can be made out that this represents his true model. Hollander (1979) has made the strongest case for regarding the general model where prices and wages deviate from their natural rates as the true Ricardo model, while O'Brien (1981 and 1982) has strongly challenged this position, but left Hollander (1982) unconvinced.

13. The proposition that either profits must be high, or wages, or both together if the stationary state has not yet been reached, and that either of these will lead to recovery is set out in R II 302–31 in a series of replies to passages in Malthus's *Principles*.

14. See Mitchell and Deane (1962) pp. 366, 396 and 402.
15. Mitchell and Dean (1962) pp. 366–8 and 402–3.
16. See, for instance, R I 82.
17. Dobb (1973) cites two passages, the one below and one from R VIII 208, to show how Ricardo believed that abolition of the Corn Laws would postpone indefinitely the otherwise inevitable tendency for profits to fall.
18. See Sraffa's *Addenda to the Memoir of David Ricardo* (1955): (R x 95–104).

7 MARX'S THEORY OF EXPLOITATION

1. Machiavelli, *The Discourses*, p. 141.
2. Keynes (1936) p. 32.
3. See, for instance, Morishima (1973), and with Catephores (1978); Robinson (1942) and (1978); and Samuelson (1957), (1971) and (1974).
4. See Bose (1980) ch. 1.
5. The way in which this occurs is set out in Cap iii Part IV.
6. See Chapter 6 above, pp. 182–6.
7. See Meek (1973) for a very full account of the issues involved in the derivation and use of Marx's 'labour theory of value'.
8. Cf. Chapter 6 above, pp. 197–8.
9. Marx's concept of 'alienation' amounts to far more than this brief summary of one of its aspects, and Howard and King (1975) provide a clear and useful account that explains its full dimensions.
10. See Morishima and Catephores (1978) ch. 5, 'Population, Growth and the Class Struggle', Rowthorn (1980) ch. 7, 'Marx's Theory of Wages', and Rosdolsky (1977), especially ch. 18 for accounts of the problems involved in interpreting Marx's theory of wages and population.
11. See Marx, *Grundrisse*, pp. 604–10, Cap i. 578–9 and TSV, iii. 61–3.
12. In Marx, *Capital*, iii. chs 9–10, competition between capitalists equalises the rate of profit in 'spheres of production' with different technical and organic compositions of capital.
13. The first formally correct solution to 'the transformation problem' was published by von Bortkiewicz in 1907. See Seton (1957) for the first solution of the 'many goods' case, and also Samuelson (1971). Meek (1977) Part II provides an admirable summary and survey of the literature on the Transformation Problem and its implications. See also Desai (1979) Part II.
14. Himmelweit and Mohun (1981) p. 248.
15. There is considerable controversy about this in the secondary literature. In particular, Steedman (1977) has argued that Marx's theory of exploitation can be understood entirely from a carefully and precisely defined economic model in which only prices of production are stated. He relies on argument derived from Sraffa (1960) where an economy's production relationships are set out entirely independently of any consideration of questions involving income distribution, with the result that the latter can be explained in the manner that Marx suggested or

indeed in many other ways. This neo-Ricardian approach has been strongly contested, for instance along the lines suggested in the previous paragraph, by Himmelweit and Mohun (1981) and Shaikh (1981).

16. Shaikh (1981) has argued that the relationship between the ratios 'surplus labour/necessary labour' and 'goods produced for capitalists/ goods produced for workers' measured at market prices will depend on the capital intensities with which workers' and capitalists' consumer goods are produced but not on the capital intensity with which investment goods are produced, because the latter will enter equally into the costs of all goods (pp. 286–7).

17. Blaug (1978) explains the relationship between total profits as a ratio of total incomes, and total surplus value as a ratio of total labour values produced, and what determines deviations between them, extremely clearly.

8 MARX'S THEORY OF THE DECLINING RATE OF PROFIT

1. Williams (1982) develops this line of argument, and the significance of tendencies towards centralisation in Marx's work.

2. See, for instance, Marx, *Wage Labour and Capital*, pp. 162–7.

3. Meek (1960) considers this line of argument vital in his essay 'The Falling Rate of Profit'.

4. Cf. Fine and Harris (1976) and Shaikh (1978) who argue that the rate of profit which could be earned if the wage was zero – in this case $(s + v)/(c + v)$ since $s/(s + v) = 1$ when $v = 0$ – will tend to fall steadily as the capital to output ratio rises, and this should in the end influence actual profit rates.

5. See Cap ii. Part III, 'The Reproduction and Circulation of the Aggregate Social Capital'. Marx's scheme of extended reproduction is set out with the assumptions of a constant rate of exploitation and a constant organic composition of capital, so he never used his reproduction scheme to work through the effects of the particular trends leading to the collapse of capitalism with which this chapter is especially concerned.

6. Marx's precise assumption which he reiterates is that constant capital, C, rises relative to variable capital, V. This generally entails that C will also rise in relation to net output, $V + S$, the assumption made here, but the two assumptions will not both hold in all circumstances. Marx does go on to say quite specifically, however, (Cap i. 583–4) that 'The relative magnitude of the element of price' (that is, of $\Pi C + V + S$) of 'the constant part of capital consumed' (that is of ΠC) will increase in line with 'the advance of accumulation'. This can only occur if $\Pi C/(\Pi C + V + S)$ rises, that is, if $1 + (V + S)/\Pi C$ falls. The ratio of constant capital to net output is, of course, $C/(V + S)$, so what Marx said in the passage cited above is equivalent to the assumption of a rising capital to output ratio which is made in this chapter.

7. Several previous mathematical restatements of Marx's argument, for instance those of Blaug (1960), and Heertje (1976) assume production

with constant returns to scale, with the result that productivity growth is largely the result of technical progress, in Heertje's case even Harrod-neutral technical progress. It will be seen that the failure to allow for increasing returns has important effects on the argument.

8. See, for instance, Blaug (1960) and Heertje (1976).

9. The proportional rates of growth with respect to x of the numerator and the denominator of the right-hand side of equation (8.10) are equal when:

$$\frac{(1 - U)\, e^{(1 - U)x}}{e^{(1 - U)x} - V_o} = \frac{(H - U)\, e^{(H - U)x}}{e^{(H - U)x} + V_o/C_o}$$

If the unit of output is so chosen that $e^x = 1$ so that $x = 0$ when the above equality holds, then at that point only: $[(1 - U)/(1 - V_o)] = (H - U)/[1 + (V_o/C_o)]$ which can be rearranged as $(H - 1)/(1 - U) = [1 + (1/C_o)]/[(1/V_o) - 1]$, and since net output $= 1$ (since $e^0 = 1$) $= V_o + S_o$ where $x = 0$: $[(H - 1)/(1 - U)] = [1 + (V_o + S_o)/C_o]/(S_o/V_o)$.

10. This quotation from Joan Robinson is from (1942) p. 36.

11. The significance of Okishio's article, and an account of the subsequent literature is discussed extremely helpfully in Roemer (1981) chs 4 and 5.

12. Dickinson's (1957) mathematical reconstruction of Marx's argument to demonstrate the tendency of the rate of profit to decline has much in common with that outlined here. Dickinson's rate of profit is, however, S/C, and not Marx's $S/(C + V)$. His restatement of a production function to which Marx's argument will apply makes no allowance for increasing returns or technical progress. Steedman (1977) also sets out some of the circumstances where the rate of profit will decline despite a rising rate of exploitation.

13. This formula is derived by using equation (8.10) to substitute for r in equation (8.17). As constant capital is $C_o\, e^{Hx}$ and variable capital $V_o\, e^{Ux}$ when output is e^x, $(C_o/V_o)\, e^{(H - U)x}$ can be substituted for C/V in equation (8.17) to produce the equation:

$$n = s_s \left(1 - B\left(Z - \frac{1}{H}\right)\right) \cdot \left(\frac{\dfrac{1}{V_o}\, e^{(1 - U)x} - 1}{\dfrac{C_o}{V_o}\, e^{(H - U)x} + \dfrac{U}{H}} \right)$$

When this is differentiated with respect to x, and the unit of output is so chosen that $e^x = 1$ (that is, that $x = 0$) where

$$\frac{dn}{dx} = 0$$

so that n is at its maximum (or minimum):

$$\frac{1 - U}{H - U} = \frac{C_o\,(1 - V_o)/V_o}{\dfrac{C_o}{V_o} + \dfrac{U}{H}}$$

and S_o/V_o, the rate of exploitation can be substituted for $(1 - V_o)/V_o$ since $1 = V_o + S_o$ when e^x, the level of net output, equals 1.

14. In Table 8.4, the rate of growth of employment is maximum where net output = 479.7_{v+s}, when constant capital = 840.51325_c variable capital = 219.02055_v and surplus-value = 260.67945_s, $C/V = 3.8375999$, and S/V, the rate of exploitation = 1.1902054. For the purposes of equation (8.18), C is the ratio of constant capital to net output at this point, so this equals 1.7521644.

For the purposes of equation (8.18) the unit of output is so chosen that this is 1 at the point where

$$\frac{dn}{dx} = 0$$

so in these units in place of those in Table 8.4, net output = 1_{v+s} in place of 479.7_{v+s}, constant capital = 1.7521644_c in place of 840.51325_c, variable capital is 0.45657817_v in place of 219.02055_v and surplus-value is 0.54342183_s in place of 260.67945_s. This change of units has no effect on C/V, which is 3.8375999, and S/V which is 1.1902054. Since $H = 1\frac{1}{2}$ and $U = \frac{1}{2}$, the left-hand side of equation (8.18) is $(1.7521644 \times 1.1902054)/(3.8375999 + 0.3333333)$ which equals 0.5000, while the right-hand side, which equals $\frac{1}{2}$ divided by 1, is also 0.5.

15. The most recent estimates are those by Matthews, Feinstein and Odling-Smee (1982) p. 164. The gross domestic product is the gross national product less income from abroad, which was 4.4 per cent of GNP in 1873.

16. Matthews, Feinstein and Odling-Smee (1982) p. 133.

17. See, for instance, Klein and Kosobud (1961).

18. See n.6 above.

19. See pp. 255–6 above.

20. See Fellner (1957).

21. See Hartwell (1971) for one of the most notable non-Marxist interpretations.

22. See Klein (1947) and Sweezy (1942) for accounts of the relationship between Marxist and Keynesian theory.

23. See, for instance, Bose (1980).

9 The Classical Theory of Economic Growth

1. Bordo and Landau (1979).

2. Hollander (1973) and (1979).

3. Hecht (1958) p. 278.

4. Finley (1973) pp. 20–3.
5. Davenant (1699) p. 23 (Scheme D) and p. 50.
6. Mirabeau (1756–60).
7. From a letter from Mirabeau to Rousseau translated and published in Meek (1962) p. 17.
8. Eagly (1974) p. 20.
9. From a letter from Mirabeau to Longo dated 11 June 1778 which is quoted from and translated in Meek (1962) p. 15.
10. From a letter from Quesnay to Mirabeau written in late 1758 or early 1759 and translated by Meek (1962) p. 108.
11. Weulersse (1910b) Book IV, *La Réalisation du Programme Physiocratique*.
12. Hecht (1958) p. 276 [E].
13. WN 672–8.
14. Jur (1762–3) and WN 340. See in particular Skinner (1979) ch. 5, 'The Development of a System', for an account of the influence of Quesnay on Smith's analysis of capital accumulation and growth.
15. TMS 35 and Tab edn3 20.
16. Weulersse (1910b) vol. I, p. 137.
17. Hicks (1965) ch. 7, 'The Fixprice Method'.
18. See, in particular, Fox-Genovese (1976) for an illuminating account of the full significance of this line of argument.
19. Hume (1752), 'On the Balance of Trade'.
20. Hartwell (1976) provides an interesting account of the significance of property rights in Adam Smith's theory of economic growth.
21. Weulersse (1910b) vol. I, p. 136.
22. WN 109.
23. McCulloch was the author of the 3 000 word article on Quesnay in the Sixth, Seventh and Eighth editions of the *Encyclopaedia Britannica*, and he devoted pp. 43–52 of his *Principles of Political Economy* (1825) to Quesnay.
24. See the citation to '*Physiocratie*' in the review article 'Spence on Commerce', *Edinburgh Review* (January 1808), which is attributed to Brougham by Semmel (1963) p. 15.
25. Pop edn1, chs 16 and 17.
26. See pp. 134–7 in Chapter 4 above.
27. Pr edn2 375.
28. Letter from Hume to Smith written on 1 April 1776 in S. Corr 186.
29. Hicks (1972).
30. See Hollander (1977) for an account of the durability of Ricardo's influence.
31. Sraffa (1955).
32. John Stuart Mill *Principles*, p. 94. The passage quoted below first appeared in the 6th edition (1865).
33. Thomas More (1516).
34. Lamond (1929) p. 15.
35. See Berg (1980) pp. 20–1, for a discussion of the data which indicates that machinery may have accounted for 5 per cent of British fixed capital in 1750 and 17 per cent in 1850.

36. Mitchell and Deane (1962) pp. 60–1.
37. Cap iii. 300–1.
38. Walsh and Gram (1980) offer a most helpful survey of the development of classical and neoclassical economic theory in the eighteenth, nineteenth and twentieth centuries, and of the fundamental differences between them.
39. The economy is divided into a market sector, which produces marketed output, and a non-market sector, which consumes marketed output and produces none, in Bacon and Eltis (1976).
40. See, in particular, Friedman (1957) and Modigliani (1966).
41. See p. 218 in Chapter 6 above.
42. The implications of this line of argument are developed in Kalecki (1939).
43. See, for instance, Jorgenson (1971).
44. Hicks (1975) pp. 19–21.
45. This line of argument is developed in Bacon and Eltis (1976) and (1979).

References

Adelman, Irma (1962) *Theories of Economic Growth and Development* (Stanford: University Press).

Arrow, Kenneth, J. (1962) 'The Economic Implications of Learning by Doing', *Review of Economic Studies*, vol. 29, June.

Bacon, Robert and Walter Eltis (1976) *Britain's Economic Problem: Too Few Producers* (London: Macmillan).

——(1979) 'The Measurement of the Growth of the Non-Market Sector and its Influence: a Reply to Hadjimatheou and Skouras', *Economic Journal*, vol. 89, June.

Bailey, Samuel (1825) *A Critical Dissertation on the Nature, Measures and Causes of Value* (London).

Barkai, Haim (1969) 'A Formal Outline of a Smithian Growth Model', *Quarterly Journal of Economics*, vol. 83, August.

Barna, Tibor (1975) 'Quesnay's *Tableau* in Modern Guise', *Economic Journal*, vol. 85, September.

Barro, R. J. (1974) 'Are Government Bonds Net Wealth?', *Journal of Political Economy*, vol. 82, November–December.

Barton, John (1817) *Observations on the Circumstances which Influence the Condition of the Labouring Classes of Society* (London).

Baudeau, L'Abbé (1770) *Explication du Tableau Economique à Madame de *** (Paris). Included in Daire, E. (ed.) (1846) *Physiocrates* (Paris).

Berg, Maxine (1980) *The Machinery Question and the Making of Political Economy, 1815–1848* (Cambridge: University Press).

Black, R. D. C. (1967) 'Parson Malthus, the General and the Captain', *Economic Journal*, vol. 77, March.

Blaug, Mark (1958) *Ricardian Economics: A Historical Study* (New Haven: Yale University Press).

——(1960) 'Technical Change and Marxian Economics', *Kyklos*, vol. 13, 4.

——(1978) *Economic Theory in Retrospect*, 3rd edn (Cambridge: University Press).

Bordo, M. D. and D. Landau (1979) 'The Pattern of Citations in Economic Theory 1945–68: an Exploration Towards a Quantitative History of Thought', *History of Political Economy*, vol. 11, Summer.

Bortkiewicz, Ladislaus von (1907) 'On the Correction of Marx's Fundamental Theoretical Construction in the Third Volume of *Capital*'.

Translated and published with Eugene von Böhm-Bawerk (1949) *Karl Marx and the Close of His System* (New York: Kelley).

Bose, Arun (1980) *Marx on Exploitation and Inequality* (Delhi: Oxford University Press).

Boulding, K. (1955) 'The Malthusian Model as a General System', *Social and Economic Studies*, vol. 4, September

Brems, Hans (1970) 'Ricardo's Long-Run Equilibrium', *History of Political Economy*, vol. 2, Fall.

Candela, Guido (1976) 'La Fisiocrazia Secondo Eltis', *Rivista di Politica Economica*, Anno 66, Aprile.

Cantillon, Richard (1755) *Essai sur la Nature du Commerce en Général* (London). Edited and translated by H. Higgs (1931) (London).

Caravale, Giovanni A. and Domenico A. Tosato (1980) *Ricardo and the Theory of Value Distribution and Growth* (London: Routledge & Kegan Paul).

Casarosa, Carlo (1974) 'The Ricardian Theory of Distribution and Economic Growth', *Rivista di Politica Economica*, Anno 64 (Supplement to No XII) December.

——(1978) 'A New Formulation of the Ricardian System', *Oxford Economic Papers*, vol. 30, March.

——(1982) 'The New View of the Ricardian Theory of Distribution and Economic Growth', in Mauro Baranzini (ed.), *Advances in Economic Theory* (Oxford: Blackwell).

Clapham, J. H. (1926) *An Economic History of Modern Britain: The Early Railway Age 1820–50* (Cambridge: University Press).

Corry, B. A. (1959) 'Malthus and Keynes – a Reconsideration', *Economic Journal*, vol. 69, December.

——(1962) *Money, Saving and Investment in English Economics 1800–50* (London: Macmillan).

Davenant, C. (1699) *An Essay Upon the Probable Methods of Making a People Gainers in the Ballance of Trade* (London).

Desai, Meghnad (1979) *Marxian Economics* (Oxford: Blackwell).

Dickinson, H. D. (1957) 'The Falling Rate of Profit in Marxian Economics', *Review of Economic Studies*, vol. 24, February.

Dobb, Maurice (1973) *Theories of Value and Distribution Since Adam Smith: Ideology and Economic Theory* (Cambridge: University Press).

Dupâquier, J. (1968) 'Sur la Population Française au 17e et au 18e Siècle', *Revue Historique*, Janvier-Mars.

Eagly, R. V. (1969) 'A Physiocratic Model of Dynamic Equilibrium', *Journal of Political Economy*, vol. 77, January–February.

——(1974) *The Structure of Classical Economic Theory* (New York: Oxford University Press).

Eatwell, J. (1975) 'The Interpretation of Ricardo's *Essay on Profits*', *Economica*, vol. 42, May.

Fellner, William (1957) 'Marxian Hypotheses and Observable Trends Under Capitalism: A "Modernised" Interpretation', *Economic Journal*, vol. 67, March.

Fine, B. and L. Harris (1976) 'Controversial Issues in Marxist Economic Theory', *Socialist Register*.

Finley, M. (1973) *The Ancient Economy* (London: Chatto & Windus).

Fitzherbert, J. (1534) *The Booke of Husbandrye*.

Foley, V. (1973) 'An Origin of the *Tableau Economique*', *History of Political Economy*, vol. 5, Spring.

Fox-Genovese, Elizabeth (1976) *The Origins of Physiocracy* (Ithaca: Cornell University Press).

Friedman, M. (1957) *A Theory of the Consumption Function* (Princeton: University Press).

Godwin, William (1793) *An Enquiry Concerning Political Justice and its Influence on General Virtue and Happiness*, 1st edn (London).

——(1797) *The Enquirer, Reflections on Education, Manners and Literature* (London).

Gordon, B. J. and T. S. Jilek (1965) 'Malthus, Keynes, et l'Apport de Lauderdale', *Revue d'Economie Politique*, vol. 75, Janvier.

Gray, Jack (1972) 'The Chinese Model: Some Characteristics of Maoist Policies for Social Change and Economic Growth', in Alec Nove and D. M. Nuti (eds), *Socialist Economics* (Harmondsworth: Penguin).

Hahn, F. H. and R. C. O. Matthews (1964) 'The Theory of Economic Growth: A Survey', *Economic Journal*, vol. 74, December.

Hartwell, R. M. (1971) *The Industrial Revolution and Economic Growth* (London: Methuen).

——(1976) 'A Comment on the Historical Background', in T. Wilson and A. S. Skinner (eds), *The Market and the State: Essays in Honour of Adam Smith* (Oxford: University Press).

Hecht, Jacqueline (1958) 'La Vie de François Quesnay', in *François Quesnay et la Physiocratie* [abbreviated as Q], 2 vols (Paris: Institut National d'Etudes Démographiques).

Heertje, A. (1976) 'An Essay on Marxian Economics', in M. C. Howard and J. E. King (eds), *The Economics of Marx* (Harmondsworth: Penguin).

Hicks, J. R. (1939) *Value and Capital* (Oxford: University Press).

——(1965) *Capital and Growth* (Oxford: University Press).

——(1972) 'Ricardo's Theory of Distribution', in Bernard Corry and Maurice Peston (eds), *Essays in Honour of Lord Robbins* (London: Weidenfeld & Nicolson).

——(1975) 'The Scope and Status of Welfare Economics', *Oxford Economic Papers*, vol. 27, November.

——and Samuel Hollander (1977) 'Mr. Ricardo and the Moderns', *Quarterly Journal of Economics*, vol. 91, August.

Himmelweit, Susan and Simon Mohun (1981) 'Real Abstractions and Anomalous Assumptions', in Ian Steedman *et al.*, *The Value Controversy* (London: Verso and NLB).

Hishiyama, Izum (1960) 'The Tableau Economique of Quesnay – its Analysis, Construction and Application', *Kyoto University Economic Review*, vol. 30, April.

Hollander, Samuel (1962) 'Malthus and Keynes: a Note', *Economic Journal*, vol. 72, June.

——(1969) 'Malthus and the Post-Napoleonic Depression', *History of Political Economy*, vol. 1, Fall.

——(1973) *The Economics of Adam Smith* (Toronto: University Press).

——(1975) 'Ricardo and the Corn Profit Model: Reply to Eatwell', *Economica*, vol. 42, May.

——(1977) 'The Reception of Ricardian Economics', *Oxford Economic Papers*, vol. 29, July.

——(1979) *The Economics of David Ricardo* (Toronto: University Press).

——(1982), 'The Economics of David Ricardo: A Response to Professor O'Brien', *Oxford Economic Papers*, vol. 34, March.

Howard, M. C. and J. E. King (1975) *The Political Economy of Marx* (London: Longman).

Hufton, Olwen (1974) *The Poor of 18th Century France, 1750–1789* (Oxford: University Press).

Hume, David (1752) 'On the Balance of Trade', in *Political Discourses* (Edinburgh).

James, Patricia (1979) *Population Malthus: His Life and Times* (London: Routledge & Kegan Paul).

Jorgenson, D. W. (1971) 'Econometric Studies of Investment Behaviour: A Survey', *Journal of Economic Literature*, vol. 9, December.

Kaldor, N. (1955–6) 'Alternative Theories of Distribution', *Review of Economic Studies*, vol. 23, 2.

——(1966) *Causes of the Slow Rate of Growth of the United Kingdom* (inaugural lecture) (Cambridge: University Press).

——(1972) 'The Irrelevance of Equilibrium Economics', *Economic Journal*, vol. 82, December.

Kalecki, M. (1939) 'The Principle of Increasing Risk', in *Essays in the Theory of Economic Fluctuations* (London).

——(1954) *Theory of Economic Dynamics* (London: Allen & Unwin).

Keynes, John Maynard (1933) 'Thomas Robert Malthus: The First of the Cambridge Economists'; *and*

——(1935) 'Thomas Robert Malthus: The Centenary Allocution'. Both articles on Malthus are republished (1972) in *Essays in Biography* which is vol. X of *The Collected Writings of John Maynard Keynes* (London: Macmillan).

——(1936) *The General Theory of Employment Interest and Money* (London). Republished as vol. VII of *The Collected Writings of John Maynard Keynes*.

Klein, L. R. (1947) 'Theories of Effective Demand and Employment', *Journal of Political Economy*, vol. 55, April.

——and R. F. Kosobud (1961) 'Some Econometrics of Growth: Great Ratios of Economics', *Quarterly Journal of Economics*, vol. 75, May.

Lambert, P. (1956) 'The Law of Markets Prior to J. B. Say, and the Say–Malthus Debate', *International Economic Papers*, vol. 6.

——(1966) 'Lauderdale, Malthus and Keynes', *Annals of Public and Cooperative Economy*, vol. 37, January.

Lamond, E. (ed.) (1929) *A Discourse of the Common Weal of this Realm of England* (1581) (Cambridge: University Press).

Lange, O. (1938) 'The Rate of Interest and the Optimum Propensity to Consume', *Economica*, vol. 5, February.

Leibenstein, H. (1980) *Beyond Economic Man: A New Foundation for Microeconomics* (Cambridge, Mass: Harvard University Press).

Leontief, Wassily W. (1941) *The Structure of American Economy, 1919–39* (New York: Oxford University Press).

Levy, D. (1976) 'Ricardo and the Iron Law: a Correction of the Record', *History of Political Economy*, vol. 8, Summer.

Link, R. G. (1959) *English Theories of Economic Fluctuations, 1815–48* (New York: Columbia University Press).

Lowe, A. (1954) 'The Classical Theory of Growth', *Social Research*, vol. 21, 2.

——(1975) 'Adam Smith's System of Equilibrium Growth' in Andrew S. Skinner and Thomas Wilson (eds), *Essays on Adam Smith* (Oxford: University Press).

Machiavelli, Niccolo (1519) *The Discourses*. Reprinted and translated (1940) (New York: Random House).

McCulloch, J. R. (1825) *The Principles of Political Economy*, 1st edn (Edinburgh).

Malthus, Thomas R. (1798) *An Essay on the Principle of Population as it Affects the Future Improvement of Society* [abbreviated as Pop], 1st edn (London). 2nd edn, 1803; 3rd edn, 1806; 4th edn, 1807; 5th edn, 1817; 6th edn, 1826.

——(1811) 'Publications on the Depreciation of Paper Currency', *Edinburgh Review*, vol. 17. Reprinted in Bernard Semmel (ed.), (1963) *Occasional Papers of T. R. Malthus* [abbreviated as Occ] (New York: Franklin).

——(1814) *Observations on the Effects of the Corn Laws* (London).

——(1815a) *The Grounds of An Opinion on the Policy of Restricting the Importation of Foreign Corn* (London).

——(1815b) *An Inquiry into the Nature and Progress of Rent* (London). This and the two above pamphlets are reprinted in (1970) *The Pamphlets of Thomas Robert Malthus* [abbreviated as Ess] (New York: Kelley).

——(1820) *Principles of Political Economy Considered with a View to Their Practical Application* [abbreviated as Pr] 1st edn (London). 2nd edn, 1836.

——(1827) *Definitions of Political Economy* [abbreviated as Def], 1st edn (London).

Marshall, Alfred (1890) *Principles of Economics* (London).

Marx, Karl (1849) *Wage Labour and Capital*.

——(1865) *Wages Price and Profit* [abbreviated as WPP]. This and the above are reprinted in (1969) *Karl Marx and Frederick Engels: Selected Works*, 3 vols (Moscow: Progress Publishers).

——(1867–83) *Capital* [abbreviated as Cap], 3 vols. Republished in 1974 (Moscow: Progress Publishers for Lawrence & Wishart).

——(1873) *Grundrisse* (London: Penguin).

——(1969–71) *Theories of Surplus Value* [abbreviated as TSV], 3 vols (Moscow: Progress Publishers for Lawrence & Wishart).

Matthews, R. C. O., C. H. Feinstein and J. C. Odling-Smee (1982) *British Economic Growth, 1856–1973* (Oxford: University Press).

Meek, R. L. (1960) 'The Falling Rate of Profit', *Science and Society*, vol. 24, Winter.

——(1962) *The Economics of Physiocracy* (London: Allen & Unwin).

——(1973) *Studies in the Labour Theory of Value*, 2nd edn (London: Lawrence & Wishart).

——(1977) *Smith, Marx, and After* (London: Chapman & Hall).

Mill, James (1808) *Commerce Defended* (London).

Mill, John Stuart (1848) *Principles of Political Economy with Some of Their Applications to Social Philosophy*, 1st edn, 2 vols (London). Republished J. M. Robson (ed.), (1965) as Vols II–III of *Collected Works of John Stuart Mill* (Toronto: University Press).

Mirabeau, Victor de Riqueti, Marquis de, and François Quesnay (1756–60) *L'Ami des Hommes* [abbreviated as AH] (Avignon). Reprinted (1972) (Scientia Verlag Aalen).

——(1763) *Philosophie Rurale* [abbreviated as PR], 1st edn (Amsterdam). A 1764 Amsterdam edition has been reprinted (1972) (Scientia Verlag Aalen).

Mitchell, B. R. and Phyllis Deane (1962) *Abstract of British Historical Statistics* (Cambridge: University Press).

Modigliani, F. (1966) 'The Life Cycle Hypothesis of Saving, the Demand for Wealth and the Supply of Capital', *Social Research*, vol. 33, Summer.

More, Thomas (1516) *Utopia*.

Morishima, Michio (1973) *Marx's Economics: A Dual Theory of Value and Growth* (Cambridge: University Press).

——and George Catephores (1978) *Value, Exploitation and Growth* (London: McGraw-Hill).

O'Brien, D. P. (1975) *The Classical Economists* (Oxford: University Press).

——(1981) 'Ricardian Economics and the Economics of David Ricardo', *Oxford Economic Papers*, vol. 33, November.

——(1982) 'Ricardian Economics: A Rejoinder to Samuel Hollander', *Oxford Economic Papers*, vol. 34, March.

Okishio, N. (1961) 'Technical Change and the Rate of Profit', *Kobe University Economic Review*, vol. 7.

O'Leary, J. J. (1942) 'Malthus and Keynes', *Journal of Political Economy*, vol. 50, December.

——(1943) 'Malthus' General Theory of Employment and the Post-Napoleonic Depression', *Journal of Economic History*, vol. 3, November.

Pasinetti, Luigi L. (1960) 'A Mathematical Formulation of the Ricardian System', *Review of Economic Studies*, vol. 27, February.

Petersen, W. (1979) *Malthus* (London: Heinemann).

Petty, Sir William (1662) *A Treatise of Taxes and Contributions* (London). Republished in C. H. Hull (ed.) (1899) *The Economic Writings of Sir William Petty*, 2 vols (Cambridge: University Press).

Phillips, A. (1955) 'The *Tableau Economique* as a Simplified Leontief Model', *Quarterly Journal of Economics*, vol. 69, February.

Place, Francis (1822) *Illustrations and Proofs of the Principle of Population* (London).

Price, Richard (1769) 'Observations on the Expectations of Lives; the Increase of Mankind; the Number of Inhabitants in London; and the Influence of Great Towns, on Health and Population', a Letter to Benjamin Franklin, Esq., LLD and FRS, *Philosophical Transactions of the Royal Society*, vol. 59, April 27.

——(1771) *Observations on Reversionary Payments, Etc.* 1st edn, 2 vols (London). 2nd edn, 1772; 3rd edn, 1773; 4th edn, 1783.

Quesnay, François (1756) 'Fermiers'.

——(1757) 'Grains'.

——(1757) 'Hommes'.

——(1757) 'Impôts'. These four articles are reprinted in L. Salleron (ed.), (1958) *François Quesnay et la Physiocratie* [abbreviated as Q], 2 vols (Paris: Institut National d'Etudes Démographiques).

——(1758) *Tableau Economique*, 1st edn (Paris). 2nd edn, 1759; 3rd edn, 1759. Republished and translated in Marguerite Kuczynski and Ronald L. Meek (eds), (1972) *Quesnay's Tableau Economique* [abbreviated as Tab] (London: Macmillan).

——(1766) 'Répétition de la Question Proposée dans la "Gazette du Commerce" au Sujet du Bénéfice que la Fabrique des Bas de Soie Etablie a Nîmes Produit a la France' (Paris) [reprinted in Q].

——(1766) 'Analyse de la Formule Arithmétique du Tableau Economique' [reprinted in Q].

——(1766) '(Premier) Problème Economique' [reprinted in Q].

——(1767) 'Second Problème Economique' [reprinted in Q].

Rankin, S. C. (1980) 'Supply and Demand in Ricardian Price Theory: A Re-interpretation', *Oxford Economic Papers*, vol. 32, July.

Ricardo, David (1815) *An Essay on the Influence of a Low Price of Corn on the Profits of Stock* (London). Reprinted in Vol. IV of Piero Sraffa (ed.), (1951–73) *The Works and Correspondence of David Ricardo* [abbreviated as R], 11 vols (Cambridge: University Press).

——(1817) *On The Principles of Political Economy and Taxation*, 1st edn (London). 2nd edn, 1819; 3rd edn, 1821 [Vol I of R].

——(1820) 'Notes on Malthus's *Principles of Political Economy*' [Vol II of R].

——(1820) 'Funding System', *Encyclopaedia Britannica*, Supplement to the 4th edn [Reprinted in Vol IV of R].

——*Speeches and Evidence of David Ricardo* [Vol V of R].

——*The Correspondence of David Ricardo* [Vols VI–IX of R].

Robbins, Lionel (1958) *Robert Torrens and the Evolution of Classical Economics* (London: Macmillan).

Robinson, Joan (1942) *An Essay on Marxian Economics* (London: Macmillan).

——(1978) 'The Organic Composition of Capital', *Kyklos*, vol. 31, 1.

Roemer, John (1981) *Analytical Foundations of Marxian Economic Theory* (Cambridge: University Press).

Rosdolsky, Roman (1977) *The Making of Marx's Capital* (London: Pluto Press).

Rowthorn, Bob (1980) *Capitalism, Conflict and Inflation* (London: Lawrence & Wishart).

Salleron, Louis (1958) 'Editorial Notes' to [Q].

Samuelson, Paul A. (1957) 'Wages and Interest: A Modern Dissection of Marxian Economic Models', *American Economic Review*, vol. 47, December.

——(1959) 'A Modern Treatment of the Ricardian Economy: 1. The Pricing of Goods and of Labour and Land Services; 2. Capital and Interest Aspects of the Pricing Process', *Quarterly Journal of Economics*, vol. 73, February and May.

——(1962) 'Economists and the History of Ideas', *American Economic*

Review, vol. 52, March.

——(1971) 'Understanding the Marxian Notion of Exploitation: A Summary of the So-Called Transformation Problem Between Marxian Values and Competitive Prices', *Journal of Economic Literature*, vol. 9, June.

——(1974) 'Marx as Mathematical Economist: Steady State and Exponential Growth Equilibrium', in G. Horwich and P. A. Samuelson (eds), *Trade, Stability and Macroconomic Essays in Honor of Lloyd A. Metzler* (New York: Academic Press).

——(1982) 'Quesnay's "Tableau Economique" as a Theorist would Formulate it Today', in Ian Bradley and Michael Howard (eds), *Classical and Marxian Political Economy: Essays in Honour of Ronald L. Meek* (London: Macmillan).

Schumpeter, Joseph A. (1943) *Capitalism, Socialism, and Democracy* (London: Allen & Unwin).

Semmel, B. (1963) 'Malthus and the Reviews', in [Occ.].

——(1965) 'Malthus: 'Physiocracy' and the Commercial System', *Economic History Review*, vol. 17, April.

Seton, Francis (1957) 'The Transformation Problem', *Review of Economic Studies*, vol. 24, June.

Shaikh, Anwar (1978) 'Political Economy and Capitalism: Notes on Dobb's Theory of Crisis', *Cambridge Journal of Economics*, vol. 2, June.

——(1981) 'The Poverty of Algebra', in Ian Steedman *et al.*, *The Value Controversy* (London: Verso and NLB).

Skinner, A. S. (1969) 'Of Malthus, Lauderdale and Say's Law', *Scottish Journal of Political Economy*, vol. 16, June.

——and Thomas Wilson (eds) (1975) *Essays on Adam Smith* (Oxford: University Press).

——(1979) *A System of Social Science: Papers Relating to Adam Smith* (Oxford: University Press).

Slicher van Bath, B. H. (1963) *Agrarian History of Western Europe, 500–1850* (London: Arnold).

Smith, Adam (1759) *The Theory of Moral Sentiments* [abbreviated as TMS], 1st edn (London). 2nd edn, 1761; 3rd edn, 1767; 4th edn, 1774; 5th edn, 1781; 6th edn, 1790. Republished, D. D. Raphael and A. L. Macfie (eds), (1976) as I of *The Glasgow Edition of the Works and Correspondence of Adam Smith* (Oxford: University Press).

——(1776) *An Inquiry into the Nature and Causes of the Wealth of Nations* [abbreviated as WN], 1st edn, 2 vols (London). 2nd edn, 1778; 3rd edn, 1784; 4th edn, 1786; 5th edn, 1789; 6th edn, 1791. Republished, R. H. Campbell, A. S. Skinner and W. B. Todd (eds) (1976), 2 vols, as II of *The Glasgow Edition of the Works and Correspondence of Adam Smith*.

——*Lectures on Jurisprudence* [abbreviated as Jur], delivered in 1762–3 and 1766. R. L. Meek, D. D. Raphael and P. G. Stein (eds), (1978), V of *The Glasgow Edition of the Works and Correspondence of Adam Smith*.

——*The Correspondence of Adam Smith* [abbreviated as S. Corr], E. C. Mossner and I. S. Ross (eds) (1977), VI of *The Glasgow Edition of the Works and Correspondence of Adam Smith*.

Sowell, T. (1963) 'The General Glut Controversy Reconsidered', *Oxford Economic Papers*, vol. 15, November.

——(1972) *Say's Law* (Princeton: University Press).

Spengler, J. J. (1945a) 'Malthus's Total Population Theory: A Restatement and Reappraisal', *Canadian Journal of Economics and Political Science*, vol. 11, February and May.

——(1945b) 'The Physiocrats and Say's Law of Markets', *Journal of Political Economy*, vol. 53, September and December.

——(1959) 'Adam Smith's Theory of Economic Growth', *Southern Economic Journal*, vols 25–6, April and July.

Sraffa, Piero (1951) 'Introduction' to David Ricardo, *On the Principles of Political Economy and Taxation* [Vol I of R].

——(1955) 'Addenda to the Memoir' of David Ricardo and 'Ricardo in Business' [Vol X of R].

——(1960) *Production of Commodities by Means of Commodities* (Cambridge: University Press).

Steedman, Ian (1977) *Marx After Sraffa* (London: NLB).

Stewart, Dugald (1793) 'Account of the Life and Writings of Adam Smith, LL.D.', *Transactions of the Royal Society of Edinburgh*. Republished in W. P. D. Wightman, J. C. Bryce and I. S. Ross (eds) (1980), III of *The Glasgow Edition of the Works and Correspondence of Adam Smith* (Oxford: University Press).

Styles, E. (1761) *A Discourse on Christian Union* (Boston).

Sweezy, Paul M. (1942) *The Theory of Capitalist Development* (New York).

Thweatt, William O. (1957) 'A Diagrammatic Representation of Adam Smith's Growth Model', *Social Research*, vol. 24, 2.

Turgot, A. R. J. (1770) *Réflexions sur la Formation èt la Distribution des Richesses* (Paris). Translated and edited by R. L. Meek (1973) in *Turgot on Progress, Sociology and Economics* (Cambridge: University Press).

Tutain, J.-C. (1963) 'La Population de la France de 1700 à 1959', *Cahiers de l'Institut de Science Economique Appliquée*, Supplément no. 133, Janvier.

Vatter, H.G. (1959) 'The Malthusian Model of Income Determination and its Contemporary Relevance', *Canadian Journal of Economics and Political Science*, vol. 25, February.

Voltaire, J. B. de A. (1768) *L'Homme aux Quarante Ecus* (Paris). Republished (1942), in *Contes et Romans de Voltaire* (Paris: Cluny).

Walsh, Vivian and Harvey Gram (1980) *Classical and Neoclassical Theories of General Equilibrium* (New York: Oxford University Press).

West, Edward (1815) *Essay on the Application of Capital to Land* (London).

Weulersse, Georges (1910a) *Les Manuscrits Economiques de François Quesnay et du Marquis de Mirabeau aux Archives Nationales* (Paris).

——(1910b) *Le Mouvement Physiocratique en France de 1756 à 1770*, 2 Vols (Paris).

Williams, Phillip L. (1982) 'Monopoly and Centralisation in Marx', *History of Political Economy*, vol. 14, Summer.

Woog, H. (1950) *The Tableau Economique of François Quesnay* (Berne: Francke).

Wright, J. F. (1965) 'British Economic Growth, 1688–1959', *Economic History Review*, vol. 18, August.

Zinke, G. W. (1942) 'Six Letters from Malthus to Pierre Prévost', *Journal of Economic History*, vol. 2, November.

Index

Adelman, I. 346, 357
Africa 69, 112, 113
agriculture: Quesnay 3–15, 27–31, 42–7, 49–67, 314, 320, 339; Smith 73–4, 89, 100–4, 318–21; Malthus 107–8, 130–8, 156–7, 170–2, 321–3; Ricardo 186–8, 193–7, 199–201, 208–9, 211–16, 324–6
alienation 259, 278, 351
America, North 64–5, 88, 102–3, 106–7, 109, 112, 130, 139, 227, 305, 310, 314, 336
Aristotle 245
Arrow, K. J. 69, 71, 72–3, 345, 357
Australia 139

Bacon, R. 356, 357
Bailey, Samuel 348, 357
Barkai, H. 346, 357
Baring, Alexander 222–3
Barna, T. 341, 357
Barro, R. J. 222, 357
Barton, John 223–5, 228, 255, 357
Baudeau, L'Abbé 339, 342, 357
beggars 56
Berg, M. 355, 357
Berkeley, George 137
Black, R. D. C. 348, 357
Blaug, M. 302, 346, 348, 349, 352, 353, 357
Bordo, M. D. 354, 357
Bortkiewicz, Ladislaus von 351, 357
Bose, A. 351, 354, 358
Boulding, K. 348, 358
Brems, H. 350, 358
Britain 10, 26–7, 88, 125, 147, 166, 216, 219, 223, 231, 303–5, 310, 319, 329, 339, 342, 355
Brougham, Henry 185, 223, 321, 355
Brus, W. xiii

Candela, G. xii–xiii, 67, 358
Cantillon, Richard 10, 17, 106, 313, 339, 340, 358
capital
  accumulation and growth: Quesnay 42–7, 58–65, 345; Smith 69, 75–86, 93–4, 96–8, 100–1, 315, 319; Malthus 116–19, 122–4, 126–8, 131–3, 142–6, 157, 167–76, 323–4; Ricardo 192–3, 202–5, 216–18, 225–9, 325, 327–9, 350; Marx 253–8, 274–8, 281–5, 286–8, 296–303, 331
  constant and variable 242–3, 253–7, 268–9, 281–5, 291–6, 297–9, 303–5, 352
  depreciation of 13, 26, 30–1, 34, 35, 62–3, 243
  fixed and circulating 62–3, 75, 79, 85–6, 96–9, 167–9, 224–9, 345
  markets 8, 163, 178, 336–7
  per worker and productivity 7–10, 55, 57, 91, 185, 204, 223–9, 245–6, 249–53, 255, 265–8, 281–5, 291–6, 301–2, 327–9, 330–1
  to output ratio 63–4, 90, 94–6, 98–100, 281, 304–5, 352
Caravale, G. A. 350, 358
Casarosa, C. xiii, 201, 205, 350, 358
Catephores, G. 351, 362
Chilosi, A. xiii
China 67
Clapham, J. H. 349, 358
classical theory of economic growth see growth, classical theory of
coercion of workers, the power to, and income distribution 242, 262, 308
Colbert, Jean-Baptiste 40, 57, 67
colonies 102, 320
competition 14–15, 83–5, 90, 259–60, 261–3, 265–7, 293–4, 319

Condorcet, Antoine-Nicolas de 129–30
contraception 129–30
Corn Laws 136–7, 230–2, 351
corn, special significance of in
    determining wage and economic
    surplus xiii, 14, 74, 88–9, 100,
    199–201, 240–1, 325–6, 335, 340, 350
Corry, B. A. 348, 349, 358
cyclical fluctuations 117–19, 140–8,
    274–9

D'Alembert, Jean le Rond 1
Danguel, Marquis de Plumart 10
Davenant, Charles 312, 355, 358
Deane, P. 351, 356, 362
Debt, National 219, 221–3, 231, 336
de-industrialisation 306
depreciation of capital *see* capital,
    depreciation of
Desai, M. 351, 358
Dickinson, H. D. 353, 358
Diderot, Denis 1
distribution, income *see* profits, rent,
    wage
division of labour 68–9, 71–3, 86, 91–2,
    100–2, 105, 250–2, 265–6, 281–5,
    310, 315
Dixon, R. xiii
Dobb, M. 351, 358
Domar, E. 310
Douglas, Major C. H. 233
Dupâquier, J. 343, 358

Eagly, R. V. 313, 340, 348, 355, 358
Eatwell, J. 350, 358
Edinburgh Review 140, 348, 355
education 3, 329–30
Eltis, W. 356, 357
Europe, Western 130, 138, 305
European Economic Community 232

Feinstein, C. H. 304, 354, 361
Fellner, W. 306, 354, 358
Fine, B. 352, 358
Finley, M. 311, 355, 358
Fitzherbert, John 339, 358
fixed capital *see* capital, fixed and
    circulating
fixprice and flexprice models 318, 323,
    324, 327, 331–2
Foley, V. 340, 359
Fox-Genovese, E. 340, 355, 359
France: economy of 10, 26, 39–41,
    57–8, 138, 319, 340, 342; finances of

government 39–40, 54–8, 62, 315;
    revolution 55–6, 62, 67, 314
Friedman, M. 356, 359

Gatcombe Park 327
Germany 138
Gesell, Silvio 233
Ghosh, R. N. 345
Glyn, A. xiii
Godwin, William 119–24, 347, 359
gold (and silver) mining 183–7, 226, 349
Gordon, B. J. 348, 359
Gram, H. 356, 365
Gray, J. 345, 359
growth of output: Quesnay 33, 39–67,
    314–15; Smith 75–86, 92–100,
    317–21; Malthus 148–77, 321–4;
    Ricardo 198–232, 324–7;
    Marx 280–303, 329–32
classical theory of: defined vii;
    summarised 310–38
of capital *see* capital, accumulation
    and growth
of population *see* population

Hahn, F. H. 345, 359
Harcourt, G. C. xiii
Harris, L. 352, 358
Harrod, R. F. 310
Harrod-neutral technical progress 310,
    353
Hartwell, R. M. xii, 346, 354, 355, 359
Hecht, J. 339, 355, 359
Heertje, A. 352, 353, 359
Hennings, K. xi
Hicks, J. R. xiii, 93, 200, 201, 203, 205,
    318, 326, 337, 346, 350, 355, 356, 359
Himmelweit, S. 351, 352, 359
Hishiyama, I. 340, 344, 359
hoarding 178–9
Hollander, S. xiii, 87, 182, 201, 203,
    205, 311, 345, 346, 347, 348, 349,
    350, 354, 355, 359–60
Howard, M. C. 351, 360
Hufton, O. 343, 344, 360
Hume, David 319, 324, 355, 360

Industrial Revolution 68, 245, 303–5
industry: Quesnay 11–14, 15–18, 25–6,
    31–2, 42–9, 66; Smith 101–4,
    317–19; Malthus 113–14, 130–7,
    170, 321–3; Ricardo 196–7,
    199–201, 211–13, 325–6;

industry *cont.*
    Marx 245–6, 249–53, 265–8, 301–2,
    330–1; *see also* machinery
interest, rate 177–8, 218, 219, 276:
    in Quesnay (where it refers to
    depreciation allowances) 13, 26,
    30–1, 34, 35, 62–3, 341
input–output tables 1, 29, 318
investment, and saving, including
    possible discrepancies between, *ex
    ante* 78–9, 85–6, 160–4, 166, 174–7,
    178–81, 218, 273–5; overseas 180,
    349; and growth *see* capital,
    accumulation and growth
invisible hand 85, 319
Ireland 129, 328
Italy 138

James, P. 347, 348, 360
Jilek, T. S. 348, 359
Jorgenson, D. W. 356, 360

Kaldor, N. 199, 310, 345, 347, 360
Kalecki, M. viii, 155, 348, 356, 360
Kaser, M. C. xiii
Keynes, John Maynard viii, 105, 141,
    177, 233, 307, 332, 348, 351, 360
Keynesian economics xii, 1, 69, 181,
    307, 345, 354
King, J. E. 351, 360
Klein, L. R. 354, 360
Kosobud, R. F. 354, 360
Kuczynski, M. 363

labour: force *see* population; theory
    of value *see* value, labour theory
Lambert, P. 348, 360
Lamond, E. 355, 360
land: availability and quality of 10–11,
    66–7, 107–8, 320–1; division of
    landed property 159–60, 162–3;
    significance of length of agricultural
    leases 59–61, 66–7, 166, 314–5; *see
    also* rent
Landau, D. 354, 357
Lange, O. 349, 360
learning by doing 68, 69, 71
Leibenstein, H. 348, 360
Leontief, W. W. 1, 339, 360
Levy, D. 347, 360
limited liability 336
Link, R. G. 348, 360
Lowe, A. 347, 361

luxuries, effect of consumption of 41,
    48–9, 114, 197–8, 211–13, 215, 220,
    249, 252, 273–4, 305–6, 335, 345

McCulloch, John Ramsay 321, 332–4,
    355, 361
Machiavelli, Niccolo 233, 351, 361
machinery 71–3, 185, 204, 223–9,
    245–6, 249–53, 253–8, 265–7,
    327–31, 338, 355
Malthus, Thomas R. viii–ix, xv, 66,
    106–81, 187, 193, 201, 202, 213–14,
    216–21, 234, 260, 307, 310, 311,
    320–6, 329, 331, 333–7, 347–50, 361:
    and Quesnay 66, 132–3, 321–3; and
    Smith viii, 106–7, 131–2, 140, 154,
    320, 321–2, 324; and
    Ricardo 140–1, 150, 187, 193, 201,
    202, 213–14, 216–21, 324–6, 350; and
    Marx 181, 234, 260, 273, 307, 329,
    331; and Keynes viii, 141, 177, 181
theory of population 106–39, 142–4,
    164–5, 167–73, 260, 321–3, 335–6,
    347–8: positive and preventive
    checks to 109–14, 123, 138;
    social implications of 119–29
theory of effective demand viii,
    140–81, 322–4, 348–9: saving and
    investment, possible *ex ante*
    discrepancies between 160–4,
    166, 174–7, 178–81; explanation of
    general gluts 146–7, 166, 181;
    case for unproductive
    expenditure 147–8, 153–4, 162,
    323; implications for
    policy 147–8, 161–3, 323–4
*relationship between accumulation and
    growth* 116–19, 122–4, 126–8,
    131–3, 142–6, 157, 167–76, 323–4:
    determination of productivity
    growth 138, 148–51, 165,
    169–73; motivation to work and
    invest 138, 149–52, 159–60,
    169–70, 180–1, 322; benefits from
    trade 148–50, 156–7, 170; social
    institutions needed for
    growth 113, 119–29
*correct balance between industry and
    agriculture* 113–14, 130–7,
    170–2, 321–3: diminishing returns
    in agriculture viii, 107–8, 321;
    case for agricultural
    protection 134–7; divide
    between productive and

unproductive 178–9, 333–4
determination of wages 114–19,
122–4, 126–8, 135–6, 142–4,
146–7, 164–5, 167–73, 335:
profits 142–6, 154–66, 167–75;
rents 156–7, 171–2
Mao Tse Tung 67
market and non-market sectors 334–5,
356
Marshall, Alfred 233, 361
Marx, Karl ix–x, xv, 1, 33, 48–9, 67,
105, 181, 185, 233–309, 310, 311,
320, 328–32, 335, 336, 337, 338, 339,
351–4, 361: and Quesnay 1, 33,
48–9, 67, 234, 307, 329, 330, 331; and
Smith 105, 234–5, 250–2, 254, 265,
272, 285, 320, 329, 330, 331; and
Malthus 181, 234, 260, 307, 329,
331; and Ricardo 185, 234, 235,
244, 249, 255, 260, 265, 280, 306,
328–32; and Keynes 233, 307, 332,
354

theory of exploitation ix, 235–64,
307–9, 329–30, 351–2:
determination of rate of 243–53,
258–60, 263–4, 266–8, 303–5,
307–9; length of working day
and 243–7, 252–3, 263–4,
269–71; coercion and 242, 262,
308; determination of
profits 237–43, 246–7, 261–4,
272–7, 303–5, 307–8, 330; social
implications of 245–8, 252,
258–60, 264, 277–9, 307–9

theory of value 235–44, 261–4, 280–1,
351–2: value in use and value in
exchange 237–42; money in
explanation of 234–40; the
transformation problem 261–4,
351; determination of uniform rate
of profit 261–4

accumulation and growth 253–8,
274–8, 281–5, 286–8, 296–303,
331: mechanisation and
productivity growth ix–x, 245–6,
249–53, 265–8, 281–5, 291–6,
301–2, 330–1; significance of
difference between constant and
variable capital and tendency of
ratio of constant to variable capital
to rise 242–3, 253–7, 268–9,
281–5, 291–6, 297–9, 303–5, 352;
reproduction schemes 280,
297–8, 352

*theory of reserve army of the
unemployed* 253–60, 279, 285–8,
296–303, 303–6, 328–9, 338:
determination of wages 237–8,
246–8, 255–60, 270, 294–6, 303,
307–8, 329, 335, 338, 351; divide
between productive and
unproductive labour 242, 305–6,
329–30

theory of declining rate of profit 234,
268–72, 274–8, 288–96, 300–6,
307, 331, 352–3: crises 274–9,
307–9, 331; role of money
in 276–7; realisation problem
in 272–7, 307; possible excess
of *ex ante* saving over
investment 273–5; tendencies
towards monopolisation,
concentration and
centralisation 265–7, 272, 278,
352

*historical predictions, accuracy
of* 294, 303–9
mathematics, in the history of economic
thought x–xi, 2, 21, 177, 311, 341
Matthews, R. C. O. 304, 345, 354, 359,
361
Meek, R. L. xiii, 32, 59, 340, 341, 342,
344, 351, 352, 355, 361, 363, 365
mercantilism 140, 312
Mercier de la Rivière 318
Mill, James 346, 361
Mill, John Stuart 233, 328, 355, 361
Mirabeau, Victor Riqueti, Marquis
de xii, xiv, 2, 40–1, 44, 45, 132,
312–14, 320, 321, 341, 344, 355,
361–2
Mitchell, B. R. 351, 356, 362
Modigliani, F. 356, 362
Mohun, S. 351, 352, 359
money 23, 27–8, 161, 183–7, 234–40,
267, 276–7, 319
monopolisation 265–8, 272, 317
More, Thomas 355, 362
Morishima, M. 233, 351, 362

Napoleonic wars 125, 136, 137, 147, 216

O'Brien, D. P. 141, 348, 350, 362
Odling-Smee, J. C. 304, 354, 361
Okishio, N. 295, 353, 362
O'Leary, J. J. 348, 362

Pasinetti, L. L.   182, 199, 349, 362
Petersen, W.   347, 362
Petty, Sir William   184, 362
Phillips, A.   341, 362
Physiocratic school of economists   vii,
    2–3, 57–8, 68, 132–3, 140, 315–18,
    320–1, 348: *see also* Quesnay *and*
    Mirabeau
Place, Francis   129, 347, 362
Poor Laws   124–9, 245–6
population, determination of:
    Quesnay   10–11, 39, 64–5;
    Smith   86–9, 92–3; Malthus
    106–39, 142–4, 164–5, 167–73,
    321–2; Marx   260; general   335–6
Price, Richard   106, 347, 362
prices, determination of   183–8, 226,
    261–4, 293–4, 318–19, 323, 324, 327,
    331–2
productive and unproductive, distinction
    between: Quesnay   11–15, 66;
    Smith   75–8; Malthus   130–3,
    178–9; Marx   242, 305–6;
    general   317–18, 321–2, 332–5
profits: Quesnay   14, 42–7, 49–57,
    58–65, 66; Smith   89–90, 94–6,
    98–100, 104–5; Malthus   142–6,
    154–66, 167–75; Ricardo   189–92,
    205, 209–10, 211, 214, 216, 217–18,
    228–9, 325–6; Marx   237–43, 246–7,
    261–4, 272–7, 303–5, 307–8, 330
    rate of, tendency to decline: in
        Smith   70, 90, 95–6, 98–100,
        104–5, 234, 320; Ricardo   192–3,
        205, 209–10, 230–2, 325–6, 327,
        338; Marx   234, 268–72, 274–8,
        288–96, 300–6, 307, 331, 352–3

Quarterly Review   140, 348
Quesnay, François   vii–viii, xii–xiii, xiv,
    1–67, 68, 132–3, 198, 234, 307,
    312–20, 321–3, 329, 330, 331, 337,
    339–45, 355, 362–3: and
    Smith   vii–viii, 48–9, 66–7, 68,
    315–20, 355; and Malthus   66,
    132–3, 321–3; and Ricardo   9,
    48–9, 66–7, 198, 321; and Marx   1, 33,
    48–9, 67, 234, 307, 329, 330, 331; and
    Keynes   xii, 1
    '*Tableau Economique*' *of*   vii, 1–38,
        40–2, 42–7, 49–53, 56–7, 62–3,
        313, 314, 318, 322, 339–44:
        circulation of money in   23, 27–8,

340, 341; role of trade in   24–5,
    26–7, 32–3, 34–8, 57–8, 342, 343
*agricultural techniques of
    production*   3–10, 55, 57, 339:
    quality and availability of
    land   10–11, 66–7, 320; capital
    requirements   7–10, 13, 55, 62–5,
    66–7, 339; generation of economic
    surplus (*produit net*) in agriculture
    and its significance   3–10, 13–15,
    27–31, 58–61, 66–7, 314;
    determination of farmers'
    incomes   3–10, 14–15, 42–7,
    49–57, 58–65
*determination of rents according
    to*   14–15, 44–7, 49–57, 58–61,
    66–7: influence of on effective
    demand   15–21, 27–31; multiplier
    in work of   1, 19–20, 24, 340;
    influence of demand on extent of
    industry and commerce   15–21,
    25–6, 31–2, 42–9, 54, 343–4;
    sterility of industry and
    commerce   11–14, 66, 316–17,
    321
*capital accumulation and
    growth*   42–7, 58–65, 345:
    population growth   10–11, 39,
    64–5; determination of
    wages   12–13, 14, 340
policy implications of argument   vii,
    41, 49–57, 57–8, 61–7
Rankin, S. C.   349, 363
rent: Quesnay   14–15, 44–7, 49–57,
    58–61, 66–7, 314; Malthus   156–7,
    171–2; Ricardo   193–6, 208–9,
    212–16, 324–5, 350
reproduction schemes   3, 21–4, 33, 280,
    297–8, 352
Ricardo David   viii–ix, xiii, xv, 9, 48–9,
    66–7, 100, 103–4, 140–1, 150,
    182–232, 233, 234, 235, 244, 249,
    255, 260, 265, 280, 306, 310, 311,
    320, 321, 324–32, 335, 336, 337, 338,
    347, 349–51, 363: in House of
    Commons   ix, 185, 221–3, 229, 231;
    and Quesnay   9, 48–9, 66–7, 198,
    321; and Smith   viii, 100, 103–4,
    201, 202, 320, 324, 326–7, 347; and
    Malthus   140–1, 150, 187, 193, 201,
    202, 213–14, 216–21, 324–6, 350; and
    Marx   185, 234, 235, 244, 249, 255,
    260, 265, 280, 306, 328–32
theory of value   183–7, 198–9, 200–1,

206–7, 226–7, 349: gold mining in 183–7, 226, 349; food and manufactures in units of output xiii, 196–7, 199–201, 211–13, 325–6; corn model version of Ricardo xiii, 199–201, 325–6

determination of wages 188–9, 201–2, 205–7, 209–10, 217–18, 223–6, 327, 335, 350: profits 189–92, 205, 209–10, 211, 214, 216, 217–18, 228–9, 325–6; rents 193–6, 208–9, 212–16, 324–5, 350; declining rate of profit 192–3, 205, 209–10, 230–2, 325–6, 327, 338

capital accumulation and growth 192–3, 202–5, 216–18, 225–9, 325, 327–9, 350: effects of productivity growth 186–8, 191–2, 210–16, 223–9, 327–9; influence of machinery 185, 204, 223–9, 255, 327–9; elastic supply of entrepreneurs 218

policy implications of theory 218–23, 229–32, 325–6, 351: unproductive consumption as brake on growth 220–1; benefits from abolition of Corn Laws 229–32, 325–6, 351; repayment of National Debt 219, 221–3, 231, 336

Ricardo effect 226–8

Riqueti, Victor, Marquis de Mirabeau *see* Mirabeau

Robbins, L. 349, 363

Robinson, J. 233, 294, 351, 353, 363

robots 338

Roemer, J. 353, 363

Rosdolsky, R 351, 363

Rousseau, Jean Jacques 312, 355

Rowthorn, B. 351, 363

Salleron, L. 339, 362, 363

Samuelson, P. A. 182, 196, 233, 294–5, 339, 340–1, 343–4, 349, 351, 363–4

saving: contribution of thriftiness to growth 79–82, 101, 217–21, 317, 319; possible discrepancy with *ex ante* investment 160–4, 166, 174–7, 178–81, 218, 273–5; optimum 175–7, 323–4, 349; whether derived entirely from non-wage incomes 78–9, 85–6, 336–7

Say's law 75, 137

Schumpeter, J. A. 1, 2, 339, 364

Semmel, B. 348, 355, 364

Seton, F. 351, 364

Shaikh, A. 352, 364

Skinner, A. S. xi, 348, 355, 364

slavery 112, 262

Slicher, van Bath, B. H. 339, 364

Smith, Adam xi–xii, xiv–xv, 48–9, 66–7, 68–105, 106, 131–2, 140, 154, 201, 202, 234–5, 250–2, 254, 265, 272, 285, 310, 311, 315–22, 324, 326–7, 329, 330, 331, 332, 334, 335, 337, 338, 345–7, 355, 364: and Quesnay vii–viii, 48–9, 66–7, 68, 315–20, 355; and Malthus viii, 106–7, 131–2, 140, 154, 320, 321–2, 324; and Ricardo viii, 100, 103–4, 201, 202, 320, 324, 326–7, 347; and Marx 105, 234–5, 250–2, 254, 265, 272, 285, 320, 329, 330, 331; and Keynes 105

division of labour and industrial productivity 68–9, 71–3, 86, 91–2, 100–2, 105, 251–2, 310, 315: productivity in agriculture 73–4, 89, 100, 320–1; extent of market determines extent of division of labour 71–4; desirable balance between industry and agriculture viii, 101–4, 318–19

productive and unproductive employment 75–8, 317: connection between saving and investment and ratio of unproductive employment 78–9, 85–6, 100–1, 319–20, 338; importance of frugality 79–82, 101, 317, 319

capital accumulation and economic growth 69, 75–86, 93–4, 96–8, 100–1, 315, 319: growth with a circulating capital model 75–86, 93–4; effect of fixed capital on argument 86, 96–9, 345

determination of wages 68–9, 86–9, 100, 105, 319–20, 335–6: population growth 86–9, 92–3; profits 89–90, 94–6, 98–100, 104–5; falling rate of profit 70, 90, 95–6, 98–100, 104–5, 234, 320

significance of property rights and social institutions xii, 75, 80–1, 319, 346: gains from international trade and case for free trade

Smith: *property rights and social institutions cont.*
 83–5, 101–2, 319;
 implications for public
 policy 81–5, 100–1, 104–5,
 319–20
Sowell, T. 146, 347, 348, 364
space, limitation of 139, 338
Spengler, J. J. 342, 345, 346, 348, 364–5
Sraffa, P. 345, 349, 350, 351, 355, 363, 365
stationary state 33, 104–5, 193, 208–9, 214, 216, 217–20, 230, 319
Steedman, I. 351, 353, 365
Stewart, Dugald 345, 365
Styles, Edward 106, 347, 365
surplus: Quesnay 3–10, 13–15, 27–31, 58–61, 66–7; Smith 78–86, 102–4; Malthus 130–3, 178–9; Ricardo 193–6, 197–8, 204–5, 208–9, 212–16, 225–9; Marx 237–43, 247–53, 261–4, 303–5, 307–8; general 311–14, 316–18, 321–2, 326–7, 329–30, 332–8
Sweezy, P. 354, 365

taxation 49–57, 61–2, 126–8, 161–2, 174, 218–23, 311, 314, 335–6, 349
Thweatt, W. O. 347, 365
Tosato, D. A. 350, 358
trade, international 24–5, 26–7, 32–3, 57–8, 83–5, 101–2, 134–7, 148–50, 156–7, 170, 229–32, 269, 325–6
trade unions 259–60, 264, 307–8, 337–8
transfer prices 264
transformation problem 261–4, 351
Turgot, Anne Robert Jacques 58, 66, 315, 317, 318, 345, 365
Tutain, J.-C. 343, 365

unemployment 146, 181, 253–60, 279, 285–8, 296–303, 303–6, 328–9

unproductive *see* productive and unproductive, distinction between
usury laws 178

value, theory of: Ricardo 183–7, 198–9, 200–1, 206–7, 226–7; Marx 235–44, 261–4, 280–1; labour theory of 186, 237–44, 261–4, 280–1
Vatter, H. G. 348, 365
Verdoorn's law 345
Voltaire, François Marie Arouet de 15, 316–17, 340, 365

wage, determination of:
 Quesnay 12–13, 14; Smith 68–9, 86–9, 100, 105; Malthus 114–19, 122–4, 126–8, 135–6, 142–4, 146–7, 164–5, 167–73; Ricardo 188–9, 201–2, 205–7, 209–10, 217–18, 223–6; Marx 237–8, 246–8, 255–60, 270, 294–6, 303, 307–8; general 319–20, 327, 329–30, 335–6, 338
Walsh, V. 356, 365
West, Edward 66, 187, 193, 324, 349, 365
Weulersse, Georges 339, 340, 341, 344, 355, 365
Williams, P. L. 352, 365
Wilson, T. xi
women (and children), effect of work of 164–5, 247–8
Woog, H. 340, 342, 365
workhouses 129, 245
Wright, J. F. 347, 348, 365

X-efficiency 348

zero-sum game 236–7, 240–1
Zinke, G. W. 349, 365